Oedipus;
or, The Legend
of a Conqueror

# STUDIES IN VIOLENCE, MIMESIS, AND CULTURE

# Oedipus; or, The Legend of a Conqueror

**Marie Delcourt**

**Translated by Malcolm DeBevoise**

Michigan State University Press · *East Lansing*

♾ The paper used in this publication meets the minimum requirements
of ANSI/NISO Z39.48-1992 (R 1997) (Permanence of Paper).

Michigan State University Press
East Lansing, Michigan 48823-5245

LIBRARY OF CONGRESS CATALOGING-IN-PUBLICATION DATA
Names: Delcourt, Marie, author. | DeBevoise, M. B., translator. Title: Oedipus :
or, the legend of a conqueror / Marie Delcourt ; translated by Malcolm DeBevoise.
Other titles: Œdipe, ou, La légende du conquérant. English
| Studies in violence, mimesis, and culture.
Description: East Lansing : Michigan State University Press, 2020.
| Series: Studies in violence, mimesis, and culture
| Includes bibliographical references and index.
Identifiers: LCCN 2019043637 | ISBN 9781611863512 (paperback)
| ISBN 9781609176259 | ISBN 9781628953879 | ISBN 9781628963885
Subjects: LCSH: Oedipus (Greek mythological figure) | Oedipus (Tale)
| Oedipus complex. | Oedipus (Greek mythological figure)—In literature.
| Oedipus (Tale) in literature. | Oedipus complex in literature.
Classification: LCC BL820.O43 D4513 2020 | DDC 809/.93351—dc23
LC record available at https://lccn.loc.gov/2019043637

Book design by Charlie Sharp, Sharp Des!gns, East Lansing, MI
Cover design by David Drummond, Salamander Design, www.salamanderhill.com.
Cover art: detail from Oedipus Asking the Sphinx Riddle Greek Mythology Tale,
by delcarmat, Shutterstock vector ID#1542409481
Author photo courtesy of Université de Liège, Belgium

Michigan State University Press is a member of the Green Press Initiative and is committed to developing
and encouraging ecologically responsible publishing practices. For more information about the Green
Press Initiative and the use of recycled paper in book publishing, please visit *www.greenpressinitiative.org.*

Visit Michigan State University Press at *www.msupress.org*

# Contents

# Foreword

*Vinciane Pirenne-Delforge*

Oedipus is known today mainly for the "complex" to which Freud gave his name. It is not this aspect of the Oedipus legend that Marie Delcourt seeks to explore in her book, first published in 1944 and now translated into English for the first time. She sees the Oedipus complex as nothing more than the latest version of the myth of a Theban hero whom the Greek poets had made the murderer of his father and the husband of his mother. It is the Oedipus of ancient tragedy and epic, not of modern psychoanalysis, that Delcourt wishes to consider.

She studies six themes, in as many chapters, that together make up the legend of a conqueror—exposure of the infant, murder of the father, victory over the Sphinx, the riddle of the Sphinx, marriage to a princess, and incest with the mother—and sets them in a broad historical context incorporating a range of parallels drawn from Greek narrative traditions and, to a much lesser degree, comparable traditions from outside the Greek world. This legendary corpus is then rigorously analyzed with reference to the different types of sources that transmitted these traditions and to the relations that the various episodes bear to one another.

Translated by Malcolm DeBevoise

To some extent Delcourt's purpose in this book is associated with a style of historiography that has fallen out of favor in the intervening decades. For better or for worse, few scholars today would follow her in attempting to reconstruct the prehistoric origins of legendary themes by identifying the decayed and gradually forgotten religious rituals that gave rise to the many variants preserved in later mythological accounts. Delcourt's real subject, it is important to keep in mind, is the prehistory of sovereign power among the Greeks, and its dim reflections in the legend of a conqueror such as Oedipus, whose heroic biography was given its classic form by the genius of the tragedians.

In the meantime, structuralism and postmodern deconstruction have raised an apparently insuperable epistemological barrier between Delcourt's work and our own view of the legend. And yet reading her *Oedipus* remains a fascinating experience, not only because of its philologically impeccable contextualization of all the available documentary evidence, but also because of its painstaking detection and explication of mythic themes—what she aptly calls "fabulous cells," by analogy with biological cells. Moreover, she emphasizes that a fabulous cell must never be examined in isolation from its neighbors, because contact with other cells over time has modified its coloring. This insight is no less valuable today than it was seventy-five years ago, and the lively and penetrating intelligence from which it sprang cannot help but delight a new generation of readers, as they will discover at once in the pages that follow. But these pages do not say everything that needs to be said about their author. For this book was written by an altogether extraordinary woman, about whom I would now like to say a few words in paying tribute, not merely to her intellect, but also to her personal courage and her generosity of spirit.

Marie Delcourt was born in 1891 in Ixelles, a suburb of Brussels, where her father, a career military officer, had been posted. Her mother was from Arlon, in the south of Belgium, and it was there that she spent much of her early childhood. At the age of three she contracted poliomyelitis. She was to suffer her entire life from the limitations imposed by what she called her "ungovernable leg." But this was not the only handicap she had to overcome. For all but a very few girls at the beginning of the twentieth century, even in much of Europe, the obstacles to higher education were almost insurmountable. In Belgium, secondary schools of the period did not consider it part of their mission to prepare young women for professional careers. But Marie Delcourt did not let this stand in her way. In 1911, at the age of nineteen, having been granted the diploma in Greco-Latin humanities by a national board of examiners, she entered the University of Liège to study classical philology. The First World War interrupted her studies, and also deprived her of her father, who died at the front in 1914. She then became involved in an underground network of partisans gathering information on German troop movements for the British War Office. In recognition of her role in the Belgian resistance, and for her services to the allied cause, she was made an Officer of the Order of the British Empire (OBE). Following the war she resumed her studies, earning her doctorate in 1919 and then going to Paris for two years of postgraduate work. On her return she became an instructor in a girls' secondary school, the Institut supérieur des demoiselles (today the Lycée Léonie de Waha), devoting her considerable energies to helping young women gain admission to institutions of higher learning.

In 1929 she was appointed the first female lecturer at the University of Liège, joining the department of classical philology, whose conservative orientation and casual misogyny prevented her from ever really feeling at home there. In spite of the barely disguised hostility she frequently encountered among her colleagues, and no doubt in reaction to it, she was revered by the many students she taught over the course of three decades. One of them, the distinguished classicist Marcel Detienne, fondly recalled how different what everyone called "Marie's courses" were from the stodgy lectures delivered by the department's senior members. Among the subjects she taught was the history of humanism, one of her passions, along with Greek antiquity and literature; she was the first to offer it there. It was not until 1940 that she was appointed to a full professorship in Liège, allowing her finally to quit her position at the Institut, where she had taught Greek for almost twenty years.

As a handicapped, independent-minded, and nonconformist woman (her husband, the writer Alexis Curvers, was fifteen years her junior), Delcourt refused to be confined by conventional prejudices of any kind. In her professional career, possessed of a strong and distinctive voice and sustained by an indomitable will, she made her own way in the field of classical scholarship and the humanities more generally. But there was much more to her life than that. As a young woman, in the 1920s, together with the pioneering Belgian feminist and Walloon activist Léonie de Waha (1836–1926), the founder of the school for girls where she taught for so many years, she campaigned for women's rights, both in politics (universal suffrage was not achieved in Belgium until 1948) and in the workplace. In the 1960s, she contributed a regular column to *Le Soir*, the nation's major newspaper—further proof of the diversity of her interests, but also of a rare talent for placing scholarly erudition in the service of a wider public interest.

In her later years she also wrote lovely short stories, recently reissued in a single volume, while continuing to carry on an extensive correspondence with colleagues and friends, both in Belgium and abroad. All those who knew her vividly recall her exceptional capacity for hard work and her irrepressible urge to write. Roland Crahay, another one of her students, and later a collaborator, memorably said that her style of writing, marvelously well suited to the ideas she sought to communicate, made putting words to paper a source of great happiness to her, and reading her words a source of great happiness to others.

Marie Delcourt was a versatile and prolific scholar. Her work falls into three main categories: biography (lives of Euripides, Aeschylus, Pericles, and Erasmus), translation (the tragedies of Euripides, Thomas More's *Utopia*, and much of Erasmus's voluminous correspondence), and the mythology and religion of ancient Greece. It is to this third category that her study of Oedipus belongs, together with *Les grands sanctuaires de la Grèce* (1947), *L'Oracle de Delphes* (1955), and *Héphaistos; ou, La légende du magicien* (1957), among other books.

Not the least of her writings is a splendid little cookbook that appeared in 1947 under the title *Méthode de cuisine à l'usage des personnes intelligentes*. Written during the war, a time of economic hardship and food shortages, it shows that she was a humanist not only in the classroom but also in the kitchen. She meant to make available to everyone, men and women alike, not a series of recipes dispensed by a famous male chef (as all famous chefs were in those days) who has lost touch with the real world, but a method for cooking in an intelligent—which is to say a thoughtful—manner that takes due account of the exigencies of daily life, the availability of ingredients, and the variety of individual tastes. The Introduction to the book is a small gem, and tells us a great deal about the character of its author. "A woman who must look after her children all by herself," she writes, "and see to all the household chores by herself, will not have the time every day of the week to cook elaborate dishes. Unless she is to work herself to death, she will have to choose between two tasks. . . . [But] between scamping and serving the culinary priesthood, surely it must be possible to strike a sensible balance." Here the defense of women's rights is extended to the home.

———————————

Marie Delcourt died at the age of eighty-seven, two years before I began my studies at the University of Liège in 1981. The memory of her teaching was still fresh in everyone's mind, and reading her books nourished my passion for ancient Greek religion from the very beginning of my time there. In the years since I have also come to appreciate how truly fine a person she was. My hope is that this brief remembrance will inspire others to discover for themselves the very original and important body of work that she handed down to future generations.

# Translator's Note

have worked from the 1981 Les Belles Lettres edition, which corrects some
(but by no means all) of the errors in the original 1944 Droz edition, mainly
in the transcription of the Greek. Marie Delcourt was evidently prevented
by the circumstances of the war from reviewing galley proof, and seems never
to have had the opportunity afterward to revise either text or notes. The
second edition, published two years after her death, contains translations of
the Greek, Latin, and German passages quoted by Delcourt, due to M. l'abbé
André Wartelle, dean of the faculty of letters at the Institut Catholique de
Paris. I have followed his renderings for the most part, while comparing them
with the best English versions and, in a few places, making my own transla-
tions.

The presentation of the material in the French edition has been altered
in two respects, by moving in-text citations to the notes and by relocating the
Pisander scholion and related summaries in a separate Appendix. As a cour-
tesy to non-specialist readers I have glossed technical terms, translated Greek
phrases [in square brackets], and filled in missing citations to classical sources
wherever possible. Many references to the scholarly literature are incomplete.
I have done my best to put them into standard bibliographical form, and
again, as far as possible, to rectify occasional inaccuracies. Minor errors in

the French text have been silently corrected. Where the reason for making an alteration to the text is not obvious, or where the implication of the text is unclear, I have added a note of my own, sometimes also mentioning the results of more recent scholarship. In a few places where Delcourt seems to have been obliged to write in haste, particularly toward the end, and once more no doubt owing to the difficulties of publication during the war, I have sparingly interpolated enough information, implicit in the original text and understood by specialists, for general readers today to follow the argument more easily. Finally, I have considerably expanded the index of passages cited from classical authors, skeletal in the French edition, so that scholars may have ready access to a complete inventory.

I am grateful to Donald J. Matronarde, Emeritus Melpomene Professor of Classics at the University of California, Berkeley, for his careful review of a draft version of the translation; and to both him and Professor Maurizio Bettini at the University of Siena for recommending Vinciane Pirenne-Delforge as the ideal person to write a brief appreciation of this formidable and unjustly neglected scholar. I am very much indebted also to Sean Knowlton, the digital resources librarian at Howard-Tilton Memorial Library, Tulane University, and to Jane Pizino, formerly the director of the Rare Books Collection there, for their help in locating a great many obscure references.

# Introduction

The legend of Oedipus has come down to us through late poems, since all the epics of the Theban cycle are lost. Yet it is also one of those legends in which the mythic elements, because they are the most easily discerned, are also the most intelligible. Six episodes are recounted in it, one after another, in such a way as to compose a biography. All six are accorded equal value, and all of them stress the same themes: greatness, conquest, domination, the right to rule. Each episode occurs in other legends, but no other legend presents them together. If they have ended up being considered interchangeable with one another, their origins are nonetheless very different, which is to say that, taken as a group, they transpose to the realm of fable a particularly rich group of rites that, despite being the products of quite diverse historical beliefs and circumstances, are all bound up with the idea of *kingship*. The tale of Oedipus is certainly the most complete of all the political myths. Carefully and patiently examined, it has much to teach us about the prehistory of sovereign power among the ancient Greeks. This is by no means an insignificant thing, for by classical times the Greek language had actually lost the Indo-European word for "king."[1]

The texts concerning the legend of Oedipus were collected and studied some years ago by Carl Robert in a magisterial work that it would be pointless to attempt to rewrite.[2] But there is no reason we should not follow a different guiding thread than the one he chose. Robert sought to discover the various ritual forms that the legend might have assumed in different sanctuaries, and the various literary forms that poets might later have given it. But because he could not penetrate the biographical shell of the legend, he was unable to properly appreciate its mythic elements, whose nature and significance become clear, as we shall see, only once the shell has been peeled away and they stand fully revealed. Robert criticized these elements as one would the chapters of a work of fiction. Ancient themes underwent considerable alteration, however, as a result of their having been compressed to fit the limits of a single human lifetime. Mythic fragments cannot be subjected to the procedures of fictional composition without being distorted in ways that vary from legend to legend. In the case of Oedipus, the principal fact—that Oedipus ruled Thebes—has several explanations, any one of which by itself would have been sufficient. Yet the ancient epic poets, instead of choosing among them, presented them all together, in a jumble of contradictions that somehow had to be made to submit to the unifying demands of *duration* and *verisimilitude*. It was only owing to the prodigious art of Sophocles that audiences did not scratch their heads. Why did the gods wait twelve or fifteen years before manifesting their wrath against a murderer? How could an adventurer who conquered a kingdom fail to display the least curiosity concerning his predecessor? And so on. Aristotle quite rightly saw that the implausibilities of *Oedipus the King* were ἔξω τῆς τραγῳδίας [outside the tragedy],[3] that is, they had to do with the subject itself and not the way in which Sophocles treated it. All these implausibilities result from an accumulation of episodes that differ in their origin and fictive structure, but that are identical in respect of their religious content. They are doubles of one another, for they all illustrate a single idea or closely related ideas: entitlement to exercise power and the legitimacy of conquest by force of arms.[4] The episodes of the Oedipus myth have been made to fit together by reason of their similarity. In the legend of the Atreidae, by contrast, the episodes are united by an internal need of justification, and gain in cohesiveness and logic in proportion as the attempt at justification succeeds.

Robert accepts without discussion that Oedipus was an actual person before he came to be credited with a mythological heritage. I propose that we move from an entirely opposite premise, namely, that some events, anonymous and elusive to begin with, then grouped together, ended up constituting a distinct and individual personality. This difference in point of departure—the result of adopting the point of view of religious history, rather than the point of view of literary history—is not a trivial one. In the first place, we will be excused from having to ask ourselves at the outset whether the primitive Oedipus was an authentic king of Thebes, as Farnell and Rose suppose; a sun god, as Müller and Bréal suppose; or a chthonic hero, one of Poseidon's escorts, as Robert supposes. There was no primitive Oedipus. What is primitive are the themes that, in coming to be linked up with one another, came first to describe the feats of Oedipus, then his life, and finally his character. These themes derived in turn from rites that were much more ancient than they were. That these rites, transcribed in literary form as brief episodes, should eventually have given birth to an altogether singular, vividly delineated, and unforgettable figure is one of the miracles of Greek poetry.

The attempt I make here to go back to the origins of a particular Greek legend is also a study in mythopoeia, which is to say religious psychology. The questions that scholars have posed for two centuries now concerning the origin of myths have received a variety of responses, each of which implies a different view of the human mind.

If legends are an anthropomorphized transcription of natural events, primitive man must be attributed the gift of contemplation—a capacity for wonder and astonishment at the succession of night and day, of winter and summer, producing a perpetual unease that caused him to imagine these alternations as a kind of combat whose origin was a matter of chance. The Greek creators of religion who emerge from Usener's works were possessed of just such a gift. These are works of incomparable fruitfulness, but they are dominated by an indemonstrable idea, namely, that mythmaking sprang chiefly from a sense of gods as primitively identical with natural forces and immanent in them. A god, in this system, is a remote cause, and his worshippers must be supposed to have had an exceptionally agile and disinterested intelligence.

Scholars who saw gods as spirits of vegetation, or of rain, or disease, or the dead, had the great advantage over sun-god theorists of being able to appeal to modern religious facts similar to the ones they postulated for antiquity. Still they placed too much emphasis, it seems to me, on the notion of a divine person, which, I believe, came into existence only over a very long period. We may nonetheless venture to suggest how this came about. Spirits were understood to be immediate causes, but ambivalent in their effect, capable of either helping or harming. To induce them to give help or to prevent them from doing harm, men turned to rites whose efficaciousness was likewise considered to be immediate. An individual divine personality began to take shape through the condensation of a multiplicity of attributes, with the result that little by little a proper name came to be substituted for a sprinkling of adjectives. The proper name started out, in other words, as an adjective whose value changed when the person took precedence over his attributes. But at the same time, though the traditional rites continued to be performed, the old conviction in their immediate efficaciousness was gradually lost. Gods, having been personalized, were now dissociated from the objects of which formerly they were the animating *soul*, and rites, in order to communicate with them, were obliged to take a longer and less direct route. Ritual gestures now ceased to be understood for the most part. To explain them, myths and legends were invented, accounts that, like the gods themselves, were the product of a process of singularization. At first it was said: "To obtain such and such a result, one must perform such and such a rite." Later it was said: "To honor the god who will grant such and such a result, one must perform such and such a rite, which will please the god because it recalls such and such a moment of his story." Henceforth the whole logical interval that separates the rite from the god was filled by myth.

Scholars such as Frazer, Reinach, and Nilsson, who investigated rites in search of the origin of myths, no longer laid stress in speaking of gods and heroes on the notion of *person*, but on that of *acts*. From there it was but a short step, which they took at once, to say that many religious figures were acts before they were persons; that legends, issuing from events, were primary realities and gave rise to the beings that came to be at the center of them. Typically, however, a unitary character was assigned to each of the personifications these scholars identified. It is this tendency that I try to overcome in the present work. A legend is unintelligible so long as it has not been taken apart piece by piece, for each episode may very well have its own separate origin and meaning. The deep-seated synonymy of all the acts of Oedipus, which impresses itself upon our minds so forcefully, may or may not be exceptional. To decide the matter, it will be necessary to determine

whether identity of thematic significance plays the same role in the arrange-
ment of elements in other legends that it plays in the Oedipus legend. My
own view is that it does not.[5] What we can be sure of (leaving to one side for
the moment the question of meaning and restricting our attention solely to
that of origins) is that the events constituting the Theban hero as he is known
to us today are associated with very different layers of liturgical history. What
is more, several of them do not have a unique origin or even a purely ritual
origin. The *exposure of the newborn* seems to derive both from a rite aimed at
driving away evil beings and from rites of initiation. The *combat against the
monster* is situated at the intersection of two beliefs, one in winged beings
in whom are incarnated the souls of the dead, the other in ominous demons
who cast their dark shadow in nightmares; in this case the mythopoetic influ-
ence of a physiological reality, alongside rites and superstitions, seems fairly
clear. As for *incest with the mother*, it appears somehow to have been con-
nected with the detection of omens, which may have had a ritual substrate;
this substrate, if it ever actually existed, must have been rooted in a kind of
sympathetic magic.[6] At all events it is clear, too, that a liturgical explanation
is not capable by itself of explaining everything. To determine how far it is
sufficient, each episode must be carefully scrutinized. It will then be found
that several beliefs converge to produce an act, and that several such acts in
combination come to constitute a hero.

Here we are rather far from the ancient substantialist conception, which
places all heroes in a classic dilemma: are they mortals honored in death or
are they fallen gods? For my part, I doubt very much that any hero was a
historical figure. Probably many of them were, not fallen gods, but minor
gods who did not prosper. Usener, in his magisterial *Götternamen*,[7] well
described the humanization of minor deities. Robert ranked Oedipus in this
category and as a result, quite correctly it seems to me, began by looking at
the various centers of worship in the ancient Greek world: Eteonus, Sparta,
Colonus, Areopagus; only the first of these, he felt, was ancient and "primi-
tive." Nilsson, reviewing Robert's *Oidipus*, was skeptical of the relevance of
such a method in the present case. Arguing that "legendary themes [may]
arise without relation to any religious or devotional reality and that cults
have wholly emerged from myths,"[8] he claimed to detect the trace of mythic
themes in the episodes of the malefic child, the triumph over the monster,
the marriage with the princess, and so on.[9] In all of this I wholeheartedly

concur with Nilsson—on the condition, however, that we take the incidence of myth in such cases as a point of departure and not as the point at which our investigations will end. Fairy tales (*Märchen*) are homogeneous with myths, whereas legends are already a first step in the direction of historicization.[10] In fairy tales, as in myths, the parts have remained sufficiently distinct for it to be possible to study them separately, whereas legendary accounts, which are more elaborate, cloak disparate elements in the folds of a single garment, as it were, and so conceal their heterogeneity.

Oedipus is neither a historical figure nor an anciently humanized minor god. He is the very type of all heroes of essentially—if not uniquely—ritual origin, whose acts are prior to their person.

That the Greeks should have been able to convert these acts into distinct personalities is due to their poetical genius, not to their religious genius. The poets had inherited from popular religion heroes of divine origin, who were scarcely more than phantoms, and heroes of liturgical origin, who were scarcely more than mannequins. The poets made them admirable figures, at once human and superhuman, capable of imparting—and this is what was new—moral instruction. From a few personalized rites, from a few obscure superstitions, hero worship in Carlyle's sense was first able to be brought forth.

The problem for us therefore will be to establish a precise correspondence between *practices* and *beliefs*, on the one hand, and *legends*, on the other. It is our misfortune that only in a very few cases, thanks to their transcription into the language of myth, is it possible to identify well-known rites with certainty. If Demeter fasts in her sorrow at having lost her daughter, this is what must explain the role of abstinence in the Eleusinian mysteries; if she undertakes her search by the light of a flaming torch, this is what must account for the use of flambeaux in the mysteries. These things present no problem. Difficulties emerge when one has reason to suspect that a myth corresponds to practices of which ancient Greece has retained few memories, or none at all, and which are attested only in other cultures. Thus Dumézil thinks that the myth of a mutilated Uranus transposes an Indo-European liturgy for the coronation of a sovereign; thus Jeanmaire thinks that Theseus's exploits transpose ceremonies marking the passage to adulthood. But the ritual of the sovereign is well known only through the literature of ancient India; initiation rites are well known only through documents concerning

African peoples. The equations of the comparativists rest, as we shall see, on the assumption that the social substrate and the beliefs on which this substrate is founded are everywhere similar.

Every culture, working from an initial correspondence between rites and legends, develops a poetic tradition in accordance with its own native talents. The Greek talent for narrative invention was exercised preferentially on ritual practices that had already entered into a phase of chronic decline, whether because they had fallen into disuse or because no one any longer knew how to make sense of them. In the Hellenic world, social and political liturgies disappeared long before agrarian liturgies. Their transcription into legendary accounts therefore dates from an early period. Whereas the ritual basis of agrarian legends remained intact, social legends very quickly assumed, in the absence of continuing support from liturgical practice, the appearance of autonomy; indeed, so completely were they detached from such support, they might almost be mistaken for creations of fictive genius. Prehistoric social practices nonetheless left enough traces in worship, in institutions, and in the private life of some particularly conservative regions, such as Sparta and Crete, that we may dare, with regard to the tales of the poets, to sketch at least the outlines of a plausible account of the situation in ancient Greece.

Even so, I am under no illusion whatever as to the persuasive force of the hypotheses that are advanced in the pages that follow. In such matters it is not possible to go beyond mere probability. I have done no more than juxtapose assumptions, placing them on the same level rather than subordinating some to others; I refuse, in other words, to consider one as demonstrated and therefore capable of buttressing another. At the same time I have made a point of grouping together only Greek tales, and in order to explain them I make reference only to facts of Greek history, except in a few instances where the temptation cannot be resisted to appeal to the authority of some Latin text or Christian element in which evidence of a classical survival is indisputable. What often weakens the arguments of the comparativists is that they are constructed with hastily assembled materials. Hartland's work on the legend of Perseus, for example, like that of Potter on the Persian legend of Rostam,[11] brings to bear a great amount of documentary material, but almost all of it is studied superficially. The interesting points remain obscure because they result on the whole from apparently trivial details that a summary can dispense with. The same may be said of the traditions collected by Frazer relating to the Flood. For each culture one would need to make careful studies in an attempt to get to the bottom of a particular legend. These monographs will acquire their full value only when comparativists, indirectly having clarified certain perplexing points, succeed in setting new problems in an unexpected light. At that point, and only then, a meticulous cross-examination of ritual practices and legendary accounts having been carried out in the meantime, it will be possible to profitably survey the largely unexplored territory of historical memory where practices are losing their ancient sense, where the earliest tales speak their first stammering words, where poets then set to work and begin to give them a meaning no one had yet thought of.[12]

---

The sources of our knowledge of the Oedipus legend are in general readily decipherable. Only one of them poses a problem that, in the present state of our knowledge, remains insoluble.

At verse 1760 of Euripides's *Phoenician Women*, the M A B codices[13] all give a scholium of some thirty lines that begins with the words Ἱστορεῖ Πείσανδρος [Pisander relates that . . . ] and ends with ταῦτά φησιν Πείσανδρος [This is what Pisander says]. Are these the words of a poet, or of a mythographer who summarizes a poem? The text bracketed by these two phrases, set off in effect by quotation marks, nonetheless does not appear to be all of a piece, for it contains a discussion of the Sphinx that interrupts a tale devoted to Laius. Bethe, in *Thebanische Heldenlieder* (1891),[14] interpreted this passage (in which he also detected a gap and several interpolations) as a summary of the *Oedipodea*, the first epic of the Theban cycle—an opinion that provoked several refutations and yielded a whole crop of new hypotheses. The most recent of these is due to Deubner, who accepts the epic origin of lines 5–11, devoted to the Sphinx; of lines 31–33, concerning Oedipus's second marriage; and of the scholium subsequently conserved by Monacensis gr. 560, where the only surviving verses of the *Oedipodea* are found. Deubner interprets the rest as a summary of two plays by Euripides, *Chrysippus* (now lost) and *Oedipus* (lost but for a few fragments).[15]

The latter claim stands in stark contradiction to everything that we know about these two plays. Deubner was able to propose it only by arbitrarily leaving to one side two sources of cardinal importance. Indeed, the Pisander scholion (I would rather it were more commonly called "Pisander's summary," not least for the amphibological quality of this epithet) cannot be profitably studied without examining it alongside two other plot summaries: the argument (or hypothesis) of Euripides's *Phoenician Women*, due to Aristophanes of Byzantium and preserved by Codex Vaticanus gr. 1345, and the brief mythographic summary of the same play contained in Codex Laurentianus gr. 32.33.[16] This latter text is certainly a summary of *Chrysippus*: Laius, coming from Thebes, encounters along the way Chrysippus, son of Pelops, becomes enamored of him, and seeks to bring him back to Thebes; when the young man refuses his advances, he abducts him without Pelops's knowledge; Pelops suffers greatly from the loss of his son and, on learning the truth of the matter later, lays a curse upon Laius, condemning him never to have children or, if he does, to die at the hand of his son.

These few lines give the gist of another summary by Aristophanes of Byzantium, this one of Aeschylus's *Seven against Thebes*, the first part of which also has Pelops calling down a curse on Laius and his descendants, while the second part describes the circumstances that form the point of departure for *Phoenician Women*: Oedipus is now blind and mistreated by his sons; there is no suicide by Jocasta, who lives on; the two brothers have concluded a treaty that Eteocles refuses to honor. The last lines of this exposition have been skewed, so as to introduce Aeschylus's play,[17] but the text in every essential detail certainly comes from a Euripidean mythopoeia, for two verses of *Phoenician Women* (lines 18 and 19) are quoted in it, separately. The two arguments, of *Seven against Thebes* and *Phoenician Women*, must have *Chrysippus* as a common source, for Aristophanes mentions *Phoenician Women* in conjunction with another lost play by Euripides, *Oenomaus*. Aristophanes's text is unfortunately very damaged, and the last part cannot be pieced together with certainty. Since a didascaly is mentioned just prior to it, however, there is every reason to believe that Aristophanes was citing *Oenomaus* and *Chrysippus* as belonging, not only to the same group of legends, but also to the same trilogy as *Phoenician Women*.

The mythopoeia described by the accounts found in Vaticanus and Laurentianus resembles that of the Pisander scholion, but it is by no means identical with it. In Pisander's summary, Hera avenges the rights of marriage by sending the Sphinx against the Thebans, which is to say that she punishes less Laius himself than his people, though they are guilty only of having failed to punish a criminal king. The Sphinx seems to have appeared during Laius's lifetime. In Vaticanus and Laurentianus, it is a wrathful Pelops who calls down a curse upon Laius and his descendants. The appearance of the Sphinx, which bears no relation to the suicide of Chrysippus, is placed after Laius's death. Notice that in *Phoenician Women*, although Chrysippus does not figure there, the Sphinx appears, as in the two manuscript accounts, after the death of Laius (l. 45); and it is sent, not by Hera, as in Pisander, but by Hades (l. 810). Furthermore, the summary of *Seven against Thebes*, like *Phoenician Women* (l. 805), speaks of the *golden* pins used to pierce the child's feet. All of this therefore aligns *Phoenician Women* more closely with the two accounts than with Pisander's summary. It bears repeating that *Chrysippus* probably belonged to the same trilogy as *Phoenician Women*.[18] We should keep in mind, too, that in Pisander it is Laius's transgression that unleashes the Sphinx against the Thebans; in the two other summaries, the Sphinx strikes at Laius through his son. The first conception, in which an entire group pays for the misdeeds of one wrongdoer, is nearer to ancient ideas about the interdependence of criminal responsibility and punishment; the second is nearer to Euripides's own ethics. What is certain is that it is impossible to discover *Chrysippus* in *both* the Pisander scholion *and* the two arguments. It is necessary to choose between two mythopoeias that, if one takes the trouble to look at them closely, can be seen to be strongly divergent. All the evidence suggests that the arguments in Vaticanus and Laurentianus are accounts of a play that was performed before *Phoenician Women*. What we find in the Pisander scholion, then, is not an account borrowed from *Chrysippus*. I feel quite sure, along with Bethe, that Euripides drew from an earlier legendary source.[19]

Deubner points out a striking anacoluthon in line 18 of Pisander, in which the verbal phrase κτείνας [having killed] takes as its subject Οἰδίπους [Oedipus], whose name appears in the accusative case in the previous sentence. Deubner sees this inconsistency as evidence of a change in source: the mythographer, done with summarizing the plot of *Chrysippus*, goes on next to summarize the plot of *Oedipus*. We know very little about this latter play. According to a scholium on line 61 of *Phoenician Women*, ἐν τῷ Οἰδίποδι οἱ Λαΐου θεράποντες ἐτύφλωσαν αὐτόν [Οἰδίποδα]. ἡμεῖς δὲ Πολύβου παῖδ᾽ ἐρείσαντες πέδῳ ἐξομματοῦμεν καὶ διόλλυμεν κόρας [In *Oedipus*, it is Laius's servants who blind (Oedipus): "Holding the son of Polybus to the ground, we tore out his eyes, we crushed the pupils"]. This *Oedipus* must be the one by

Euripides, for if not the scholiast would have mentioned the author's name. The fact that Laius's servants called Oedipus "son of Polybus" places the disfigurement before the moment of recognition. I myself find it impossible to imagine a version of the legend that could satisfactorily accommodate this strange episode, but in any case it stands in total contradiction to Pisander's summary. Deubner then goes on to argue that the *Oedipus* referred to by the scholium is not in fact the one by Euripides,[20] and that there is a lacuna in the manuscript at the place where the name of the unknown author would occur. We must be careful not to pile up hypotheses on top of one another in this fashion. Changes of subject such as the one at line 18 of Pisander are frequent in Herodotus;[21] they are more rarely encountered in Attic prose and in the Koine. If one does not wish to admit that what is at issue here is negligence on the part of a bad writer, a gap in the text would explain the inconsistency better than the intervention of a new source. Reading the text without any preconceived notions, one is struck by the role played in it by Hera in her capacity as goddess of marriage, the famous Hera Gamastolus of Mount Cithaeron, who is mentioned once before and once after the point that Deubner considers to be the hinge between the two sources. One would therefore have to assume that this cult was conspicuous in both sources. But Hera was not an especially prominent divinity in the fifth century BCE. Is it not simpler to suppose that the whole text describes a unique mythopoeia? Recall, too, that Hera as a guiding force is absent from Aristophanes's summaries of both *Seven against Thebes* and *Phoenician Women*. In the latter play, however, Oedipus is exposed λειμῶν' ἐς Ἥρας καὶ Κιθαιρῶνος λέπας [in the meadow of Hera, on the rock of Cithaeron] (l. 24), which suggests that Euripides found the figure of Hera in a legendary source, from which he borrowed as the essential motive not the goddess's wrath, but Pelops's curse; nevertheless, in a corner of this mythic landscape, he made room for "the meadow of Hera," unknown in either Aeschylus or Sophocles. Once again we are led to conclude that the mythopoeia known to us through Pisander's summary was very probably the source of two tragedies by Euripides that were performed before *Phoenician Women*.

Was this source an epic? Bethe, Wecklein, and Wilamowitz thought so. But other critics refuse to recognize a set of epic traditions in lines 1–4 and 12–30, and this for two reasons that seem to me indecisive.

   1. *The love of Laius for Chrysippus could not be an epic theme.*[22] How could

anyone be sure of such a thing? Aeschylus, in the *Myrmidons*, showed Achilles in love with Patroclus.[23] His source was probably a narrative poem, which led Bethe to advance the following argument in connection with Euripides: the indignation of Pelops and Hera cannot be explained, any more than the shame of Chrysippus can, in an age when pederasty was honored in Greece; Euripides, as we know, lived in a milieu in which masculine love of young men was considered equal or superior to love of women; if he treated the legend of Chrysippus, it was therefore because it had already been established by the time he was writing. On this view, the theme goes back to the Dorian invasions, which, by introducing pederasty to Greece, must have provoked a backlash in the form of tales hostile to the new morality.[24] This is a great deal to claim regarding a subject about which everything is uncertain and contradictory. How can Pelops's anger toward his son's seducer be reconciled with the legend recounted by Pindar in the first *Olympiad*, where Pelops himself is portrayed as Poseidon's darling and implores his divine lover to help him win the hand of Hippodamia—a request the god is pleased to grant? This episode proves at a minimum that pederasty existed prior to Laius's time and that young men were not therefore prevented from dreaming of marriage. Nor did the fact that Euripides's audience knew this prevent the poet from portraying the Theban house as overwhelmed by Pelops's curse. This malediction, rather than going back, as Bethe supposed, to an epoch when pederasty was something new and repugnant, might just as well have come from a more recent way of thinking, no less hostile to male romantic desire for young men. Perhaps one should distinguish (something neither Bethe nor any other critic has done) between two different judgments. In Pisander, Laius is made to die on account of a love that is contrary to nature; in the two other summaries, Vaticanus and Laurentianus, because he rapes Chrysippus. Euripides may well have disapproved of the brutality of the act, though not the sentiment that inspired it—on the same ground that, in *Ion*, he criticizes not the love of a god for a young woman, but Apollo's rape of Creusa. In this way he may have been able to consider pederasty otherwise than the people of his time were inclined to do, deliberately taking a view opposite to that of Pindar, who found nothing objectionable about Poseidon's desire for Pelops. At all events, Euripides was not afraid to express a minority opinion. I therefore shall not endorse Bethe's conjectures about the origins of a legend that we know only through the summary of a careless author. One should say simply that the legend may perfectly well come from an epic source. There is no reason that pederasty, absent from the *Odyssey* and replaced in the *Iliad* by passionate friendship, might not have figured explicitly in other epics. Bethe would have it that Pisander was recapitulating the *Oedipodea*. It is this particular claim that is incautious. Nothing forecloses the possibility that we are reading here the summary of a less ancient work, marked already by a taste for fictive narrative. However this may be, I believe the work is surely prior to Euripides.

2. *The use of means of knowledge, it is said, indicates a Euripidean influence.* Jocasta rediscovers Oedipus not once but twice: through the weapons of Laius, she recognizes the murderer of her first husband;[25] through the swaddling clothes and the pins that pierced Oedipus's feet, she recognizes her exposed son. "This recognition [*Anagnorismos*]," Deubner says, "and more particularly its second stage, arising from objects that permit the character to be identified and that belonged to the exposed child, is as foreign to an epic poem as it is common in drama."[26] This is a curious thing to say, considering the abundance of signs that Odysseus cleverly exploits on returning home at the end of the *Odyssey*. He is recognized by Eurycleia thanks to the scar; he wins Penelope's trust by describing to her the coat he wore on his departure from Ithaca as well as its golden brooch, decorated with the image of a hound preying on a fawn; later she lays a trap that he evades by describing to her their nuptial bed; finally, Odysseus causes Laertes to recognize him by showing his scar and by enumerating the trees of the orchard he knew as a child.[27] There can be no doubt that the poet who wrote the last books of the *Odyssey* took at least as much pleasure as Euripides himself in the game of recognition. In showing his scar to Laertes, Odysseus sought to deprive him of any possible reason for doubt; for the same reason, he hastened to recall which trees Laertes had given him when he was little, reminding his father that they used to walk together in the orchard. Similarly, in *Iphigenia in Tauris*, Orestes mentions to Iphigenia objects that were known only to the two of them: the tapestry she wove as a young girl representing the tale of the golden lamb; the vase containing the perfumed water for the nuptial bath sent by Clytemnestra to her daughter in anticipation of the pathetic marriage in Aulis; the lock of hair Iphigenia sent back to her mother, to be buried in her place following the sacrifice; finally, Pelops's spear, kept in the gynaeceum—admirable evocations all, whose Homeric character was wholly

misunderstood by Aristotle.[28] At least Aristotle has the merit of not making an aesthetic distinction between signs that are described and signs that are presented. Moreover, how else do those who suppose that *gnōrismata* [things recognized] are foreign to epic poetry interpret the discovery of Oedipus in the lost epic that is the source of a famous passage of the *Nekyia*[29] if not in terms of the use of signs? Note too that these signs cannot be memories, as in the case of Odysseus, but must be objects—perhaps the weapons that in Pisander the patricidal son stripped from his father.

The mythopoeia known to us through the Pisander scholion could therefore come either from an epic or from a tragedy. At all events, the text contains an error that must be the fault of the author rather than of a copyist: υἱὸν ὄντα [she is unaware *that he is her son*] rather than Λαΐου φονέα ὄντα (*that he is Laius's murderer*] (l. 26); and the sequence of events, if one has a mind to search for narrative verisimilitude in it, poses difficulties. Robert was not in the least troubled by them: a skillful narrator distracts his readers just as a dramatist distracts his audience, without permitting them the leisure to ponder puzzling details. As for the will to detect in this clumsy and interpolated summary a precise literary form displaying a coherent authorial style and aesthetic, this, it seems to me, is a waste of time.

One line of argument that seems not to have occurred to any critic inclines me to ascribe an epic origin to the Pisander scholion. The author of the *Nekyia* says that Oedipus killed Laius and stripped him of his arms. The theme of appropriating the father's weapons no longer figures, so far as one can tell, in any tragedy, nor in the summary of *Seven against Thebes*, otherwise so detailed and explicit. Yet it survives in Pisander. In several other cases, which I will study below, the versions of the legend that the scholion suggests, or that it explicitly contains, appear—so far as one may speak of a legend evolving over time—to be intermediate between the *Odyssey* and the tragedies we have been considering. For the moment it is impossible to say anything more precise. What is more, for our purposes, it is in no way necessary to say more. The inquiry that follows is concerned, not with literary forms, but with legendary forms. These latter forms must be examined wherever they are occur, regardless of the uses to which they have been put.

Before we begin, however, it will be well at least to touch on two questions that are inseparable from one another. How many intermediate versions might there have been between the full account of which the Pisander scholion permits us to have a glimpse and the paltry résumé, the scholium itself, that remains our sole evidence of it today? Who was the enigmatic Pisander mentioned twice in our text?

It is probable that Pisander was a poet from Laranda, known through a note by Suidas[30] and several quotations, who wrote down in sixty books of verse the history of the world from the wedding of Zeus and Hera until the events of his own time, and who recounted other events in prose.[31] Everything else that concerns this Pisander is disputed, even his dates. According to Suidas he lived during the reign of Alexander Severus (222–235 CE); Macrobius, on the other hand, maintains that Virgil had much earlier borrowed the entire beginning of the second book of the *Aeneid* from him.[32]

Jacoby and Keydell suppose that, apart from the versifier from Laranda, there existed another Pisander, a mythographer, dates and origin unknown, to whom they attribute various fragments, among them our scholium from *Phoenician Women*.[33] It will be readily apparent that this hypothesis results, not from what is known, but from what is not known.

Pisander of Laranda was an epitomizer of the epic cycle who wrote sometimes in verse, sometimes in prose, and who prided himself on a lively and eloquent style.[34] We may be certain that he invented nothing. Whether our scholium goes back to him or to Keydell's mysterious Pisander XIII, one thing seems to me clear, namely, that we are dealing here with a summary, nothing more. In that case it would be rash to try to conclude anything very definite from a document that stands at a more or less great distance from the lost source of which it represents a drastic abridgment. This source, I believe, is an ancient work, probably a poem of the Theban cycle, perhaps the *Oedipodea*, as Bethe and Wecklein supposed.[35] In the Pisander scholion, however, we have a report of it that is too incomplete and too garbled for it to be possible to go beyond anything more than mere hypothesis.

*Liège, 1939–1944*

# Exposure of the Infant

---

In an earlier work I tried to show that Oedipus is one of those malefic newborn children whom ancient communities did away with because their deformity was a proof of divine wrath.[1] I did not sufficiently insist there on the fact that the exposed infants were scapegoats. Their sacralization, in the event they were rescued, had the effect of bringing about a reversal of values, so that what had been seen as evil was now considered to be good. Similarly, a divine judgment, involving a trial from which the child emerges alive, ended not in an acquittal, pure and simple, but in the *preferment* of the accused and the *punishment* of the accuser. And every exposure entailed a divine judgment.

Nonetheless it would be a mistake to reduce all tales of exposed infants to a single type. In most of them the evil character does not appear at all, or else is introduced belatedly when a psychological explanation is wanted for each of the acts that make up such tales. This leads us to recognize, alongside the theme of the *misshapen child*, which has its origin in a known rite meant to ward off barrenness, the themes of *submersion in water* and *rearing in the mountains*, which must go back to ancient rituals of initiation, tests whose usual purpose was to induct a young man into the class of adult males. It may be that the most painful tests corresponded to the highest investitures; this is in any case implied in the event that they come to be transposed into legend.

Indeed, paradoxical though it may seem, the two ritual orders discernible in the theme of the exposed infant—the judgment of malefic newborns, on the one hand, and the testing of youths on the other—end up producing synonymous legends: the abnormal infant who is rescued and the youth who survives initiation are both destined to a brilliant future. There can be no doubt that, as legendary narratives gradually took shape, this idea was more clearly brought out by secondary influences whose operation has yet to be fully understood.

---

Oedipus was exposed as an infant. The poets of classical Greece tell us why: Laius and Jocasta were warned by the oracle of Apollo at Delphi that their issue would bring misfortune upon Thebes. Aeschylus and Euripides place the warning before the conception of Oedipus; Sophocles, after his birth. Sophocles considers the prohibition pronounced by Delphi to be groundless. Euripides justifies it by Laius's shameful love for Chrysippus, son of Pelops; and while he seems not to have invented this reason,[2] he did place it in a new context. He interpreted the will of the gods more strictly than Sophocles did, and found it difficult to accept that their decisions might be arbitrary.

Let us emphasize first the reason for the exposure, namely, the *sanction* announced by the oracle in case of disobedience. Thebes as a whole was liable to suffer if a child born of Laius and Jocasta were allowed to grow up. This theme is exceptional in tales of exposed newborn children, which suggests that Aeschylus may have found it in an early version of the legend. Subsequently, once the sentimental elements of the legend had supplanted the political elements, the oracle also announced patricide and incest.[3] These were late additions borrowed from analogous but somewhat different accounts, in which a newborn is persecuted by someone who fears he will grow up to be an enemy one day. The persecutor is generally the mother's father. The baby is miraculously saved through the intervention of a god, of whom he is the son. Oedipus, son of a mortal father, is the only child (along with Paris) to have been exposed at birth by his own parents, obliged to choose between their son and the city to which they owe allegiance. Atalanta was also exposed by her father, Iasos, but this because he was disappointed at having no sons. Additionally, there was later added to the legend of Iasos an oracle warning that his life would be threatened by his daughter and by her descendants—a detail that was to figure in every legend of this type once it had become commonplace. Yet there are no synonymous legends in Greek folklore. If one goes to the trouble to compare all those having a common theme, one realizes that the theme reflects a particular context in each case, with the result that it takes on a unique meaning. It will be useful, then, to begin by methodically classifying the tales of exposed infants.

These tales have been collected by several authors, but never in their entirety. Usener, studying the myth of Deucalion, a sort of Greek Noah, rightly suspects that he was an exposed infant to begin with. This leads him to perceive similarities with other such adventures. He attaches too much importance to the detail of the floating chest, however, which he takes to be the equivalent of a theophoric boat or fish. Seeing exposures of divine off-spring as a mythical transcription of the epiphany of a sun god, he arbitrarily neglects the theme of exposure in the mountains, though it figures in several legends (Dionysus, Oedipus, Telephus) as a variant of exposure on the water in a chest. These alternate motifs need to be studied in tandem. Usener also neglects semihistorical accounts, such as those involving Cypselus, Cyrus, and Ptolemy Soter. Glotz detects in all these legends a transposition of ordeals of legitimation, and he closely studies those that bring an accusation of unchaste behavior against the mother (Danaë, Auge, Semele, Rhea Silvia). Sir James Frazer, who does not cite Glotz, arrives at the same conclusion after systematically analyzing almost all the parallels with the story of Moses.[4]

They are numerous. At Nineveh one finds an inscription from the eighth century BCE that had been deposited in the royal library. The inscription is a copy of the biography that King Sargon the Great, who lived around 2600 BCE, is supposed to have commissioned of himself. It mentions the name of his mother, Agade, a young woman of lowly birth, who conceived him by an unknown man and secretly put him out into the world. She hid him in a reed basket and left it to float down a river; but the basket did not sink, and a gardener rescued the baby. Later Sargon was beloved of the goddess Ishtar and enjoyed a glorious reign. Alone among the heroes of this type, Sargon acknowledges that he is a bastard. The others are almost invariably declared to be sons of a god. One thinks of Karna, son of the Sun and a princess who exposed him from fear of his father the king, according to the account in the *Mahābhārata*; also of Romulus and Remus, as well as the story of Moses, though all these lie too far afield.[5] By contrast, the legends of Semiramis,

Gilgamesh, and Cyrus were known in Greece, and for each of them at least one Hellenic version has come down to us.

Semiramis, daughter of the goddess Derceto and a mere mortal, is exposed by her mother in the mountains and raised there by doves.[6] The theme of the animal savior, found in many legends of this type, led Aelian to recount the tale of Gilgamesh in his book on the nature of animals.[7] The Chaldeans warn the king of Babylon, Seuechoras, that the son of his daughter will overthrow him. The king therefore imprisons his daughter, who mysteriously becomes pregnant and gives birth to a child who is hurled from the window of the citadel by her guards. The falling infant is intercepted in midair by an eagle and gently laid down in a garden; the gardener, sensing perhaps that the child is destined for great things, takes it upon himself to raise the child, who indeed later succeeds his grandfather on the throne of Babylon.

The story of Cyrus reached Herodotus less than a century after the king's death, though by then it had already been completely transformed under the influence of legends relating to exposed children. Let us briefly examine those legends that were known in Greece. They are both curious and rich enough to warrant special consideration.

Perseus is doomed by his grandfather Acrisius, king of Argos, on being told by an oracle that he would die at the hand of the son of his only daughter. Danaë declares before the altar of Zeus Herkeios that the child she has brought into the world is the son of the god. Acrisius locks the mother and her child in a large chest and throws it into the sea, from which it is fished out near the island of Seriphos. The circumstances of Danaë's rescue, of which there exist several versions, do not interest us here. Later Perseus was to return to Argus, found Mycenae, and accidentally strike his grandfather with a discus, killing him.

Telephus is the son of Heracles and Auge. Auge's father, Aleus, king of Tegea, angry with his daughter for having (or so he believed) allowed herself to be seduced, set her adrift in a chest together with her child. The sea carried them to the coast of Mysia, where they landed. This story has several variants. The casting out upon the sea of the mother and child is generally described as a punishment for unchastity. Only one author, Alcidamas,[8] says that Aleus acted out of prudence, as Acrisius had done, because the Delphic oracle had warned him that his sons would be killed by the child of his daughter; but he does not say that Aleus took steps to prevent Auge from conceiving. According to a tradition recorded by Pausanias in Arcadia itself, the young woman, like Danaë, defended herself against paternal accusations by alleging that Heracles had violated her, and afterward gave birth on Mount Parthenion.[9] There were many rivers and springs of this name in Greece, associated with stories of virginal baths and tests of virginity.[10] The Arcadian Mount of the Virgin therefore proudly claimed to be the birthplace of Telephus. The child was suckled by a doe, then raised by the shepherds of Korythos, an ancient Peloponnesian god later superseded by Apollo Kourotrophos.[11] Whereas Telephus is said to have been exposed by his grandfather (or by his mother) on Mount Parthenion, Aleus hands Auge over to Nauplius, in some versions so that Nauplius may sell her in a distant land, in which case he brings her to Mysia and gives her to the king, Teuthras, who marries her; in others so that he may kill her, in which case he drags her behind the stern of his ship and sails to Mysia, where, Auge still being alive when they arrive, he spares her.[12] Nauplius was evidently entrusted with Auge for the purpose of *testing* her, and this by means of an ordeal so terrible that it seems equivalent to a death sentence. It is tempting to consider traditions that separate the mother and the son as later variants, because they permit the pathetic moment of mutual recognition suggested by Hyginus's account. Hyginus relates that Teuthras, king of Mysia, did not marry Auge, but instead adopted her, then promised her as a reward to whoever could deliver his country from a monster.[13] Telephus vanquished the monster and was on the verge of marrying his mother, who, wishing to belong to no one after having been loved by Heracles, was on the verge of killing her son. Despite the echo here of the theme of Euripides's lost play about Oedipus, influenced by Sophocles's *Oedipus the King*, the exposure of Telephus on Parthenion is probably an old Tegean tradition. On the other hand, the two different trials imposed upon mother and child are consistent with very old ideas: for the newborn, exposure on a river or at sea and exposure on a mountainside are interchangeable; the ordeal of virginity is always administered by water, however, and it is to this one that Auge was subjected, whether she is supposed to have been placed in a chest with Telephus or strapped alone to the stern of Nauplius's ship.[14] In a version that is perhaps not earlier than the fifth century BCE, Telephus kills (without recognizing) his uncles Hippothoos and Nereus, whom he outwits.[15]

Anius is the son of Apollo and Rhoeo, daughter of Staphylus. Staphylus locks up Rhoeo in a chest, which is thrown into the sea and by good fortune lands at Delos. There she gives birth to Anius, who himself will have three daughters, Oeno, Spermo, and Elaïs, which is to say three goddesses of vegetation, heroines respectively of the vine, seeds, and olive tree. Staphylus himself is the eponymous god of the grape; his daughter, Rhoeo, is named for the pomegranate.

At Brasiae, a coastal town in western Laconia, Pausanias recorded a singular version of the story of Dionysus that is related to these other ones.[16] Cadmus locks Semele in a chest with a child to whom she has just given birth. When the chest washes up at Brasiae, Semele is no longer alive and her sister Ino nurses the baby Dionysus in a cave. From this it may be inferred that Ino's cave was at Brasiae and that Semele was buried in a tomb there as well. Pausanias's narrative combines two themes that alternate in the childhood of Telephus: exposure at sea and rearing in the mountains.

To these legends Usener adds the story of Tennes, who as an adult undergoes a trial by water. Tennes, son of Cycnus, himself the son of Poseidon, is traduced by his stepmother, who treats him as Phaedra did Hippolytus. Cycnus puts Tennes in a chest, either alone or, according to the most common version, with his sister Hemithea. They land on the island of Leucophrys, which Tennes was to name Tenedos after himself. The legend is known solely through late accounts (no poet, to my knowledge, ever spoke of it) and was probably influenced by the legend of Phaedra. However this may be, the summaries that have come down to us leave the physical abuse visited upon Hemithea unexplained. Conon is the only mythographer who seeks to justify it, saying that she had displayed undue distress at the punishment inflicted upon her brother. It is possible that in the oldest version the stepmother had accused Tennes, not of plotting against her, but of incest with his sister. In that case exposure in the chest would have been a double ordeal meant to prove the purity of each of them. The sister may also have been joined to her brother as Helle was to Phrixus, engulfed by a tide of emotion of the sort that forms the heart of stories involving a wicked stepmother. Tennes is in any case sent back to the sea, as if to a judge. Poseidon saves him, according to a scholium on the *Iliad*, because he was chaste and because he was Poseidon's grandson.[17] This formula (διὰ σωφροσύνην καὶ διὰ τὸ εἶναι υἱωνόν) juxtaposes two different tests, one applied for the purpose of demonstrating *innocence*,

the other for demonstrating *filiation*. The latter, a test of legitimacy, also fig-
ures in Theseus's Cretan adventure. The former, which in this context seems
to be the older of the two, occurs in an account given by Pausanias, who, after
mentioning the safe arrival of brother and sister at Tenedos, says that Cyc-
nus, now aware of the true state of affairs, sets sail for the island in order to
publicly acknowledge his error and his offense.[18] Neither Pausanias nor any
other author says how Cycnus came to be disillusioned, and for the Greeks,
at any rate, it did not matter: Tennes was innocent because he had survived.
Even those who no longer knew what an ordeal was interpreted the fact of
his having escaped a very grave danger as a verdict of innocence. Pausanias
concludes his account by saying that when Cycnus landed at Tenedos, his
son, in a fit of anger, cut the mooring ropes with an ax. This anecdote, in its
detail, seems to be the *aition* [cause or reason] of the proverbial expression
"to cut with a Tenedean ax."[19] But it is interesting, in its spirit, for expressing
a hostility toward the hero's family that is characteristic of a whole series of
legends. I suppose that the episode of the severed ropes must be interpreted
as implying that the ship drifted out to sea and that Cycnus died. It has disap-
peared from our versions of the myth because Cycnus later came to be identi-
fied with a homonym, the Cycnus who was killed by Achilles. The shadow
cast by Achilles also influenced the ending of Tennes's story, the later variants
of which do not interest us here.

---

Usener's reading of this series of legends is well known. The character inside
the chest, he says, is always a god, or the descendant of a god, who crosses
the sea and arrives safely in a foreign land. The legend, in other words, is
a romantic transposition of a divine epiphany. To the same race of heroes
belong Oedipus and Deucalion, whose name Δευκαλίων (or Δεύκαλος)
means "little Zeus," "son of Zeus."

Glotz and Frazer adopted Usener's grouping of the legends and gave
them another common denominator: the undergoing of an ordeal. Here
we are in the domain of material facts. Glotz shows very clearly that there
were several kinds of ordeals. This is why the tales, while they resemble one
another, do not coincide in every detail. An explanation of this sort shows
little concern for the specifically religious element of the myth of the exposed
infant, however, and it wholly ignores a detail to which Usener rightly drew

attention, namely, the hero's deportation from his native land. As a result
of the persecution of which he is a victim, and of the ordeal to which he is
then subjected, an innocent child is removed from the country of his birth:
either he comes back to it later (Oedipus, Perseus) or he goes on to conquer
other lands and to found cities (Tennes, Telephus, Anius); but in any case
he grows up far away from the place where normally he would have been
raised. In what follows I shall try to cast some light on this obscure motif.
But first it will be necessary to consider a few more legends, pointing out
their distinctive features as well as the difficulties they present. The most
curious is certainly the legend of Deucalion. No critic has made a study of
it that amounts to anything more than a collection of local Greek traditions
concerning a flood, a saved man, and the place where he came ashore.[20]

---

Deucalion escapes the flood in a λάρναξ or in a κιβωτός, which is to say in
a square chest. Whichever word is used, there can be no question that it
refers to the instrument of the actual ordeals that shaped—if they did not
in fact give birth to—the myth of the exposed innocent. It must have been a
closed crate, just large enough for the child's survival to be improbable, but
not impossible. "Confinement in a chest was retained throughout [ancient]
Greek history in the penal law concerning the family," Glotz says, "and this
punishment with suspensive effect always seemed to be an invitation for the
gods to intervene. . . . Moreover, in Italy, the *arca* was always used as a punish-
ment for slaves."[21] This amounts to saying that Deucalion was saved under
conditions in which, normally, he ought to have perished. The difference
between his story and that of Noah, in the state in which the two tales have
come down to us, is that Noah escapes the flood *because* he has taken refuge
in a boat, whereas Deucalion survives *in spite of* having been placed in an
object that was supremely unsuited for ensuring his safety over the course of
a long and difficult journey by sea. Yahweh, in Genesis, does all that can be
done to save Noah. Zeus, by contrast, is indifferent to Deucalion's fate at the
outset; Deucalion is saved, not by Zeus's counsels, but by those of Prometheus
(according to Apollodorus) or thanks to an idea that came to him (according
to Ovid). Following the child's rescue, Zeus begins to look favorably upon
him. Thereafter everything happens as if Zeus had wished, not to *spare* him,
but first and foremost to *test* him. This would indicate that the god was able

to appeal to a jurisdiction higher than himself, which is not at all surprising since, to the ancient Greek mind, pure elements (water among them) had a force capable of immediately punishing anyone who is guilty.[22] The story of Noah is coherent. The story of Deucalion is absurd, if it must be accepted that Prometheus had put him (or that Deucalion had put himself) in the chest in order to ensure his safety. Ovid, who subjects everything to the laws of bare probability, takes care not to speak of a chest: he describes only the arrival of Deucalion and his wife at Mount Parnassus, with its twin peaks, where the fortunate couple had landed in a *parva ratis*.[23] The reader is free to imagine a raft or a small boat, as he likes; in any case, something remotely plausible.[24] Genesis rationalizes much more boldly, lodging Noah in a quite large boat—a floating house, in effect, having three decks. I shall come back to the stories of Noah and Deucalion in due course. For the moment let us simply say, with regard to Deucalion, that in the earliest traditions it seems as though he must have been saved alone, and not with his wife, Pyrrha. This may be inferred from the episode of the "generative stones." If a husband and wife are saved, they hold within themselves the future of the world, and therefore have no need of Zeus's favor in order to ensure the perpetuation of the human race. But if, owing to exactly this favor, Deucalion is surrounded by male companions, Zeus having promised him that they will be born from stones that he has thrown behind him, it is because no woman is any longer alive on the surface of the earth. No one, ancient or modern, seems to have noticed that the presence of Pyrrha renders the episode of the generative stones useless (and vice versa), except for Pindar, who is plainly surprised that the "nuptial bed" did not serve to create a new race.[25] Glotz very clearly saw why Pyrrha—a red-haired woman—entered into the Deucalion legend, and I shall take up his explanation later, when it will be necessary to come back to some of the difficulties that flood myths commonly conceal. Usener, it will be recalled, was convinced that Deucalion in the earliest version of the legend was a *Zeusknäblein* [infant Zeus] saved at birth, like Perseus and Telephus. I would not dare to assert anything of the kind myself. Divine descent, it seems to me, must be a secondary feature in legends of miraculous rescue. If one sees them instead as fictionalized accounts deriving from the ordeal as a historical practice, they may be at least roughly explained. Let us therefore look at them from this perspective and try to see how they differ from one another.

Several of the legends seem to involve tests of chastity. Here exposure in a chest has an equivalent: a young woman is plunged into the sea and tied to the stern of a boat; if she is still alive at the end of a more or less long journey, it is because the sea has declared her to be innocent of the charge brought against her. Among the Hellenic traditions of Cyrene, Herodotus encountered the tale of Phronime, an exact replica of the Tennes legend.[26] Phronime likewise has a cruel stepmother who accuses her of indecency. Her father Etearchus, king of Crete, gives her to Themison with orders that she be drowned at sea. Themison attaches Phronime with ropes to his boat. On discovering that she is still breathing when they arrive at Thera, he hands her over to Polymnestus, who takes her as a concubine. The semantic transparency of the names themselves is enough to establish the stylization of the account: a True Leader (Etearchus) hands over a Good Girl (Phronime) to a Dispenser of Justice (Themison), who rules that the trial was favorable to the accused. Herodotus no longer understands that the ruling depended on the outcome of an ordeal, however, for he interprets the trial as a punishment; and yet for him, as for all his contemporaries, the fact that Phronime survives the terrible voyage settles the matter of her innocence. The only difference between the story of Tennes and that of Phronime is that chastity is required exclusively of young women. If a man figures in a trial of this kind, it is not because he is lacking in self-restraint, but because he is suspected of having violated the wife of his father, which is to say of having encroached on his father's prerogatives. The Auge legend clearly shows the equivalence of the two ways of administering the test: in certain versions, Auge is put in a chest; in others she is dragged behind a ship.[27]

When an infant is exposed together with his or her mother, it is because the mother has claimed that the child was fathered by a god, which automatically excuses maternity outside marriage. The young mother justifies herself by invoking the god's will; she is not believed; her salvation and that of the child proves that she had spoken the truth. This episode in found in the tales of Danaë, Auge, Semele, and Rhoeo. If Semele was said to have been dead on her arrival at Brasiae, it is because the people of this land felt a need to authenticate a monument to her that was to be seen there. The decisive point is that the chest, however improbably, managed to come ashore, thus demonstrating the innocence of the accused.

Those who have studied the theme of the ordeal have nevertheless neglected one aspect of it. They are solely interested in the fate of the accused, never the fate of the accuser. Now, the legends that have come down to us prove that, to the Greek mind, one does not appeal to the justice of the gods without putting oneself in danger. Readers of Glotz's book might suppose that a divine judgment absolves or condemns only that person who is explicitly subject to it. Not at all—the trial always ends in an acquittal or a conviction. If the accused is found innocent, his persecutor, even in the event he has acted in good faith, pays for his error. Acrisius dies at the hand of Perseus, Aleus loses his sons because of Telephus, Cycnus is at least placed in danger by Tennes. The flood myth, which certainly implies an ordeal (even if the myth signifies something else as well), concludes with the salvation of the one who has been tested and the death of everyone else. Later we will speak about the murder of Laius.

The expiation of the accuser, as it is described in the legends, has two constant features:

1. Patricide is presented as involuntary or nearly so. Perseus kills his grandfather inadvertently; Tennes cuts the mooring ropes of his father's boat in a fit of anger; Oedipus, in the versions that we have, has many excuses for having killed Laius. The saved infant is a sympathetic figure, merely an instrument of the divine wrath aroused by the suspicions of his persecutor.

2. Eventually it came to be forgotten that punishment of the accuser automatically follows acquittal of the accused. On the other hand, the structure of the legends prevented the punishment from being represented as an act of vengeance performed through the rescued child. The child acts solely as an intermediary between those on high who are responsible for the administration of earthly justice and the person who unwisely appealed to them, in vain. Because error is no longer imagined to reside in the accuser, his misfortune is represented instead as the fulfillment of an oracle. It is owing to a dream, or to a divine threat, that a man persecutes his offspring—a useless precaution that in the end is turned against him. That the theme of the oracle was a late addition to legends of this kind becomes clear on closer inspection. It is absent from very old accounts that have been discovered through other versions, for example the tale of Semele's exposure; and absent as well from accounts that have never, or only seldom, received literary treatment, for example the tale of Rhoeo and Anius. By contrast, it is found in the story of Cypselus and, later, in the legend of Cyrus, which was elaborated over a

quite brief period whose extent is exactly known, since Cyrus died in 529 BCE and Herodotus must have prepared the first book of the *Histories* about 450. Sometime around the end of the sixth century, then, the legend of a child chosen by the gods must have arisen from the idea of a threat of divine origin. As a motif of tragic drama, this idea was all the more convenient as it allowed the elements of the plot to be closely connected with one another, and made it possible to foreshadow the denouement in the prologue and to establish the innocence of all the actors of the drama, the convicted persecutor no less than the persecuted elect. It must have been a motif of late invention as well, for the oracles themselves are not very old.[28]

It remains to discover how, in the absence of an oracle, another motif could explain the sequence of events. Danaë, Auge, and Semele may have been persecuted, like Tyro and Melanippe, because they had become mothers without having married, and indeed Glotz sees the exposed infant essentially as a bastard who emerges victorious from a legitimation ordeal. Apollodorus attributes to Auge yet another misdeed: in hiding her infant son in a precinct sacred to Athena she brought a great scourge upon the land, with the result that it remained barren.[29] In the legends of Cypselus and of Cyrus, the oracle is indispensable in imparting narrative consistency to an account constructed from folkloric materials that are roughly consistent with historical fact. Cyrus could not be given a god for a father, since everyone knew he was the son of Cambyses, nor could he be made Astyages's murderer, since everyone knew he had treated his grandfather rather generously.[30] The hostility shown by Astyages toward the son of Mandane could therefore be explained only by a threat issuing from a god.

And if Laius had received no divine warning, the exposure of Oedipus would have no readily apparent explanation. We therefore find ourselves back where we started. Let us pause here to consider the points on which the story of Oedipus differs from the stories we have just examined.

Oedipus's existence in no way threatened the lives of either his grandfather or his maternal uncles. We know of no archaic version that mentions an oracle. The oldest one that has come down to us, Aeschylus's *Seven against Thebes*, says simply that, should Laius die without issue, he will save Thebes.[31] In Sophocles's *Oedipus the King*, the oracle announces—after the birth of the child, and so too late for calamity to be averted—that the newborn will kill his father.[32] In Euripides's *Phoenician Women*, the announcement is placed, as in Aeschylus, before the birth; the oracle predicts the death of the father and the quarrel of the sons, which is to say the civil war for control over Thebes. Here Euripides's skillfulness in exploiting the innovations of his predecessors is manifest. The prediction never involves marriage with the mother, except in the version due to Nicolaus of Damascus: "The god says to Laius that he will sire a son who will kill him and who will marry his own mother";[33] and in John Malalas, who mentions only the marriage with the mother and not the murder of the father.[34] The sources from which Nicolaus of Damascus and Malalas draw are unknown, and probably no longer extant. Both authors refer to the legend as they recollected it from memory, neglecting to distinguish between the first response of the oracle, at Delphi, given to Laius in connection with the birth of his son, and the response given twenty years later to Oedipus when he came to Corinth to submit to the god his doubts concerning his birth.[35] If the mythographers confused the two warnings it is because, between Aeschylus's time and theirs, the legend had evolved: political in its beginnings, it became more and more *sentimental*, and the theme of incest steadily gained in importance; in Aeschylus, political motives were still predominant. Let us therefore take as our point of departure the oracle's response as it is formulated in *Seven against Thebes*. This way of proceeding is recommended additionally by the fact that the threat conveyed by the oracle in this case is not the same as the one that frightens Acrisius, Aleus, or Astages. It does not express the familiar prediction that the newborn will grow up to be the murderer of his grandfather or of his uncles—an adventitious detail that ultimately was to enter into all the legends of this type.[36] It expresses a motif that is peculiar to the legend of Oedipus. I therefore think that, while it is foreign to the primitive myth, it nonetheless has to have appeared at a much earlier time than the one in which all tales of an exposed infant came to be stereotyped on the story of Perseus.

The idea that a child must be sacrificed because, if he lives, he will bring misfortune to an entire community is encountered, so far as I am aware, in only three legends, those of Oedipus, Paris, and Cypselus. I leave to one side that of Romulus, which is closely related to them, but whose independence—or lack of independence, as one may well be inclined to suspect—cannot be argued here.

The exposure of Alexander is known to us solely through texts in which one detects the influence of tales concerning Oedipus and Cyrus.[37]

In Homer, Alexander—like the other Trojan princes—herds his father's flocks to graze on Mount Ida. There is no mention of his having either been exposed or raised in the mountains. A fragment of Pindar speaks of a frightening dream in which Hecuba is warned of the misfortune that will befall Troy if Paris survives.[38] In the lost plays entitled *Alexandros* by Sophocles and Euripides the legend is found in its complete form, though we are unable to determine to what extent it had already been worked out before them. The infant is exposed on Ida, nursed by a she-bear, and raised by a shepherd who names him Paris. He soon surpasses all the companions of his childhood in strength and beauty, and vanquishes all who attempt to raid his flocks, as a result of which he is called Alexandros ["protector of men"]. His parents organize games at Troy in honor of their exposed son, whom they believe to have died long ago. Paris returns and emerges victorious in competition with his brothers, notably Hector and Deiphobus, who threatens to kill him.

To be sure, it is difficult to say which part of this account is likely to be old. Hecuba's dream could be a replica of Astyages's dream: the Trojan prince distinguishes himself in competition with his rivals exactly as the Persian child does. Nevertheless it must be recognized that the Greek playwrights, in elaborating the legend, preserved not only the religious coloring of each episode but also what might be called its archaic efficaciousness, as I will attempt to show in a moment.

Cypselus's childhood is known to us through Herodotus, who seems to have been determined to drive later historians to despair, so carefully does he obscure the religious content of his narratives. Deciding how much archaic reality lies concealed in a tale reported by Pausanias or Apollodorus is not especially difficult, for they frankly reproduce details they no longer understand. Herodotus rationalizes everything he touches, covering over authentic traditions, as well as the links he establishes between them in order to make them more acceptable, with a varnish of bourgeois plausibility. Let us therefore make due allowance for a certain folkloric element implicit in what he says of Cypselus.[39]

The Bacchiadae reign at Corinth. They have a daughter named Labda, who is afflicted with lameness. None of the men of the family wish to take her as a wife. Finally she is wed to Eëtion, son of Echecrates, from the township [deme] of Petra. Echecrates himself is descended from Caeneus, a Lapith.

Time goes by. Eëtion and his wife are still unable to conceive. Eëtion consults the oracle, which answers: "Eëtion, none esteem you though you are worthy of many honors. Labda is pregnant; she will give birth to a round boulder [ὀλοοίτροχος]. It will fall among royal men; it will punish the Corinthians."

The oracle is reported to the Bacchiadae. It reminds them of another, much more enigmatic one that they had long known without having ever been able to interpret it: "A fertile eagle among the rocks; it will bring forth a strong lion that will break the knees of many men. Mind you well, Corinthians, who live near lovely Peirene and haughty Corinth."

The Bacchiadae perceive that the two predictions concern the same child. When Cypselus is born, ten men from the Bacchiad clan are sent at once to the deme where Eëtion lives (ἐσ τὸν δῆμον, ἐν τῷ κατοίκητο ὁ Ἀετίων) with orders to seize the newborn and kill him. But the infant smiles, disarming the envoys; and after each one has passed him to the next in the hope that one of them would finally have the courage to "smash [him] against the stone threshold" [the Greek verb, προσουδίσαι, literally means to dash against the ground], in keeping with the plan they had agreed upon, they give him back to his mother. Labda hears them reproaching one another, understands the danger, and hides the infant in a round chest—a *cypselē* [κυψέλη], hence the name later given to her son—where, on their return, they do not think to look for him.

This story, like that of Cyrus, was influenced by the tale of Perseus, whose popularity must have been great in preclassical Greece. The child is a menace to his maternal relatives; warned by an oracle, they seek to make him die. It is awkward to leave the prophecy of an oracle unfulfilled, however, and Nicolaus of Damascus was later to relate that Cypselus, in order to seize power, kills a Bacchiad, whom the manuscripts first identify as Hippoclides, then as Patroclides. On the other hand, the folkloric spirit that suffuses this legend bears the trace of earlier beliefs that caused malefic infants to be exposed. Exposure is always described as the action of an entire community.[40] This is why the ten Bacchiad envoys presented themselves to the local authorities before entering Eëtion's home. What they were demanding was a sort of right of extradition, for in antiquity, except for precisely this case of *apothesis*, the father as paterfamilias had absolute authority over his offspring. The envoys obtained the permission they sought because the Bacchiadae had been shrewd enough to identify their cause with that of Corinth as a whole. The father on his return rescued the infant, hidden in a chest used for measuring out grain, and brought him to Olympia as a supplicant of the god.[41]

The laws relating to *apothesis* all say that the infant must be exposed immediately following birth. The head of the house of the Bacchiadae sends his messengers the moment Labda has delivered her child (ὡς δὲ ἔτεκε ἡ γυνὴ τάκιστα). But he made their mission a dangerous one by charging them, not with exposing the infant, but with killing it on the spot. An ancient Greek had few scruples about sending a guilty person to a certain death; he had many more when it was a matter of shedding blood, particularly that of someone who, in dying before his time, was liable to become a particularly dreaded ghost. None of the Bacchiad envoys wished to bring upon himself the stain of such a murder, or run the risk that would result from it. This is why, Herodotus says, they decided between them that the one to whom the mother handed over the infant would be responsible for smashing it on the ground. When the moment came, no one had the courage to carry out the plan. Herodotus, always ready to rationalize, would have us believe that the reason was not *fear*, but *pity*, and in order to make the envoys' reaction more plausible he adds that the infant smiled—without realizing that this embellishment is incompatible with the exact instruction[42] he had quoted earlier, namely, that the execution take place at the moment of birth, for a newborn baby does not smile.

We must not take our leave of Cypselus without saying a few words about the names of his companions in legend. His father is called Eëtion—in Doric both Aëtion and Aëtos, for the oracle given to Cypselus as an adult[43] calls him Ἠετίδης [Eëtides (son of Eëtion)] and not Ἠετιονίδης [Eëtionides (descendant of Eëtion)]; similarly one finds in the *Iliad*[44] Δευκαλίδης [Deucalides (son of Deucalion, or of Deucalos)] rather than Δευκαλιονίδης [Deucalionides (descendant of Deucalion)]—suggesting the form Δεύκαλος, from which Usener was able to conclude so much. Aëtion, the Eagle or the Son of the Eagle, is descended from the Lapith Caeneus, who did not die. He had been buried alive under a great mound of tree trunks by his enemies, the Centaurs; and from deep within the piled-up trunks, Nestor recounts in Ovid, there flew up a bird with golden wings ("which I then saw," the old hero says, "for the first and last time").[45] Caeneus, who was a young girl named Caenis, beloved of Zeus, before becoming an invulnerable warrior, immortal, and then finally being transformed into a bird, may well be the most ancient incarnation of the myth of the phoenix.[46] If that is so, it must be accepted that already in Greek antiquity the Eagle and the Phoenix were identified with each other: the bird that Ovid describes resembles the Phoenix, and a man named Eagle claimed to be descended from Caeneus. The myth of Caeneus is so obscure, however, that it is impossible for us here to go beyond mere hypothesis.

The village of Petra near Corinth is unknown to us. The name was probably inferred—perhaps by Herodotus himself—from the oracle, which says that the Eagle will inseminate among rocks. One may wonder whether ἐν πέτρῃσι κύει does not simply mean to fertilize unproductive land, that is, *to sow on stony ground*. The issue of Eëtion and Labda (which must be smashed against the ground [a "stone threshold"]) will be fatal in the manner of a "round boulder that a stream swollen by the storm has thrown down from the rock that it crowned." It is to the fall of one such boulder that the *Iliad* compares charging Hector.[47] One must not try to read too much into images selected by an oracle that couches very simple realities in enigmatic terms. The oracle can only mean that Cypselus, son of an eagle inseminating stony ground, will be hard for Corinth, just as his mother was. His mother's name, Labda, poses several problems, however.

The first of these is determining since which period, and in which parts of Greece, *labda* and *lambda* were understood to signify a particular disability, that is, lameness. The entry for βλαισός in the *Etymologicum Magnum* says: "Knock-kneed, paralyzed, someone whose feet are turned outward like the letter λ. It is for this reason that Eëtion's wife, mother of the tyrant Cypselus, was called Lambda."[48] *Labda*, which is not an adjective, is known as a proper name only through the passage in Herodotus. The phrasing of the *Etymologicum Magnum* proves that its author did not know, any more than we do, the least thing about the word's literary use outside of Corinthian history. But as a nickname it has all the characteristics of a piece of slang, and may very well have been current in the popular tongue.[49] If the word, in the fifth century, designated someone who is lame, Herodotus, encountering the story of a woman named Labda, could have interpreted it as a nickname and inferred from it what he says about the young woman's infirmity. But in that case how are we to explain the strange parallelism of this tale with that of Oedipus, whose grandfather is called Labdacus?

Labdacus is a grandfather, Labda the mother, of a newborn [Oedipus and Cypselus, respectively] who is declared before his birth to be evil and who is destined to die. None of these characters has a proper name. They have nicknames, taken in the case of the ascendants from an infirmity, and in the case of the descendants from an episode in which their lives were saved. At least this is how the Greeks understood, how they interpreted, the words *Oidipous* and *Cypselos*.

The two tales cannot have had any influence on each other. Both are recent and may be at least roughly dated. The names of Labda and Labdacus could have acquired the meaning indicated by the *Etymologicum Magnum* only after the introduction of the Phoenician alphabet. At Thebes, so far as we know, the letter *lambda* was written not ⅂, but ʟ.[50] Labdakos, a character without any accompanying legend, must have been a late interpolation between Polydorus and Laius in the line of Theban kings. Cypselus reigned in the mid-seventh century. The mythopoetic imagination that created his legend was constrained, as in the case of Cyrus as well, by the need to take into account historical facts that had not yet completely faded from memory.

The legend of Oedipus, like that of Cypselus, was, I believe, transcribed from an actual practice, the habit of exposing deformed newborn children from birth. But Cypselus and Oedipus are both victorious, and the ancients could not accept that their heroes might have been physically defective; the maleficent infirmity was therefore attributed to a forebear, a grandfather or a mother—mere personifications of the illness that is at the very root of legendary creation.

As for Cypselus's name, it is certainly independent of the *cypselē* that is supposed to explain it. The choice of an *aition* here is all the more significant as it shows the prestige that the story of Perseus enjoyed in people's minds not only in the seventh century, but also in the sixth and the fifth. A tyrant, a conqueror such as Cypselus or Cyrus—or, later, Romulus—had to have undergone some childhood adventure that made him more like a son of Zeus. The *cypselē* would therefore have had to become as similar as possible to the chest thrown into the sea on the order of Acrisius, for everyone in the seventh century saw the chest, not as an instrument of trial, but as a means of punishment transformed by the gods into an instrument of salvation, and then into a sign of election. It was therefore necessary that the *cypselē* likewise serve to save Labda's son. A *cypselē* is a cylindrical vase; the *larnax* and the *kibōtos* are square. Now, the object that was venerated at Olympia, and that was called the chest of Cypselus, was square.[51] Pausanias, who describes it, disposes of the difficulty by saying that at some earlier time the Corinthians had given the name *cypselē* to a *larnax*—an explanation evidently invented for the occasion. It would appear, then, that folk etymology connected the name of the hero, Cypselus, with a *cypselē*; the myth of the exposed infant caused the *cypselē* to be identified with the chest of the ordeals; and the sculpted chest found at Olympia was considered to be the votive offering of the tyrant who, as a baby, was saved in a chest.

Let us summarize what has been established so far. We have recognized, in the stories of exposed infants, two groups that may roughly be characterized as follows.

First group: *A woman is subjected to a test of chastity. She is exposed at sea together with the child to whom she has given birth, or else she is subjected to a trial by water and the infant is exposed on a mountainside. They are saved. The accusers die a miserable death. This is the nucleus. Then, in keeping with the rule that the beginning of a story generally be modeled on the conclusion, the catastrophe that befalls the accusers is predicted by an oracle that serves at the same time to justify the virginity imposed on the mother. The oracle represents the infant as a danger to its maternal relatives.*

Second group: *An infant is exposed alone because it is judged to be a source of evil for an entire community. It is the community, or a person who represents it, who commands the exposure.*

Let us add one further point, which concerns not the mother but the infant:

*In both cases there is an ordeal: the god is left with room for intervention, allowing him to save the infant tested by it. The two ordeals differ in spirit, though not in their methods, which are indifferent as to exposure at sea or exposure in the mountains: if a miracle occurs, the waters carry the chest to safety and a wild animal nurses the infant. In both cases the ordeal involves a risk for whoever resorts to it unwisely.*

------

The ancients were familiar with two versions of the exposure of Oedipus.

1. In the one case he is placed in a chest and cast into the sea. It washes up ashore at Sicyon or at Corinth. The scholiast and the mythographer to whom

we owe this information do not tell us the names of whoever it was who recounted this version of the story, but it had to have been current because it was treated by ceramists.[52] The arrival at Corinth or Sicyon is explained by the rival claims of several cities—claims either grounded in local traditions or merely authorized by a poetic text.

2. Otherwise he is abandoned on Mount Cithaeron.

The two methods alternately occur in legends relating the legitimation of a divine *parthenios*. Both are also encountered in attested customs concerning the exposure of evil offspring. With regard to this latter point, however, it is necessary to distinguish between times and between places.

In Sparta, evil offspring are relegated to a place called the Repository, "located near [Mount] Taygetus, full of holes," as Plutarch puts it in his account of Spartan laws. In Athens, they are hidden in a mysterious and unknown place according to Plato, who describes a custom that by his time had fallen into disuse. In Rome, under the Republic, they are brought to the sea in a chest and dumped into the sea far off the coast, without ever having touched the ground. If their deformity is such that they are no longer recognizably human, they are burned and their ashes thrown into the sea—the fate reserved for monstrous animals.[53] It seems therefore that the extermination of evil offspring by drowning is peculiar to Rome and not attested in Greece. The extreme aversion expressed by Greek authors must nonetheless be taken into account, as well as the physical aspect of such monsters and the treatment that they were made to undergo; Livy, who is not ashamed of national superstitions, is more explicit. Finally, we know nothing whatever about the "holes" Plutarch mentions, the mysterious places where exposures were carried out in Sparta. Perhaps they were channels carved out by torrential mountain streams.

However this may be, we arrive at the following conclusion: in Hellenic *legend*, predestined bastard children are exposed at birth, either at sea or in the mountains; in the archaic *customs* of Greece and Italy, malefic newborns suffer the same fate, exposed in the mountains in Greece, on a river or at sea in Italy.

Strange as it may seem, both kinds of infant were treated similarly. It will be necessary to come back to this parallelism later and try to explain it. First, however, let us consider the two versions of Oedipus's exposure. Which one is likely to be the older of the two? One is tempted to reply: exposure at sea. First, because it is not mentioned by any of the poets whose works have come down to us, and cannot serve to explain the name given to the infant who is rescued. Exposure on Mount Cithaeron would presumably have been invented, and then preferred, so that the detail of the pierced feet could be inserted, which had the dual advantage of giving a sign that could be recognized later and also of furnishing an *aition* for the name. At this juncture, however, a few observations will be in order.

The detail of the pierced feet is absurd under any construction that may be placed upon it. A newborn infant abandoned in the countryside or at sea is liable to perish whether or not his feet are bound. Several ancient grammarians were well aware of the difficulty and sought to resolve it. One scholiast, commenting on line 26 of Euripides's *Phoenician Women*, says that Oedipus was mutilated by his parents to prevent him from being rescued and raised to adulthood. It is true that in the historical period, on finding exposed infants, people who otherwise had not the least humanitarian feeling gave shelter to boys who showed promise of growing up to be robust and to girls who were likely to be pretty. Another scholiast commenting on the same verse, as well as Nicolaus of Damascus,[54] thought to dispose of this vexing detail simply by saying that Oedipus's feet had become swollen on account of his swaddling clothes.

The scars left by Oedipus's wounds do not assist recognition in any of the primary works that have come down to us, only in two summaries and then without any indication of sources. The first is the Second Vatican Mythographer, who says that "one day, as Oedipus was putting on his sandals, his mother saw his scars, and, recognizing her son, wept and moaned miserably."[55] It is probable, as Keseling suggested and Robert concurred, that this passage summarizes a partially lost commentary on the beginning of Statius's *Thebaid*. The second is Hyginus: "Menoetes, the old man who had exposed Oedipus, recognized him as the son of Laius by the scars on his feet and his ankles."[56] It has been supposed that old Menoetes had to have been a character in the lost *Oedipus* by Euripides, or at least had to belong to a mythopoeia influenced by *Oedipus the King*. It did in fact occur to Sophocles to make two secondary characters, the Corinthian shepherd and the Theban shepherd, responsible for identifying Oedipus. We have no idea, however, which poet in a later fable gave the Theban shepherd a name and a personality. There are several mythological figures named Menoetes or Menoetius, but there is no obvious reason why one of them should have been incorporated in the

Oedipus legend. On the other hand, the tragic poets never gave a name to episodic characters whom they created solely for the purpose of moving the plot along, unless it is the nominal equivalent of an adjective: Kopreus, for example, or Lycus. Hyginus's formula *Menoetes senex* therefore poses several problems that, in the current state of our knowledge, are insoluble.[57]

In the poems that have been preserved, Oedipus is never identified by the scars on his ankles. In the *Odyssey*, the gods reveal to Jocasta the identity of her husband; we do not know which signs could have served them as an instrument, perhaps the weapons taken from Laius. In Pisander's summary, Jocasta first recognizes the *murderer*, from Laius's weapons, then her formerly exposed *son*, by the swaddling clothes and the clasps still in the possession of the stableman from Sicyon who rescued the infant Oedipus.[58] It is obvious that if the signs (whatever they may have been) were there for Jocasta to see, then, on pain of implausibility, the moment of recognition must have immediately followed her marriage to Oedipus. Some poets tried to postpone the recognition until after the birth of their four children; but this meant having to deprive Jocasta of everything that could have enlightened her. In *Oedipus the King*, Sophocles makes her ignorant in the presence of the two shepherds, who, between them, could give a complete account of the exposure and salvation of the infant. I am inclined to believe that this episode was suggested to the poet by Herodotus's account of Cyrus's childhood. In the Sophoclean mythopoeia, Jocasta does not know that Oedipus's feet had been pierced. The wound was inflicted on the infant by the Theban shepherd, who points to the scars as proof of his own avowals—a useless proof since Jocasta, on the one hand, and the Corinthian shepherd, on the other, were both witnesses, the one at the beginning, the other at the end of the story. The old man does not say why he pierced the infant's feet. No one questions him about this inexplicable and unexplained act.

Nor would anyone watching Sophocles's play have noticed that the detail of the pierced feet was incongruous. And yet if so great an artist, so skillful a dramatist keeps an episode that is at once absurd and superfluous, it is because this episode was imposed upon him by a prior mythopoeia. Since the wound appears not to have served any purpose in bringing about recognition, unless perhaps in later accounts, it must have been invented in order to explain the name.

Here it is impossible not to think of the hero Melampus, whose name (literally, Black Foot), related to that of Oedipus (Swollen Foot), was explained in the same way, by a clumsily contrived episode that no poet was able to link up with the rest of the story; in this telling, he had a tanned foot because his mother neglected to protect it against the rays of the sun. The story of Melampus exhibits several features analogous to that of Oedipus,[59] but none is more striking than the fact that the reason for their names is not understood. In each case the name must be older than the tale that purports to justify it.

The question arises whether *Oidipous* did in fact primitively signify "Swollen Foot" (or "Feet"). For once linguists accept the etymology proposed by the ancients, and, for once as well, a Greek hero bears a transparent name, as meaningful as one could wish, wholly similar to the descriptive names that the heroes of folktales typically bear.[60] But the translation, however certain it may be, creates more problems than it clears up. Let us consider the two following hypotheses:

1. There was a hero named Swollen (i.e., Misshapen) Foot, who was the mythic personification of the old Greek custom of exposing deformed newborn infants. This one miraculously survived. His destiny was at once glorious and terrible, for he avenged himself more or less voluntarily on those who had condemned him to death. Later, because on the one hand what is related about him is incompatible with the loss of strength implied by an infirmity, and because on the other hand Greek legend ignores illness, physical suffering (unless it results from a wound or from some mysterious cause), and natural death, the deformity gradually faded from memory. It was replaced by a lesion sustained after birth that is capable of explaining the name. In this case, however, exposure is unmotivated. It will therefore be given an extrinsic cause: an oracle forbidding the parents from establishing a lineage.

This hypothesis accounts for the names borne by Oedipus's father and grandfather:

- Labdacus (*Labdakos*, "lame") was inserted in Cadmean genealogy because the circumstance that originally motivated the exposure had not yet been wholly forgotten. The physical defect was carried back from the grandson to the grandfather.
- The name Laius (*Laios*) is equivalent to the Latin names *Publius* and *Publicola*, according to a hypothesis proposed some years ago now,[61] but

still accepted. No one has been able to justify this etymology, however. Let us recall that the presence of a deformed newborn was considered to be a danger to the community as a whole; and that it is the representatives of the community who take the decision to do away with it, as much in Sparta as in Rome or in Athens. Oedipus is the only infant exposed by his father. But this father (interpreting his name literally) is called "He who is of the people." Faced with so many telling facts and revealing names, I think it is difficult not to recognize in the legend of Oedipus a mythical transcription of *apothesis*.

2. The name of the hero cannot originally have had the form and meaning that was given to it later. The content of the legend was able to act upon the word and to make it mean what it needed to mean. Whether the word had been meaningful from the first, or whether it became so only after a more or less long period of uncertainty, is scarcely of any importance. In the first case, the name and the myth were invented together; in the second, the myth sought to provide itself with a hero. The most we can say is that, as far as we are able to go back, the hero had already been found.

The moment when a custom is most likely to be transformed into a myth is when it begins to fall into disuse, or else when, while continuing still to be practiced, it ceases to be understood; for if it is no longer its own justification, if it is no longer immediately efficacious, an attempt must be made to explain it by means of a distinctive story, associated with a particular character. We have no information concerning *apothesis* in the immediate vicinity of Thebes. All we know is that Aelian mentions a Boeotian law restricting the rights of the father in respect of *ekthesis*.[62] Unfortunately, he does not say to what period the law he mentions belonged. But it is certain that it had to stand in contrast to the customs of the rest of Greece. It is therefore not impossible that *apothesis* had also disappeared in Boeotia sooner than in the rest of Greece.

The various accounts of Atalanta's early life were likewise inspired by *ekthesis*. Her father exposes her because she is a girl and he had hoped for a boy. The custom of exposing unwanted infants, especially girls, was practiced throughout historical Greece. It is therefore from a contemporary custom that the reason for the heroine's being raised in the mountains was taken. According to other versions, her father condemned her to death on the advice of an ominous oracle. The oracle is a recent invention in this legend, as in others of the same type. It is plain to see, comparing the two stories, how an archaic religious custom is transposed into a myth, whereas a utilitarian custom, intelligible to all, enters as an intruder into a legend whose incoherence requires a rational justification, and as a result transforms it into a romance.

I am prepared to believe that, in the various accounts of Oedipus's early life, the versions of exposure at sea and exposure in the mountains are equally ancient. The two are also found in the case of Telephus. What is more, the storytellers who accepted Oedipus's exposure in the mountains described his rescue in several different ways. The Beugnot amphora, a work in the style of Phideas, shows a young horseman carrying the infant Oedipus in his arms to King Polybus, an episode unknown to other sources. Now, an artist depicts only scenes that are familiar to his audience. Whether or not Carl Robert was right to detect in Oedipus's features an expression of physical suffering, the painter of the amphora manifestly does not indicate the faintest sign of a lesion on Oedipus's feet.[63]

---

Exposed infants made to undergo the trial of the chest and deformed infants who were excommunicated as portents of evil were both treated in a way that in many respects resembles the fate of adult *pharmakoi*. How far are we entitled to assimilate these three categories to one another? Let us begin by studying the obvious kinship between pharmakoi and abnormal children.

Recent researches have clarified the dual character ascribed by the Greeks to scapegoats.[64] The act by which a *pharmakos* was solemnly expelled from the community was intended both to increase the fertility of its land and to ward off evil in the person of one who has been made to bear the full weight of the community's transgressions. To the modern mind these two ideas are quite different, and it was a long time before the scapegoat was recognized both as a "sin-eater" [purifier], weighed down with the accumulated burden of so many individual culpabilities, and as someone related to the "spirits of vegetation" who is thrashed in order to ensure a bountiful harvest. This dual quality is nonetheless certain, with the expiatory character of the pharmakos probably being the more modern of the two. Little by little, it would appear, agrarian rites were transformed into "atonements."[65] This evolution will become clear if we compare scapegoats with abnormal infants who were exposed.

In both cases one encounters the same psychological components: fear in the face of the wrath of mysterious forces (to speak here of the gods is probably an anachronism); anxiety in the face of an unknown transgression that is more or less explicitly conceived as the cause of the harm to the community; a desire to transfer this harm to an individual who then can be excluded from the community.

Let us lay stress on the common elements, and also on a few details that until now have not been satisfactorily explained. We will see at once why a magical act meant to ensure fertility appears at the same time to be an expiatory rite.

1. *Identity of harm and remedy.* The wrath of the gods is manifested not only by barrenness, but also by the birth of misshapen infants. Once exposed, these infants serve as a remedy by counteracting the harm of which they are the symptom and by preventing it from spreading. In Rome they figured in all collective calamities. With the outbreak of war, if the enemy threat became dire, abnormal individuals—which is to say all those who had been lucky enough to have been ignored at the time of their birth—were rounded up. Instead of being exposed, they were executed at once: aversion to shedding blood gave way to fear and the need to find expiatory victims as soon as possible. The very intensity of the evil they were thought to embody made them especially well suited to become healers, so long as one knew how to make use of them in accordance with the will of the gods. Bouché-Leclercq had drawn attention earlier to the ambivalent—malign or beneficial—character of persons who had been "dedicated." Riess emphasized the identical role played in magic by *aori* [ones who have died untimely deaths]: "An early and violent death renders the soul capable of becoming a magical *paredra* [sacred consort]."[66]

Let us now turn again to the evidence regarding Greek antiquity. Unfortunately, we have nothing here as valuable as Livy's admirably simple and candid testimony concerning the treatment of deformed newborns in Rome.[67] But a Greek poet is credited by the Byzantine commentator John Tzetzes with an observation similar to the one made by the Roman historian. Tzetzes relates that in Ionia, according to Hipponax, τῶν πάντων ἀμορφότερον ἦγον ὡς πρὸς θυσίαν [the most deformed of all they conducted as to a sacrifice].[68] The Greek word ἄμορφος may mean "ugly" or "deformed." The same ambiguity is found in a scholium on Aristophanes, which seems to confirm the sacrifice of "wretches and those whom nature had mistreated."[69] Gebhard has tried to explain the fact by the apotropaic character of caricatural ugliness.[70] But I believe that the question here is much less one of ugliness than of deformity. Note that in the passage quoted from Aristophanes one finds mentioned, among the dregs of humanity, redheads.[71] The dominant conception here is not ugliness, but strangeness. It is exactly this quality that governs the expulsion of newborns.

2. *Ordeal.* As a rule, misshapen infants are simply exposed in conditions such that they could scarcely avoid death. Similarly, pharmakoi were chased away under a shower of stones. This does not mean they were always killed. Harpocration (see the entry for φαρμακός) says that the expulsion of the scapegoat in the Thargelia commemorates the execution of Pharmakos, thief of Apollo's holy cups, who was stoned by Achilles. But an *aition* is invariably more precise and more intelligible than the rite it claims to justify. Two isolated grammarians say that the pharmakos was *sacrificed*,[72] but in addition to the fact that θυσία and θύειν, in later writing, may refer to any religious act whatever, they are probably employing a rough and ready shorthand to express the idea that death sometimes followed the brutal expulsion of the unfortunate surrogate. Nevertheless one should not too hastily reject the account reported by Tzetzes, who says that the victim, after having been beaten, "was burned on a rough-hewn pyre, and the ashes then cast into the sea, to the winds, in order to purify the stricken city, as Lycophron also recalls in connection with the Locrians."[73] Gebhard wholly discredits this testimony, arguing that it can only be due to confusion with another rite, the postmortem cremation of the priestesses sent from Locris to Ilion to atone for the sacrilege committed by Ajax.[74] I am not so sure that the detail of the incinerated corpse comes from a foreign context. In Rome, monstrous animals were burned and their ashes cast into the sea. The same treatment is mentioned once in connection with a misshapen infant having a particularly frightening appearance.[75] The fates of scapegoats and malefic abnormal infants are so closely related that the information furnished by Tzetzes must have some basis in fact. The most one can say is that the events he attests were isolated and probably rare, and that cremation can only have taken place under exceptional circumstances, perhaps when the scapegoat, having been

fatally wounded by the stones hurled at him by his pursuers, died before he could escape their territory. Tzetzes's information might even have its source in a layer of very archaic beliefs (while implying nothing whatsoever with regard to the era in which the event was actually witnessed), beliefs that were associated with harvest rites in which a creature is immolated in order to restore to nature the forces residing in it. Gradually these rites seem to have become charged with expiatory significance. Once this evolution was complete, the sacrificed creature having in the meantime come to be seen as a "bearer of sins," its killing was no longer necessary. Now excommunication was enough—and this all the more as it resulted from a *race* between pursued and pursuers, which is to say from a rite that in the very remote past seems to have possessed an inherently cathartic or stimulating quality.[76]

Let us leave this unverifiable hypothesis to one side, however, along with any uncorroborated information from which no conclusions can be drawn. We may nonetheless be certain is that, in the historical era, the scapegoat was handed over to the will of the gods, exactly as in the case of the exposed infant. To avoid death by stoning he probably had to flee, hoping to be able to run fast enough that he could find refuge beyond the borders of the territory from which he was being expelled. Nothing more was asked of him. This much stands out from a passage in Strabo describing the "leap" of pharmakoi who, on the island of Leucas, were forced to throw themselves from a great height into the sea during the annual sacrifice performed in honor of Apollo: "At the foot of the rocky promontory a circle of small boats waited to rescue [any who survived the leap] and, as soon as they had been taken on board, to conduct them safely outside the territory." Strabo also says that attached to the body of the scapegoat were "wings and birds of all kinds to break the fall,"[77] a detail that Glotz takes literally but that must be seen through the lens of myth. The survivors probably offered to the god who saved them a monument that pictured them holding one or more birds, symbols of a harmless fall, just as the survivors of a shipwreck were shown in sculpture on the back of a dolphin. In the story of the cocks offered as a gift by Meles to Timagoras, J. Hubaux has quite rightly detected an *ation* invented to explain a monument that had become incomprehensible. I think nonetheless that the monument was not a funerary stele, but a votive stele: after all, if the youths had died, what meaning could the birds—symbols of a fortunate journey through the air—possibly have had?[78]

3. *Rescue of the pharmakos.* In Strabo's time, those forced to make the ritual leap at Leucas were persons accused of having committed crimes, which scapegoats certainly were not, at least not at first. Moral reasoning had become more sophisticated in the interval, and a community no longer dared to saddle an innocent victim with its transgressions. Instead the community sought to reconcile its belief in the efficaciousness of banishment with its growing need for justice by selecting as a surrogate someone presumed to be guilty of a crime. In earlier times it is probable that some poor misshapen creature was chosen, someone who could not defend himself. The first quality has a religious value, the second a rational value. In Aristophanes, *pharmakós* is more or less equivalent to the French word *misérable*, in both of its senses [impoverished, wretched]. There is also a sense of contempt implicit in the Greek word, whose shades are so subtle that it is difficult to distinguish between a moral nuance, a social nuance, and even an aesthetic nuance. The poor and ugly pharmakos belongs to the scum of humanity, even if to his naturally abject condition no specific crime is added. In Marseilles, in Petronius's time, the scapegoat was a pathetic soul who gladly accepted the following offer: for a year he would be well fed, and after that he would take his chances.[79]

Now, with regard to these criminals who leapt into the sea at Leucas, an attempt was made to rescue them and give them safe conduct outside the territory. This is rather curious, for all sources are agreed that they were presumed to be guilty of crimes and could justly have been abandoned to their fate, leaving the gods free to save them if they were innocent. It is tempting to explain such surprising indulgence in terms of a general softening of moral attitudes. Similarly, during the classical period in Greece, deformed newborns gradually ceased to be exposed. In Rome, Livy speaks of abnormal adults, which indicates that some were spared at birth, though we know nothing about the circumstances under which they were reared. Did their parents keep them, or were they exposed in such a way that their lives could be saved? I believe that it was not only on account of pity that scapegoats and deformed offspring were given the greatest possible chance of survival. All the legends that we have studied so far have a common theme: one who has been consecrated, and whom the gods have chosen to save, becomes a source of good. The forces weighing upon him remain no less burdensome, but their character has undergone a reversal. Let us recall how Hubert and Mauss describe the fundamental ambiguity of the notion of the sacred:

What is pure and what is impure are not mutually exclusive opposites; they are two aspects of religious reality. The religious forces . . . can be exerted for good as well as evil. . . . Thus is explained the way in which the same mechanism of sacrifice can satisfy religious needs the difference between which is extreme. It bears the same ambiguity as the religious forces themselves. . . . [T]he victim represents death as well as life, illness as well as health, sin as well as virtue. . . . It is the means of concentration of religious feeling; it expresses it, it incarnates it, it carries it along. By acting upon the victim one acts upon religious feeling, directs it either by attracting and absorbing it, or by expelling and eliminating it.[80]

This complexity exists, not only in ritual, but also in legend, for example in that of Oedipus, driven out of the community in the first place as a malefic "spirit," then elected by the gods, so that the more wretched he was, the more powerful he would be.

---

Expulsion of pharmakoi and exposure of abnormal offspring therefore appear to be closely related. Is it possible to see the memory of an analogous rite in legends concerning exposure of divine bastards?

Glotz replies in the affirmative. Having persuasively shown that the exposures of deformed children described in Livy are an expiatory rite, he goes on to say:

They were resorted to in times of epidemic or of public calamity in order to appease divine wrath, and sometimes cruelty was pushed to the point of causing to perish with newborn monsters those who had already attained a certain age. Instead of limiting [the rite] to casting the victim into the sea, it was shut up alive in a chest. But a small city such as early Rome could not constantly provide the gods with two-headed fetuses or infants of indeterminate sex. The newborns that at that time were set adrift [on the Tiber] were disabled, or simply bastards. If they were placed in an ark,[81] it is because, in offering them to the divinity, it was desired that the right to spare them be reserved to it. Note, moreover, the name of the place where legend has the trough containing Romulus and Remus land. This place, near which grew a sacred tree, the life-giving fig tree of the goddess

Rumina, was called *Germalus*. If this name ever had a meaning, it can only have designated the place where newborns were legitimated.[82]

Glotz very clearly recognizes, first, that exposure was always a trial by ordeal; second, that misshapen newborns served as pharmakoi. But I do not think that he is right to liken abnormal offspring to what he calls "disabled"—which is to say, I imagine, weak or sickly—infants. Glotz is influenced here by a law that Plutarch attributes to Lycurgus. He interprets this text by rationalizing it, and in so doing confuses two kinds of idea that primitive logic was careful to distinguish. To the ancient mind, a *monster* was recognized by signs that bore no relation to strength or weakness, to sound or unsound constitution. A child born from a breech presentation, feet first; or a child born with teeth, or one in whom the upper incisors come through before the others; or a child who speaks at birth, or suffers from cryptorchidism, or has supernumerary teeth—any of these things was a sign of divine wrath, and sufficient reason, on account of the religious terror it inspired, for such a child to be expelled from the community. But no ancient text says that a sickly child was treated as a scapegoat.[83]

Nor is there any mention whatever of bastards being excluded on this ground alone.[84] All those whom we discussed earlier (except for Sargon, though his legend is not of Greek origin) were the children of a god and a mortal woman. I see only one category of divine bastards that could be compared to abnormal offspring: twins, who frequently appear in divine genealogies. Dual births are considered to be monstrous by many primitive peoples and always appear to convey a strong religious impulse, so that they are thought to have a favorable or, to the contrary, an unfavorable influence on harvests and the fertility of livestock. Never are they regarded with indifference. One recognizes here the curious reversibility that we noticed earlier in connection with those who are expelled. It is therefore possible that, in some very ancient period, twins were expelled because they aroused fear. They would have been treated, in other words, as scapegoats. Apart from this case one finds nothing of an expiatory character in the excommunication of divine bastards.[85]

If this is so, what sentiment, what superstition, what rite may one expect to meet with at the origin of these legends? Glotz feels that they arise from an ordeal ordered by the father, who wishes to maintain a pure line of descent within the *genos*. "The ordeal," he says, "has its origin in the family. . . . In primitive justice, the procedure is not complicated enough for the mode of proof to be clearly distinguished from the sentence itself. . . . The bastard is exposed at sea or on the rivers so as to be swallowed up or legitimated."[86] All that is true, and it may explain why infants were put in chests; but it can by no means explain why they gloriously emerged from them, ready to vanquish monsters, found cities, win wars. Moreover, the ordeal of legitimation cannot be more ancient than the scruples of bourgeois morality that it implies. One has only to read Homer to see that houses were pleased, indeed proud, to trace their lineage back to a *parthenios* born of a god and a mortal woman. In the *Nekyia* he recounts in all innocence the story of noble Tyro, wife of Cretheus, who was enamored of the river Enipeus. Poseidon assumed the appearance of Enipeus in order to make love to her, and gave her two fine twin boys, Pelias, who grew up to be the father of Alcestis, and Neleus, the father of Nestor (note that, in an archaic version of the legend, twins were children of the river). In the hands of mythographers, fortunate Tyro was to become poor Tyro—a persecuted creature, finally rehabilitated after many tribulations by her children, who had been exposed and then were saved; by a rare stroke of luck, they had kept the trough in which they had been exposed, and which later allowed them finally to be recognized. The lost play that Sophocles devoted to Tyro's misfortunes seems to have been a lachrymose tragedy in the manner of Euripides's *Ion*. It is this play that influenced the accounts of Apollodorus, Diodorus Siculus, Tzetzes, and, through them, the picture that Glotz drew of fathers angry with a virtuous and unjustly suspected daughter.

In older forms of the legend, trial by exposure, either in a water-borne chest or on a mountainside, is intended not so much to prove the chastity of the mother and the legitimacy of the child as to show that the infant is worthy of becoming king. Often, as in the case of Perseus, Dionysus,[87] Anius, and Romulus and Remus, the child's maternal grandfather is a king who has no son. Another characteristic feature, which nonetheless has not been pointed out by commentators, is that a brother of the king is closely involved with the young mother, almost as a rival of the god. Thus it is that, according to one version, Proetus, brother of Acrisius, was the father of Perseus. Tyro is married to Cretheus, brother of her father, when she conceives the twins (Pelias and Neleus); this Cretheus, at once uncle and husband, a sort of "passive rival" of Poseidon, already figures in the *Odyssey*.[88] The enemy of Rhea Silvia is Amulius, brother of Numitor. The enemy of Antiope is her uncle Lycus, whose wife Dirce accuses them of being secret lovers. Robert considers the version related by Hyginus, in which Antiope is married to Lycus,[89] to be a later development; one might well be inclined to believe him if so many parallels did not invite us to assign the role of the jealous and malevolent uncle a rather ancient heritage.[90]

On the other hand, it often happens that the infant is saved and nursed by an animal: Semiramis by doves, Gilgamesh by an eagle,[91] Cyrus by a bitch,[92] Telephus by a doe, Romulus and Remus by a she-wolf. Trials of this type are well known. They seem to have a remote origin in zoolatrous beliefs: a child is proved to belong to a clan if the animal of the clan can approach it without harming it. Those who found this episode in old myths no longer understood it, and in the course of transmitting it deprived it of its meaning.[93]

A legend like that of Telephus or Cyrus indisputably implies a twofold ordeal: first, the infant survives under conditions in which normally he would perish; second, he is recognized by an animal from which he receives nourishment. At the end of this dual trial he appears destined to achieve great things. And that leads us to see these ordeals much less as the memory of a *familial* rite than of a *political* rite that authorizes the admission of a newcomer, welcoming him into a social group that initially had tried to reject him. The practices covered by the myth of the exposed infant must have been applied to people who, in one way or another, were *intruders*, or, if one prefers, men who were obliged to conquer the place where they wished to settle, a place where to begin with they had no right of entry. In the historical period, this reality was transposed in terms borrowed from a new body of law, which is to say family law. The conquerors became sons of an improperly married woman, that is, a woman who is married to someone other than her nearest agnate, who in turn and for this very reason becomes her enemy. The theme of the "evil uncle/lover" must therefore go back to the earliest familial regimes; and though it is not truly archaic, it nonetheless cannot be considered a romanticized detail that was added later.

Legends of the exposed bastard therefore exhibit two constant features. In the first place, the father of the hero is a god; if the hero is a historical figure, his father is treated with undeserved scorn.[94] Second, the hero's maternal relatives are hostile both to him and to his mother. What actual rites could have given rise to the myth of the exposed infant? Here one must carefully distinguish between themes that are typically encountered in a composite and confused form. In some cases it will be possible to go back to known *rites*. In others we will only be able to arrive at other *legends*, making it necessary to search for the rites that gave rise to them. Two attested *customs* crop up repeatedly in the accounts that have come down to us. The purpose of each of them is to legitimate a newborn. Sometimes, however, it is a question of legitimacy in relation to a *clan*, sometimes of legitimacy in relation to a *father*.

1. *The totemic animal of a clan recognizes the children of the clan.* Aelian speaks of the harmonious relationship that the Psylli, a tribe of Libyan origin, enjoy with the horned viper (κεράστης) of the Sahara: not only do these snakes not bite them, but the Psylli can cure others of their bites. Strabo mentions the relationship between serpents and the Ophiogeneis [Serpent-born], a tribe in the Hellespont founded by a snake that had metamorphosed into a man. Now, Lucan was still aware that the Psylli tested the legitimacy of their children by subjecting them to the bites of certain snakes. Since immunity was thought to be shared by the entire clan, it was indeed a test of social rather than familial legitimacy. What one wanted to know was not whether a child was the son of a husband, but whether he was the son of a male member of the clan. The clan's totemic animal was responsible for determining this.[95] When the same theme is found in Greek and Latin legends, their authors often fail to understand its deeper meaning. Sometimes they say that the infant emerged victorious from the trial thanks to his exceptional vigor and courage (as in the legend of Heracles, the serpent-slayer); sometimes they transform the relation between tester and tested into a benefit rendered and received, which converts the trial into a sort of miracle that rewards goodness. In legends of an exposed child, this moralizing tendency is nowhere to be found. The benevolence of the animal is interpreted as a proof of the *infant's election*.

2. *The ordeal of legitimacy by water.* In archaic Greece, this ordeal seems actually to have been applied to mothers suspected of unchastity, but never to have been accompanied by the legitimation of newborns. In the historical period, the Celts set adrift on the water, in a shield, children whose line of descent appeared to them doubtful. This custom seems to have made a great impression on the Greeks and Latins.[96] Now, an analogous practice underlies several stories involving children sired by a river or a sea god. The

mother appeals to the god by whom she has conceived, and beseeches him to recognize his child, whom she has placed in conditions that the son of a human father could not endure. Cycnus, son of Poseidon and Calyce, is exposed next to the sea. Neleus and Pelias, sons of Poseidon (or perhaps, in a primitive version, the river Enipeus), are put in a trough and consigned to the waters. The poets to whom we owe these traditions completely misinterpret the discriminatory character of the trial. They reason as Aristotle did in ascribing a rational motivation to the custom of plunging newborns into the water, saying that it was for the purpose of making them stronger, hardier. Similarly, if the Muse who gave birth to Rhesus, conceived by the river god Strymon, throws her son into the river, it is, the author of the tragedy bearing the child's name says, "out of shame." Strymon saves the newborn and has him raised by nymphs, among whom he grows up to be tall and handsome. Chione, Apollodorus says, conceived Eumolpus by Poseidon and threw him into the water "to hide her sin." No one any longer grasped the kinship of these accounts with the story of the sea nymph Thetis putting her sons out on the waters to see whether they shared her marine and divine nature, or only the purely human nature of Pelias. Very soon this story ceased to be understood, and Thetis was said to have acted out of hostility toward her husband.[97]

Romulus and Remus are also exposed on the water, although their father, in a late legend, is not a sea god. Yet it must not be forgotten that, after their birth, their mother is said sometimes to marry the Tiber, sometimes the Anio, depending on the version. Might this be the vestige of an archaic tradition in which the river is the father of the children?[98] Moreover, just like Tyro's sons, Romulus and Remus are twins, which is to say persons who, in the prehistoric period, may have been considered to be evil by Mediterranean peoples, as they were by many others. In that case they would have been set afloat on the water in an act of excommunication, whereas in other cases the river was asked to recognize its paternity. In the case of still other divine bastards, the ordeal rather quickly ceased to be understood as a test, but instead as an act of persecution against the mother. Thereafter, for sentimental reasons, poets were inclined to associate the infant with cruel treatment. On closer examination, however, this explanation appears to be altogether inadequate.

Every ordeal that ends favorably for the one subjected to it amounts to a preferment. Infants who survive a test of legitimacy are therefore ipso facto destined for great things. Nevertheless this trial does not by itself constitute an *investiture*, as Picard wrongly believes.[99] In order to acquire this meaning, it had to absorb the ideas associated with a *ritual leap*, which has a wholly different origin.

We now come to two other themes, the *rearing of a child in the mountains*, on the one hand, and the *chest*, on the other. They do not yet lead us to rites, only to groups of legends that are easier to decipher than the ones we started out from. Both themes imply the election of the one subjected to trial and his promise of a higher destiny.

1. *Rearing in the mountains.* This theme is common in accounts of the early childhoods of heroes and gods. Zeus, Dionysus, and Aeneas are all raised by nymphs. Achilles is raised by the wise centaur Chiron, or else by Naiads, who are also nurses of Rhesos; Aristaeus by the Horae (Hours). Similarly, in the great forests of Mount Pelion, Chiron raises Jason, who was secretly sent to him after his birth. On reaching his twentieth year, the adolescent reappears in Iolcus, his hair still flowing over his shoulders, to lay claim to the throne that is rightfully his by inheritance from his father. Jeanmaire detects in these tales a memory of rites of initiation: "The account of the 'childhoods' of gods and heroes is the myth—more exactly, one of the myths—of rites of puberty and of the period of retreat, away from towns and cities, that actually and symbolically, in the ancient Hellenic world as elsewhere, was the characteristic solemnization of them."[100] He also points out that whereas the rites were applied to adolescents, such myths invariably speak of *bambini*, even if otherwise they require the presence of children who are already grown up. Thus the *Iliad* recounts that Dionysus's nurses were pursued by the murderous king Lycurgus, whom the god escaped by diving into the sea.[101] How old was this divine child, still being cared for by nurses when he was already so robust? The rearing of a child in the mountains, still a theme of adolescence in the legends of Achilles and Jason, became a theme of infancy in those of Zeus, Dionysus, Oedipus, Telephus, Atalanta, Semiramis, Paris,[102] Rhesus, and Cyrus. This is because etiological legends always have something more assertive about them, something more excessive, more raw, than the rite that they claim to explain—and understandably so: since they present the rite as a commemoration, as a dim reflection of the event they relate, this event must be striking, easily understood; the legends paint it in bold and distinct colors, stretching the limits of credibility at every turn.[103] To Jeanmaire's remark

concerning the antiquity of the theme of rearing in the mountains must be added another. Little by little, the idea of *the outdoors* grows in importance, extending its reach back to earlier episodes in the legends. A child is born in the countryside; now it is also conceived in the countryside. Amphion and Zethus, Neleus and Pelias, Iamus, and Evadne are all born outdoors; their names are explained by some detail of their exposure or of their rural upbringing. According to Hyginus, Egisthus is suckled by a goat after being exposed.[104] Hippe, daughter of Chiron, having been seduced by Aeolus, gives birth in the mountains to a daughter, Melanippe, who herself, having been seduced by Poseidon, brings forth twin boys whom she places among a herd of cattle.[105] All these romances are of late invention. What in archaic tales is a significant detail is here no more than a minor descriptive element. The poets, incapable of innovation, limit themselves to repeating the same details, to juxtaposing equivalent variants, with the result that beneath the overwrought effects and picturesque exaggeration the original coloring can still nonetheless be discerned.[106] The rationalizing Homer is scarcely familiar with these rustic unions,[107] with these childbirths somewhere in a forest— imaginative extensions both of the theme of rearing in the mountains. As for the theme itself, it is probably, as Jeanmaire supposes, the transcription of a test of initiation. For the cases I have just mentioned, I would say rather: the transcription of a test of qualification or entitlement.

2. *The chest.* This theme raises a series of questions that the researches of Usener and Glotz did not resolve. Glotz sees the *larnax* as a wooden chest, identical to the one that must have been used for the earliest ordeals and that survived in Roman criminal law as an instrument for the punishment of slaves. He believes that, originally, the closed chest was always thrown into the sea; and, furthermore, that because of this authentic memory the theme of the chest came to be introduced in legends in which there is no ordeal, for example those of Erichthonius and Adonis. It is nonetheless highly implausible that an object capable of being used in so many ways should have given rise in Greece to only one type of story.

Usener thinks, to the contrary, that what matters in these legends is the presence of a chest, not what it was used for. This is why he compares the case of Perseus with that of Eurypylus, who, after the fall of Troy, finds himself in possession of a mysterious chest. Inside it he discovers an effigy of Dionysus, the sight of which drives him mad. On the advice of an oracle he goes to the town of Patrae and founds a cult of Dionysus there, thanks to which he is able to recover his sanity and to free Patrae from the painful obligation of having each year to make a human sacrifice until such time as the cult of a foreign god is established. From this Usener derives the theory that chests and vessels he considers to be related to them, namely, boats and fish, serve as the vehicles of a divine epiphany.[108]

I do not believe for a moment that one can regard, as Usener does, chests, small boats, and savior dolphins as interchangeable in myths of a roaming god. But certainly one has not exhausted the mythic significance of the *larnax* by defining it as an instrument of divine judgment. Here Usener points us in the right direction, I think. In the Achaean version of the legend, the chest contains the image of a god, and this image, once seen by Eury-pylus, causes him to lose his mind. In the Attic version, a chest is given to the daughters of Erechtheus on the strict understanding that it is not to be opened; two of them disobey the order, are driven mad, and kill themselves in view of the snake child (or else a baby guarded by a snake) they discovered on opening the lid.[109] There is also the legend of Adonis. After Myrrha, trans-formed into a tree, has given birth to him, he is cared for by Aphrodite. She places him in a small chest and entrusts it to Persephone, who, on opening the lid, is so captivated by his beauty that she refuses to give him back. The dispute between Persephone and Aphrodite is finally settled by an agreement to share custody of the child.

These legends are meaningful only if the *larnax* is closed when it is handed over. The prohibition against opening it, necessary to explain the madness of Eurypylus, is explicit only in the legend of Erichthonius. Now, we know very well where this latter legend comes from: it is an etiological tale meant to explain why on a certain night every year the young *arrhephoroi* had to carry a cist [κίστη], whose contents they were forbidden to know, from the Acropolis to an underground precinct sacred to Aphrodite of the Gardens.[110] Jeanmaire sees in this "mystery of the cist" a ceremonial schema modeled on a theme of initiation.[111] It must have had a clearer religious significance. The chest of Eurypylus, like the one that Erechtheus's daughters had been given, probably elucidates a rite associated with a mysterious object whose display, forbidden in normal times, was permitted at certain particularly solemn moments. Pausanias recounts the voyages of Eurypylus at length.[112] Unfortunately he says nothing of the ceremonies performed in connection with the mysterious image of Dionysus. He reports simply that a *mnēma* [memorial] of Eurypylus was found in the temple of Artemis Laphria on the acropolis of Patrae. Artemis's authority, more than that of any other divinity, was exerted over adolescents. Coins from Patrae dating from the imperial period still bore the image of a chest—a round cist—placed either next to the town's tutelary spirit or in the arms of Eurypylus, who is preparing to place it on an altar.

This leads us to reconsider the difficult and obscure story of Thoas, who was spared by his daughter Hypsipyle during the massacre by the women of the island of Lemnos of their male relatives. Georges Dumézil, who recently proposed an interpretation of these women's crime,[113] recognizes that the episode involving Thoas is ancillary to the principal legend, and seeks to explain it on the basis of the version presented by Valerius Flaccus in the *Argonautica*.[114] It opens with Hypsipyle hiding her father in the temple of Bacchus; then, in the first light of dawn, she disguises Thoas as Bacchus, makes him climb up on a chariot whose reins are covered with ivy, and adorns herself with ivy. Brandishing the thyrsus, she conducts the supposed god from his temple into the city on the pretext that he going down to the sea, so that he may be cleansed and purified; instead she leads him to a forest. On the coast she finds a raft that will take Thoas to Crimea, where, in contempt of all fabulist chronology, he will become the barbarian king from whom Iphigenia and Orestes later escape.

Dumézil interprets this adventure as the transposition of a rite of spring or of summer solstice: the procession to the sea, then the immersion there of a man disguised as the daimon of vegetation. It is perhaps to the credit of an account so encumbered with literary allusion that someone would wish to give religious meaning to each of its component details. Thoas/Bacchus puts one in mind of the false Athena put on parade alongside Pisistratus with the complicity of Megacles.[115] The evasion under pretext of purification in the sea comes from Euripides's *Helen* and his *Iphigenia in Tauris*. The raft and the arrival in Crimea are mere rationalizations of a parallel account due to Apollonius of Rhodes. Moreover, Dumézil is probably right to see Thoas the Swift as a spirit of the earth. "Thoas disguised as Dionysus; [Thoas] son of Dionysus, brother of Oenopion and of Staphylus, which is to say [brother] of Wine and of the Grape; Thoas whose grandchildren bear golden grapes as their emblem—[this figure] is no doubt only the Lemnian hero of an annual rite of vegetal disguise, procession, and immersion."[116] But this in no way explains why his legend came to incorporate the theme of the chest.

This theme appears here in the same bizarre form it assumes in the myth of Deucalion. Prometheus puts Deucalion in the chest, just as Hypsipyle does Thoas, *in order to save him.* As Apollonius of Rhodes says:

λάρνακι δ' ἐν κοίλῃ μιν [ὕπερθ] ἁλὸς ἧκε φέρεσθαι
αἴ κε φύγῃ ... (1. 621–622)

[In a deep chest she abandons him to the drifting sea, in the hope that he might be saved ... ]

And just as Ovid omits this detail, considering it to be absurd, so Valerius Flaccus transforms the chest into a raft, considering a raft to be more plausible. What did it signify in archaic legend? The chest of Thoas cannot be reduced to the account of an ordeal, no more than those of Eurypylus, Erichthonius, and Adonis can. But this strange tale prompts several observations that will allow us to go further.

Thoas is the son of Dionysus, who as an infant was subjected to the trial of the chest, and the brother of Staphylus, who inflicted the same test on his sister Rhoeo when she was pregnant with Anius. The three legends of Dionysus, Thoas, and Rhoeo were developed independently of one another, and a transfer of theme, a proliferation by similarity, is unlikely, for they never formed a group of related literary texts.

Eurypylus brings back from Troy a closed chest containing an image of Dionysus, the sight of which makes whoever is reckless enough to open the chest go mad. Hypsipyle rescues a chest that contains a son of Dionysus —disguised as Dionysus himself, one would hasten to add if one were sure that Valerius Flaccus's account goes back to an ancient tradition. The one hero is called "Wide Gate" [Eurypylus], the other "High Gate" [Hypsipyle]. It is tempting here to apply Usener's hypothesis of divine epiphanies in a variant form.[117] Usener saw these myths as the transposition of a *sentiment* inspired by the spectacle of nature; I would rather see it as the transposition of a *ceremony*, the opening of a habitually closed tabernacle and the solemn revelation of mysterious objects the sight of which is normally forbidden. Something similar had to have occurred in Valerius Flaccus's source, for among the various objects with which Hypsipyle surrounds Bacchus he mentions "caskets [*cistae*] filled with a secret dread."[118]

But one must look at the rest of the story of Thoas, such as it is found in Apollonius of Rhodes. He is saved by fishermen near the island of Oenoë ("The Vinous"). He marries a local nymph bearing the same name, and from their union is born a son, Sicinus, who will later change the island's name, replacing it with his own. Here we are brought back to one of the themes of the legend of Tennes, eponym of Tenedos. Thoas and Tennes are, along with Deucalion, to whom I will return further on, the only adult men who are shut up in a chest. For all of them, the trial and fortunate rescue mark *the beginning of a new life*. In the case of Thoas this is all the more curious since when he arrives at Oenoë he is already the father of an adult daughter, which is to say, recalling the cliché of Greek epic, an old man.[119] It goes without saying that Thoas, father of Hypsipyle, and Thoas, lover of Oenoë, might primitively have been two different individuals and that the identification of the two, not attested before Apollonius of Rhodes, may not be very old.[120] It was nevertheless invented by people who were still sensitive to the Dionysian character of this figure. What interests us here is that, in order to associate the two episodes with each other, someone had thought to use precisely the idea of being shut up in a chest, the ultimate origin of which seems to be a ceremonial act of display. This therefore proves—as the story of Cypselus very exactly attests for the period between the seventh and the fifth centuries BCE—that still quite late the episode had the meaning that emerges from a rereading of all related legends: *enclosure in a chest implies a new birth, a life begun again (often under a new name), a transplantation and, in the new land, an increase in power.* The hero reveals his divine quality. He assumes a hostile and haughty attitude toward the family that earlier had mistreated him.

The theme of transplantation has attracted no critic's attention. When a hero appears in several places, his ubiquity is justified by saying that the poets wished to reconcile the pretensions of rival cities, each of which claimed at least one episode of the great man's life as its own. I do not believe that this explanation is sufficient. It is true that Heracles won fame in the course of his travels, and that his legend was created by assembling the various episodes. But exposed infants are entitled to power by virtue of the displacement from one country to another that is entailed by the trial they undergo, and as a result of the adventures they experience during this displacement. Either they conquer a country other than their own, or they return as conquerors to the land from which they had been expelled.[121]

---

An infant cast adrift on the sea in a chest or exposed in the mountains is therefore the object of a ceremony that, in the minds of the ancients, had immediate effect: anyone who survived such a trial emerged from it stronger. When the two rites ceased to be practiced and understood—the first probably well before the second, which still existed in Sparta in the form of a stage of military training known as *krypteia*—they came to be seen instead as a torture committed by a persecutor upon an innocent who triumphs in the end. Let us leave to one side what makes each of them an occasion of divine judgment, for this aspect of the matter has been adequately studied, and examine them as efficacious rites.

Exposure in the mountains is probably the mythic transcription of initiation retreats. What are we to make of the theme of immersion in a chest, whose underlying significance appears to be richer and more complex? The two themes, interchangeable in late legends, seem to have had very different origins.

One thinks first of *ritual leaps*, the cathartic character of which was demonstrated independently by Hubaux and Jeanmaire. One who hurls himself into the sea emerges from it purified, transformed, ready to recommence his life, sometimes under a new name.[122] He has forgotten what in a previous existence was harmful to him. Sappho threw herself from the rocky outlook at Leucas in order to free herself from a hopeless love. The priests of Eleusis changed their name on assuming their office, following, it would appear, a sacred cleansing in the sea analogous to the one undergone by the initiates [μύστης] themselves, on 16th Boedromion.[123] The "leap" figures among the rites through which *baptae* were initiated into the Cottyto mysteries.[124] It signifies something more than a mere immersion, because it implies a *rupture*, a brief hiatus in the succession of states of consciousness. The sinner Aridaeus who dies, then is brought back to life under the name of Thespesius and thereafter leads an exemplary life, "feels taking place in him [just as he is losing consciousness] a change like the one a helmsman might experience at first on being plunged with his ship into the depths of the sea."[125] Leucas is preeminently the White Rock [*petra Leuka*], the most famous of all those places seen by the Greeks as a gateway to the kingdom of the dead—where one can enter the hereafter and then immediately come back from it, as though through a second birth.

But there was in the rite of the leap something other than a power of individual purification. Leaps that were thought to be capable of releasing a person from the weight of his past were made until a late period at Leucas, together with oblations involving pharmakoi. I spoke earlier of these accused criminals (τινα τῶν ἐν αἰτίαις ὄντων), who were forced to jump from the rock in an expiatory sacrifice (ἀποτροπῆς χάριν), and I have tried to explain why the Leucadians went to so much trouble to save them.[126] At the moment when he rises to the surface, the scapegoat—who represents an entire community—is cleansed of all his sins and, along with him, all those who hurled him into the sea. Even more importantly, sacralization endows him with the beneficent force that we have already noticed in those who were subjected to ordeals and saved. If he survives, it is because the gods approve of his starting over again, together with the whole group he represents; of his beginning a new life, better than the one he had led until then. Thus it becomes possible, I believe, to explain the fact that both leaps of oblivion and leaps of expiation were performed at Leucas. The leap is a ritual complex, a set of related elements uniting three distinct purposes: *entering into a new life*; *offering a victim to the gods*; *submitting to divine judgment.*[127] Glotz laid particular emphasis on the third motive, recourse to an ordeal; Hubaux on the first, rebirth. Jeanmaire brought out, albeit in rather too summary a fashion, the links among the three. We can, I think, quickly dispose of Picard's attempt to explain the leap in terms of a "folklore of the sea."[128]

Immersion in a chest is therefore a mythic translation of the rite of the leap, just as exposure in the mountains is a mythic transcription of rites of initiation.[129] But why should a newborn child be shut up inside the *larnax*? The rites performed on adolescents and adults appear to have been transformed rather easily into myths associated with birth. Here a special reason intervenes to justify the transformation. For the leap signifies: "You shall be born again." It must cause the whole of a person's previous existence to be utterly forgotten. Altogether naturally, then, the rebirth was symbolized by a newborn child. But where the hero of the rite is not an adolescent or a grown man, he can no longer be imagined to make the leap unaided; he will have to be thrown into the water in an object that can sink and then come back to the surface and float.

This leads us to the chest, which resembles a *coffin*. Surely it is on account of this resemblance that it is suited to the purposes of an ordeal. Those who are to be subjected to the judgment of the gods are offered up to them in the paraphernalia of death—with acquittal being tantamount to a glorious resurrection. The Greeks themselves, in establishing the equivalence τελευταν [to finish (die)] = τελεῖθαι [to be complete (initiated)], intended to signal that initiation in the mysteries meant new life.[130] Moreover, in many societies, the simulation of death plays a role in the initiation of adolescents. Unfortunately, we know little about the actual details of this practice in the Hellenic world. Whereas among primitive peoples initiation rites maintain their original meaning, which allows them to be readily and irrefutably equated with the myths to which they give rise, in Greece they scarcely exist apart from Spartan institutions, where their original meaning came to be more and more rationalized, so that in the historical period we are able to have some sense of it only through legendary transcriptions. Now, I am trying in this book not to argue on the basis of extraneous evidence.[131] And while the tale of Glaucus, brought back to life after having fallen into a jar of honey, is well known,[132] I know of none in which rebirth follows interment in a chest.

In this connection, however, the significance assumed by the *forbidden chest* in trials analogous to the ones that were imposed upon the young *arrhephoroi* must not be neglected. Every object that appears in a myth is liable to have several sources.[133] It is part of a multiplicity of images that sometimes have only one point of intersection, but that in other cases may be partially overlapping. Suppose that, in a certain set of archaic rites, the object arouses a certain kind of emotion. It then comes to be incorporated in two or more stories, having a particular meaning in each one, variously colored by the narrative context to which it now belongs. Sometimes it is the *affectus* of one ceremony, sometimes the *affectus* of another that appears in the foreground, reviving in an unforeseen manner a very ancient emotion that, in its purely religious form—which is to say, liturgical form, still unencumbered by any romantic construction—had long been forgotten. It is in chests that one puts the mysterious things that the gods covet and that human beings never touch without putting themselves in danger: the log snatched from the fire by Meleager's mother, the lamb with golden fleece found by Atreus, the egg produced by Leda.[134] Others contain gods or divine images, the sight of which fills with terror anyone careless enough to open the sacred box. Phyllis gives a *forbidden casket* to her husband Demophon when he goes away. If Demophon opens the box, which contains an object sacred to Rhea, he will never see Phyllis again. Far away from her, Demophon disobeys the prohibition; a ghost rises up from the box and both he and his wife die. Here one can easily make out an ancient foundation, however insubstantial, beneath the later embellishments that weigh upon it.[135]

Moreover, the chest may cause what was contained in it mysteriously to disappear. When the *larnax* in which Alcmene was buried is opened, only a stone is found inside.[136] The same theme occurs in more fully developed form in the story of Cleomedes, from the deme of Astypalaea, who was disqualified in the Olympic boxing competition of 488 BCE after killing his opponent. According to Pausanias, he went mad and, after a further series of misadventures, the infuriated populace of Astypalaea chased him away under a shower of stones.[137] He ran to the temple of Athena and took refuge in a chest, pulling down the lid, which his pursuers then tried in vain to open. At last they managed to pull apart the boards of the chest, only to find that Cleomedes was not inside. The Pythian priestess at Delphi subsequently bid them to honor him as a hero, indeed as the last hero. This may not be as late a version of the story as it seems, however, for ancient fables often crystallize around historical names. What is certain is that we find here one of the characteristic themes in tales of predestined infants: one who enters a chest comes out from it magnified in stature. This is what happens, for example, with the goatherd Comatas in Theocritus's ode.[138] Conversely, too, such tales were influenced by the mysterious, frightening nature of the forbidden chest: when Perseus and Telephus emerge from the *larnax*, they are less terrifying, but no less formidable, than Erichthonius and Dionysus themselves. Qualified in this fashion, Usener's theory concerning divine epiphanies has perhaps an element of truth, namely, that the chest is a sort of tabernacle in which demigods are created. Its image arouses very vivid and distinct emotions associated with danger and the presence of a divinity: though the chance of survival is small, the hope of triumphant salvation is nonetheless not extinguished. Enclosure in the chest represents what today we would call, more abstractly, an *absolute beginning.*

On the other hand, all these legends betray an adamant hostility between the hero and his family. We know that a profound tension existed between familial authority and the preparation of young boys for adulthood, to the point that a male adolescent who entered into the ranks of men was supposed to have died and to have been reborn under a new name.[139] Sociologists will naturally be tempted to reduce such legends to mere rites of initiation. I think that they have a deeper, more general, and also more religious significance. One sees in them children rejected by their family, sent away from their country, emerging alive from the belly of death and going forth to meet a glorious, yet terrible destiny. If in fact these admirable myths originated solely in certain rites of adolescence, one would have to speak once more of a "Greek miracle." But they are illuminated also by the mysterious light that envelops the "forbidden chest." Furthermore, their heroes are brothers of the *Grabkinder* of the German Middle Ages, of which Jacob Grimm says: "In the north, when a poor *Freigelassner* exposed children, they were put together in a trench, without food, so that they could not but perish. If one survived the others he was pulled out from the grave and raised by the lord." Similarly, according to the Lombard custom, the one who alone among a group of exposed infants grabbed hold of the king's spear, thus proving his superior vitality, was saved.[140] And Macbeth, meant like Oedipus both for greatness and for crime, was born of a dead mother. Whoever emerges from an ordeal is adorned with a dual prestige deriving on the one hand from death, which momentarily claims him as its own, and on the other from divine favor, which restores him to life.

---

We are now brought back to the story of Deucalion. It will be well to begin by distinguishing between two aspects: the Flood, and the legend of the Sole Survivor.

The origin of flood stories is unknown. They exist among many peoples, but not among all, being absent from most of Africa. A map of their diffusion may be found in Frazer's study. As for theories concerning their origin, several pages would be required in order to enumerate them all. Let us limit ourselves to classifying their authors as follows.

First, there are the *realists*. They hold that a great cataclysm occurred at the end of the Ice Age, about 8000 BCE (though this assumes that the people of the Stone Age had a very long and faithful memory), or else they see in the Flood an image, enlarged by the passage of time, of authentic but limited inundations (though Frazer, who proposes this explanation, cannot help but himself recognize that several of the diluvian traditions lack any geographic substrate).

Second, there are the *symbolists*. They detect, beneath the literal language of our traditions, the appearance of sun gods and the voyage of the dead toward the divine world (though it may be wondered whether this does not amount to attributing to the primitive imagination a poetic genius of which it has never been known anywhere to give another proof).

Third, there are those who advance *liturgical* explanations. Together such explanations form a school of thought, popular today, that sees the Great Cataclysm as the transcription of a rite. Immediately, however, a difficulty presents itself. If one adduces a known rite of limited extent in space and time, then the myth's quasi-universality needs somehow to be explained. Boyancé, for example, regards the Flood as the *aition* of the Athenian Hydrophoria. But how could the mere existence of a Greek festival (of which we are in any case almost wholly ignorant) by itself account for so widespread a myth? Surely there must be a certain proportion between the importance of the rite that is supposed to give rise to the myth and that of the myth itself. Between an episodic rite and an enduring myth, however, there is nothing of the kind. The alternative is to search in the domain of magical practices for evidence of immediate efficacy. But none of the practices known to us seems to have been able to conjure up the image of a submerged world. Lord Raglan, who is inclined to look favorably upon the ritual explanation, altogether gratuitously assumes the existence of ceremonies in which effigies of the year just passed were thrown into the sea.[141]

I believe any attempt at explanation that is based on poorly studied traditions, from among which it is impossible to isolate similar elements and to draw parallels with any precision, is ill-advised. A series of monographs would be needed first, to establish the psychological and religious tonality of each narrative. Nothing of the sort has yet been begun; indeed, even the Greek traditions have been studied only superficially. For the time being, then, let us turn our attention to several points of interest in the legend of the Sole Survivor.

Deucalion survives the flood in a *larnax*. Here the chest is an instrument of testing and, as I hope to have shown, of authorization, of qualification for the exercise of power; it is not an instrument of salvation.

Was the flood the memory of an ordeal? If so, it would have been neither on the advice of Prometheus, nor on his own initiative, that Deucalion was put in the chest: he would have been shut up inside it by other men, who sacrificed him in order to appease divine wrath. The ordeal would have redounded to the advantage of the *scapegoat*, who alone would have been spared; and since a legendary ordeal is a procedure that entails a risk for whoever improperly institutes it, it would have been turned back against his persecutors. In that case the legend of Deucalion would be the equivalent, on a universal scale, of the legend of divine infants persecuted by a wicked grandfather. But nothing in the Greek traditions justifies us in rewriting the story of the Survivor in this fashion. In order to discover its psychological elements it will be necessary to penetrate to a deeper layer than the one where we find evidence of the ordeal as an instrument for judging.

The Hebrew flood narrative exhibits curious parallels with the Deucalion legend, even with regard to the difficulties that it presents. In saying as much I am by no means unaware that I am trespassing, unwisely perhaps, upon a field in which my claim to expertise is nil. I shall therefore limit myself here to pointing out only a few uncontroversial details concerning the *form* of an ark, and considering how far this may support the idea of an archaic kinship between an ark and a probative chest.

Noah climbs into an ark at Yahweh's command. It is described with the greatest care, as a boat containing a house with three floors. The term used to name it nevertheless does not usually designate a small boat. It is the Hebrew word *tevah*, which occurs only in two places: first in Genesis, in connection with Noah's embarcation; then in Exodus, in connection with the reed basket coated with pitch in which Moses's mother placed her infant son. This basket is indisputably an instrument of exposure and ordeal. Might Noah's *tevah* originally have been an analogue of Deucalion's *larnax*?[142] Here, curiously, where the Hebrew and Greek legends converge, it is not Noah's plausible boat that later carried him along in the Greco-Roman imagination, but Deucalion's absurd chest. From the time of Augustus onward, Apamaea in Phrygia (anciently Celaenae) bore the nickname *Kibōtos*. A coin from the third century CE, struck under Macrinus and Philip the Arab, shows what amounted to the city's armorial emblem: a square chest sailing on the water.

Pictured inside the chest, to the left, are a man and a woman, standing—a sign that they eventually disembarked. Are they Deucalion and Pyrrha? No, the chest bears the name of Noah, together with a dove at the peak of the raised lid. An odd piece of syncretism, this. Whereas the *stories* transformed Deucalion's chest into a bark, a small boat, the *engravers* of Apamaea attributed to Noah the chest of an old Greek legend. And Mâle, stressing the purely Greek character of many "distinctive details" in the art of medieval catacombs, writes: "The monster of Jonas resembles the monster of Andromeda; Noah's ark is similar to the peculiar square chest of the coins of Apamaea."[143] On the other hand, Contenau, in his book on the Babylonian flood myth, gives the following table (dimensions in meters):

|                      | LENGTH | BREADTH | HEIGHT |
|----------------------|--------|---------|--------|
| Noah's ark           | 156    | 26      | 15.5   |
| Utnapishtim's vessel | 156    | 62.5    | 62.5   |
| *Lusitania*          | 228    | 45      | 29     |

Of the Hebrew *tevah* he says: "It was an enormous flat-bottomed chest, watertight and capable of carrying a considerable load." It is a pity we cannot conduct an experiment, for it is highly doubtful that a flat and very tall vessel could maintain its equilibrium as easily as Contenau supposes. Even so, the composer of Genesis seems to have rationalized the traditions on which he worked, for Utnapishtim's vessel, with its height equal to its breadth, is even less suited to navigation. *The relation between its three dimensions* ($2.5 \times 1 \times 1$) *is roughly what one finds in sarcophagi.* These proportions, which evidently have nothing to do with those of actual boats, must come from monuments decorated with reliefs depicting a rectangular chest whose presence could no longer be explained, and so came somehow or other to be transformed into a boat. "The Akkadian text," Contenau says, "speaks of a boat or of *a sort of box*; the Sumerian [text] speaks of a seafaring vessel."[144] Is it not strange that here we find the very method later employed by Ovid, who transforms Deucalion's *larnax* into a *parva ratis*? The very method employed by Valerius Flaccus, who does the same thing with Thoas's chest? All these variants do indeed seem to occur at intervals along a line whose starting point is the narrative of a *trial* and whose end point is the narrative of a *rescue*. Everywhere one finds an attempt to recast in a more plausible and reasonable form a story that, having been displaced from its original center of gravity, has become incoherent. It is nevertheless true, if one wishes to make a serious study of flood myths in general, that one cannot avoid taking as a point of departure the strange detail of the quadrangular chest. More modestly, let us come back to the Deucalion legend.

Earlier in this chapter I distinguished between two aspects of this story that are juxtaposed in all the traditions known to us, but that must have been independent to begin with: the creation of a race of people from stones, with the pun λᾶες [stones] / λαοί [people (born of stones)]; and the presence of Pyrrha, mother of Protogeneia. Pyrrha the Redhead, as Glotz rightly saw, is a woman subjected to a trial by fire, whereas Deucalion is a man subjected to a trial by water. Evidently she is a close relation of those heroes—Meleager, Demophon—whom a goddess attempts to make immortal by causing them to pass through flames.[145] Why the Deucalion cycle should have drawn from her legend therefore becomes clear.

It is now necessary to come back to a detail, known only through Ovid, that all critics (even Glotz and Hubaux, otherwise so attentive to the profound realities contained even in the most absurd legends) consider to be a romantic invention, both late and ridiculous: Deucalion throws himself into the sea from the White Rock at Leucas, as Sappho had done, in order to cure himself of a love that Pyrrha had spurned.[146] If Ovid did in fact invent this detail, it is the only invention in all the poems of the *Heroides*, where otherwise he faithfully follows the most classical sources, step by step, without ever adding to them on his own account, at least not with regard to events. His imagination could not be more impoverished—except in one respect: only when it is a question of finding reasons for the events that tradition furnishes him with does he let himself go, devising motives in the manner of a novelist who shows no discrimination in such matters. Thus when he says that Deucalion suffered from lovesickness, as Sappho did, we can be sure that it is indeed Ovid who is speaking. But I do not believe that he invented the event itself, that is, the leap. If he had, I think that he would have described Pyrrha as being driven to despair by her husband rather than Deucalion made miserable by his wife's indifference; and he certainly would not have limited himself to a mere allusion, so brief that it can only refer to something known by everyone. The high quality of Ovid's sources in the rest of the *Heroides* inclines me to suppose that this episode, not found in any other source, nonetheless comes from a sound tradition.

I do not think, however, that the anagram *Leucadion/Deucalion* suffices to explain the unexpected presence of the Sole Survivor at the White Rock. Hubaux adopts this hypothesis from Birt while recognizing that it does nothing to dispel the enigma.[147] To associate Deucalion with Leucas, Ovid had to find a tradition founded on something more than a grammarian's play on words, a legend that we no longer know apart from that. Stripped of the absurd romantic plot with which Ovid awkwardly embellished it, and examined in the context of other flood myths, it can be seen to be a curious variant of the legends that appear in stories of Telephus, Oedipus, and Dionysus. In the case of Telephus and of Oedipus, the trial is sometimes exposure on a mountainside, sometimes exposure on water; in the case of Dionysus, sometimes exposure on a mountainside, sometimes exposure on water, sometimes the leap. Here, in the case of Deucalion, the leap alternates equally with exposure on water. It would be very surprising if a late fabulist should have artificially introduced in his legend, alongside the theme that had long been at its heart, another theme, exactly synonymous with the first—only the synonymy in this case is prehistoric, one that the late fabulist himself could neither understand nor appreciate, and that indeed he so poorly grasped that he joined to it an utterly heterogeneous psychological motivation: unrequited love. What we know of Ovid's method, on the one hand, and of his total lack of imagination, on the other, suggest that anciently there existed a version in which Deucalion—as the result, perhaps, of some unstated persecution—had to throw himself into the sea.

Usener quite rightly saw Deucalion as a brother of Perseus, Oedipus, and others who were predestined to greatness. But while all of these ones, in the popular imagination, were put to the test shortly after birth, the Deucalion of legend was a man in the prime of his life. Accordingly, nothing stood in the way of having him leap into the sea and then emerge from it reborn. (The same two themes, it will be noted, also alternate in the legend of Dionysus.) The flood probably played no role in the version featuring the leap, and may even explain why this version fell into oblivion: once Deucalion had essentially become the hero of the Great Cataclysm, any variant associating him with an infinitely less interesting adventure was apt to be forgotten. The theme of exposure on water was therefore preserved by every author working in this tradition, including Ovid himself in the *Metamorphoses*. The theme of the leap is preserved solely in verses 166–170 of the fifteenth poem of the *Heroides*.

A second hypothesis nevertheless remains plausible: there existed a *hero of the leap*, named Leucarion, known—if one may put it this way—through an enigmatic gloss of the *Etymologicum Magnum* that seems to regard *Leucarion*, *Deucalion*, and *Leucadion* as doublets. Usener may be right to consider the form *Leucarion* originally to have been independent of *Deucalion*.[148] In that case Deucalion would have been rescued from the sea in a *larnax*, and Leucarion after one of those spectacular trials by leaping that took place at the White Rock. The two characters would then have been assimilated, so completely that grammarians later took their names to be variants of a single name. The Greek floods and the story of their heroes (Ogygea, Dardanus, Deucalion himself) are so poorly known that here we may well suppose that between the legends with which we are acquainted there is a large gap.

Deucalion is therefore the Renewed One par excellence, who owes his second birth to the fact that he has been chosen, made one of the elect. Noah emerges from the ark and concludes a covenant with Yahweh. The Babylonian flood is related in the epic of Gilgamesh, who, as a child, underwent adventures quite similar to those of Perseus. The Babylonian Noah was not Gilgamesh, however, but his ancestor Utnapishtim. Immersion, for the individual, is a promise of resurrection. Would the flood have had the same meaning on the scale of the world itself? One may propose this hypothesis, but I do not see any way to go beyond it, that is, to identify the intermediary ritual that must have served as a point of transition between the idea and the myth. For we are scarcely willing any longer to accept that abstract thoughts are directly transcribed into images, into stories, into figures. So long as the myth of the flood cannot be associated with a liturgy as widespread as the myth itself, it will indeed be necessary to resign ourselves to regarding it as one of the most difficult, and also one of the most fascinating, enigmas in the history of religion.

---

One who is predestined accedes to a new life after having been offered up to the gods; the gods, rather than accept the offering, adopt the one sacrificed, thus signaling his election or else, in late versions influenced by family law, his divine descent. The Oedipus legend, as we know it, fits the first schema. But an unknown version came to be attached to the later conception, making Oedipus a son of the Sun.[149] Unfortunately, we know nothing whatever about this version. It had to be very different from the versions that have come down to us, whose other episodes we now need to study. Let us keep in mind the dual meaning that we have drawn from the first episode:

*Following exposure, from which he emerged alive, Oedipus—like his brothers, the* Grabkinder—*is promised a new life, happiness, and power.*

Alone among them, however, he was exposed by his father, as a malefic being, which is to say as a scapegoat of the community that rejected him. His salvation reversed the effect of the powerful religious influence that weighs upon beings dedicated to the gods: henceforth this force worked to favor him.

# CHAPTER 2

# Murder of the Father

A god's judgment always culminates in the pronouncement of a sentence. If the god finds in favor of the accused, it is the accuser who will perish. In legends, divine justice must likewise be swift and decisive: a character who has survived persecution will at once strike down his persecutor. But anyone who has been tested and not found wanting cannot help but be a sympathetic character. Things will therefore be arranged in such a way that he kills or wounds involuntarily. And because his persecutor is no more a wicked man than he is, an oracle must be invented to warn that person, at the beginning of the tale, of a grave menace facing him. In the versions contrived by the tragedians of the fifth century, everything hangs together, events succeed one another in unbroken sequence, and each party is excused—the persecutor because he acts in response to a divine warning, the persecuted (though he has now become a murderer) because he is only a blind instrument in the hands of the gods.

Oedipus, having been exposed by his father, Laius, will have his revenge upon him. And yet no crime, to the ancient Greeks' way of thinking, was more horrible than patricide. The tragic poets all mitigate the act's vindictive quality, first, by stipulating that Oedipus and Laius are unknown to each other; next, by diminishing Oedipus's responsibility at the moment he

71

delivers the fatal blow. Mind you, the poets could have gone further in this direction. They could have imagined that Oedipus kills Laius as Perseus does Acrisius, by a clumsy and wholly inadvertent gesture. That would not have changed Oedipus's position in relation to the gods in the least, since it was not criminal intention but the fact of the murder itself that brought their disfavor upon him; and in that case the sequence of events would have been easier to accept from a psychological point of view. If the poets did not do that, if they treated the theme of patricide without further modification, it is because this theme was imposed on them by a prior mythopoeia, a mythopoeia marked by a much more pronounced hostility between generations than the one that survives in the plays of the fifth century that have come down to us. This hostility cannot be explained with reference to tales of exposure. It arises from a different legendary context: the struggle between father and son.

This struggle figures in many legends belonging to all of the world's literatures. Some forty years ago Potter undertook to study them together in the hope that a standard basis for comparison could be discovered.[1] He came to believe that they have a common origin in primitive customs (exogamy, matriarchy, polyandry and polygamy, premarital sexual freedom, divorce) that, once abandoned or superseded, acquire a peculiar aspect that finds expression in tales of various kinds. Thus a father and son are imagined to come into conflict without knowing each other, and only after the death of one of them does the survivor recognize the identity of his adversary from some sign.

It becomes clear on a close reading of Potter's book that he explains—or seeks to explain—all the incidental circumstances of the murder, but not the crux of the tale itself, that is, the conflict between generations. The background is rehearsed by the storytellers in great detail in order to make it seem plausible that the son should have grown up far away from his father. Usually a husband has left a pregnant wife, though sometimes the son has been separated from his parents at birth. These are the themes that Potter takes as a point of departure, because he takes it for granted that the tale was first conceived in a family context. The struggle itself, whether it ends with the death of the father or with that of the son, is the product of a prior state of society, before the family became the fundamental social unit.

Freud applies a method that could not be more different from Potter's, since instead of studying peripheral episodes he goes at once to the heart of the matter, namely, conflict. But nonetheless he starts out from the same assumption, since he accepts as demonstrated that the primitive kernel or nucleus of the tales is indeed a struggle between father and son. On Freud's view, myths arise from the most profound human sentiments: in the mother, love for her children; in the father, an ambivalent feeling compounded of admiration and affection for his male offspring, on the one hand, and jealous hatred of them on the other. This amounts to saying that the Theban legend is the keystone of his theory, to which I will return below.[2] For the moment, however, it will suffice to say that while psychological impulses may well have acted to fix certain mythic themes, and to give them an exceptional vividness and celebrity, I do not think that they could have created them. In the second place, rather than lay stress on feelings of sexual jealousy experienced by the son as a small child, I believe that greater emphasis must be placed on the impatience with which the son as an adult endures persistent domination by an aging father. The hostility between them seems to me much less likely to be caused by a repressed libido than by a will to power. If that is true, we are entitled to compare the legend of Oedipus with that of Pelops, for example, where one finds a father in conflict with his daughter's suitor. Here the essential thing is not a duel between father and son, but conflict between generations.

Let us start instead from the assumption that what is primordial in the tale is antagonism between a young man and an old man. Let us suppose furthermore that this central theme only later became incorporated in the context of the family. The young man and the old man become a father and his son, and now their antagonism is criminal. All the circumstances that serve to explain why they are unknown to each other have been invented to make it less odious. It will therefore be necessary to see these circumstances not as the residue of memories of a bygone social state but as a more recent form of justification, as with the theme of the oracle in the story of the exposed child.

I do not know what would come of applying this assumption to the many foreign legends assimilated by Potter—a bit prematurely, it seems to me—but it does appear to hold the key to Hellenic tales that treat the same subject. Hostility between father and son (or between father-in-law and son-in-law) is invariably accompanied in them by a *contest for power*. This contest (contrary to what one finds, for example, in the Iranian legend) inevitably concludes with the triumph of the son. Without wishing to prejudge non-Greek versions here, I feel justified nonetheless in claiming that the struggle between father and son had its genesis in a rite—the battle to the death through which, in primitive societies, a young king was able to succeed an old king. The whole familial structure, together with the moral problems it implies, was added only later, once patrilinear succession had become regularized. The subconscious tendencies illuminated by psychoanalysis may well have favored the recasting of the myth within the framework of the family, but I do not think that they could have done more than that.

If I am right, then, Oedipus's patricide, in which classical authors no longer see anything other than a crime, was primitively a *rite for the conquest of power.* It is this that now needs to be demonstrated.

––––––––––––

Among the illustrious dead whose shades Odysseus encounters in the *Nekyia*, the author mentions "the mother of Oedipus, beautiful Epicaste, who did a terrible thing unawares, having married her own son. Oedipus killed his despoiled father and married Epicaste. At once the gods revealed everything to men. Oedipus, cruelly tested in fair Thebes, ruled over the Cadmeans owing to the disastrous designs of the gods. Epicaste went down to Hades, the strong Gatekeeper, in her sorrow having knotted a noose from the high ceiling. She bequeathed to Oedipus many woes, all those that a mother's Furies bring to pass."[3]

Ὁ δ' ὃν πατέρ' ἐξεναρίξας / γῆμεν, says the poet [He (Oedipus), having robbed his father, married his mother].[4] The verb ἐξεναρίζειν means *to despoil one who has been killed* (usually a foe slain in battle), which explains why it admits of two constructions: with a personal complement, the idea of *killing* is paramount;[5] when the complement is a thing, the idea of *removing* or *depriving* is uppermost. In the present passage it is plain that ἐξεναρίξας [having despoiled (a slain foe)] cannot be taken as a simple equivalent of συλήσας [having robbed or plundered (in general)], making it impossible to interpret Oedipus as having stripped his father of his arms or possessions without killing him. The context clearly indicates that he married Epicaste after she had been made a widow.

Oedipus deprived his father of his sword and belt—a detail that no

longer survives in any of our poems, but which probably still figured in
accounts where spoliations helped to advance the narrative. The Pisander
scholion recounts that Oedipus brought Laius's horses to his adoptive father
Polybus, as an expression of thanks for the education he had received from
him. The sending of θρεπτήρια (gifts offered to adoptive parents under such
circumstances) in no way implies that at the moment of the murder Oedipus
knew that he was the adoptive, not the real, son of the king of Corinth:
Robert has cataloged the passages in which one sees a child address θρεπτήρια
to his natural father.[6] Laius's belt and sword permitted Jocasta to recognize
her second husband as the murderer. In this archaic context, spoliations play
a purely fictive role. They no longer have any such role in the tragedies of the
fifth century.

What meaning could they have had for the author of the *Odyssey*? In
the Homeric poems, one despoils an adversary only after an exceptionally
fierce struggle. The use of a term as energetic as ἐξεναρίζειν indicates an acute
hostility between the two combatants. The legend to which the author of
the *Nekyia* refers portrayed a bitter and protracted combat, not the sort of
suddenly fatal misunderstanding suggested by both the tragedians and the
author of the Pisander scholion.

One may wonder whether the significance of Laius's weapon was not
clearer in the archaic mythopoeia than in the Pisander scholion. Indeed, an
object possessed by means of physical force is liable to assume rather different
meanings, depending on the case.[7] These meanings can be represented along
a scale of gradations:

1. The plundered object, in showing who killed and who was killed,
establishes the identity of the two rivals. It is thus in the epic poem that is
known to us through Pisander's summary of it.

2. The plundered—or sometimes simply possessed—object stakes a
claim to power. It is by itself a symbol of royal investiture, as with Laius's
weapon; with the earring of Danaus taken by Abas, son of Lynceus; the ax of
the Lydian queens; the tripods of the Hylleans; and, firmly in the historical
period, the trident of the Eteoboutades.[8] The magic character of conquered
or possessed arms is also implied in legends in which a victory is promised,
not to a particular hero, but to his bow or to his sword, regardless of who
uses it. This narrative theme must have been dear to the Greeks since in the
late fifth century, at the height of an age of rationalism, Sophocles was able

throughout the entire course of a tragedy, *Philoctetes*, to keep his audience in suspense as to whether Odysseus would finally seize hold of the great archer's bow for himself.

3. What entitles a conqueror to exercise power is not mere possession of the object, but his strength and skill in making use of it. Here taking possession of a weapon matters less than the test of fitness to which it gives rise. This theme is found in the legend of Heracles wielding the harvesting scythe; in the childhood of Theseus; also in the *Odyssey*, where the one who can string Odysseus's bow will become king. This bow came from Eurytus, who had it from Apollo. If Telemachus's prowess proves to be the equal his father's—if he manages to bend the bow and shoot an arrow through the rings of a dozen axes—his mother will no longer have to leave her home, for he would at once be recognized as fit to rule in Ithaca.[9] The *Little Iliad* probably ended with the investiture of Neoptolemus, who, alone among the Greeks, was able to avail himself of Achilles's spear.[10] Notice that in all these accounts weapons and armor pass from the hand of a father or grandfather to the hand of a son, in order to crown a young king in the place of an old king. One encounters here, in fictively immature form, one of the themes of conflict between generations, to which I will return in due course.[11] The epic poets must have perceived the faith in the magic character of arms still dimly transmitted by archaic legends. Yet the ferocity with which armor is attacked and defended in the *Iliad* seems to be explained by their material value, by the pride that they inspired in the conqueror. There the old belief is not, strictly speaking, rationalized; it has been eclipsed by utilitarian considerations.[12]

Robert criticizes Pisander's summary for its bald lack of verisimilitude, finding it absurd to suppose that Oedipus could have worn Laius's belt without Jocasta's immediately noticing it; absurd, too, that the moment of revelation should be postponed until the journey they make together that brings them to the split road,[13] exactly where the patricide occurred. Unquestionably this is difficult to accept—yet no more difficult than the plot of Sophocles's *Oedipus the King*, whose claim to plausibility cannot withstand even mild scrutiny. The reason for the lack of verisimilitude in such tales is that they are composites, assembled at some later date from primitively independent elements and then to one degree or another adapted and adjusted. The poets who looked to archaic legends for inspiration sought to distract the audience's attention from their weak points, redirecting it toward an arresting bit of description or a memorable piece of characterization. Let us try to imagine how the Oedipus story might have been modified in connection with the sword stripped from Laius.

A trophy is usually displayed because it brings a young conqueror recognition. But here the conqueror's first interest must be to remain unknown. Once the conquest of the father's arms and marriage with the mother came to form two episodes of a single legendary sequence, the first was bound eventually to be overshadowed by the second, since the sword no longer serves the purpose of investiture, only of recognition. And just as the poets, to the extent that they sought to give the legend a richer psychological content, were more and more inclined to delay recognition, so too the theme of despoliation, far from helping to carry the narrative along, increasingly got in the way. It is still mentioned in the Pisander scholion. Whereas the implausibility of this dry and clumsy account impresses us as its outstanding feature, readers of the lost epic Pisander summarizes may have been less troubled by it. The tragic poets, for their part, at least so far as we know, no longer spoke of a trophy.

If, in the archaic legend, there had been a desperate struggle between Oedipus and Laius, how is it that the murderous son was not hounded by his father's Furies as the old horseman Phoenix was for a crime that he had merely contemplated committing, without actually carrying it out?[14] The silence of the avengers in this case seems to have surprised no one, neither among the ancients or the moderns, with the exception of Pindar. Pointedly adding a detail in which it is difficult not to detect a rebuke of Homer, Pindar says that that "when the sharp-sighted Erinyes saw [the patricide], they punished him by the mutual slaughter [of his warrior progeny]"—thus, with the deaths of Eteocles and Polynices, exterminating a noble line.[15] Not a word here of the mother's Furies, who are present only in Homer. Between Homer and Pindar, the conception of the Erinyes had changed. In Homer they seem to pursue only those transgressors whom they have been especially sent to torment; in Pindar they have become enforcers of moral authority, responsible for punishing criminal behavior generally. A fierce combat, in Homer, implies no stain, no dishonor for anyone who spills blood. It may very well be that, in the archaic mythopoeia, Laius had nothing to reproach his murderer for. The wrath of the dead, a theme wholly absent from the *Nekyia* but expressly developed by Pindar, takes up the whole beginning of

*Oedipus the King.* Why did the gods send the scourge to Thebes? Because Laius's murderer has not been punished. Who is Laius's murderer? The whole play depends on the idea of patricide. Incest is discovered only incidentally; as a religious offense, it plays no role in the drama.

The theme of maternal anger loses importance as the tradition develops. The Homeric Oedipus is pursued by his mother's Furies. In order to enlist their service a formal summons had to be issued, the urgency of which was probably all the greater as it was a matter of life and death. Epicaste's hanging holds a particular interest in this connection as the earliest example of *an avenging suicide*.[16] The author of the *Nekyia* was acquainted moreover with the suicide of Ajax, who still in death remained so consumed with hatred for Odysseus that he turned away from him, without a word, on encountering him again at the gates of the underworld—a detail that Virgil retained in dramatizing Dido's abiding rancor toward Aeneas. The Epicaste of epic seems therefore to have taken her own life, not from despair, as with the Jocasta of tragedy, but from a desire to *punish* her son. But what reason did she have for bearing a grudge against Oedipus? So deep-seated an anger points to a different mythopoeia from the one we know from the plays of the classical period. Sophocles's Jocasta is rather more Oedipus's wife than Laius's widow; Homer's Epicaste, by contrast, seems to have taken the side of Laius against Oedipus. Moreover, when one examines the Homeric text more closely, one notices that Epicaste is said to have married her son without knowing it: ἣ μέγα ἔργον ἔρεξεν ἀιδρείῃσι νόοιο—literally, who committed a grave deed in the ignorance of her mind;[17] but it does not say that Oedipus shared this ignorance. Nothing more than this negative proposition can be asserted with confidence. The only thing that emerges clearly from the Homeric text is that there the hostility between Oedipus and Laius is more pronounced than in the tragic version; so too, perhaps as a consequence, the hostility of Oedipus's mother/wife toward him. Oedipus is portrayed as an "accursed conqueror" who reigns in Thebes by the "disastrous designs of the gods," suffering "many woes" on this account. The same curse is brought down upon Pelops following his altogether similar triumph over Oenomaus.

The combat between Oedipus and Laius, like the one between Pelops and Oenomaus, appears to me to be a mythic transposition of the rite that Frazer unforgettably described in connection with the priest at Nemi who had to be killed by his successor. Let us call this the struggle between a young king and an old king, while keeping in mind that, in myths, it is often a question of two gods, and that Frazer himself cast his argument in terms of conflict between priests and magicians.

The *rite of succession by murder* appears to have totally disappeared in Greece in historical times, by which point survivals were no longer to be observed even in Latium. Nevertheless it did leave traces in legends. All of these, in the form that they have come down to us, date from an epoch when sons regularly inherited titles and property from their father. Only at that point do our legends speak, not of a young and an old king, but of a father and a son. This relocation of a ritual combat within the framework of family law and custom is a result of the contamination of an old mode of succession by a new one based on heredity. But the legends thus transformed now found themselves burdened with a *moral* problem, since a ritual murder had become a homicide—the most serious crime of all, in fact, a patricide. No poet dared to present a son consciously killing his father: in epic, Oedipus and Telegonus kill without knowing their adversary; the tragedians, considering this attenuation still to be insufficient, transformed Oedipus's deed into a sort of road accident. These slight alterations notwithstanding, and even in a culture where patricide was the gravest of all transgressions, legendary tradition almost always set fathers against sons in a relation of mutual hostility. Nearly every legend concerning an exposed child bears the trace of generational conflict as well, beginning with the fabulous tale of Alexander murdering his father Nectanebus.[18]

Succession by murder is founded on the principle of the *incapacity of an old man* to carry out the duties of kingship. At bottom the reason is magical: a king who has lost his physical potency is no longer able to transmit it, no longer able to impress his will on the world through the emanation and radiance of his personality, as a good king ought to be able to do. We should expect to find this principle rationalized where some more or less small trace of it can yet be discovered. Senile incapacity is still discernible in legends in which a king has been dispossessed by a son who takes his place the moment the old man has become too feeble to reign. Consider the curious case of Odysseus's father, Laertes, still alive in the *Odyssey* but no longer capable of administering the affairs of Ithaca.

Few critics have wondered why Laertes, who must have been still a man of considerable vigor when Odysseus left Ithaca, had by then already yielded power to his son and why, having done this, he did not exercise a sort of regency while Telemachus was still a minor. Lamer, to his credit, does perceive the problematic nature of Laertes's position, but he disposes of the difficulty a little too easily by excusing it as a piece of poetic license.[19] Westrup, on the other hand, observing "that personal merit is a necessary condition for ascending the throne of one's ancestors and that persistent and energetic activity is indispensable in holding on to royal power,"[20] rightly calls attention to the passage of the *Nekyia* in which Achilles uneasily contemplates the possibility that Peleus is now held in lesser regard, wondering

ἢ ἔτ᾽ ἔχει τιμὴν πολέσιν μετὰ Μυρμιδόνεσσιν,
ἢ μιν ἀτιμάζουσιν ἀν᾽ Ἑλλάδα τε Φθίην τε,
οὕνεκά μιν κατὰ γῆρας ἔχει χεῖράς τε πόδας τε. (11.495–497)

[whether he is still honored among the Myrmidon hordes, or whether he is a figure of contempt in Hellas and Phthia, because old age restrains him by both hand and foot.]

Now, these three lines pose a puzzle whose importance no critic has sufficiently insisted upon. An old king is in no sense a retired sovereign, he is a *scorned* and *mistreated* man. Such is the wretched condition of Laertes (δύσμορος Λαέρτης), who lives miserably in the countryside (ἀπάνευθεν ἐπ᾽ ἀγροῦ πήματα πάσχων), resting on a bed of fallen leaves, pulling weeds in his garden and wearing filthy clothes.[21] The poet gives us to understand that if the old man lives this way it is because he wishes it thus. What is more, he is shown the greatest respect on all sides; indeed, the whole epic is filled with the warmest sentiments between parents and children. Reading Odysseus's splendid exchanges with Telemachus and with Laertes, one is apt to forget that the legend itself still bears traces of generational conflict: one is Odysseus's murder at the hands of Telegonus, which was known to the author of the *Nekyia*;[22] another is Laertes's pitiable existence. "Your father lives in the fields," says Anticlea, "he no longer comes to the city. No longer does he have a bed to lie down on, nor blankets and bright coverlets; no, through the winter he sleeps [in the house] where the slaves sleep, in the ashes by the fire,

covered by tattered clothes. When summer comes, and [through the] pros-
perous autumn, fallen leaves on a slope of the vineyard make a bed for him.
There he lies, sorrowing, gnawed at by regrets, longing for your return."[23] It
is evident that moral reasons do not suffice to explain a degradation of this
order. It attests to an older state of the legend, in which Laertes was forced
most unwillingly to endure the same terrible scorn that Achilles feared for
Peleus. One has only to read the twenty-fourth book of the *Odyssey* to appre-
ciate how curious and how striking is the natural scenery that surrounds the
elderly prince. Laertes has still some of the traits of the King of the Wood,[24]
even if in other respects his legend had been revised to suit the scruples of a
new civilization.

The principle of senile incapacity is found again in three plays by
Euripides. Pheres in *Alcestis* has bequeathed power to his son, Cadmus in
the *Bacchae* to the son of his daughter, Peleus in *Andromache* to the son of
his son. In the last of these, Neoptolemus reigns in Phthia while nonetheless
leaving Pharsalus to his grandfather, Andromache says, declining to take the
scepter as long as the old man lives.[25] The reluctance of Peleus's grandson
to seize power is presented as an exception to the rule, namely, dispossos-
sion of an elderly prince. In Euripides's play, moreover, which takes place in
Phthia, Peleus is never called ἄναξ [king, or chief]; this title is reserved to
Neoptolemus and to Hermione.[26] Peleus is shown to be an energetic leader,
authoritarian, capable of commanding obedience, a leader who owes his
ascendency to his personal qualities, not to any royal entitlement, which in
any event he never invokes.

From these four legends, in the form in which they have come down to
us, the theme of hostility between generations has been completely erased. In
each case the old king is the father, or grandfather, of a unique descendant—
the muffled echo of a time when power passed from a reigning sovereign to
a younger man, the one person who had managed to wrestle his throne from
him. In archaic Greece, at least in the north and west of the country, such
tales seem to attest to a state of affairs where the king ceased to be fit to rule
the moment he lost the virility he had enjoyed in the prime of his life. All
hypotheses about the nature of the test administered to prove incapacity are
evidently futile. It is not impossible that there once was a time when the son
succeeded his father while he was still alive, an intermediate regime between
murder and inheritance. All that can be inferred from the legends, however,

is that a king's reign was more or less brief, limited by the duration of his manly vigor.

In contrast to those legends in which the principle of senile incapacity is still present, though the sentiments that nourish generational conflict have been forgotten or otherwise discarded, there are other tales that throw light on the *hostile act* by which a reign is violently interrupted. To this class belongs the story of Pelops, who won Hippodamia and conquered the kingdom of Pisa by vanquishing Oenomaus. Oenomaus had promised his daughter's hand to whoever could defeat him in a chariot race. As he had no intention of allowing her to marry, however, he contrived to kill off her suitors, one by one, by coming from behind and then thrusting a spear in their back just as he was about to overtake them. Hippodamia, with the aid of her father's charioteer, Myrtilus, betrayed Oenomaus so that Pelops might win. Afterward, according certain versions, the old king was put to death by his young conqueror; in others, he killed himself in despair. The contest assumes the form, in other words, of a challenge that must end with the death of one of the rivals.

One sees here how the poets were obliged to modify ancient themes to the extent that archaic motives ceased to be understood. Hostility between a rising generation and their elders could no longer be taken for granted, for it no longer expressed a normal state of affairs. It therefore had to be provided with extrinsic motivations. If Oenomaus wished to prevent his daughter from marrying, this was now said to be because an oracle had warned him that his son-in-law would rob him of his crown; so, too, Acrisius is warned to beware his grandson. The task imposed on the suitors therefore assumes a benign aspect, presented as a precaution taken to prevent the realization of a divine threat—in the event, a useless precaution: Acrisius is killed by his grandson, as it was foretold; Oenomaus by his son-in-law. The original story has been so thoroughly transformed that its central theme, murder, now seems altogether incongruous. For if Oenomaus is able to overtake the suitors and win the race every time, why does he need to kill them? And why does Pelops, once he has won Hippodamia's hand, have any need of killing Oenomaus, having now become his rightful heir by marriage? Evidently the idea of a fight to the death is no longer understood. One sees also how the poets reconciled succession by murder with succession by entitlement: the conqueror is now made to be the husband of the old king's daughter and heiress. Thus the primal myth is reconfigured, adjusted in whatever way is needed to suit the law and customs of a later epoch.

The legend in which the theme of the murdered king stands out most clearly is perhaps that of Phorbas, king of the Phlegyans, who lived under an oak tree next to the road leading to Delphi. Phorbas appears to have been not so much a king as a sorcerer, a venerable shaman possessed of dreadful secrets who stopped pilgrims and forced them to take part in contests from which he invariably emerged the victor, then cut off their heads and hung their bodies from the oak. It is curious that Frazer did not recognize Phorbas as a brother to the Italian king of the wood. One should have thought that two things would have caught his attention: the oak and the sinister old man's name—literally, the Nurturer. This last detail is less perplexing than it may seem at first sight: it is exactly because a king must be the nurturer, the foster-father of his people, that he must also be young and vigorous. Unfortunately for Phorbas, and for our inquiry, his story comes to a sudden end. Apollo presents himself one day as a competitor and vanquishes the aged brigand; lightning destroys the oak. A Delphic solution, as it might be called, that sidesteps the vexing problem of succession to power.

Hostility between an old man and a young man is encountered in many tales related to that of Oenomaus by virtue of the fact that all of them treat the theme of a competition for the hand of a royal fiancée. The young man does not immediately accede to power upon defeating and killing his elder; he becomes king only after he weds the princess. Evenus, for example, challenged the suitors of his daughter Marpessa, killed them, and nailed their heads to the wall of the palace. Finally he was vanquished by Idas, who then married Marpessa, and killed himself in despair. I shall consider this and other such tales in the following chapter. Their common characteristic is that a *sentimental element has now superseded the political element*. What is more, the death of the old man is often represented, not as a deliberate murder, but as the result of a mistake, an unintended consequence. Whereas Hesiod still says that Amphitryon killed Electryon, father of Alcmene, in a combat, Apollodorus maintains that Amphitryon killed him inadvertently when, hurling a club in self-defense at an onrushing cow, it bounced off and struck Electryon in the head.[27] Again, according to Apollodorus, Peleus wed Antigone, daughter of Eurytion, who gave him a third of his kingdom of Phthia, but then, in the Calydonian hunt, Peleus took aim with his javelin at a boar and accidentally struck his father-in-law dead.[28] The relations of Heracles and Eurytus, king of Oechalia, are more complicated. The king had promised his daughter, Iole, to anyone who could outdo him in feats of archery. Heracles triumphed over Eurytus, but the king refused him Iole and in retaliation Heracles sacked Oechalia. In one tradition, Eurytus is in love with his daughter, a theme that also appears in the tale of Oenomaus.[29] I do not think that here the theme of incest forms part of an ancient layer. In explaining paternal hostility in this way, the poets yielded to a modernizing impulse that transformed old political myths into romantic legends. To begin with, the hatred of an old man for a young man had no need of justification. Later this changed. I examine the question more closely in Chapter 6.

There is almost no legend in which a struggle between generations does not occur. Jason comes into conflict with Pelias, his father's brother, whose power he covets. Pelias promises to cede to Jason the contested kingdom if he brings back the Golden Fleece and kills the fire-breathing oxen. This challenge leads Jason to Aeëtes, father of Medea, in Colchis. An oracle had warned Aeëtes that he would die by the hand of a descendant of Aeolus, Jason's grandfather. Aeëtes commands Jason to yoke two fire-breathing bulls and to sow the earth with the teeth of a dragon. Jason accomplishes these tasks and vanquishes the giants that sprang from the dragon's teeth. Aeëtes then sets further traps that the Argonauts manage to evade with the help of Medea. The description of these heroic feats has the cumulative effect of obscuring the primitive subject of the struggle between a young man and two old men. Aeëtes ends up dying by the deed, if not by the hand, of his son-in-law. One tradition has it that the conqueror did not return to Greece, but stayed in Colchis and reigned there.[30]

Earlier I pointed out an analogy between the tales of Oedipus and Telegonus. The oracle of Dodona warned Odysseus against his son, which the king interpreted as referring to Telemachus; in fact it is Telegonus who will arrive in Ithaca, sent by his mother in search of Odysseus. Driven to desperation by the pangs of hunger, he and his companions steal some cattle and, in the confusion, Telegonus kills his father with a needle-tipped spear. The misapprehension created by the oracle and the semi-involuntary nature of the murder recall the Theban legend, and it may be wondered whether one of the two tales did not influence the other. However this may be, the story of Telegonus does indeed seem to belong to a very ancient mythic layer:[31] the theme of raiding herds and the use of a sharp pointed stick as a spear have an archaic color. The conflict between generations thus appears twice in the legend of Odysseus,[32] pitting him first against his brother-in-law Icarius (see my discussion in Chapter 5), then against his son Telegonus. As for Theseus, let us not forget that he inadvertently brought about the death of his father Egeus (and also of his son Hippolytus).

It will be clear, then, that accounts in which the battle between old and young kings is personified by a father and his son are rare. The hereditary element figures only when the two adversaries are unknown to each other (Oedipus, Telegonus, Alexander), or else in legends concerning the gods. Either dethronement is substituted for patricide or the murder of the father occurs by mistake. In both cases the poets avoid having to portray what to their mind was the most shocking of all crimes. That, in spite of their horror of patricide, they should have so often felt obliged to deal with the theme of lethal animosity between men of different generations shows how important a place succession by murder must have occupied in prehistoric Greece. The most curious transcriptions of this archaic rite are found in theogonies. Let us now consider two of these.

*Rivalry of Uranus and Cronus.* Dumézil has so clearly isolated the political aspect of the myth of Uranus that we may limit ourselves here to summarizing his argument.[33] Even if Uranus—a god of legend, though one with no shrine—is imagined above all (indeed almost exclusively) as a naturalistic and scarcely personified figure, the Sky, the qualities of kingship are no less essential to him than to Cronus or Zeus. He was the first to rule over the whole world, as Apollodorus says in the opening line of his *Library*, and Diodorus Siculus recalls that, among the forty-five children of the Sky, the eldest daughter is called *Basilea*.[34] The Orphic cosmogonies, even more than that of Hesiod, are basileogonies.[35] What is at stake in every feat performed by Uranus and his children, and the motives underlying them, are ἀρχή, δύναμις, ἡγεμονία [rule, power, hegemony].[36] Uranus feared and detested his sons because they were strong. As a precaution, he bound them in chains. In a way, Dumézil observes, the bonds of Uranus were

> not at all moral but wholly political, [for they] protected the sovereign against his "natural dethroners," the males of the family. Obviously [they] bound only his sons, because they are his heirs and rivals (δεινότατοι

παίδων [the most terrible of children], says Hesiod); because he knows
they will strip him of his authority (ἐκπεσεῖσθαι αὐτὸν ὑπὸ τῶν παίδων τῆς
ἀρχῆς μαθών [having learned that he will be toppled from power by his
sons], say the Orphics); because they are physically formidable (μεγέθει τε
ἀνυπέρβλητοι καὶ δυνάμει [they are unsurpassed in size and strength], says
Apollodorus)—and experience proves him right, not only his own experi-
ence, but that too of Cronus, vulnerable to the same fears and victim of the
same revolts. The political meaning of the adventure . . . is that between the
bearers of the same royal blood there is a natural competition [marked by]
threats and violence. The story of Uranus is one of a transmission of power
at once dynastic and revolutionary, at once bloody in its form and regular,
even lethal, in its principle.[37]

Dumézil seems here to consider the familial aspect of the competition to
be archaic, and on this point I must sharply differ from him. Primitively, I
believe, the conflict involved two men unknown to each other, and that their
inclusion within the same *genos* is the result of adapting to a relatively recent
social structure. Otherwise Dumézil's account of the influence of old rites
concerning the violent conquest of power on the myth of Uranus seems to
me exactly right.

*Rivalry of Cronus and Zeus.* Pohlenz has quite correctly pointed out
that, in the archaic mythopoeia, Zeus is Cronus's only son.[38] This is still
implied in a passage of Hesiod's *Theogony*: Cronus devours his children after
an oracle told him he would be *vanquished by his son* (ἐῷ ὑπὸ παιδὶ δαμῆναι).[39]
Here again we encounter the device of a threat from on high, convenient
for explaining a hostility the reasons for which were once understood by all
but now have been all but forgotten. The myth of Cronus came to be com-
plicated in other respects as well. First, because several gods and goddesses
were taken in the interval to be brothers and sisters of Zeus, they all became
Cronids, with the result that the struggle between the children and their
father was intensified. Additionally, there was at Delphi a stone, not very
big, says Pausanias, on which oil was poured every day and which every year
was crowned with filets of white wool.[40] The Greeks soon ceased to recog-
nize fetishes of this sort as gods, attaching them instead to a divine or heroic
legend in which they figured as relics. Already in the *Theogony* one finds an
etiological legend concerning the stone crowned by filets of wool at Delphi,[41]

primitively a stone wrapped in swaddling clothes that Rhea makes Cronus swallow in the belief that he is devouring the last of his children.[42] Once several or more children are menaced by an ogre and then eaten by it, one after another, the savior must be the youngest of them, the one who miraculously escapes and takes revenge on behalf of his siblings—a theme familiar to us from many later folktales. Zeus became this last-born. We can still make out the stages by which the myth assumed the form we know today, moving from an original version that opposed, not a father to his children, but an old leader to a young man who lusts after power. *Basileus* is the habitual epithet of both Cronus and Zeus. The priests of Cronus in Elis, in the Peloponnese, were called *Basilai*. From the kinship between Cronus and Zeus sprang hostility, nothing else. The reason is that, in the rite that the legend transposes, they were strangers and rivals. They became father and son once, and only once, succession took place within the framework of the family. From that point on rivalry between them became morally repugnant, and since Zeus was increasingly seen as a just god, Cronus had to be made the aggressor. But Cronus himself could not be seen as altogether unjust. This is why he was made to act under the influence of an oracle. The same psychological forces were at work in shaping the legend of Oedipus's patricide. But the theme of violent conquest was so thoroughly a part of Cronus's legend that it figures there still, in a form different from the one attested to by the *Theogony*.

It is to Pausanias that we owe this precious tradition: Δία δὲ οἱ μὲν ἐνταῦϑα παλαῖσαι καὶ αὐτῷ Κρόνῳ περὶ τῆς ἀρχῆς, οἱ δὲ ἐπὶ κατειργασμένῳ ἀγωνοϑετῆσαί φασιν αὐτόν [Some say that Zeus wrestled with Cronus (in Olympia) for the throne; others say that (Zeus) established an athletic contest to commemorate the defeat (of Cronus) after his reign had begun].[43] It is also related that Heracles, in founding the Olympic games, issued a challenge to all comers. Only Zeus accepted it, and so found himself obliged to compete against his own son. The contest was judged to end in a tie. Zeus thus became known for having achieved a peaceful resolution of the conflict between generations.[44] One might suppose that combats of this sort, at Delphi (in the legends of Phorbas and of the stone wrapped in swaddling clothes swallowed by Cronus) and at Olympia (between Cronus and Zeus and between Zeus and Heracles), are etiological legends deriving from games. But it is more probable that these games, like the legends themselves, originated in ritual tests, among which conquest by murder figures as a particular case.[45] The etiological elements are readily discerned and interpreted. For example, if Diodorus Siculus tells us that Oenomaus sacrificed a black ram before entering the arena, it is evidently in order to explain that this animal was still sacrificed then to Pelops in accordance with a fairly specific ritual.[46] The rivalry between an old king and his future successor belongs to a much more ancient layer, now partially eroded and difficult to recognize. Yet it can still be made out very clearly in tales that closely associate three things: generational conflict, battle, conquest of power.

It is curious that no one has thought to compare the struggle between Oedipus and Laius with the one between Zeus and Cronus. The parallelism of the two legends is striking, not only in respect of the myths that form their warp but also of the psychological insights and moral justifications that form their weft. Generational conflict figures in each case twice: there is enmity between Cronus and Zeus, as earlier there had been between Uranus and Cronus; there is enmity between Laius and Oedipus, as there was to be later between Oedipus and his sons.[47] According to Euripides, Oedipus was locked away in a dungeon by his sons,[48] as Cronus had been by Zeus. I will come back to this story of the sons, which is foreign to the primitive mythopoeia. For the moment let us see how legends inspired by rites, among which the rite of Nemi has been the most carefully studied, acquired new meaning in the minds of the poets.

A king who seized power by killing his predecessor or by reducing him to impotence was now considered to be *culpable.* His offense was mitigated, however, by the fact that the old king was disloyal and had abused his authority. Nevertheless the old king was not wholly blameworthy, because an oracle had warned him that his successor posed a mortal threat to him. A cycle was thus set in motion in which, strictly speaking, there was no longer any aggressor: each of the two adversaries thought only of defending himself. Even so, victory is not a happy occasion, for it puts an end to nothing; quite to the contrary, it gives rise to a new series of violent episodes. One thinks of *Prometheus*, where Aeschylus portrays Zeus, immediately after his triumph over Cronus, as hateful, jealous, and tyrannical. But Zeus himself, like Cronus before him, was troubled by an oracle that warned him against a son who would surpass him in strength—which brings us back once more to the conflict between generations. Phorbas is a highway bandit who subjects pilgrims to terrible tests before mutilating and violating their corpses. In killing

Phorbas, Apollo makes Delphi and its vicinity safe from deadly harm—a wholly moral victory that permits him to escape the odium that weighs on Zeus, Pelops, and Oedipus. Oenomaus is a treacherous old coward who eliminates his rivals by stabbing them in the back. But Pelops himself triumphs through disreputable means, with the aid of Hippodamia, who treats her father as Proteus's daughter did hers, and through the betrayal of Oenomaus's servant Myrtilus, whom Pelops drowns at sea after having obtained from him the help and support needed to prevail over his master. The story of Myrtilus, who rendered service to both father-in-law and son-in-law in turn, is marked by the same dual culpability to which, in all the accounts we are considering here, victor and vanquished alike are liable.

The sentimental version of this last adventure is reported by Pausanias. Myrtilus, son of Hermes, is in love with Hippodamia. By his skill as a chariot driver, he maneuvers Oenomaus's horses in such a way that the suitors are invariably caught up with and slain. The competition is rigged, in other words, to the advantage of the old king. Pelops corrupts Myrtilus by promising him that, in exchange for his aid in defeating Oenomaus, he will permit Myrtilus to sleep with Hippodamia for one night. Once victory has been achieved, he rids himself of a henchman who proves to be overly eager to claim his reward.[49] But Pelops's triumph is cursed from the moment it was won. The *Nekyia* says that Oedipus reigned in Thebes owing to the calamitous wishes of the gods, and amid much woe.[50] These lines would have appeared less enigmatic to commentators if they had considered them in the light of an epode in Sophocles that expresses the same sentiment with regard to Pelops. The women of the chorus encourage Electra by giving her hope that Clytemnestra's dream portends an abrupt change of fortune. Then, as if suddenly realizing that the dawn they wish for will soon be darkened by a fresh murder, they sing:

> O fatal ride of Pelops, your advance toward this land, in days of old, brought only sorrow. Since the day that Myrtilus, plunged into the sea, fell asleep, torn from his golden chariot by an ill-fated blow, never more since that day has torment left this opulent palace.[51]

As in the verses from the *Odyssey*, the poet places *riches and power* alongside the *torments* that resulted from the blow struck (αἰκία).

Some poets suppressed the theme of succession by murder and replaced it by a less shocking version. Consider, for example, the Homeric legend of the golden scepter, the emblem of royal authority confided by Zeus to Pelops, handed down by Pelops to Atreus and passing next, without incident, to Atreus's brother Thyestes, and finally to Agamemnon. Aristarchus concluded from this passage that Homer was unaware of the rivalry between the two brothers. In that case, however, it would have to be admitted that Homer was also unaware of Oenomaus's death, and this is most unlikely. What is more, never—not in Homer or any other author—do we find a younger brother inherit the throne directly from an older brother who has sons. This story is too edifying for it not to be tendentious. Homer was perfectly familiar with the crimes of the house of Pelops, but in recounting Agamemnon's feats he preferred to embroider a version that cast his hero's family in a more honorable light.[52] Similarly Aeschylus, though he was well acquainted with the traditions concerning Apollo's triumph over Python, deliberately substituted for them a peaceable agreement between Gaia/Themis and the young god who succeeded her in legend. Nor did the tragedians take any notice of Homer's optimistic view of succession among Pelops's descendants, any more than Euripides took notice of Aeschylus's optimistic view of Apollo's accession to power in Delphi. The author of the *Nekyia* did not have the same reasons for sparing Oedipus's descendants that the author of the *Iliad* had for sparing the memory of Pelops's descendants; hostility between father and son is frankly acknowledged in the *Odyssey*. It was not until the great tragedies were composed, or perhaps before them in some lost epic, that the theme of generational antagonism was to be handled in a milder way.

In the Pisander scholion the battle is said to have arisen from an altercation between travelers. Two chariots arrive at the same time at a crossroads and a quarrel ensues over which one has the right of way. Laius has a driver with him, Oedipus seems to be alone. On being struck by Laius's whip, Oedipus kills the two others and then buries them with their clothes. He keeps Laius's belt and sword for himself and brings the horses to his foster father, Polybus. Burying the dead, it should be kept in mind, is an act of respect—and a detail that probably was new to this mythopoeia, for the narrator emphasizes it. What is more, a tradition that was still known to Apollodorus in the second century BCE has it that the two murdered men (evidently left on the side of the road by Oedipus) were later found and then buried by Damasistratus, king of Plataea. This tradition was repeated much later by Pausanias in connection with the split in the Daulis road, site of Laius's supposed tomb.[53] The burying of the victims by their murderer seems therefore to be an invention peculiar to Pisander's summary that failed to become established in the works of later poets. On the other hand, the summary describes Oedipus as being struck by Laius's whip. A whip is not a weapon. Its use here suggests a reflexive and tactless gesture that was bound to anger someone who was all too ready to take offense. Similarly, in *Oedipus the King*, the son receives a blow from his father and gives him one in return[54] that proves to be fatal.[55] In both cases it is a matter simply of an exchange of blows between an old man and a young man who, being more vigorous, hits back too hard, without meaning to do harm. Neither one of the two adversaries is inspired by hatred. Perseus kills his grandfather by mistake, with a poorly aimed discus. An episode of this kind would have well suited Sophocles's purpose, for he seeks as far as possible to excuse Oedipus. Neither Pisander nor Sophocles is prepared to make Oedipus a willful murderer, but both are obliged to incorporate the theme of combat, imposed by a prior mythopoeia.

The skill with which Sophocles constructs the episode of the crossroads has been much admired. Oedipus encounters Laius and his servants alone, which is to say that when the fighting starts Oedipus is legitimately acting in self-defense. He kills all his adversaries except for one, who manages to escape, permitting the solitary traveler to massacre the others. Later the one who fled lies about the incident, out of shame. To mask his cowardice he says that they were attacked by bandits—a falsehood that puts Oedipus on the wrong track. According to the unknown work summarized by the Pisander scholion, Oedipus faced only two adversaries, this probably in order to further diminish the patricide's crime.

These texts raise a question: what form did the ritual contest that our myth transcribes assume? Was it a *combat* or a *race*? Success in both racing and wrestling were proofs of entitlement to rule. It needs to be kept in mind that all the traditions, however much they may diverge in other respects, are agreed in treating the first Olympic contest as a struggle for power. Earlier we considered the struggles between Zeus and Cronus and between Heracles and Zeus. They combined three elements: generational conflict, battle, accession to the throne. Another legend relating to the institution of racing, rather than wrestling, combines at least the two last elements: Endymion created the games by competing against his own sons. One of them, Epeius, triumphs and obtains the prerogatives of kingship for himself. Plutarch recalls also that racing on foot was to begin with the only Olympic competition, with the prize of the throne going to the winner, and that initially it assumed the form of a battle to the end: "In olden times there were duels at Pisa that ended only with the death of the vanquished rival."[56] The legend of Pelops and Oenomaus is an exact transcription of these two trials, race and duel to the death, combined. Is it not possible to find them both in our versions of the death of Laius as well?

In Pisander, Laius travels in a chariot; in Sophocles, in a mule-drawn wagon. In both versions Oedipus is on foot. Curiously, Apollodorus insists that they are both in chariots, which proves in any case that the four-wheeled ἀπήνη of Sophocles had not been substituted in the popular imagination for the ἄρμα of the old legend, where Oedipus surely was also himself in a chariot.[57] In both Sophocles and Euripides he is a pedestrian, first so that he would be alone and could not be considered the aggressor, but also in order to make the belated identification of the murderer more plausible. And yet two chariots no doubt better explain the nature of the altercation.

The Pisander scholion says that the encounter took place at *the* cross-roads, but it does not tell us where this junction, apparently known to all, actually was. It figures in every text that has come down to us, but the poets do not put it in the same place: Aeschylus locates the junction near Potniae in Boeotia, Sophocles near Daulis in Phocis.[58] It is very curious that the *layout* of this crossroads should have been a conspicuous feature of the legend from early on, whereas its *location* was never fixed and remained an object of dispute. This is because the bifurcation of a highway is well suited to the meeting of two men, each of whom arrives by one of the two branches and whose paths cross at the intersection with a common trunk road.[59] Could it be that both of their journeys were invented solely for the purpose of justifying this image: two chariots disputing a right of way? Sophocles, in *Oedipus the King*, describes a narrow road at the bottom of a small valley, hemmed in on either side by an oak grove where the two travelers approach from opposite directions without seeing each other:

Ὦ τρεῖς κέλευθοι καὶ κεκρυμμένη νάπη
δρυμός τε καὶ στενωπός ἐν τριπλαῖς ὁδοῖς (ll. 1398–1399)

[O triple way! hidden vale! grove of oaks!
Narrow passage at the split between two roads!]

Apollodorus, for his part, speaks simply of a narrow road. All this suggests that what we find everywhere is the memory of a race, transformed with the passage of time into a chance encounter between two travelers that ends in violence. That would explain why the name of Laius's driver has been preserved, a character who plays no role apart from being killed with his master and whom there is no apparent reason to remember by name. The detail would be relevant, however, if Laius's driver were with him, as Myrtilus was with Oenomaus, in order to assist him in a contest where something of great moment was at stake. Pherecydes calls him Polypoites.[60] Pausanias says that he was buried with his master by Damasistratus.[61] The driver has become a herald in Apollodorus, who calls him Polyphontes[62]: this shows the influence of Sophocles (who replaces the chariot by a humble carriage that Laius drives himself, causing the driver to become a herald)[63] and of Euripides (who still mentions the driver, but simply to say that he addresses Oedipus and tells him to give way, acting in effect as a herald).[64] No one seems to have found it surprising that a herald or a servant was given a name, as talented charioteers were in Homer,[65] or that he was entitled to share the tomb and the memorial of his master. In the Pisander scholion, the driver is killed and buried by Oedipus; one should think that there are few other examples of slaves interred by a young prince. What happened in this case, I believe, is that the race was no longer remembered in the historical mythopoeia, and the traditions relating to the driver and his name became confused. It will be recalled, finally, that Laius grows fond of Chrysippus while teaching him how to drive a chariot.

If this conjecture is correct, the legends of Oenomaus and Oedipus would naturally develop in quite different ways. In the first case, the theme of racing came to the fore as the memory of a physical struggle receded, to the point that sometimes the vanquished competitor kills himself, sometimes is killed by the victor. In the second, the memory of a race faded while the theme of physical struggle survived in all its vivid detail.

Earlier we compared the legend of Laius with that of Cronus. They are the only ones in which the ancient principle of succession by murder is reconciled with the later hereditary principle, which implies that the two rivals are a father and a son. There could not have been many such legends: if the son normally inherited his father's estate, what would be the use of confronting and vanquishing him? It would make sense only if, for whatever reason, a son were to be deprived of his inheritance, or if one immortal being were to dispute the power of another immortal—which does not mean that the Greeks invented the conflict in order to explain Cronus's partial dispossession,[66] but that, finding the myth in an unsettled state, as it was at the time of its origin in a rite performed at Nemi, they took advantage of an unforeseen opportunity to associate the myth with the tale of an immortal whose prestige was waning. In the case of Oedipus, the patricide was no longer deliberate; for Aeschylus's audience, this alleviated its horror in some measure. It will be plain, then, in view of the need to balance narrative verisimilitude with the demands of contemporary morality, how fortuitous the success of the Theban legend was.

---

What place must we reserve in the story told by the various traditions of the Oedipus myth for the Minyan version recounted by Nicolaus of Damascus?[67]

Laius departs from Thebes for Delphi with Epicaste and at Orchomenos, in Boeotia, encounters Oedipus coming from Corinth. Oedipus is said to have left ἐπὶ ζήτησιν ἵππων [in search of (the) horses], which may mean either that he had set out on a raid or that he sought to recapture the horses stolen from Polybus. The travelers fall to quarrelling over who has the right of way. Oedipus strikes the herald with his ax and then kills Laius when he comes to his servant's rescue, while leaving untouched the woman who accompanies them. Then he takes refuge in the wooded mountainside. Epicaste buries the two men where they were struck down, on Mount Laphystion. After a certain time Oedipus returns from Orchomenos to Corinth and gives Laius's mares to Polybus. The aftermath of these events is known to us from other sources.

If Epicaste was in Laius's carriage at the moment of the murder, she must have seen Oedipus. How could she have failed to recognize him, considering that he had sought her hand after having triumphed over the Sphinx? There is something here that we do not understand.

As for Oedipus's flight into the forest, it plays no role in the very tradition in which it is mentioned. Perhaps it is to be explained as a contamination of the Theban legend by the sacrifice of the Athamantids made at the sanctuary of Zeus Laphystius (the Ogre)—assuming that Laphystion does in fact derive from λαφύσσειν [to devour]. In that ritual, every descendant of the Boeotian king Athamas who entered the town hall of Halos was driven out and up into the mountain, and if he was captured he was killed. Perhaps other tales of murder and flight were told in connection with Laphystion. I shall not try to deduce anything whatever from this slender reed of a hypothesis, no more than I shall seek traces of ancient mythopoeias in the medley of strange versions rehearsed by the scholiast of *Phoenician Women* 26:

> Some say that Oedipus was the son of the Sun. Others relate that Hippodamia, wife of Oenomaus, had slandered Oedipus to her husband and that [Oedipus] killed Laius while coming to the aid of Chrysippus, whom Laius was attempting to kidnap. Since Jocasta had come to bury the body, Oedipus married her and begot children [*sic*], and then, having guessed the enigma, he was identified. Others relate that Polybus blinded him after having heard an oracle foretelling that Oedipus would kill his father. Others, that it was his mother who blinded him and that he killed not only the Sphinx but also the Teumessian fox, as [the lyric poet] Corinna maintains.

Around a basic story, then, which must summarize a romance of recent date and poor quality, a grammarian seems to have assembled willy-nilly the most eccentric variants of certain long-established episodes. How are we to separate archaic fragments from the gratuitous inventions of authors infatuated with novelty?

---

There is little to be learned from the other legends concerning Laius. At Thebes there were several traditions that told of the founding of the city and of its past in different ways. Historians set them alongside one another so that each had its place in a coherent account. That made it necessary to admit frequent changes of dynasty. Cadmus, namesake of both the Cadmea, the citadel of ancient Thebes, and the Cadmeans, was celebrated on just these grounds by the two great poets of the land, Hesiod and Pindar. On the one hand, in order to demonstrate his blood relationship to Dionysus, Cadmus was given two daughters, Semele, the god's mother, and Ino, his nurse after being orphaned. The *Catalog of Women* (Γυναικῶν Κατάλογος) annexed to

Hesiod's *Theogony* attributes two more daughters to him, Agave and The-onoe, as well as a son, Polydorus, who served simply to assure continuity with the Labdacus-Laius-Oedipus line. On the other hand, mythographers had to introduce the tradition of the Spartoi,[68] which to begin with was independent of the legend of Cadmus. Cadmus was now said to have killed the dragon, sown its teeth, and married his daughter Agave to one of the Spartoi, Echion. One may perhaps still faintly sense in *Antigone* an opposi-tion between the indigenous Spartoi and the immigrant Labdacids; but this theme, the importance of which Robert has surely exaggerated, may well be an invention of Sophocles. It was also said, however, that Thebes had been built by Zethus and Amphion, twins born of Zeus and Antiope, a claim that cannot be reconciled with that of Cadmus as the city's founder. Here again things had to be tidied up: either the twins constructed Thebes, which was destroyed by the Phlegyans and then rebuilt by Cadmus; or they came after Cadmus (in some versions before the reign of Polydorus, in others before that of Laius), and only the construction of the ramparts around the lower city is attributed to them.[69]

Polydorus and Labdacus are both characters in search of a legend. Laius, by contrast, is the hero of two episodes that probably in the beginning were independent of each other; in the one he marries Jocasta and is killed by their son; in the other he rapes and kidnaps Chrysippus, as a consequence of which he is accused of helping to introduce pederasty to Greece. Earlier, in the Introduction, I briefly considered this charge, whose history depends on how one interprets the Pisander scholion and the summary of *Phoenician Women* due to Aristophanes of Byzantium (see Appendix 1). Laius, the son of Labdacus, and Laius, the violator of Chrysippus, were probably at first, as I say, distinct characters who subsequently were identified on the strength of a more or less complete homonymy once the figure of a Boeotian king had become established in the work of the epic poets. There is a Theban prince in Homer who is called *Leitos*, which Wilamowitz sees as a doublet of Laius.[70] This identification is likely to have been favored because Laius, like Oeno-maus, is an old king who is killed by his successor: Laius punishes Pelops in the person of his son Chrysippus, and will be punished in turn by his own son Oedipus. We saw earlier that the chariot theme already appears in this episode of Laius's youth, when he first becomes enamored of Chrysippus. But in order to bring them together in the first place, the Theban character had to be relocated to Elis, in Arcadia. Labdacus was said to have died, leaving behind a one-year-old son who was now to be raised by his maternal great-great-uncle Lycus.[71] Lycus reigned in Laius's place for twenty years, then was killed by Amphion and Zethus, who sought to avenge their mother Antiope. Laius, obliged to flee, arrived in Elis, where he was given shelter by Pelops, king of Pisa. After Amphion's death Laius went back to Thebes and ruled there. In this complicated story, recorded by Apollodorus,[72] one suspects invention on the part of poets in order to link the Theban and Pisan adventures, and on the part of authors of traditional prose histories in order to make room, in the annals of ancient Boeotia, for all the royal names of which heteroclite traditions yet retained some memory.

In Pausanias, Lycus was entrusted first with responsibility for raising Labdacus and then, following his premature death, for raising Laius.[73] The house of Amphion and Zethus was ravaged by an epidemic, which permitted Laius, once their reign had come to an end, to resume his father's succession. Nicolaus of Damascus says that Laius reached an agreement with the twins and compensated them for the mistreatment of Antiope by Lycus and his wife Dirce.[74] These are evidently ad hoc explanations devised to account for awkward inconsistencies and contradictions. They contain elements of local traditions, but the connections between them are arbitrary and no doubt added later.

Only one detail perhaps deserves closer examination: the name of the uncle/guardian, *Lycos* (literally, "wolf"). Theseus's guardian, who bears the same name, is a highly unsympathetic character. The Theban Lycus behaves correctly toward his ward, but very badly toward his niece Antiope, who is avenged at last by the divine twins, her sons by Zeus. Here one is tempted to agree with Jeanmaire, who regards royal guardians and tutors bearing names such as *Lycurgus*, *Lycomedes*, *Lycas*, and *Lycus* as characters "belonging to a species of monsters and devils whose novitiates are terrified until the moment when, instructed by initiation itself, they win their liberty, going so far as to retaliate against the masqueraders who terrified them."[75] Jeanmaire does at all events make us reconsider the following points: the Edonian king Lycurgus threatened Dionysus as a child, and Dionysus, in order to escape him, leapt into the sea; Lycomedes, maternal grandfather of Achilles, brought the boy up, disguised as a young girl, in his own home (the role of leaps and transvestism in ritual initiation is rather well known, as we have already seen);

Lycus is the wicked uncle of Antiope.[76] To these instances that Jeanmaire has grouped together let us add one more that escaped his notice: Euripides, in *Heracles*, gives the name Lycus to a usurper who murders Creon, father of Heracles's wife Megara, seizes power in Thebes, and then, just as Heracles is about to return, prepares to kill the hero's family. The character, evidently invented by Euripides out of whole cloth, is described simply as a descendant of the Cadmean Lycus.

By about 425 in Athens, then, the Wolf was already a stock character, the child-butchering throne-stealer. Laius, on the other hand, by contrast with Dionysus, Achilles, Theseus, and Heracles, is a very curious figure. Zethus and Amphion are more interesting heroes, and it is between them and Lycus that a primitive relation must be sought, not between Laius and Lycus. If Lycus is the personification of a wolf, a werewolf who sadistically instructed novices, his terrified pupils must originally have been the divine twins themselves, whom he tormented up until the day that they took their revenge upon him. The legend as it has come down to us breaks this theme down into three elements:

1. Lycus is the guardian of Laius (or of Labdacus and Laius).
2. Lycus, with his wife Dirce, cruelly mistreats his niece Antiope.
3. The twins kill them both.

So long as the connections between these elements are not perceived, it will be impossible to understand the least thing about what happens subsequently.[77] We need to recognize first of all that the tale of Lycus tells us nothing about Laius. Far from giving his character greater depth, the episode of Lycus's tutelage is better simply removed from Laius's biography altogether.

———————————

Studying shrines and their oracles will tell us much more. Herodotus relates that Dorieus, second son of the Spartan king Anaxandrides, was advised to go to Sicily and found the city of Heraclea there. This advice was given to him by Antichares of Eleon in Boeotia, on the basis of his interpretation of the oracles *of* Laius (Λαΐου χρησμοί). It is almost impossible to see how these oracles could be interpreted as oracles given *to* Laius.[78] After all, why should a Theban king have received advice meant for a Spartan Heraclid? What is more, Herodotus never mentions advice of this kind without saying where it comes from. The genitive that he uses here is a source reference, intended to inspire confidence. A few lines further on he will recall that Dorieus consulted the oracle at Delphi in order to learn whether circumstances were propitious for acquiring the land that Antichares assured him would be his. The Λαΐου χρησμοί must therefore refer to prophecies uttered by Laius or prophecies of which, at the least, Laius was the depositary. Robert supposes that Antichares was an itinerant dispenser of oracles and that Laius was primitively a god or a Cthonian hero who had a sanctuary at Eleon where he prophesied, as Trophonius did at Lebadea and Amphiaraus did at Orapus.[79] Any conjecture that might be made about an unknown shrine at Eleon is obviously insecure. Let us simply bear in mind that succession by murder is encountered precisely among regal magicians such as the *Rex Nemorensis* of the Roman countryside.

Let us suppose that Eleon had anciently been a seat of prophecy where the rite of Nemi was practiced. Earlier we identified Laius's death as a literary transcription of this rite. We may therefore imagine that a number of different oracles were sold under Laius's name at Eleon. Laius need not have been either a god or a Cthonian hero. If this name, Laius, figured in a legend in which a king is killed by his successor, it might have been tempting to give the same name to some less illustrious shaman of whom only one specific memory survived, namely, that he too had been overthrown and killed. Furthermore, if some collection of prophecies had come in this manner to be attributed to Laius, there can be no doubt that sellers of oracles (*chresmolo-goi*) rapidly added to it. To assume this much is therefore to accept that the Theban legend was composed before Laius's name was given to the oracles of Eleon. The legend must have consisted of at least two episodes: the abandonment of the child and the murder of the father. Indeed, since the names of Laius and Oedipus come from the rite of apothesis (as we saw in Chapter 1), it is there that we are most likely to find the primitive kernel of the legend.

Herodotus also relates that the Lacedaemonian family of the Aegids (Aegidae), which claimed a Theban origin,[80] seeing all of its children die, one after the other, inaugurated at the urging of an oracle the worship of the Furies of Laius and Oedipus. Herodotus may well have been accurately informed about the form this cult assumed in his time, but he provides no supporting evidence, and damage to the rest of the text prevents it from being reliably reconstructed. The very sense of the key sentence is in doubt, for ἱρόν ἱδρύειν may mean "to dedicate a temple" or "to found a sacrifice." Jeanmaire adopts the second reading, unwisely,[81] for the first, which is much more common in Herodotus, seems to be confirmed by other traditions. Indeed, Pausanias speaks of the story as though it were still well known in his time, and in giving Polynices's genealogy he says: "The wrath of the Furies of Laius and Oedipus was unleashed not against Tisamenus, but against Autesion, his son, with such force that the god's oracle instructed him to go live among the Dorians."[82] In his time, in other words, everyone still knew the story of the Furies' anger at a descendant of Polynices. This descendant, it used generally to be said, was Tisamenus. Pausanias evidently had reasons, which he does not reveal, for thinking that it was Autesion. Now, Herodotus seems to place the founding of the cult (*hieron*) during the time of Aegeus or a little after, which is to say three generations after Autesion.[83] The two authors, in disagreement on this point, diverge also with regard to the events that followed. Herodotus says that the Aegids who saw their children die had long been established in Sparta. Pausanias speaks of Autesion being exiled in the aftermath of a calamity whose cause he does not mention. It would appear that the source for both Herodotus and Pausanias was a sacerdotal tradition whose details varied over the centuries. If that is so, the ἱρόν of which Herodotus speaks would not be a mere sacrifice instituted by the Aegids, but a temple that they constructed. It is probable that their claims to nobility were much debated and that they sought to strengthen their position by clarifying the circumstances of their coming to Sparta.

Most modern commentators are agreed in seeing the ἱρόν as a temple. Several theories have been proposed. Studniczka reckons that the founding does in fact go back to the Lacedaemonian Aegids and detects an insincere attempt to bolster their pretensions to royal descent from Cadmus through Polynices's son Thersandrus. Robert, for his part, doubts that the sanctuary was a pious fraud and holds that Aegeus, the family's ancestor, really was a Theban noble whose *genos* traced its origin to the sowing of the dragon's teeth. If this view is correct, then the Spartan temple would attest to the presence of Boeotian legends in Laconia from an ancient period. The claims of the Aegids to descend from the Labdacids would have belonged to a later time.[84]

Rereading these nine chapters (145–153) from the fourth book of Herodotus's *Histories* today, it is difficult not to see them as a rationalization of folkloric and religious traditions in which archaic rites are dressed up as historical accounts. Again, several explanations have been given for these narratives.[85] Just one detail of the strange and confused story they tell seems certain to be true, because it is vouched for by a known fact concerning the temple of the Furies.

If the argument developed in Chapter 1 is correct, we should not be surprised to find Laius and Oedipus and their Furies associated with the mysterious death of newborns. Nevertheless we must distinguish here between several elements that belong to religious layers of varying antiquity. Precisely how they might have come to be combined is not easy to say.

The dying Laius cursed his murderer. The mistreated Oedipus cursed his sons. The Erinyes, once aroused, were not readily placated. They continued to hound the Aegids who descended from Polynices. Perhaps sacrifices would appease them. The reasoning is sound, but its premises are derived from late literary works. If the Spartan cult was in fact a pious fraud invented by Aegids in order to assert a Labdacid origin, the founder of the *hieron* might well have been inspired by such a memory. But if, as seems to have been the case, the founding was more ancient, then it must have relied on less elaborate traditions, influenced not by poetical legends but by rites whose efficacy was supposed to be immediate.

Let us not forget that, on the one hand, Oedipus was primitively a malefic newborn who had been expelled as a scapegoat in order to ward off barrenness; and that, on the other hand, it was in the conservative city of Lacedaemon that abnormal infants, signs of divine wrath, were most dreaded in all of Greece and for the longest time. It is by no means impossible that a legend analogous to that of Oedipus had retained an archaic character there that it lost elsewhere under the influence of epic. But it seems likelier that a cult did exist, created for the purpose of exorcising hostile forces that cause misshapen infants to be born and then to be condemned to death. This cult would have been associated with the name of the hero who personified the old rite—and we have no reason to suppose, moreover, that this hero was called Oedipus in Sparta. All this was later *modernized*, which is to say that all the characters would have been given names that had been hallowed by literature during the interval. The protective divinities of birth would have become Erinyes, who were still invoked as late as the *Eumenides* of Aeschylus against infant sickness and fatality,[86] and the heroes of the rite would have been expressly identified with the two Theban princes. In a third and final step, by way of consecrating the newly revised traditions, a Spartan noble claiming to be of Theban origin would have constructed or restored an edifice in honor of his lineage. I have long thought that the scourge described by Sophocles[87] was part of a prior and possibly archaic mythopoeia—a hypothesis that would fit rather well with the one I have just sketched. But I well recognize that there is no point trying to explain obscurities by things that are still more obscure.

---

Let us summarize what the present chapter teaches us, first with regard to the theme of old and new kings in Greek legend:

1. What is at stake in the *conflict between generations* is always the *conquest of power.*

2. Its central episode is a *combat* or a *race*, at the end of which the defeated competitor must die.

3. *The old man is always vanquished*, except in the story of Zeus and Heracles, which can only end in a reconciliation.

4. The two rivals are sometimes father and son, but more often an old man and a young man who is in love with the old man's daughter. The theme of generational conflict is therefore combined with that of *marriage to a princess*, which I will study below in Chapter 5 and which moreover has the same ultimate meaning: both are concerned with accession to the throne. The linking of the two themes caused the first one to be modified, coloring an old political tale with fictive elements and sentimental feeling.

5. The ritual nucleus of the myth is a contest that entitles the victor to wield power. Archaically, this competition certainly entailed the death of the vanquished contestant. The legend's retelling in a family context dates from a later epoch when the rite, exhausted of its original meaning, now unintelligible, came to be transposed into a variety of distinct narratives. This same rite was the source of sporting competitions in ancient Greece.

6. The central motif—a battle between two men—was not overlaid by incidental circumstances in the first instance, by the inventions of poets anxious to explain how it could be that the two adversaries did not know each other. In none of the legends as they have come down to us do we find any

trace of the primitive customs relating to marriage in which Potter sees the origin of a combat between father and son.

With regard to the incorporation of the theme in the legend of Laius, I shall limit myself to the following observations:

1. The details of the struggle between an old man and a young man must have long remained unsettled, as the great number of variants of which we are aware goes to show. If, once family life had acquired a stable character, the struggle became transformed into a duel between father and son, an ingenious poet must have been tempted to associate it with the figure of Oedipus, separated from his parents from birth and, as a consequence, unknown to his father. This does not mean that the theme of combat is more recent than that of exposure, simply that its crystallization around the name of Oedipus seems to have come after the theme of combat was first elaborated. The antiquity of this theme is guaranteed by the fact that the names that figure in it come from the rite of apothesis.

2. Laius seems to have been honored as a prophet in Eleon. It seems to me useless in this case to ask which is more ancient, the myth or the cult; but very interesting, by contrast, to ask on the basis of what association of ideas did an archaic cult come to be designated by a legendary name.

3. In Sparta, Laius, Oedipus, and their Furies were linked to the premature death of newborns. Here again I believe we are dealing with a primitively anonymous cult that subsequently came to be associated with a legend that had been elaborated in the interval.

4. Nevertheless the name given to the prophet of Eleon and the Spartan cult for the protection of newborns must go back to an earlier time when the meaning of the two rites—bound up with combat and exposure of malefic infants—was still intelligible.

# CHAPTER 3

# Victory over the Sphinx

---

Oedipus is famous for having vanquished a fabulous creature. This theme figures in so many legends, Greek and other, that one could hardly list them all. The classification of variants is difficult because storytellers' imaginations led them to take liberties with an archaic myth, which nonetheless may yet be glimpsed beneath the embellishments and exaggerations of the revised versions.

First, a word about the archaic myth. Evidently it would be unwise to postulate a single source for several hundred—perhaps several thousand—more or less similar tales. In every case, however, two things need to be distinguished: the victory of man over monster and the monster itself. And while a unique origin cannot plausibly be assigned to so many different types of monster, their defeat has an identical significance from one legend to another.

"The duel of the hero and the monster, and, naturally, the victory of the former," as Jeanmaire summarizes the matter, "is the enabling exploit of kingship."[1] To this one must add: the *victory* is almost always separated from the *taking of power* by an intermediate episode, the *marriage of the victor to a princess*. Later I shall try to explain why the marriage and the triumph are presented as related events. First, however, let us try to determine what place the defeat of the Sphinx occupies in the legend of Oedipus, considered as a literary composition.

This legend, as I say, treats in succession all the signs that mark out a man for greatness. He undergoes a trial, either of the chest or of the mountain. He kills an old king. He solves a riddle. He vanquishes a monster. Finally, he marries a princess. In other legends one finds two or three of these themes more or less artfully combined. Thus Pelops conquers and kills the old king and marries the princess, whose hand entitles him to rule. Perseus, having undergone the trial of the chest, kills a monster and wins a princess, after which, having established his claim to kingship, he accidentally kills his grandfather. In the Theban legend as the tragedians received it, all five themes interact and shape one another, forming a complex in which the victory over the Sphinx is central, for it alone confers power. The other episodes do no more than prepare the way to this principal moment, or else are a consequence of it. Their concatenation can therefore be described in the following manner: *after* having endured the ordeal of the chest (or of the mountain) *and* having killed the old king, Oedipus, *thanks to* his solving of the riddle, vanquishes the monster, which gives him at once the princess and the kingdom. In this narrative, the first two episodes wholly lose their character as *trials*. They serve simply to conceal Oedipus's true identity and to ensure the vacancy of the Theban crown. We have had to study these two themes separately, searching for counterparts to them in other legends in order to restore their primitive religious content, for on a first reading they seem to be a fictive means of improving the plausibility of an exceptionally unlikely sequence of events, nothing more. The struggle against the Sphinx, by contrast, has kept its mythic character: it alone is presented as guaranteeing the hero's ascension to the throne.

Now, this central episode appears never to have been treated by the poets. To the same extent that Perseus's feats came to be enriched by everything that in the folklore of all nations celebrates this sort of prowess, so Oedipus's triumph has remained, by contrast, a bare and unadorned fact. Not one account of it has come down to us. We do not even know the events that led up to it, nor exactly what happened between the two adversaries once the traveler had pronounced the decisive words. Our literary sources limit themselves to brief allusions. Figuratively decorated monuments suggest that the literature that has been lost to us would not tell us anything more. They

represent the Sphinx atop a column or pillar and Oedipus at its base, ponder-
ing her riddle—seldom anything else, nothing in any case that would point
to versions unknown to us, no hint whatsoever that more explicit versions
once existed.

Again, it is by placing the legend in comparative perspective that we find
the most telling argument against the existence of lost accounts that might
have been more detailed. In almost all tales involving a vanquished monster,
narrative ingenuity has been guided by two main ideas. First, *the hero receives
help from the gods.* Perseus is aided by nymphs and the Phorcides; Heracles
in the land of the Hesperides is aided by Prometheus and by Nereus. Second,
*his final triumph results from a prior series of victories.* Perseus, searching for
the land of the Gorgons, arrives among the Phorcides and tricks them into
showing him the way; they send him on to nymphs who provide him with
winged sandals, a satchel, and a cap of invisibility. Heracles, searching for
the land of the Hesperides, is advised by nymphs to query Nereus, whom
he forces to reveal the route he must take. It would be a simple matter to
multiply examples of this kind.

There is nothing of the sort in the Theban legend, where the theme of
the vanquished Sphinx is introduced at once, without the least delay. That it
has had no literary progeny is due mainly to two things:

1. The victory over the Sphinx results from the solving of a riddle. A
match of wits does not readily lend itself to picturesque description, however.
Because it excludes just those romanticized elements that are to be found in
abundance elsewhere, helpful animals, metamorphosed monsters, and the
like, a sterile cerebralism is scarcely avoidable.

2. Greek literature gives only an *expurgated* version of the traps laid by
the Sphinx. If sculpted and painted memorials teach us nothing further
about her duel with Oedipus, they can by contrast instruct us with the great-
est precision about her nature and her appetites. What they have to say in
this regard is rather different from what the texts have to say. The character
and the role of the Sphinx were modified because her struggle against the
hero had previously been stripped of all its episodes except one, the solved
riddle, which, in tales of this kind, is either exceptional or added to other tests
that impress themselves on the imagination more forcefully. Here it occupies
the entire center stage. It could not do this without at once intellectualizing
both antagonists, who have now become rivals in a wholly abstract mental

competition. But the primitive mythopoeia must have contained something completely different, and it is this transformation that we must begin by studying. Apart from the legend of Oedipus, the Sphinx hardly appears in literature. The texts that I cite here therefore serve the immediate purpose of the present book.

––––––––––––––––––

Hesiod knew of a monster near Thebes, lurking in the gorges of Mount Phikion and lethal to the Thebans, that he called the Phix.[2] It has been wondered which of the two is the more ancient, the name of the place or the name of its inhabitant. Scholars today think that it is the latter, and that Phikion is to Phix as Typhaonion is to Typhon.[3] Scholiasts regarded the form "Phix" as a Boeotian name for the Sphinx: like everyone in Greece, they considered the two creatures to be one and the same. Other forms existed, attested by Hesychius and by a passage of the *Cratylus*.[4] In addition to Φίξ there appears to have existed a form Σφίξ that very soon was drawn by folk etymology into the orbit of σφίγγειν [to hold tight, to grasp, grip, squeeze, crush]. Attesting to this are manuscripts of Hesiod in which the correct reading Φῖκ' is kept—in one case by a scholiast, also in a recent copy (though there with a mistaken accent), together with a variant mention in another copy; the rest give Σφίγγ' or Φίγγ'. The Theban *Phix* might have had a vivid place in popular and local beliefs long afterward, alongside the *Bikas* known to Hesychius in the fifth century CE, but it disappeared from literary texts. The derivative form "Sphinx" (stem Σφίγγ-) no doubt benefited from its phonetic resemblance to σφίγγειν, whose semantic value naturally suited the image of a constricting demon. One may wonder whether it is a sign of anything more than the alteration of a slightly different theme under the influence of folk etymology. One may also wonder (and this is no less an unanswerable question) whether Hesiod knew a legend that associated the Phix and Oedipus. That he omits to mention Oedipus in the passage I quoted from the *Theogony* proves nothing. His silence might be explained in one of two ways: either he was unaware of the struggle between the monster and the king, or he was familiar with other legends, lost to us, in which the monster confronted other adversaries. It is possible, after all, that Laius's son did not always enjoy, in relation to the Sphinx, the sort of monopoly that the poets of the fifth century granted to him and that he retains in our imagination still today.

The Hesiodic Phix's mother is Echidna, who conceived her by her own son, Orthrus. According to Lasus of Hermione, the Sphinx is the daughter of Echidna and Typhon.[5] Euripides, according to a bizarre formula in *Phoenician Women*, makes her the daughter of Echidna and Gaia: γᾶς λόχευμα νερτέρου τ' Ἐχίδνας [offspring of Earth and infernal Echidna].[6] His audience, I imagine, was put in mind of those monsters that were given birth to *by* their mother *in* caves. In archaic legends, they certainly would have been born of Earth/Gaia herself. This is the version that Euripides preserved in connection with the birth of the Sirens: πτεροφόροι νεάνιδες παρθένοι χθονὸς κόραι Σειρῆνες [young goddesses, winged virgins, daughters of Earth, O Sirens!].[7] They were born, Eustathius of Thessalonika says,[8] from the blood that fell on the ground from the horn of Achelous. These conceptions owe more to popular sentiment than do those of the poets, who make the Sirens daughters of a Muse. It was only later that the need was felt to give monsters, first, a semihuman mother, then a father and a mother in the fashion of human families. The passage in *Phoenician Women* juxtaposes the first and the second of these three conceptions.

—————————

The mythical creature that the Greeks wound up calling the Sphinx derived from two basic notions. The one expresses a physical reality, the actual experience of an *oppressing nightmare*; the other, superimposed on it, is religious in nature and arises from a belief in ghostly spirits—*souls of the dead*, which were pictured as having wings. These two conceptions were combined to produce something original. They have many points in common, notably their erotic character, whose significance is all the greater as the nightmare and the ghost, once overcome, bequeath to whoever vanquishes them treasures, talismans, and kingdoms—which brings us back once again to the fundamental meaning of the Oedipus legend: Oedipus as conqueror. As for the many more or less confused images of the Sphinx in surviving texts, all of them crystallized around the figure of a winged lion-woman that Greek art inherited from the southern Mediterranean.

These two aspects of the Sphinx have been studied, but always separately. So far as I know, no one has thought to associate the physiological Sphinx with the psychical Sphinx. And yet the more closely they are examined together, the more both texts and monuments illuminate one another and acquire new significance.

The physiological aspect of the Sphinx was studied for the first time more than fifty years ago by Laistner in a curious, highly intelligent, and very penetrating work devoted to *inquisitorial demons*.[9] To be sure, it is now partly obsolete. And it is to be regretted that, not content with having so insightfully described the role of the tormentor in folklore and legends, he should have tried to explain much of Greek mythology in terms of this figure alone. But these criticisms do not apply to the pages devoted to the Sphinx, which, despite the work's title—*The Riddle of the Sphinx*—are few in number. And though they are few, they ought to have been enough to point astute readers in the right direction. Yet when Roscher took up the theme of *crushing demons* a decade later, he did not mention the Sphinx among them.[10] And neither Ilberg, who wrote the entry on the Sphinx in Roscher's *Lexikon* (1909), nor Lesky and Herbig, who were jointly responsible for the same entry in companion articles in Pauly-Wissowa (1929), devoted a single line to the Sphinx so well described by Laistner. This omission is all the less pardonable as Ilberg and Herbig both were familiar with the archaeological monuments that Laistner had not taken into account and in which Roscher showed scarcely any interest.[11] The inadequacy of what has been written about the Sphinx is nonetheless explained by the fact that textual evidence is rare; what little there is speaks almost exclusively, and then only in the most summary fashion, about her struggle against Oedipus. Weicker, however, had the bright idea of making a thorough study of ancient conceptions of the Sirens.[12] They do not appear solely as principal actors in a legend. We know many things about them that we would know nothing about if we were familiar only with literary sources, especially the famous passage in the *Odyssey* in which Odysseus prevails over them.[13] The Sirens were no less ennobled by Homer than the Sphinx was by Sophocles. And yet, in spite of Sophocles, we know rather more about the Sphinx than is commonly supposed.

The Sphinx belongs at once to two quite distinct categories of mythological creature. As a kindred spirit to Ephialtes, she is a *crushing demon*; as a kindred spirit to the Sirens, she is a *tormented soul*.[14] Let us begin by summarizing what Weicker established with regard to the Sirens.

The Sirens, like the Keres, the Erinyes, the Harpies, and the Stymphalian birds, are *spirits* of the dead. Just as there are several Sirens, so too there would be several Sphinxes if an overly fortunate legend had not assigned to one of them so remarkable a fate that the others fell into oblivion. All these creatures have one thing in common: they thirst for blood and crave erotic pleasure. Weicker has assembled the various literary documents and figurative representations that tell us which different kinds of bodily fluid permitted souls to replenish their chronically depleted stores of vitality. It will be instructive to consider his argument, which is conclusive.[15] Around the Sirens he groups their relatives the Keres, Erinyes, Striges, Moirai, Harpies, and Lamiae, along with Baubo, Empusa, Mormo (or Mormolyce), and other individual spirits. If Weicker scarcely mentions the Sphinx, at least he draws attention to monuments in which figures of the Siren and Sphinx types are mixed together and confused, and in a note he remarks: "The Sphinx received her name from the borrowed and wholly finished type [*fertig übernommen*] of the woman/lion who killed men; later she became a demon of death generally; in the case of the Siren, it is the general sense that created the specific type."[16] It needs to be kept in mind that the peoples of the Mediterranean commonly pictured the soul in the form of a bird, and that the Sirens, like all their sisters who menacingly sing and fatally enchant, came for this reason to be associated with music. A sculptor could represent the idea only by putting a musical instrument in their hands,[17] on which account they became bards, poets, or muses, all the while remaining, for the comic poets, deadly temptresses of young boys.[18] This much we can assert with confidence about the Sirens. It would be reckless, without anything more in the way of evidence, to liken the Sphinx to them. Greek mythology is a well-formed language, which is to say that no exact synonyms are to be found in it.

When Weicker speaks of the leonine type of Sphinx that the Greeks borrowed ready-made, he has in mind chiefly the Egyptian versions, which are wingless and male. The wings and female sex originated in the Euphrates Valley. It is in this guise that the Sphinx passed into Europe, in the first instance to Crete and Mycenae. The Cretan Sphinx crouches on the ground; so too the one in Mycenae, where the wings are shown spread, with the uppermost feather projecting furthest from the body, as in the case of the Sirens.[19] On account of her wings, the Greeks saw the Sphinx as the representation of a soul; on account of her name, she was identified with the Theban Phix, and it may be that this identification helped to make her a single creature and not a plurality, for otherwise her spiritual nature would more naturally have suggested a species rather than an individual specimen.

But the Sphinx is something more than a soul-bird, a *Seelenvogel*; it is also one of those oppressing demons to whose number belong so many disturbing figures of classical and medieval folklore. Laistner and Roscher are agreed in thinking that they all derive from what in German is called *Alptraum*, a term that we may translate simply by the French *cauchemar* [nightmare], so long as the full etymological import of this word is not neglected.[20] Laistner gave his study a scope that may be excessive. Grouping together all the stories in which he believed could be found one of the themes associated with the crushing demon, he sometimes overlooked the fact that two tales related to some third tale need not themselves be related. Passing from one variant to the next, and paying greater attention to similarities than to differences, he was often liable to lose sight of his starting point. What is more, many of the legends that he collected appear to have been influenced by a belief in sorcery, widespread in Central Europe during the Middle Ages, less so in the Mediterranean region. It is true that the physiology of sorcerers is plainly modeled on that of incubi. A superstitious belief in sorcerers, the product of conceptions analogous to ones that were common in classical antiquity and that exist in the folk mythologies of all nations, must have enjoyed an unusually favorable environment for it to have undergone further development. But we must not forget that this milieu was Christian and that a positive doctrine colored even tales of the most inferior quality, introducing in them most notably the idea of salvation, for both persecuted human being and persecuting demon—an idea wholly foreign to classical antiquity. Keeping this in mind, we may now consider how Laistner describes oppressing demons, male and female.

They arrive in a whirlwind.[21] They pose questions that must be answered on pain of death or of paralysis. They are capable of assuming the form of any animal. They constrict, crush, or smother their victims. They require sexual pleasure but succeed in satisfying this desire only with difficulty, for their appearance is always frightening and sometimes hideous. The treasures with which they have been entrusted they surrender to their conquerors, sometimes ones who are able to solve their riddles and answer their questions, sometimes ones who are able to withstand their overwhelming strength. Furthermore, in many of the legends studied by Laistner, the problem has two aspects: Will the hero be delivered from the demon's deadly embrace? Will the demon be delivered, thanks to its conqueror, from its infernal

condition? Laistner devotes a very long chapter to the *Erlösung der Lorin*.[22]
A man who has triumphantly endured a trial of this sort often manages to
free himself from the demon and to restore to it a human form and way of
life. In this case the demon is female and the hero marries her: the legend has
become a romance with pronounced Christian overtones. Marriage is not
the end of the tale, however, and with the birth of children the parents come
to sense the inequality of their origins. We may leave to one side these further
developments, which are of no interest for a study restricted to the Hellenic
Sphinx. Greek fables did not treat the theme of a rescued and rehabilitated
demon in moral terms.[23] But it is curious that Laistner and Roscher could
have read classical and later folktales without realizing that, if the oppressing
female demon is to be explained as the personification of nightmares, she
must also be a *lost soul*, which explains the concern that was felt for her fate
in the Christian world.[24]

Roscher, considering the problem studied by Laistner more narrowly
while at the same time stating it more clearly, examined the incarnations of
the *Alpdaemon* in classical antiquity: Ephialtes and Typhon in Greece; Pan,
Faunus, Inuus, and Incubus in Italy. He did not include the Sphinx in this
family. He certainly would have done so had he studied Laistner's argument
more carefully and against the background of the figurative monuments that
I will describe in a moment. To his credit, he very well describes the elemen-
tary and unvarying myths to which the figure of the midnight demon, the
Nightmare, gave rise in the classical world. The demon crushes its victim and
then, if the victim after a long struggle yet manages to prevail, he receives
from the demon a treasure, or a talisman, or a secret—a sort of benediction
pronounced by the vanquished spirit just before it disappears. This theme is
found in much richer, much more developed form in the European folklore
analyzed by Laistner. Indeed, certain themes attested in Slavic and Ger-
manic tales seem to have been unknown in antiquity; they were probably
elaborated later, under the psychologically formative influence of two things:
the Christian doctrine concerning the salvation and destiny of the soul, on
the one hand, and an extensive popular mythology concerning sorcery, on
the other. Certain features are constant, however, both in time and space.
Ancient tradition invariably sees the Nightmare as a mysterious supernatural
being, consumed, like tormented souls, by erotic desire. In calling him Inuus,
the Latins said rather crudely what they thought of him.[25] Saint Augustine

described with the greatest precision the dangers to feminine virtue repre-
sented by Silvani and Pans. "The people," he says, "call them *incubi*"—which
proves that, in the Latin world of the late fourth century CE, these maleficent
beings were referred to by their outstanding characteristic and not by their
mythological names. Augustine, for his part, did not think to doubt their
existence for a moment.[26]

The question arises whether we must reserve a particular place among
these fearsome beings for the noonday demons that have separately and
recently been studied by Roger Caillois.[27] Caillois holds that the classical
*daemon meridianus* and the medieval *Dame de Midi* are, among other things,
a personification of *insolation*. But he does not completely fail to recognize
the gloomy, funereal character of apparitions that sometimes disturb daytime
sleep, for he emphasizes that the dead cast no shadow, no more than demons
that appear when the sun is at its zenith do.

In drawing up a catalog of noonday demons, Caillois confines his atten-
tion solely to beings that are explicitly associated in legends with the noon
hour. This is why he leaves out the Sphinx. I am indebted to Mr. Maurice
Stracmans for pointing out to my friend Libon a curious story concerning
the dream of Thutmose (Thothmes) IV, known through a stele discovered in
1817 under the Sphinx of Giza. The monster appeared to the young prince at
the hour when the sun reaches its highest point in the sky and promised him
the crown of Upper and Lower Egypt, wealth and plenty, tribute from all
peoples, and a long and happy reign on the condition that he clear away the
sand that covered the statue up to its neck. When the stele was discovered
it was considered to be authentic, but subsequently doubt was cast on its
antiquity. Even if there are some who continue to see it as a later falsification,
most scholars now think that it was a work from the time of Thutmose IV
(fifteenth century BCE), destroyed under Amenhotep (Amenophis) IV and
restored by Seti (Sethos) I (fourteenth century).[28] Whether this tradition
does in fact go back to the eighteenth dynasty, or whether by contrast it con-
stitutes a pious fraud,[29] need not concern us here. We may be certain that at
least one version associated the Egyptian Sphinx with the noon hour.

What is more, I do not think that it is necessary to attach great impor-
tance to the detail of the hour. The Greeks always considered the middle of
the day to be a time fraught with mystery and danger. But the strictly meridi-
onal character of the beings who represented these dangers, assuming that it

was primitive, which may be doubted, was soon forgotten. In order to restore it to the Homeric Sirens, Caillois is obliged to identify νηνεμία [absence of wind, calm weather], a word that does occur in the text, with μεσηυβρία [the midpoint of the day, the noon hour], a word not found there, and to say: "The Sirens are not specifically demons of the noon hour, but noon, which delivers their prey to them, is the hour when their action is efficacious."

I do not believe that any demon is specifically associated in Greek mythology with the noon hour. Disturbing dreams seem to have been supposed to result from the coincidence of two things: *ghosts* that act during *sleep*, whether during the night or the day. To this was added the sacred character of the moment that divides night and day in two—a critical instant since it marks a *passage*. "Noon is a sexual hour," Caillois says elliptically.[30] Midnight as well, perhaps still more so. Meridional or nocturnal, nightmares are often erotic.[31] It may also be objected that Caillois lays too little stress on the funereal character of the apparitions in dreams.

Here let me insist on a crucial distinction that, to the best of my knowledge, has never been made. The Latins saw demons that press down on their victims on the whole as male beings who tormented women. The Greeks, by contrast, personified both nightmares and distressed souls by feminine figures. The kinship between the two in the Greek case becomes clearer the more closely they are bound up with each other. One thinks particularly of the Sirens, the Empusas, and the Sphinx. The Erinyes, at least in the works that are known to us, have lost all sexual character and been transformed into pure administrators of justice. But how is it that no one has ever noticed that *they are never seen harrying a woman*? For the forbearance shown toward Clytemnestra they give a plausible excuse, namely, that a wife is not a blood relation of her husband, whereas their duty is solely to protect and enforce birthrights. One may wonder whether, primitively, the Erinyes' indifference toward culpable women did not have different, much less respectable reasons. Laistner cites many legends[32] in which a Dame de Midi marries her savior, out of gratitude: a legendary litotes, as Laistner very rightly observes, signifying that she no longer has anything to refuse to him; and if later, the captive of her husband, she rebels against the yoke of marriage, it is because an open relationship would have better suited her unsubmissive nature as a psychical creature, a spirit. In the Middle Ages, the nightmare was imagined in its full horror as an old woman with sagging breasts.[33] According to the sixteenth-century surgeon Ambroise Paré, physicians of his time held that the nightmare [Paré refers to it by its Latin name, *Incubus*] is an evil where a person has the impression of being crushed or suffocated by some heavy weight pressing down upon the body and that it comes principally at night; the common people, Paré adds, say that it is the weight of an old woman. In Languedoc, Littré says, the nightmare is called *chaouche-vielio*, an old woman who presses, squeezes.

The Greek tragedians did not connect the Theban Sphinx with this erotic aspect of bad dreams. But we will find it elsewhere, for she is essentially a *feminine incubus*, which is to say a female being who approaches a man and lies down upon him. Old Latin knew the masculine *incubus* (more anciently, *incubo*) and the feminine *succuba*; the latter was in no way a demoniacal power, however, simply a *mulier adultera* [unchaste woman], a *subnuba* [a rival in love (literally, one who supplants a bride)]. The absence of a feminine term corresponding to *incubus* is not at all surprising; it fits with what I said earlier, that the Romans could scarcely imagine female demons tormenting men. They would have considered the existence of a feminine incubus,[34] that is, a pursuing or haunting spirit who lays herself upon men she desires, to be contrary to nature. Yet this state of affairs is exactly what Paré affirms in associating a Latin masculine name [*Incubus*] with the old woman [*une vielle*] of the nightmare in its popular conception. And it is impossible to give any other name to the Sirens, or to the Sphinx, who invariably are upright when they approach a man who lies prostrate before them.

There is a great resemblance, as I say, between crushing demons and tormented souls. This is why dreamers received their visitors during the night (or at the noon hour, in the case of ghosts). Nevertheless certain beings more closely belong to one class than the other. The Sirens, for example, are essentially psychical creatures, spirits who act on the minds of their victims. Others, such as Pan, Empusa, and the Sphinx, are found at the intersection of these two orders of imagination. The Sphinx's ambiguity derives, I think, from her name and the way in which she was pictured. On the one hand, her wings predestined her to embody a tormented soul, thirsty for blood and hungry for sexual gratification—yet a seductive one as well, for she was endowed with the gift of song. On the other hand, her leonine body and her epithet ("the Frightening One") predestined her to embody the oppressing nightmare. A fleet vampire, she hunted young men with ease; a powerfully built vampire, she crushed them with her full weight.[35] Moreover, it was not primarily, or even essentially, their life that she threatened.

The Siren is revealed to be an incubus by textual sources (above all later ones) and not by sculpted or painted works of art, except for one from the Alexandrian period that is very fine and perfectly clear.[36] Matters are entirely otherwise in the case of the Sphinx. Literature portrays her as a question-posing ogress. In the texts that have come down to us, her erotic character has left only faint traces, which would have remained unintelligible had they not been figuratively represented by a small number of archaic memorials where the erotic implication is evident. Curiously, however, the scholars who have studied these artistic images unanimously describe the Sphinx as a murderer, which she was not—or at least not in the texts that interest us—and not as a feminine incubus, which she certainly was. Nothing is more imperious than a literary reputation, and nothing interposes itself with more lasting effect between memory and reality. Let us therefore pause to examine the following series of decorated objects.

1. Black-figure Attic cup found at Gela in southern Sicily (Figure 1). Orsi associates it with the Exekias cycle (first half of the sixth century BCE, though possibly the second half), suggesting that it is a product of "that studio of foreign artists, perhaps Chalcidian, working in Attica, to whom certain cups in the Louvre are due."[37] Eight naked youths, all of them similar, flee to the right with their left arms raised. Coming after them from the left is the Sphinx, to whom the youth nearest her appears to cling by his right hand, buried in the monster's chest at the origin of her right wing. The youth's right foot and lower leg are shown between her forelegs.[38] Orsi, the first to have published this picture, sees it as a representation of Odysseus escaping from the cave of Polyphemus, but with a Sphinx being substituted for the Homeric ram.[39] This is pure fantasy. Robert nonetheless concurs, saying that "the young man holds on to the Sphinx as Odysseus [did] to the ram."[40] Wilamowitz, for his part, recognizes that the young man's position is odd, and remarks that, "far from having been carried off by the Sphinx, he gives the impression instead of having voluntarily followed it"[41]—a possibility that he then proceeds to dismiss out of hand. Malten considers the Sphinx to be a predatory *Todesdämon* [demon of death]. He too is surprised to see that the last of the eight youths appears to cling to her, but reasons that "the artist could not have done otherwise since he wished to depict the forward

motion of an upright Sphinx having no arms."[42] Evidently this explanation is worthless. The artist has illustrated, in the clearest possible fashion, an erotic entanglement, a *symplegma*.

2. A *lekythos*, carelessly wrought, with black figures on a white ground, of a type commonly found in Athenian tombs (Figure 2). According to Chanot, the first to publish it, it represents a Theban knocked to the ground by the Sphinx, who is preparing to devour it.[43] In reality, it is not a struggle that is depicted here but a sexual encounter: the Sphinx is preparing to embrace a nearly recumbent man who raises one arm toward her while falling backward, his weight on the other arm. In this very stylized scene, a tree is placed on either side of them to indicate that the encounter takes place in the countryside.

3. A carnelian scarab in the A. J. Evans Collection at the museum in Corfu, circa 500 (Figure 3).[44] A Sphinx holds down beneath her a naked young man who wraps his legs around her flanks. Sexual intercourse is indicated here in a particularly realistic fashion. Nonetheless there is something caricatural about the physiognomy of the two figures that suggests they are part of a nightmare.

4. A squat lekythos (*aryballos*) ornamented with red figures in a very beautiful style, circa 450, in the National Archaeological Museum of Athens, inv. no. 1607 (Figure 5). A Sphinx in flight, wings spread, lands on her prey and embraces it; her left hind paw holds the thigh of the young man, who is falling backward, his left arm folded across his chest. They look into each other's eyes. Here again sexual intercourse is very clearly indicated.[45]

5. Four terra-cotta reliefs discovered in different eras at Milo.[46] The first three (Figures 6, 7, 8) belong to the series of severe works that Jacobsthal places between 470 and 460; the last (Figure 9) to a middle series that he dates to between 460 and 450. The first two are similar in shape and face leftward, the last two face rightward. The Sphinx, in the severe pieces, is crouched over her victim. Of her four paws, only two are visible. She has in her grasp the torso and the thighs of the youth, who is naked except, in the first and third reliefs (Figures 6 and 8), for a garment of unknown extent that flows diagonally behind his head, torso, and arm; in the third relief, a hand is extended with fingers spread in a manner that suggests spasmodic twitching; in both these cases the other arm is raised and disappears behind the neck of the Sphinx, and the youth's head, turned away from the Sphinx, rests on his

shoulder. In the third relief, his legs form an angle with his thighs. The style of the fourth relief is more sophisticated. The Sphinx is bent over her victim, her right front paw pressing down on his chest, the left wrapped around it in back. The claws of the right hind paw are dug into his thigh. Her tail is wrapped around the leg of the youth, who is trying with his left hand to free himself from her clutches. What remains of his neck allows us to deduce that he is looking at the Sphinx.

6. Fragment of an Attic prothesis amphora (Figure 10), from about 600, which must have belonged to Furtwängler.[47] It seems to show a meeting of two Sphinxes. Between them one sees a young man, naked, who clings with one hand to the neck of the Sphinx on the left. He seems to want to slip beneath her.

7. Finally, one has only to look at the engraved gem published by Overbeck[48] to see the resemblance between the scene it represents (Figure 11) with certain encounters of Leda and the Swan. The artist plainly wished to portray sexual foreplay, not violent conflict. Intercourse will be fatal for the man. The Milo reliefs seem to show a sleeping youth who is tormented by a bad dream and struggling confusedly to free himself from its grip. In the oldest images, by contrast, the young man appears to give himself up willingly to the Sphinx's smothering embrace.

A few discerning critics have recognized the erotic character of the Sphinx in scenes of her attacking the Thebans. Unfortunately, they have mentioned this detail only in passing, without insisting on it. As early as 1847, Jahn had remarked on a kinship between the depiction of Aurora carrying off Memnon and that of the Sphinx carrying off the Thebans.[49] His commentary on the Tenos relief (Figure 6) could not have passed wholly unnoticed. Jahn also published the Leda with swan found in Argos and conserved in the British Museum (Figure 12).[50] The resemblance of this Leda (allowing for the reversal of the two sexes) with two engraved stones in which one sees a Sphinx approaching a young man struck Jahn, writing seven years before Overbeck, at once. Goldman, studying two vases at the museum in Boston more than sixty years later, drew attention to the fact that the poets spoke of a violent hostility between the Sphinx and her adversary that does not appear in the figurative monuments, which represent a popular tradition.[51]

Present circumstances have prevented me from consulting photographs of several painted vases whose description, kindly shared by Professor

Delvoye, inclines me to believe that they confirm my opinion. I present these
descriptions below. It is easy to see that in each case they concern, not a scene
of aggression, but a sexual encounter.

- White lekythos with black incised figures at the National
  Archaeological Museum of Athens (inv. no. 12964): "Seated Sphinx,
  wings spread, holding between her forepaws a naked man, thrown
  to the ground, who is trying to raise himself up by putting weight on
  his right elbow (Theban?). To the left a bearded man, legs crossed,
  stretches out his right arm in encouragement. To the right, another
  person standing and leaning on a stick; he is turned round toward the
  central group and extends his right arm from this side, fist clenched."[52]
  Apart from the lateral figures, the scene must surely resemble that of
  Figure 2. Haspels dates it to about 500.[53]
- Black-figure lekythos (Athens 2308/397), excavated in Tanagra: "A
  Sphinx with the head of a woman, crowned with leaves, face painted
  white, carries away in her arms an unbearded youth who clings to
  her."[54] No indication as to school or date.
- Four Attic black-figure lekythoi grouped together by Haspels because
  they all have the same subject: a Sphinx with its victim in the presence
  of spectators.[55] Haspels attributes them all to the same artist, whom she
  calls "the Haimon Painter" on account of his predilection for scenes
  of the abduction by a Sphinx of an adolescent; a purely conventional
  name, chosen on account of the literary tradition that makes Creon's
  son Haemon the last and most desirable of the Sphinx's victims.[56]
- Two Attic black-figure lekythoi, one at Mannheim, the other at
  Princeton, on the same subject, attributed by Haspels to an artist she
  calls "the Emporion Painter" who was in some sense a successor to the
  Haimon Painter.[57]

What is striking about these descriptions is the passivity of the young
man, consistent with the behavior we have already noted. In Figures 2–6 and
8 he seems feeble, as though paralyzed. In Figures 1, 5, 6, and 8 there is no
point of contact between him and the ground. Either the Sphinx holds him
or he holds on to her, but so insecurely that he seems bound to fall. The act
of sexual intercourse is spatially suggested, following on from the implied

movement of a feminine incubus who flies or walks.[58] There is nothing to indicate hostility, except in the most recent of the Milo reliefs, and perhaps also in the Corfu scarab. Critics would never have seen in these images a representation of a murder scene had the idea of Oedipus's combat not imposed itself on their minds, dictating a preconceived interpretation. Only one detail conveys a hint of anything at all disturbing: the desperate flight of the youths on the Gela vase. Their wild gesticulation proves that, if the artist had wished to picture rebellion on the part of the victim, he would not have been at a loss to summon the necessary means of expression.

In more recent pictorial representations, the Sphinx always appears in the company of Oedipus. Under the influence of literature, she has lost her character as an incubus. Might she nonetheless have retained it in the popular imagination? A note in Suidas, which says that prostitutes were called *Megarian Sphinxes*, suggests as much.[59] It is tempting at first sight to take these two words as a writerly paraphrase, but, on reading the note more carefully, one perceives that it is solely concerned with explicating the sense of Μεγαρικαί; the sense of σφίγγες here seems to go without saying, to the point of furnishing an explanation for σφιγκτής. Suidas is probably right that the Megarians were known for their maliciousness (a reputation given to them, he says, by the Athenians). Can we conclude that Sphinxes, in the plural, were still a recognized species in current speech? One thing is certain, that most Greeks still remembered the Sphinx's lewdness, though the poets so seldom reminded them of this aspect of her character. In the literature that has survived, this trait is rarely mentioned; so rarely, in fact, that one is hard pressed to recall texts in which one cannot help but wonder whether the author had relied on the evidence of archaeology in order to compose them. The passage in *Seven against Thebes* describing the shield of Parthenopaeus emblazoned with a Sphinx comes to mind:

Σφίγγ᾽ ὠμόσιτον προσμεμηχανημένην
γόμφοις ἐνώμα, λαμπρὸν ἔκκρουστον δέμας,
φέρει δ᾽ ὑφ᾽ αὑτῇ φῶτα Καδμείων ἕνα (541–543)

[The Sphinx, devourer of living flesh, whose
shining form is embossed and fastened by rivets,
holds beneath her a man, a Cadmean]

The last line makes it seem almost as though Aeschylus had before him the Gela vase, or perhaps was thinking of one of the motifs that decorated Zeus's throne at Olympia and that Pausanias describes thus: τῶν ποδῶν ἑκατέρῳ τῶν ἔμπροσθεν παῖδές τε ἐπικεῖνται Θηβαίων ὑπὸ σφίγγων ἡρπασμένοι [On the two front feet (of the throne of Zeus) Theban children are being carried off by Sphinxes].[60] These Sphinxes were almost surely female, but their gender is not specifically indicated.

Here Pausanias does what modern archaeologists do: he interprets what he sees in terms of the legend he is familiar with. Consider, for example, the case of Fritz Eichler, who reconstructed one of the Sphinxes from Zeus's throne with the aid of remnants found and pieced together from a replica of the Imperial era, in black basalt, that had been discovered in the course of the Austrian excavations being carried out at Ephesus.[61] Both Eichler and the sculptor who executed the design under his direction detected a murder in the scene that they were reconstituting. So great was their exactitude, however, that this preconceived notion, false though it undoubtedly is, did not succeed in altering the character of the work that they were trying to bring back to life. One sees in it quite plainly a sexual encounter similar to the ones I have just described. A prostrate young man is struggling to stand up, leaning on his right hand, his feet pulled back under him. The lower part of his face, which had been preserved, suggests the acute anguish that someone who is gravely weakened and has no hope of defending himself must feel. The monster's right forepaw rests gently on his left shoulder, a gesture that resembles a caress more than a blow (Figures 13 and 14).

Recall that the only surviving fragment of the *Oedipodea* relates that a female Sphinx had abducted Haemon, who was still handsomer and more desirable—handsomer and more desirable, that is, than her preceding victims:

Ἀλλ᾽ ἔτι κάλλιστόν τε καὶ ἱμεροέστατον ἄλλων
παῖδα φίλον Κρείοντος ἀμύμονος Αἵμονα δῖον.[62]

It is a scene of this kind, half-intelligible, that is pictured on a lekythos at the Bibliothèque Nationale in Paris,[63] a vase of pinkish clay with a flat tapered base on which a Sphinx may be seen, against a slightly reddish light-brown ground, pursuing a naked youth who turns back to look at her as he flees

(Figure 15). She is touching him with both forepaws, and it clear that he has now been caught. Two clothed persons watch the scene, which they frame, one on the left and the other on the right, without taking any part in it. Against the front of their body (their arms are not indicated), each one bears an object that must be a shield. This vase, which may be dated to the first half of the sixth century, is originally from Cervetri in Etruria.

---

Oedipus vanquishes the Sphinx, according to the classic mythopoeia, by answering her riddle. It is generally believed that the riddle is an ancient theme that came late to the legend of the Sphinx, which, in its earliest version, must have contained something quite different. Robert argued that antagonism, primitively, would have been represented in the form of hand-to-hand combat, and pointed out that a creature who is half-lion must succumb, not to the intelligence of a man who is skilled at solving puzzles, but to the physical strength of a hero. In support of this argument he cites a small red-figure lekythos at the Boston Museum of Fine Arts,[64] carelessly modeled and clumsily drawn. A wingless Sphinx is pictured on hilly ground that may perhaps stand for Mount Phikion. With one of her forepaws she threatens a naked man who holds out to her his left hand, at the level of her face, and who brandishes a club with his right. This image attests a version in which Oedipus did battle with the Sphinx, an episode no longer known to our mythopoeias, in which, merely by solving the riddle, the hero suddenly has the monster at his mercy.[65] Robert thinks that this account comes from an archaic version in which Oedipus fought against a lion with a woman's face and that this tradition did not contain the riddle.[66]

When I first read Robert's book, I thought that the hand-to-hand combat of monster and man was the expurgated translation of a more ancient mythopoeia where the hero emerged victorious from a sexual encounter in which he had succeeded in overcoming an incubus. The physical battle seemed to me to be merely a kind of understatement, an instance of mythological compression. As for the riddle, like Robert I believed it to be a late addition to the Sphinx episode. Later I came to see, however, that it could readily be explained by association with the theme of the princess, for there are many tales in which a hero wins a bride by correctly answering a difficult question. The riddle would therefore have been relocated from the episode of Oedipus's marriage to the one immediately preceding it. In the legendary schema, a young man defeats a monster and solves a riddle, with marriage to a princess as his reward; the Theban tale would have abridged the sequence of events by recounting the feat of a young man who vanquishes a monster by solving a riddle. The riddle would therefore have been substituted for the combat, which itself had already been substituted for a sexual conquest.

But this explanation cannot withstand the force of Laistner's insight, namely, that crushing demons subject their victims to three tests, in the form of their caresses, their blows, and their questions. One is therefore bound to go astray in searching for a unique archaic reality that lies concealed under the question posed to Oedipus. The question is part of a primitive mythopoeia that was richer than the one the poets stylized and embellished. Similarly, the theme of hand-to-hand combat is not, as I had once supposed, more recent than the sexual encounter and older than the riddle. The earliest tales must surely have included all three variants. The poets kept only one of them, the one that best served their purpose.

---

It remains to determine what exactly Oedipus's triumph amounts to. One is tempted to compare it to Odysseus's triumph over those other incubi, the Sirens. But this begs another question: what exactly did Odysseus's triumph amount to?

The author of the *Odyssey* composed this episode so skillfully that no one thinks to ask what would have happened if the hero had not been deaf to the songs of the enchantresses. One would imagine, considering the dread they inspired, that they killed their victims. The poet says nothing about this, except to allude in passing to the rotting carcasses at the edge of their dismal meadow.[67] From similar legends we may suspect that death must follow upon a brief and ghastly sexual assault.[68] Odysseus escapes danger by fleeing: he is saved and he saves his companions; that is all we are told. He has won no victory. Nor does the poet say what became of the Sirens after Odysseus had passed by unscathed, though his very silence seems to suggest that they went on with their business, patiently setting traps for less wary travelers. And yet the poet certainly knew the ending of many such tales, where the monster, having failed in its attempt to kill, must perish. A single lapse deprives it of its mysterious power. Scholars who have studied the crushing nightmare see the death of the persecutor as a transcription of the joy experienced by the dreamer on awakening from it and the sense of relief at suddenly being delivered from oppression. Possibly so. Yet one wonders whether it may not be only an adventitious justification for an essential rule of popular mythology: adversaries are obliged to compete on equal terms. We have already seen that this sort of principle of fair play applies in tales of exposed infants, ordeals in general, and the struggle between the young and old kings; presently we will see it operating in connection with the riddle, and later with the contest for the hand of the princess, and even with the strange case of the hero's marriage with his own mother. A certain sentiment of justice requires that whoever stands to gain much should stand to lose much as well. Similarly, the tempting monster is itself exposed to all the dangers that it exposes its victims to.

The Sirens' suicide appears on an amphora, now in London, from the end of the sixth or the beginning of the fifth century, in which one of them can be seen throwing herself into the sea from a high promontory. There can be no doubt that well before this period it figured among the variants with which storytellers embroidered the theme of the vanquished temptress. Later, when the principle and rule of these struggles, that one of the antagonists must perish, was no longer understood, an oracle was invented condemning the Sirens to death if a ship passed by their island without stopping there.[69] Analogous variants exist in connection with the Sphinx.

In the tragedies of the fifth century, Oedipus kills his adversary. Audiences were given to understand that, once the answer to the riddle has been guessed, the Sphinx was disarmed, so that there could be no battle in the strict sense. At all events it is plain that the poets, though they have much to say about the monster's carnivorous appetites, praise the hero for his intelligence rather than for his courage. The tragic version, in which the demon is at the mercy of whoever succeeds in answering her question, admits of several different endings. Either Oedipus clubs the Sphinx to death, as on the Boston lekythos. Or, as on an aryballos found at Marion on the island of Cyprus, he delivers the fatal blow when she has already fallen at his feet.[70] Or else she kills herself in despair,[71] like the Sirens, and like so many of the vanquished enchantresses who figure in the folktales of Central Europe. Here as in so many other places, when mythographers no longer understood the mechanics of a traditional plot they introduced the theme of an oracle; in

this case, the Thebans will be delivered from the Sphinx the moment some-
one solves her riddle.[72]

Like the poets, the painters of the classical period preferred to represent
Oedipus's triumph as that of a peaceable, self-assured intellect. On a cup
from the fifth century, the traveler is seated facing the "clever virgin," his
legs crossed, chin resting on hand. They look at each other solemnly. A few
letters of the second line of the riddle stand out against the ground of the
image.[73] Documents of this kind, in which the tale has been wholly spiritual-
ized, as it were, add nothing to our knowledge that would make it possible
to answer two related questions: How was the Sphinx of popular mythology
vanquished? What did her defeat signify?

Odysseus avoids being fatally beguiled by incubi because he has been
strapped standing and upright to the mast of the ship that his oarsmen,
their ears plugged with wax, drive past the enchanted island.[74] Oedipus's
victory was certainly a more positive one. If Homer had less thoroughly
romanticized Odysseus's relationship to Circe, it might have provided us
with a useful parallel by showing how a mortal manages to gain the upper
hand over a creature of menacing intent and superior strength. Odysseus
dominates Circe because he is able to sleep with her with impunity, thanks
to the magical herb given to him by Hermes.[75] Circe is a nymph, no less
charming a companion for a mortal, if she wishes, than a water-sprite. It is
thanks to her and to her advice that Odysseus emerges victorious from the
trials set for him. Laistner has very rightly perceived that sexual intercourse
between a man and a Dame de Midi is a kind of ritual of holy marriage [*hie-
ros gamos*], with all that this implies in the way of risk and odds of success.[76]
In the medieval European tradition, whoever overcomes the spell cast by a
fairy is rewarded with riches; in the ancient Hellenic tradition, he becomes
a conqueror, sometimes for having avoided sexual entanglement (as in the
story of the Sirens), sometimes for having gladly welcomed it (as in the story
of Circe). The two branches of the alternative constitute a legendary litotes
that satisfies the Greek taste either for humanizing the hero's partner or for
dismissing the very idea of sexual partnership. Germanic and Slavic folklore
is less scrupulous. The question arises whether we must assume, considering
the prehistory of the mythopoeias that have come down to us, that a mar-
riage ritual was actually acted out between Oedipus and the Sphinx. It is true
that in modern Greek tales, Oedipus marries the Sphinx, who has therefore

simply replaced Jocasta.[77] The scythe-wielding Heracles, on the other hand, did have sexual relations with a woman/serpent, but the two tales are not at all parallel. There is no point, then, trying to determine how the Sphinx was overcome in archaic legend. It will be less futile to ask ourselves what her defeat meant.

Recall that Laistner and Roscher speak of an oppressing demon that, once vanquished, gives its conqueror talismans, secrets, and clues for locating hidden treasures. A bizarre story reported by Pausanias exploits this theme.[78] The tale is so incoherent that there is no alternative but to reproduce it in its entirety:

> Further on is the mountain where they say the Sphinx had her lair. From here she sprang, chanting her deadly riddle; though some say she was a pirate with a wandering fleet, who put in at Anthedon, occupied this mountain, and used it as a base for raiding, until Oedipus captured her with an overwhelming army he brought from Corinth. Another legend says that she was a bastard daughter of Laius, and Laius, who loved her, told her the message given to Cadmus by Delphi: no one else but the kings knew about this oracle. The oracle was handed on only to Epikaste and Epikaste's children, not to the sons of Laius by his mistresses; so if ever one of these brothers came to claim the throne from the Sphinx, she used a trick on them, saying that being Laius's children they must know the prophecy made to Cadmus; when they had nothing to answer, she condemned them to death for fraudulently laying claim to royal blood and to the throne. But when Oedipus arrived he knew the prophecy from a dream.[79]

Robert regards anything that tends to humanize the Sphinx as a late invention. And indeed the story of the woman/pirate must summarize a mediocre and absurd romance. But in the tale involving Laius's daughter,[80] one readily recognizes an old folktale that had been tidied up in much the same way as the tales collected by Perrault were to be nearer our own time. The Sphinx possesses a royal secret, and she will yield only to someone who possesses it as she does. All the brothers who come to her are disqualified, one after the other, until there arrives the last and apparently most disadvantaged one, who, thanks to supernatural intervention, knows the password. These two themes are encountered elsewhere in folklore. I do not think that they teach us the least thing at all about the archaic mythopoeia concerning Oedi-pus. But insofar as they formed a primitively independent and perhaps no less ancient anecdote, they were able to be associated with illustrious names.

Oedipus prevails here, not because he *guesses* something, but because he *knows* something—and he knows it thanks to a dream. This brings us back to victories achieved as the result of divine intervention. The Oedipus of the tragedians owes nothing to anyone but himself, and at bottom it is this fact that distinguishes him from Perseus and from Bellerophon. "We can only imagine," Robert quite sensibly remarks, "that in this version it is the Sphinx who governs Thebes after Laius's death."[81] Indeed this is probable. Note too that Oedipus, by giving the correct answer, would have been able to prove his royal lineage—another folkloric theme that is foreign to the Theban legend as it has come down to us, in which an unknown conqueror can reign only so long as no one, least of all the conqueror himself, knows who he is. Despite the fact that Laius's wife is called Epikaste, the name she has in epic, the tale summarized by Pausanias can therefore tell us nothing about the prehis-tory of the Theban legend, for archaicizing storytellers were apt to amuse themselves by adopting this old name, rather than Jocasta, precisely in order to show their independence from tragic versions; but it does give us some idea of how the folklore of the Sphinx might have developed. The schema proposed by Roscher differs slightly from this one. A vanquished demon typically divulges his or her secret; in this case, the demon is vanquished because someone else shares it with her. Unfortunately, the tale related by Pausanias does not say what became of the Sphinx after her downfall. Since she had the right to kill her ignorant half-brothers, her knowing half-brother surely has the right to kill her as well. Duels of this kind, as I say, impose the same conditions on both sides.

---

The tragedians depict the Sphinx as a *musical ogress.* Oedipus triumphed over a Sphinx *who feasts on raw flesh*; in Thebes he is honored as no one before him had been, for having freed the city *from a monster who robbed it of its men.* Thus says Aeschylus.[82] Pindar, in a lost paean, spoke of the *riddle that came forth from the young woman's ferocious jaws.*[83] The priest in *Oedipus the King* praises the one who, *in coming to Thebes, delivered the city from the tribute that it paid to the savage bard;*[84] elsewhere she is said to be *the Sphinx of the beguiling songs, the chanting bitch.*[85] The chorus thanks the hero, who, *having killed the young woman with the crooked claws who chanted her oracles,* raised himself up as a rampart and kept death from ravaging the land.[86] In *Phoenician Women,* Jocasta reveals that her hand had been promised to him who could solve *the riddle of the learned young woman; Oedipus understood the songs* of the Sphinx;[87] the chorus deplores the sorrows that had afflicted the city ever since *Oedipus, having understood a song difficult to understand, killed the savage bard the Sphinx.*[88] No commentator seems to have been surprised by the emphasis that Sophocles and Euripides place on the fact that the Sphinx *sings.* Whereas Aeschylus's epithets stress her cruelty, the two other tragic poets speak of her as a *musician*—according to their exegetes, because the enigma is set in verse. Evidently this will not do: no one in classical Greece would have regarded hexameter poetry as belonging to a musical genre; the riddle is in dactylic verses like all the oracles, yet no one considered the Pythia to be a musician on that account. The Sphinx, however, like the Sirens, is a *soul,* and souls sing in order to enchant. If, in the *Odyssey,* song is only an art of pleasure for Circe, this is owing to the poet's rationalist cast of mind; in mythopoeias more influenced by popular beliefs, there can be no doubt that the songs of a nymph had a more mysterious and more unsettling significance. Pausanias, when he says that the Sphinx sprang from her mountain lair *chanting* her riddle (which, according to Apollodorus, she had *learned from the Muses*), still recalled this essential trait of demoniacal enchantresses.[89] Apollodorus goes on to reproduce the riddle in prose—proving that, for him, the Sphinx's *musical* character was in no way associated with a versified enigma.

In the form of a *lioness/songstress* that the tragedians give to the Sphinx, the aspect of her character as an incubus has vanished almost completely. Was it more apparent in the poem known to us through the Pisander scholion? "The Sphinx," this text says, "seized and devoured young and old [alike]." She was, in other words, the most ordinary of ogresses. But the only two victims named are Haemon, son of Creon, and Hippius, son of Eurynomus: both of them young men. The ogresses of folktales prefer to eat children rather than adults; they crave tender flesh more than beauty. Yet the *Oedipodea*— according to the only two lines that have survived—said that Haemon was *the handsomest and the most desirable* of all the Thebans. The scholiast who preserved these two lines (Codex Monacensis gr. 560) adds, again apparently referring to the *Oedipodea*: "And it is said that [the Sphinx] was not a monster, as most people suppose, but a soothsayer who set riddles for the Thebans and put many of them to death when they misinterpreted her prophecies."[90] Similarly, Socrates of Argus made her into a chresmologist, a collector of prophecies.[91] All this is puzzling. The Sphinx who chose the young and handsome Haemon is still very close to an incubus. Yet the chresmologist who punishes those who misinterpret her oracles (why would she, unless she *were* a monster?) seems to belong to an entirely different realm of narrative invention. The divergence between these two strains of the tradition is so great that I am tempted to suppose that a phrase has been lost in line 37 before φασιν [it is said (or: it is recounted) that], either ἄλλοι δε [so the text would read: "others say (or recount)"] or ἔνιοι δε ["some (say or recount)"]. In this case the prophetess Sphinx would no longer come from the *Oedipodea*. Whatever assumptions we may make about these lines can only be tentative, of course, and without any great value. It is probable that the Sphinx of epic, like that of tragedy, was murderous, not amorous. And yet her sexual character was never completely forgotten. Once the young incubus of archaic monuments, then the clever virgin of classical poetry, she wound up becoming at last an old woman with withered, sagging breasts—the image, it will be recalled, that Paré used in connection with the crushing or oppressing nightmare.[92]

---

It remains for us to study a few points of detail. The classical painters almost always picture the Sphinx as seated atop a column. On the Marion aryballos, she has been knocked to the ground and lies at the foot of her vacant column, which occupies the center of the scene. On the Athens lekythos, where an incubus Sphinx is seen carrying off a young man, behind him there stands a sort of small low altar to which she seems to be bringing her prey. On a red-figure amphora in the Ashmolean Museum that Beazley dates to about 440,[93] she is seated on a high crag that resembles an irregular column, and Oedipus on a low rock ledge that resembles a small altar. Scholars have wondered what is signified by this column, which in its various forms serves her as a sort of pedestal. Because one often encounters a column surmounted by a Sphinx serving as a funerary or votive monument,[94] it has sometimes been thought that painters brought over the motif whole from its original architectural context, omitting to dispose of the pedestal, which no longer has any use. Thus a pelike due to Hermonax[95] displays a small Sphinx seated on her column in the midst of seven seated or standing Thebans. Robert finds nothing in the least odd about this because here the column is shown in its proper place in an agora.[96] If need be, a reason can always be found to explain the presence of the column in each of the many scenes it which it appears. What is bizarre is that it should appear in all of them.

One may wonder whether this not due to the custom of placing an unornamented column atop tombs;[97] plainly it served as a seat for the *soul* that haunted the body's resting place. If the painters located the Sphinx on a column, it is probably because they still sensed in her the spirit of one who had died.

That would explain the presence of a low column on the Athens lekythos. The Sphinx drags a motionless man toward a seat that has been prepared for her. Once he has been placed upon it, he too will become what the Sphinx already is, a being who belongs to the other world. To dream of being sexually united with a spirit of the dead signifies that one is about to die; when one is sick, to dream that one is flying signifies the same thing.[98] On this lekythos, the Sphinx's wings are larger than in any other image and, what is more, she has the appearance of a bird, which is to say she possesses a psychical or spiritual character. I believe therefore that the column, whether low or high, must be interpreted as a funerary symbol. But it probably has an additional function. By isolating the Sphinx, setting her apart in a sort of sacred space, it indicates her heterogeneous nature as a demon. One further point. Whoever in archaic Greece borrowed the iconography of the Cretan Sphinx would have known whether the pillar played a particular role in it. But so many doubts have been raised recently about the Minoan cult of the pillar that considering the two problems in tandem will resolve nothing. Even so it would be good to know how far they are bound up with one another. This question is extraneous to my purpose, however.

––––––––––

One passage in the Pisander scholion raises another question. Line 5 ['Ην δὲ ἡ Σφίγξ, ὥσπερ γράφεται, τὴν οὐρὰν ἔχουσα δρακαίνης] has generally been translated as "The Sphinx was such as it is seen in paintings, with a serpent's tail." Bethe pointed out that ὥσπερ γράφεται cannot mean "such as it has been painted," for then the phrase εἶχεν δέ would have had to be added.[99] He noted, too, that δράκαινα is a rare feminine form and that the Sphinx has never been represented with the hindquarters of a dragon. In the nearest case, the Sphinx's tail sometimes ends in the head of a dragon. Bethe therefore thinks that ὥσπερ γράφεται introduces a quotation from the *Oedipodea* in which the Sphinx is said to have had a dragon's tail, like his mother Echidna in Hesiod's *Theogony*.[100] But in that case the author of the scholion would have had to say λέγεται and not γράφεται. Let us leave to one side hypotheses that have been advanced concerning the reconstruction of a lost poem. On a first reading one is tempted to see this passage of Pisander's summary as proof that, in an archaic tradition—literary or pictorial, it matters little in this case—the *serpentine* aspect of the Sphinx was more pronounced than in the later treatments that have come down to us. The head of a dragon—often terminating in a tail in classical art—would be a survival of this archaic tradition. Yet the summary suggests a tripartite monster: bird, lion, serpent. Now, the role played in epic tales by threefold tests of courage, in which a hero confronts in succession a trio of dangerous creatures, introduced in ascending order of menace, is well known.[101] Here a single monster would stand for three ranked combats. This does not mean, of course, that a sufficient explanation has been given for the presence of complex monsters in the mythological bestiary by describing them as *ellipses*, each element representing a particular adversary. But the case of the Sphinx is rather special. The whole episode seems to be a sort of abridgment, in which things are indicated without being developed. The unknown beast described in Pisander's summary may well owe her dragon's tail (later removed in both art and literature) to a different version of the myth, in which Oedipus—or a hero related to Oedipus—did battle not with the Sphinx, but with a dragon. We know of another version in which he faced, in addition to the Sphinx, the Teumessian fox.[102] These variants are closely related, for the Teumessian fox is also an incarnation of the oppressing nightmare. As for the dragon, which has a funerary significance in Greece and elsewhere, its form is the one typically assumed by oppressing demons in later folklore.

---

In medieval folktales involving a monster, there is generally little concern with explaining why it should be there in the first place. A monster ravages the countryside, so naturally it must be destroyed—that's all there is to it.

But a Greek could not have helped but wonder, for example, what Demeter was up to. He would have wanted to know what exactly she was doing on the bank of that river, why she had with her the eel and the owl, and so forth. He would have sought out at once another Greek who could explain the story to him.

The hostility of the Theban Sphinx therefore came to be justified in several ways. Sometimes she was sent by Hades (a way simply of emphasizing her deadly character);[103] sometimes by Ares, angered by Cadmus's murder of the dragon;[104] sometimes by Dionysus, whose rancor against Cadmus's descendants had not abated;[105] the explanation that was most commonly adopted is the one mentioned in the Pisander scholion, which says that the scourge was sent by Hera.[106] All these justifications seem to be of purely literary origin. The last one poses a further problem. In a legend known to us through a triumphal ode by Bacchylides, the Nemean lion was sent against Heracles by Hera.[107] One of the two stories seems clearly to be based on the other. It might be possible to determine which one of the two served as a model if we could read them in their entirety, or at least extensive quotations from them. As matters stand, however, we can do no more than venture a guess on the basis of a poor summary and a mere allusion. The most that we can say is this: the mythopoeia implicit in the Pisander scholion is remarkably coherent from the religious point of view; on this point Bethe was probably right, as against all those who have contradicted him. In order to punish Laius's unnatural passion for Chrysippus, Hera inflicted on the Thebans another παράνομος ἔρως,[108] this one in the form of an incubus/ogress that devoured young men only after having chosen the handsomest ones. Between Heracles and the Nemean lion, by contrast, there is no natural hostility. But that does not necessarily prove that the Theban legend is older. A resourceful poet might have reworked a theme elaborated before him and given it an internal consistency that was lacking in the earlier version.

---

The results of our search for the origin of the legendary themes we have isolated so far justify us in drawing a number of firm conclusions. First, the theme of the monstrous adversary, like that of the chest, consists of several superimposed layers of meaning. There can be no doubt, in the special case of the Sphinx, that we are dealing with an oppressing, inquisitorial, and lewd incubus. This demon is at the same time a tormented soul—as indeed the figures of nightmares almost inevitably are. The Sphinx's relationship to the world beyond the grave explains her wings, her musical temperament, her learning, her insatiability. As for the combat to which the Sphinx dedicates herself, I believe that it preserves an ancient memory of trials of initiation, in the first place those rites of passage that every adolescent must undergo; but above all those more terrible ordeals to which future leaders must submit. Unfortunately, while we know a bit about the first kind, we know almost nothing about the second.[109] One would like to be able to write down next to each of them an exhaustive list, the one enumerating the archaic religious practices to which people were long faithful, the other the legends to which these rites were transposed when they began to fade from people's minds. The first column remains empty. With regard to tests of qualification for leadership, there have come down to us a few legends; the actual details of the tests themselves escape us almost totally.[110] It may be that we should imagine they involved dreadful persecution and terrible combat between political masters cloaked in animal disguises and those who sought to succeed them in power. We will be able to make a little more progress in this connection by studying the themes of the riddle and, above all, marriage with the princess.

1. Vase from Gela (first half of sixth century BCE)

2. Lekythos in the Attic style, with black figures on a white ground

3. Cornelian scarab from Corfu (ca. 500 BCE), A. J. Evans Collection, Archaeology Museum, Corfu

4. Chalcedony scarab (no date indicated), Naue Collection, Munich

5. Squat red-figured lekythos from Athens (ca. 450 BCE), National Archaeological Museum of Athens

6. Terra-cotta relief from Milo (470–460 BCE), British Museum

7. Terra-cotta relief from Milo (470–460 BCE), British Museum

8. Terra-cotta relief from Milo (470–460 BCE), Vlasto Collection, Marseille

10. Attic prothesis amphora
(ca. 600 BCE)

9. Terra-cotta relief from Milo (460–450 BCE), National Archaeological Museum of Athens

11. Engraved gem showing the Sphinx approaching a youth (no date indicated; published by Overbeck, 1854)

12. Marble relief of Leda with Swan from Argos (50–100 CE), British Museum

13. Remnants of the Ephesus Sphinx, from the Austrian excavation there that began in 1895

14. The Ephesus Sphinx as reconstructed by Eichler in 1937

15. Lekythos from Cervetri, in Etruria (first half of sixth century BCE),
Bibliothèque Nationale, Paris

**16.** Bas-relief of Siren approaching a peasant (Alexandrian period), Froehner Collection, Boston Museum of Fine Arts

# CHAPTER 4

# The Riddle

The riddle must be studied separately as a theme of Greek epic and tragedy, for the Theban legend uses it in a wholly peculiar fashion. In other tales, two principal schemas may be distinguished:

1. An oppressing demon poses questions. Whoever knows how to answer them will prevail against his questioner; whoever does not will die.

2. The hand of a princess is promised to whoever can solve a riddle. Whoever tries his luck and fails will pay with his life.

The test set for Oedipus is unique, but it has two meanings. The first is immediate, the second follows as a consequence. It must be noted, too, that the two schemas have one thing in common: the severity of the sanction imposed stands in striking contrast to the triviality of the contest. It will be instructive to begin by classifying different types of riddle according to their form, something that seems never to have been done before.

---

The Greeks adored conundrums and made a popular pastime of them. Homer and Hesiod, Melampus and Calchas, Alexander and the Gymnosophists all tried to outdo one other in the ingenuity of their solutions to such problems. Athenaeus devotes the entire tenth book of *Sophists at Dinner* to riddles as a form of entertainment.[1] In Hellenic folklore, by contrast, as in that of all other countries, there figures a particular kind of wager, in which a prize of very great value is promised to whoever is able to discover, whether by cleverness or by chance, some small unimportant thing. In the event of failure, the unlucky contestant will have to relinquish, by way of compensation, an advantage in which he places great store.[2] Greece has no equivalent to the riddles of Thor and Odin in the *Edda* or those of Yudhiṣṭhira in the *Mahābhārata*, but some traditions indicate that it was acquainted with the theme of a battle of wits followed by a terrible punishment: according to one, Old Homer killed himself after failing to guess the word that would have made a sailor's joke comprehensible; according to another, Calchas had to die when he encountered a seer more able than himself (probably Sophocles is responsible for introducing an oracle to this effect, identical to the one that was added at a late stage to the tale of the Sirens).[3] Both became necessary when it ceased to be understood that failure, by definition, entails death.

The theme of a monster who poses questions does not appear in ancient Greek literature apart from the Theban legend. Laistner brought together a large number of demoniacal riddles, while making no attempt to classify them. Many others could be found. In Christianized folklore the monster is replaced by the Devil, but the nature of the questions themselves scarcely varies. They can be reduced to two principal types, depending on whether they bear on something that must be *known* or something that must be *understood*. We have already encountered this distinction, which neither Laistner, nor Ohlert, nor Friedreich made, in connection with the Theban Sphinx.[4]

In general, demons require their interlocutors to give proofs of information or of memory rather than of intelligence. Usually what they demand are *secrets* or *names*. Recall the tale of the Sphinx, daughter of Laius, in the version related by Pausanias: she knows a secret from the king and kills all those who falsely claim to possess it as well. The presence of this theme makes me believe that at least small fragments of an ancient tradition can be seen in Pausanias's account. Sometimes the person being questioned must know the esoteric name of certain beings or things. In the ballad of Vafthrudnir, recounted in the *Poetic Edda*, Odin interrogates his enemy, the giant (*jötunn*) Vafthrudnir, posing questions that must be answered by proper names ("What is the name of the stallion that pulls Day across the world?"—"Its name is Skinfaxi," and so on). Finally, Odin—who has come to Vafthrudnir in disguise—asks: "What did Odin whisper in his son's ear before [his son] was burned on the pyre?" This time the giant cannot respond and is put to death. Similarly, in the ballad of the dwarf Alvis, Thor asks him for the names of the earth, the sky, and so forth in the various worlds, that is, among men, gods (the Aesir and the Wanes), elves, giants, and so on. Alvis stands to gain a fiancée, Thor's daughter. The dwarf responds correctly, but loses nonetheless because the dawning light of day catches him unawares—a frequent mishap in stories of crushing demons, who have only a limited amount of time in which to accomplish their purposes. Still it is generally the questioner who has to finish his work before a certain moment—a particular hour, often midnight or sunrise—and the one who is being questioned must do everything possible to prolong the contest until the hour when his inquisitor will have been disarmed. Not infrequently the one who is being tormented must speak the name of his tormentor. The name is difficult to remember, and it is only by happenstance or divine intervention that he manages to recall the magic syllables. No sooner has his true name been spoken than the demon flees or else is reduced to powerlessness.[5] Once Apollonius of Tyana named the Empusa, the spell with which she threatened Menippus ceased to have effect; the nuptial chamber, together with all of its preparations, disappeared.[6] This is evidently a vestige of the old popular belief that a supernatural being is deprived of its power once one has mastered its name.

The Sphinx asks Oedipus what animal has four feet in the morning, two at midday, and three in the evening. Here the answer that must be given is not the name of his inquisitor, as so often is the case, but his own name as a human being—man. This is very curious, but it can hardly be anything but mere coincidence. For the matter to be otherwise, one would have to suppose, first, that archaic tales featured a monster whose name the one being tested had to guess, and, second, that a poet was pleased to turn the theme inside out by adding to it the subtlety that it is no longer the name of an individual that is wanted, but the name of a species. This is much too complicated to be plausible. Surely it is more reasonable to suppose that, if the Theban legend contains a question that is the reverse of the one posed by all other monsters known to us in Greek legend, it is the result of pure chance. It must nonetheless be kept in mind that in the name *Oidipous* a Greek would have heard *dipous* [two-footed], which is to say that the personal name of the one who is on trial contains the collective name of the species to which he belongs.

Furthermore, one tradition maintains that Oedipus guessed the answer to the riddle by accident, without meaning to. He happened to touch his forehead, and the Sphinx understood this gesture to signify that in response to her question he had designated himself. Convinced of her defeat, she asked nothing more of him and in a fury killed herself. This is to attribute very little intelligence to the Sphinx and not more to Oedipus. But success due to chance has long been a theme of such tales, in addition to conundrums that call for sustained mental effort and tactics of delay,[7] so commonly in fact that the interest of whatever archaic fragments may survive in this anecdote is slight.

The demoniacal repertoire also contains *questions of intelligence.* When a Dame de Midi demands to know about the "sufferings of flax" or the "sufferings of barley," and the baffled victim has no choice but to try to draw out the interrogation until the hour strikes when the enchantress will suddenly lose her hold over him, we are evidently in the presence of a transcribed nightmare. We are equally in its presence when the inquisitor asks, "What is one, what is two, what is three . . . ?"[8] The essential thing in tests of this sort is not so much finding a word as finding a way to gain time.

It remains to consider true conundrums. The questioner formulates a paraphrase and the one who is questioned must discover the noun whose meaning it restates. One thinks of the puzzles put by King Heidhrekr in the riddle contest of the *Hervarar saga* to which Odin, disguised as the king's thane Gestumblindi, replies triumphantly. Demons rarely pose such questions. And yet it is to this type that the problem set by the Theban Sphinx belongs. Here again one detects in it the echo of a numerical series familiar from ancient folklore, "What is two, three, four?"

What can we say about the history of the riddle put to Oedipus? The version that is known to us from summaries of the tragedies was already current in the middle of the fifth century, since the Maître à la Guirlande[9] wrote down two lines from it on the ground of a cup on which Oedipus and the Sphinx are shown facing each other. Robert thinks that the five hexameters describing their exchange must come from an epic—a quite worthless hypothesis, since all oracular poetry was composed in hexameters. A passage in Hesiod's *Works and Days* likens an old man bent over a staff to a three-legged man.[10] The conundrum might have long been in circulation before being incorporated in a fictive context, after which it would rather naturally have been absorbed by the Oedipus tale on account of the assonance Οἰδίπους, δίπους, τρίπους, τετράπους; on account, that is, of the phonetic similarity between Oedipus's name (literally, "Swollen Feet") and the compound adjectives "two-footed," "three-footed," and "four-footed." The tragedians do not reproduce the exact wording of the problem, and the reason is not far to seek: the insignificance of the contest by comparison with the seriousness of the hero's predicament. In the fourth century, the *Oedipus* composed by Theodectes of Phaselis replaced the conundrum of the ages of man by one involving day and night. Perhaps Theodectes considered it to be more poetic, or perhaps these two sisters of Greek mythology, Day and Night, who gave birth to each other, put him in mind of the theme of incest.[11] It is not uncommon for such associations of ideas to act upon and shape literary composition.

---

We may separately classify those riddles where the prize for giving the correct answer is a bride. Of this type are the questions posed to Solomon by the Queen of Sheba (1 Kings 10:1–3), the details of which are not indicated in the biblical text. Note that *nuptial riddles*[12] always involve intelligence, never memory. They often have the form of *performative* conundrums, requiring ingenuity and patience. Thus, for example, Portia's father promises his daughter's hand to the man who, presented with three small boxes, can choose the one that contains a ring; the suitor who chooses wrongly will thereafter be unable to ask any woman to marry him. Here, as elsewhere, the gravity of the risk contrasts with the unimportance of the thing itself. With the story of Turandot, the fourth tale of the Persian epic *The Seven Beauties* by Nizāmī Ganjavī (Muhammad ibn-Yūsuf, d. 1180),[13] we draw nearer to that of Jocasta.

Turandot, a young princess, has shut herself up in an impregnable castle. Her suitors have to satisfy four conditions: they must be honest, they must locate the secret entry to the enchanted fortress, they must find and destroy a talisman, and they must obtain her father's consent. The severed heads of the many who have failed are hung in the battlements of the castle. Now there comes forward a young prince. Guided by the bird Sīmurgh, he fulfills the first three conditions. Turandot's father promises his agreement if the prince can guess three riddles that his daughter will put to him. These riddles assume the form of mysterious acts whose meaning must be discovered.

Turandot sends the prince two pearls. The prince correctly understands this to mean that life resembles two drops of water. He returns the pearls with three diamonds, which means that joy may prolong life. Turandot returns everything to him with some sugar. He rightly interprets this to mean that life is a mingling of desires and pleasures. He pours some milk into the box, which means that as the milk absorbs the sugar, so does true love absorb desire. The battle continues in this manner, preciosity vying with profundity on equal terms, until Turandot acknowledges at last the prince's triumph.[14]

Gozzi, Schiller, and Puccini have written brilliant variations on this theme, but their brilliance cannot hide the fact that it is but a meager theme. It differs furthermore from the story told of Oedipus in respect of transparency. Beneath the episode of the Sphinx's riddle as it has come down to us, we are led to suspect the existence of an earlier version: the princess will give her hand, and the crown, to whoever can guess the answer; whoever cannot will die.

Our texts say: Oedipus marries the queen because he vanquished the Sphinx, and he triumphed because he guessed correctly.

Folklore says: A conqueror marries the queen because he vanquished a monster and solved a riddle.

Certain tales choose between the two versions. The Theban legend prefers the first one to the second, and it is not hard to see why. Having become richer over time, more serious, more fully endowed with deep human psychological insight, it was more inclined to reject the trivialities with which other legends were satisfied. The victory of the hero had to have a significance that could be generally appreciated and welcomed. Like Heracles, like Theseus, Oedipus had to deliver the state from a collective scourge. This motif was well calculated to please a people who cultivated a native genius for politics. Solving a riddle seemed like child's play by comparison. It therefore was demoted in the ranks of causes, being subordinated to the victory over the monster, with the result that the mystery and the prestige surrounding a terrible duel worked to attenuate its most puerile aspects; and by being relocated in the sequence of events, coming now between patricide and incest, it became easier to overlook the fact that the event itself was of little significance next to its aftermath. Similarly, in the legend of Heracles, the poets of the fifth century discard everything of interest in *Works and Days* that, like the riddle, derived from popular folklore; they concern themselves instead with incidental deeds (πάρεργα) that associate the hero with more important adventures, more readily transposed to the moral plane. Whereas an epic poet considered the picturesque episode of the Nemean lion a worthy subject for extended treatment, Aeschylus and Euripides were happier to have Heracles save Prometheus and Alcestis. It comes as no surprise, then, that the tragedians, who never quote the riddle, should dispose of the combat against the Sphinx in as few words as possible.

---

What could be the source of the riddle myth, which is to say of the idea, central in so many tales, that one who succeeds in answering a question, in itself devoid of any interest, is thereby promised a higher destiny, whereas the downfall of one who fails may actually culminate in his death?

The theme of the riddle appears in two contexts: *struggle against a monster* and *royal marriage*. Scholars who have studied the first see the demoniacal riddle as the transposition of the intense anxiety that attends oppressing nightmares. On awakening, dreamers often recall having made futile attempts to find elusive words, to read undecipherable texts, to reply to unanswerable questions. Roscher, who stated the problem of the *Alpdaemon* in its relationship to the *Alptraum* more clearly than Laistner had done, argued that success in a test, together with the triumph and enrichment that follow from it, transcribes the feeling of deliverance that awakening brings to the troubled dreamer. This may well be. Nonetheless it is unlikely that a purely physiological phenomenon of so little intrinsic interest would have given rise to one of the most fertile of all mythic themes. More probably it had to be fortified by other elements whose traces can still be detected.

Most oppressing demons are also tormented souls. Now, everything that has to do with the other world, the world beyond the grave, involves a game of questions and answers that we have some idea of through the rites of initiation administered by mystery cults. The initiate must know various formulas, which is to say certain passwords and techniques, ways of proceeding that will enable him to avoid or otherwise overcome the obstacles that make crossing over to the world beyond the grave a perilous undertaking. A tale such as that of the Sirens involves the success of an initiate who, thanks to his special knowledge and skillfulness, evades the traps that the demons set for him. Whether his victory takes place in this world or the other one, the difference does not count for very much, and it becomes clear why such myths, though they were born of practices concerning the other world, should have come to be set in contexts in which infernal powers attack not the dead but the living. This way of stating the matter will have to be modified somewhat, of course, for demons, male and female alike, have very particular requirements when it comes to the creatures of flesh and blood they prey on. But any qualifications that may need to be made will not alter the essential point, namely, the necessity of being initiated.

Odysseus escapes the Sirens because he knows a formula, a particular technique for ensuring his safety. Here again, between the advice that Circe gives him and the word that solves a riddle, there is no radical difference. Their resemblance stands out more clearly when one compares the following situations:

- Victory results from a *course to be followed* that must be known beforehand.
- Victory results from a *password* that must already be known in order for it to be uttered at the right moment.
- Victory results from a *word* that must be found in order to answer a question correctly.

To be sure, the first two tests require memory and the third one only intelligence, but all three demand above all composure and presence of mind. We saw earlier that almost all demoniacal riddles belong to the second category. But a people as intellectually curious as the Greeks could not be content to leave matters there. As legends became more elaborate and further and further removed from their origins in superstition, mythic heroes were expected to display human qualities. Not unnaturally, then, riddles took on a more serious and probing character. The ancients never made any fundamental distinction, however, between questions of memory and questions of intelligence, with the consequence that the moderns, following their example, never thought to make it either. I believe therefore that the riddle myth may be considered to have been influenced by the same beliefs that underlay the mysteries. This term should not be understood as having the quite specific meaning and precise reference that it had in classical Greek antiquity, but in the more vague and more general sense that one is justified in postulating with regard to the customs of initiation observed in an earlier era. For peoples at all times must have thought it possible to provide living beings with formulas allowing them to triumph over infernal powers, whether these powers are met with in this world, in the form of ghosts, or in their own realm beyond the grave. Elements of these formulas that were unsuited for one reason or another to instruction in the mysteries would easily have been pressed into ancillary service as a mythic theme in which the person being tested, rather than find himself arraigned before a Queen of the Underworld or a Judge of the Dead, must manage somehow to prevail over a Siren or a Sphinx, which he sees as a monster rather than as a ghost.

In popular Latin mythology, as we have seen, incubi were typically male beings that tormented women. All such beliefs, in the Christian era, crystallized around the figure of the Devil. The question therefore arises (so far as I am aware, it has not been noticed until now) how far the abstract concept of evil was nourished by images and representations borrowed from the incubi of classical art and literature. The notion of sorcerers and witches that subsequently took shape was parasitic on the notion that had been formed of the Devil, for it was from sexual intercourse with the Devil that his emissaries drew their power. Sorcerers and witches became in their turn incubi who seduced and tormented people as the Devil had tormented and seduced them, in order to make them his slaves. But the fact that sorcerers and witches owed their loyalty to the Lord of the Damned drew them nearer to the other world—so much so that, in medieval folktales, they behave as tormented souls. The infernal world thus came to appear as a vast secret society in which knowing passwords is indispensable, whether one seeks merely to enter it or whether one wishes to move about in it without risk of dire misadventure.

By grouping together, under the theme of the riddle, beliefs in the existence of oppressing demons and tormented souls, and, more generally, in the perils of the hereafter, we should not suppose that we have thereby given a satisfactory explanation for the ending of almost all the stories that have come down to us: the triumph of a conqueror, who wins treasures, a kingdom, a fiancée. If we are to make further progress, we must recognize at once that there is something *pedagogic* about these tales. They aspire to teach. Teach what? The usefulness of initiation. What kind of initiation? A moment ago I spoke of a religious ceremony that warns and protects initiates against the dangers of contact with a certain class of infernal beings. The worldly, secular success that accompanies the solution of a riddle suggests another kind of initiation, a social initiation. Whenever a resourceful young man is seen to marry a princess, we should recall that, in many primitive societies, the entry into adulthood is inseparable from marriage: young men and women who have successfully undergone grueling trials of physical endurance and mental skill are now, by virtue of just this, entitled to membership in the class of married persons. In the next chapter I shall examine other legendary memories of the bonds of fellowship created by initiation. Solidarity of this kind is clearly illustrated by tales in which a young man wins the hand in marriage of the most beautiful young woman because he is able to answer a difficult question. In archaic Greece, masters subjected novices to extended interrogation in which success depended sometimes on memory, sometimes on intelligence. Nuptial riddles, as we have seen, belong almost always to the second category, in contrast to demoniacal riddles; this is because they generally appear in tales of a more elevated character intended for a more cultivated audience. It should be recalled, finally, that the masters of initiation ceremonies wore frightening disguises and animal masks. In this they resembled the monsters of popular superstition—so closely, in fact, that the two kinds of ceremony, the one arising from a religious belief in otherworldly forces, the other from initiation as a social institution, end up exactly corroborating each other. As for the severity of punishment, the exceedingly harsh sanctions reserved for those who fall short of what is demanded of them may have derived from the tests to which prospective leaders were submitted, the most exacting ones of all. These candidates, promoted at once in the event of success, would have been very cruelly treated in the event of failure. But this is mere conjecture, and for the moment at least we can say nothing more.

It may be that the riddle myth *originated* in a belief in oppressing and infernal demons. But it could never have developed into anything more than that if it had not been *used* as an instrument of propaganda in support of initiations—religious initiations to begin with, social initiations later. All those scholars who, a century ago, saw myths as a spontaneous creation of the contemplative faculty, a natural human response to the fear and wonder inspired by the forces of nature, a profound emotion that could not help but well up in the human heart and burst forth in the form of poetic invention, would have found it very difficult to accept that apologetic motivation plays any part. Yet a vindicatory purpose is obvious. It is detected in many later tales as well, as Saintyves showed in a work that, on this point at least, is novel and fertile.[15] One relates a story in order to demonstrate something, in order to persuade someone. The theme of the riddle demonstrates that a novice will become rich once the habit of scrupulous obedience enables him to correctly repeat everything his master has taught him.

The longer one studies myths, the better one is able to distinguish superimposed components. In the riddle myth, one first detects its physiological origin, to which Roscher surely attached too much importance; then one detects in it superstitions; and then, finally, religious and social liturgies transcribed with a favorable prejudice.[16]

# CHAPTER 5

# Marriage to a Princess

The Oedipus legend is the only one in which the solving of a riddle does not bring the conqueror total and unconditional happiness—the happiness of fairy tales. Usually the biography of a clever man of this type comes to a close once he has uttered the word that must be spoken. It is at just this moment that the Oedipus legend sets out in a new direction and acquires fresh interest. In the mythopoeia of the tragedians, Oedipus's victory over the Sphinx brings him only sorrow in the end, for the simple reason that the queen whose hand he has won turns out to be his own mother. But *marriage to a princess* and *sexual union with one's mother* are independent themes whose conjunction is nowhere found outside the tale of Oedipus. It is this conjunction that gives the tale both its distinctive coloring and its painful epilogue. In the tradition of the Homeric age, this ending had a different form from the one that has come down to us from the tragic poets of the fifth century, and more respectful of the profound meaning of the myths that we are presently studying. A man who has been invested with power by virtue of having successfully undergone several arduous trials[1] will not readily relinquish it. The archaic Oedipus became king and died king.[2] But when morality entered into the legend, when feats of valor were considered no longer to be *rites*, but *acts*, the conqueror was condemned on account of the same means by which his conquest had been achieved, and so he was forced to dispossess himself. This result was due to scruples that were of recent origin. In the legend that is known to us, an extended and carefully wrought composition, the episode of *marriage to the queen*, like all the others, was modified to fit a larger story constructed in the form of a biography. In the meantime it took on a distinctive aspect derived from the tragic fate of heroes. But enough of these preliminaries. Let us start by examining this episode alone, by analogy with a biological cell that has been isolated for purposes of analysis.

---

It is, to begin with, a complex cell. Nowhere is it more plain that a legendary theme never has a single origin, but several. Frazer, observing that in many fables kingship is transmitted through the female line, detected in the Oedipus legend the memory of an archaic, pre-Indo-European matrilineal regime. It is indeed possible that such a regime did exist and that traces of it survived in some traditions. This seems to me improbable, however, for customs that gradually undergo modification over time do not generally seem to leave a deep impression in popular memory. In order to determine what ancient realities may lie concealed beneath the theme of marriage to a queen, I would rather inquire into the different kinds of *tests* that conferred on the one who emerges from them victorious both a bride and a kingdom. A few seem to me to overlay archaic rites: the *cattle raid*, the *contest among suitors*, the *fight to the death against the fiancée's father*; under these heads one finds, respectively, *rites of passage from adolescence to adulthood*, the *custom of communal marriage*, and *conflict among generations* (the last of which we studied in Chapter 2). Other tests have a purely fabulous character: the *contest with the fiancée herself*, who is represented as having a superior and mysterious power (here we will find once again, albeit in very degraded form, some of the themes of the battle against the Sphinx), and the *combat against a monster* that holds a princess in its power. In this last case, the princess is a scapegoat who has been rescued by the hero. She is imbued, as a consequence, with a divine beneficence that belongs to those who have the blessing of the gods and that is communicated to their saviors.

The link between the themes of conquest and marriage arises essentially, I believe, from the *interdependence of initiations* in archaic times. This condition left very clear traces in Greek heortology, notably in a ritual of the

annual festival known as the Apaturia through which youths were inducted
into both their local phratry and the class of persons who are fit for matri-
mony. Legends were also influenced, however, by half-forgotten beliefs of
which we have no written record and that can be reconstructed only with
extreme caution. Among these are the *magical efficacy of the race* (whether
by foot or by chariot) and, somewhat less uncertainly, beliefs associated with
more complex rites such as the *procession* that accompanies a *sacred marriage
of spring*. In what follows I try to illuminate these themes by comparing them.
To do this I have had to examine two particularly difficult and obscure leg-
ends, one involving Melampus and the other Atalanta. Nevertheless I believe
that they make it possible to explain the absurd piece of trickery traditionally
attributed to Pisistratus and skeptically recounted by Herodotus. All this will
take us away for a moment from Oedipus, whose legend, in the overintel-
lectualized form that has come down to us, is so stripped down that we could
not make sense of it if we could not consult other more ramified fables of the
same sort.

---

There is a curious passage in *Oedipus the King* that has gone almost unno-
ticed by commentators, where Creon says that power at Thebes is shared
between three persons: Oedipus, Jocasta, and himself.[3] This claim is all the
more remarkable as Oedipus is said to rule alone in Thebes. Oedipus treats
his brother-in-law harshly, whereas Creon responds to him with deference;
and although Jocasta sharply reproves her husband for losing his temper with
Creon, there is no reason to believe that she takes any important decision.
The sharing of power that seems to be asserted here on behalf of Jocasta and
Creon therefore has no place in the play itself. If Sophocles has mentioned
it, this can only be out of respect for a prior mythopoeia in which it had a
clearer significance.[4]

Furthermore, Creon in *Oedipus the King* is a person almost wholly
devoid of character. For us moderns this poses a question that is difficult to
answer. The play is almost surely later than *Antigone*, in which Creon plays
an odious role. I am well aware that Athenian conservatives did not take the
side of Antigone, the young rebel, as readily as we do; they saw her as a dan-
gerous individualist whose ideas, had they been generally accepted, would
have quickly plunged the state into anarchy. It is nonetheless certain that the

poet blames Creon for the suicides of Haemon and Eurydice. How could the audience of *Oedipus the King* have forgotten the charges that Sophocles had already brought against this man, Antigone's uncle and Oedipus's brother-in-law? How could it have looked upon Creon impartially, dispassionately? The reason is that it was customary then to consider the tragedies as separate productions, not as a series in which one play led on to the next. The aesthetic of the classical period assigned primacy to the individual play as a work of art, a world closed upon itself and sufficient unto itself. As against this conception, the mythographers preferred to consider the hero as a man whose biography can be written from the time of his birth to the time of his death.

In *Oedipus the King*, Creon is what the title identifies Oedipus as being: a king. But Creon is a different sort of king: incapable of exercising power himself, he is authorized solely to delegate it. After the death of Laius, the crown of Thebes is his to dispose of, though it depends in the first instance on the person of Jocasta. Creon acts in the interest of his fellow Thebans by promising both crown and queen to whoever can vanquish the Sphinx. An analogous motif figures in many legends that we must now compare and try to explain, in which a woman gives power to a man of her choosing. Nineteenth-century scholars, often rather incautiously, regarded this theme as the sign of a pre-Indo-European matriarchy that was replaced by the patrilineal regime of foreign invaders. Since then the matriarchal hypothesis has fallen into disfavor, to an extent that may be unwarranted. There can be no doubt, however, that it goes too far in inferring a prehistoric state of affairs for which we have little or no corroborating evidence[5] on the basis of legendary elements that may have another origin. For the moment, at least, without wishing to exclude the possibility that traces of an archaic feminine hierarchy may be detected in the tales that interest us here, I do not think there is any reason to insist on it. If it did in fact play a role, its influence was very slight and must have been supplemented by other more decisive factors. It is these factors that we need to try to identify.

Let us reexamine Frazer's discussion of the transmission of kingship through the female line, and of ancient monarchies in which, unlike ours, it is the queen whose office is hereditary and the king whose office is elective. Frazer observes that no king of Rome was succeeded by his son, although several left a line of male descendants. Numa married the daughter of Tatius, whom he succeeded. Ancus Marcius's mother was Numa's daughter. Servius

Tullius succeeded Tarquin the Elder after having married his daughter. Tarquin the Proud likewise succeeded Servius, his father-in-law. It would appear, then, that

> the succession to the kingship of Rome, and probably in Latium generally, [was] determined by certain rules which have moulded early society in many parts of the world, namely, exogamy, *beena* marriage, and female kinship. Exogamy is the rule which obliges a man to marry a woman of a different clan from his own; *beena* marriage is the rule that he must leave the home of his birth and live with his wife's people; and female kinship is the system of tracing relationship and transmitting the family name through women instead of through men.[6]

Among the Aryans, Frazer adds,

> The system of female kinship is unknown . . . [but there are] some facts which appear to be undoubted survivals among Aryan peoples of a custom of tracing descent through the mother only. . . . Among the ancient Latins female kinship [may have] survived after it had been exchanged for male kinship in all others. For royalty, like religion, is essentially conservative; it clings to old forms and old customs which have long vanished from ordinary life. . . . A common type of popular tale which relates how an adventurer, coming to a strange land, wins the hand of the king's daughter and the half or whole of the kingdom, may well be a reminiscence of a real custom.[7]

Frazer has no trouble locating analogous traditions in archaic Greece. Newcomers, such as Cecrops and Amphictyon in Athens, married the daughters of their predecessors. On the other hand, to explain why sons did not succeed their father, as they would have had to do in accordance with the customs of a later era, reasons were invented—generally a murder, voluntary or involuntary—that obliged them to flee their homeland. After a time of wandering they conquer a kingdom and, at the same time, a bride. Aeacus reigns in Aegina. All his male descendants emigrate; almost all of them go to live in the country of their wives, Telamon in Salamis, Teucrus in Cyprus, Peleus in Phthia,[8] Achilles in Scyrus, Neoptolemus in Epirus. Calydon in

Aetolia marries the daughter of Adrastus, king of Argos. His son Diomedes, in the same fashion, becomes king of Daunia in Italy. Tantalus is king in Lydia; his son Pelops reigns at Pisa, his grandson Atreus at Mycenae, his great-grandson Menelaus at Sparta. Pelops and Menelaus reign in the lands of their wives. One ancient legend has Agamemnon reigning in Laconia, which is to say in the native land of Clytemnestra.

One could find—a little too easily perhaps—many other analogous cases. Four sons of Aeolus are kings: Athamas in Boeotia, Sisyphus in Corinth, Salmoneus in Thessaly (later in Elis), Cretheus in Iolcus. Cretheus marries his niece Tyro, daughter of Salmoneus, who has two sons by Poseidon, Pelias and Neleus, and bears three more to her husband; all five become kings. Pheres, Aeson, and Amythaon are eponyms of the cities of Pheres, Aeson, and Amythaonia. None of the three inherits his father's kingdom, which falls to Pelias. Aeson and his son Jason claim Iolcus and on this account come into conflict with Pelias. Is this evidence of a broader conflict between masculine and feminine succession? Looking to the line of kings of Megara, we see that Alcathous kills the lion of the Cithaeron, marries Iphinoe, and succeeds his father-in-law Nisus. Cases such as these seem to confirm the explanation proposed by Frazer.

But one must not forget that all these genealogies are late and that they are all liable to have been modified to one degree or another. In the *Iliad*, no kinship is indicated between Peleus and Telamon. In every era, different figures bearing the same name or similar names were identified with each other; concessions were made to claims of divine descent by families, by cities, and above all by temples. Mythographers, refusing to leave out the least detail, attempted to reconcile all of them by whatever expedient suggested itself. When they wish to explain why one legendary figure succeeds another, for example, because they have themselves grown up in a family system they readily imagine a marriage that creates a fictive bond between two strangers.[9] Arguments made on the basis of mythic genealogies therefore have no great value. Frazer's hypothesis gains far more credibility from the large number of tales in which the two conquests, one of a woman, the other of power, are conjoined.

First, let us briefly consider the fictive framework of these legends. When the poets began to work with them, they were no longer understood in every detail. In order to make them more easily accepted, they introduced whatever elements were needed to bring them into alignment with the customs of their time.

1. The old king has no sons, so that an only daughter becomes the sole heir (*epikleros*). In the historical era, however, this meant that she had to marry her closest relative in the male line of the family. An heiress never does this in the tales that have come down to us, where she always marries an adventurer who has come from abroad.

2. The adventurer comes from a royal family. This is at least a moral concession to the hereditary principle. The hero's father has not bequeathed him his kingdom. The hero's nobility of spirit nonetheless makes him worthy of the high esteem in which he will later be held in his wife's country.

3. The poets were writing for an audience accustomed to see a son succeed his father. They had to justify the exile of the hero and his resettlement in a foreign country. "A common [reason]," Frazer says, "is that the king's son had been banished for a murder."[10] Another common reason involves the persecution of a newborn by his father and his mother's uncle. But this is a primary, archaic theme, whereas banishment for murder is a mere narrative expedient (one recalls the role that it played in the inventions of Odysseus).

4. Almost all exposed newborns are the sons of a god, which is to say of an unknown father. Frazer correctly sees this as evidence of a tradition of female inheritance. Rights were transmitted, not by a daughter to her husband, but by a mother to her son. When this system was replaced by another, which privileged the paternal line of descent, poets could no longer make sense of the old tales in which only the maternal line was indicated. They portrayed fathers angry with daughters who had conceived outside of marriage, and daughters who protested their innocence by alleging the intervention of a god. This bourgeois drama, and the ordeal to which it gave rise, were recent innovations that exploited ancient themes: exposure on a mountain or in a chest, and the hostility of the mother's relatives.

5. This hostility often assumes a curious form. In several legends, as we saw in Chapter 1, a paternal uncle is the lover of his niece, not out of affection for her, but from hatred and a desire to injure her. This uncle is moreover

the enemy of his brother, the hero's grandfather. Perseus passed for the son, not of Zeus, but of Proetus, brother and rival of Acrisius, who was reconciled with him when Acrisius agreed to give him possession of Tiryns. In a version reported in several places by Hyginus,[11] Sisyphus, brother and enemy of Salmoneus, learned from an oracle that if he were to have children by his niece Tyro, these children would avenge him of Salmoneus; he rapes Tyro, who then kills his children the moment they are born. Similarly, Lycus, uncle and persecutor of Antiope, is sometimes accused by his wife Dirce of secretly making love to his niece; according to Hyginus, in his seventh fable, the uncle and his niece are married. Robert considers this to be a late invention.[12] One would readily agree with him were it not for the fact that the theme of the uncle as both lover and enemy appears in other stories of the same type.

How are we to explain this? The theme could not have entered our legends before inheritance through the paternal line had become the rule. Moreover it makes sense that the father's brother, who, under the new system, was not only the successor to his estate but also the guardian of his daughter, should have been at odds with the son, who, under the old system, inherited from his mother's father. It remains to be determined whether archaically this hostility was translated into legend at some point—a bit later in any case than the substitution of male for female inheritance—or whether it was the result of an inference by the author of the legend: since the uncle stands to inherit, he must keep a watchful eye on both the patrimony and his niece, and if she becomes pregnant without his permission, he will very probably seek to kill any male offspring at birth. This manner of reasoning is so ingenious that one is tempted to suppose that the legends transcribing it are not very old. And yet the fact that several legends exhibit the same schema, without any of them appearing to be a copy of another, seems to point to a rather ancient foundation.

---

Frazer mentions in connection with female inheritance, as a survival of this custom, conquerors who become kings after having married the *widow* of their predecessor. It is curious that he does not mention Oedipus among the short list of rulers he draws up, which contains, apart from two Lydian kings, Gyges and Spermus, only one Greek king, Aegisthus. Let us at once put aside Aegisthus, a mere usurper who, in marrying Clytemnestra, does not thereby seize power, at least not securely, since in order to hold on to it after Agamemnon's return he is obliged to kill the old king. There is nonetheless a resemblance between his story and those of Proetus and Sisyphus, and also Lycus, who, out of hatred for a brother, abducts his niece in order through her to have his vengeance. Then there is the story of Argus, which provides no evidence of inheritance through a widow. By contrast, a very clear case, which Frazer neglects in the same way that he neglects the Theban example, is that of Ithaca. It is true that extracting from the *Odyssey* anything resembling a coherent right of succession is by no means easy. In the second book, Antinous and Telemachus express two different points of view, without either of them, or the poet himself, appearing to realize that they are incompatible.[13] Antinous maintains that Penelope will give the crown to whichever one of her suitors it pleases her to do so. Telemachus regards his mother simply as a widow who will remarry one day if she so decides. Telemachus wishes in no way to limit her freedom of choice—and all the less because, if he sends her back to her father, Icarius, he will have to pay back the dowry and Penelope, in her anger, may decide to unleash the Erinyes against him. The poet wavers, in other words, between two systems of kingship, without seeming to recognize that what is at issue in the one case is a dowry given by the father, in the other a purchase price paid by the new husband. Telemachus himself later adopts Antinous's view when he says that whoever marries his mother will at once enjoy the same privileges as Odysseus.[14]

Moreover, kingship and patrimony appear to be dissociated. "There are many kings in Ithaca," says Telemachus at the outset of the tale. "May one of them reign, since noble Odysseus is dead. I, at least, will be the master of my own house and of the slaves that noble Odysseus forcibly conquered for me."[15] But who will reign? The one who will pass the tests a future king must submit to. If it is Telemachus who succeeds in bending Odysseus's bow, he will remain with his mother and rule the country,[16] and the fear Antinous expresses to Telemachus—"May the son of Cronus [Zeus] never make you king of Ithaca, which is your inheritance by birth")—will be realized.[17] But if one of the suitors should win Penelope's hand, she will follow him, quitting the house of Odysseus, which she will leave to Telemachus. In no passage of the poem do we find explicitly associated with one another the three very things that are conjoined in many legends: victory, a wife, and kingship. Nevertheless, by his triumph in the test of the bow, Odysseus regains both his wife and his kingdom. In other tales, the linkage of these things is much clearer. This is because these other tales have come down to us in brief versions, where the ingenuity of the poets has not yet been given free rein. A long work, such as the *Odyssey*, must explain the summary allusions of the old stories. And once the poets begin to explain, they cannot resist introducing details borrowed from the customs of their own time, with the result that the fabulous archaic theme, contaminated by more recent elements, is now incongruent with the original narrative. This is why the mythic foundations of the *Odyssey* can be glimpsed only by reading between the lines, in the light of simpler tales in which one sees plainly an adventurer who becomes king in marrying either the daughter or the wife of his predecessor, having first given proof of his physical courage and moral worthiness. These tests are what we must now study, with the aim of teasing out, in greater detail than Frazer was able to do, the meaning of those stories in which the kingship is elective while the queen's position is hereditary.

In almost all of them, the conquest of a kingdom depends on the conquest of a bride. It is impossible to study the two themes separately. Furthermore, in many of the stories the romantic element has come to the fore, obscuring the political element. It is for this reason that I will not try to classify accounts of heroic trials according to whether the young man wishes simply to marry a princess or whether he wishes to win a bride and a kingdom at the same time. Rather than concentrate our attention on the purpose of the test, we will have a greater chance of grasping the liturgical substrate that is transposed in the various tales if we examine the terms of the test in each case. Let us take them in the following order: a suitor must do battle with the young woman herself; the young woman is the prize of a peaceful competition among several or more suitors; marriage follows upon an abduction, with the father punishing the unsuccessful suitors; a suitor must kill a monster. This fourth and final theme I shall consider separately. As for the first three, they are too similar for it always to be possible to treat examples in complete isolation from one another.

1. The suitor must do battle with the young woman herself.

- In ancient legend, Peleus wrestles with Thetis, who initially prevails by assuming all manner of different forms, as sea goddesses are expert at doing; in the end, thanks to divine assistance from Proteus, Peleus emerges victorious.
- Atalanta, daughter of Schoineus, king of Boeotia, has no wish to marry. She therefore promises her suitors that she will wed the one who can defeat her in a race, knowing that none of them could, for she runs as swiftly as the wind. Those whom she leaves behind are doomed to die. Hippomenes is said to have escaped this fate by throwing golden apples in her way, calculating that she would slow down to pick them up. Ovid repeats this tradition in the tenth book of the *Metamorphoses*, which leaves unexplained the resignation of the defeated suitors to their end:

> Dant gemitum victi penduntque ex foedere poenas. [10.599]
> [The vanquished youths groan, suffering the stipulated penalty.]

- In a tradition reported by Apollodorus,[18] probably ancient, an armed Atalanta makes her suitors start ahead of her and then kills each one on overtaking them—a brutal method similar to the one used by Oenomaus to dispose of Hippodamia's suitors.

2. The young woman is the prize of a peaceful competition
among suitors.[19]

- Icarius, brother of the king of Sparta, holds a race, promising his daughter Penelope's hand to the winner. Odysseus triumphs but refuses to stay in Laconia, as Icarius begs him to do—possibly the survival of a version in which marriage with Penelope gave Odysseus rights of inheritance to Icarius's legacy. Odysseus then flees in a chariot with his young bride, chased by his father-in-law, who stops and turns back only when his daughter pleads with him to cease and desist. This account seems to combine two versions that alternated in the quality of their variants: abduction of a fiancée and race between suitors.

• Danaus promises the contestants in a race that they will be able to choose from among his daughters according to their order of finish. Pausanias, who recounts this story after that of Icarius,[20] does not see that the engagements of Penelope and of the Danaids were arranged in accordance with the same method. He describes the race held by Danaus as a punishment for his murderous daughters, criminals whom no one wished to marry—a late and erroneous interpretation.

• Pindar recounts that Antaeus the Libyan married off his daughter in the same manner that Danaus married off his forty-eight remaining unwed daughters, without in any way presenting the matter as a punishment: the precious virgin was won by the swift Alexidamus, who took her hand and led her through the cheering throng of Nomad horsemen.[21]

• The same theme recurs in the middle of the sixth century, illustrated now by the games of running and wrestling held by Cleisthenes of Sicyon for the purpose of wedding his daughter Agariste to the best man he could find in Hellas.[22]

3. The father of the fiancée punishes the unsuccessful suitors.

• This motif, which is at the heart of the legend of Oenomaus, leads us back to the defeat of the old king and the conflict between generations. To the accounts we studied in Chapter 2, we may now add several others that are chiefly concerned with a nuptial rite.

• Marpessa, daughter of Evenus, is said sometimes to have been abducted, sometimes to have been awarded as a prize to the winner of a race. Idas carries her off with the aid of a winged chariot given him by Poseidon. Evenus, who until then had put to death all unsuccessful suitors, pursues the couple; unable to cross the Lycormas, he throws himself into the river after having killed his horses, and henceforth it bears his name. This last detail alone is etiological. Evenus's fate may be compared to the death by suicide of Oenomaus.

• The same challenge occurs in the confused tale of Sithon and his daughter Pallene. At least one thing is certain: there is a conflict between generations that is related to a nuptial contest.

• Eurytus, king of Oechalia, promises his daughter Iole to anyone who can defeat him in archery, as Heracles succeeds in doing. Eurytus then reneges, in retaliation for which Heracles sacks Oechalia. One tradition has it that it was Eurytus himself who taught Heracles how to use a bow, giving further emphasis to the theme of generational conflict. Another tradition maintains that Eurytus refused to give away his daughter because he was enamored of her himself,[23] a detail that is encountered once more in the legend of Oenomaus.

• The marriage of Alcmene, as it is related by Pherecydes of Athens,[24] curiously intertwines the themes of nuptial feats of valor and generational conflict. The Teleboans having killed Alcmene's brothers in a raid, she promises her hand to one who will avenge their death. The avenger is Amphitryon, who killed Alcmene's father, Electryon. Out of love for her brothers, then, the young woman marries her father's murderer. The legend would be psychologically unintelligible if one were not able to make out in it, as a primary nucleus or kernel, now degraded almost beyond recognition, the struggle of an old man and a young man combined with the theme of female inheritance. Tradition, however, had given to Electryon sons who, in accordance with the male regime of inheritance, would have succeeded their father. The poets solved the difficulty by imagining that Alcmene's brothers were killed and that it was in order to avenge this crime that she agreed to take as a husband the one who had made her an orphan. Explaining the marriage of Hippodamia was a less complicated business: in Hesiod, Amphitryon kills his father-in-law in a combat; in Apollodorus, he kills him by inadvertence—a frequent legendary litotes in tales in which the two themes, murder of a king and marriage to a princess, are found together.[25]

---

The story of Melampus, difficult to classify since it does not correspond exactly to any of the schemas we have examined so far, will permit us at least to get a firmer grip on the theme of nuptial tests.

Neleus promises his daughter Pero to whoever can bring him the cattle of Iphiclus, which are guarded by a dog that no one can get past. Bias, son of Amythaon, manages the feat thanks to the divinatory intelligence of his brother Melampus. Melampus understands the language of animals and knows many things that ordinary mortals do not. Moreover, he himself had won a bride, Iphianassa, and a third of the Argive kingdom for having cured

Proetus's daughters of their madness. This time, to aid his brother, he allows himself to be taken prisoner by Iphiclus, to whom he gives proof of his talents as a seer, thus winning his confidence. Finally, the last step in his plan of conquest, he cures Iphiclus of impotence, in compensation for which Iphiclus gives him the cattle. A phrase conserved by one scholiast suggests that, in another version, Iphiclus refused to give up his cattle and that hand-to-hand combat between the two men ensued; Melampus, though he had been vanquished, was reassured by Zeus that he should not be disheartened.[26]

Several details of the Oedipus legend figure in that of Melampus, though the perspective in each case is different. Both do battle with a king; both win a princess, Oedipus for himself, Melampus for his brother; both conquer thanks to their intelligence; both bear names that the legend feels obliged to explain by an episode of their childhood that plays no role in what follows. Any analogy that may obtain between their names, Swollen Foot and Black Foot, remains quite obscure, however, as we saw earlier.

---

What actual prehistoric circumstances might these legends conceal? The *theft of cattle* is a well-known theme in the tests to which adolescents are subjected as an initiatory rite. Hermes can effortlessly make off with entire herds: this is what makes him worthy of being treated as an adult. After rustling Apollo's cattle on the evening of the day of his birth, he is received into a higher world by the god, who gives him his herald's staff, the caduceus; though scarcely out of the cradle, Hermes has already taken his place among the masters and initiators. The successful raid seems to me to be not only a condition of entering into adulthood, but also a test of fitness in the *selection of a leader*. Frazer points out that, in legends that appear to involve female inheritance, one has the impression that kingship is elective and queenship hereditary.[27] Now, in many primitive societies, there is a leader in times of peace, whose office is hereditary, and a leader in times of war, who is elected and who must demonstrate his qualification by performing feats of valor. A young man aspiring to leadership might announce, for example, that a dream told him to undertake a raid. If the expedition is successful, if the young man and his companions come back with cattle, then he is accepted as leader; if the expedition fails, he is rejected now and forevermore.[28] In the tale of Melampus, we are tempted to consider the hand-to-hand combat with

Iphiclus as more archaic than the version in which he allows himself to be taken prisoner, secure in the knowledge that he will prevail in the end owing to his powers of divination. Robert, interpreting the Boston lekythos, had similarly inferred an older version of the Oedipus legend in which Oedipus prevails over the Sphinx thanks to his club. And yet, in almost all the tales that have come down to us, victory depends as much on a ruse or superior knowledge as on force. Peleus vanquishes Thetis because he knows that she will run through the cycle of her metamorphoses only once. Hippomenes tricks Atalanta by distracting her with golden apples. Idas abducts Marpessa as Pelops does Hippodamia, with the aid of swift chariot-horses given them by a god. Divine interventions are welcome in such accounts, where the winner does not insist on the honor of triumphing all alone, by virtue of his own strength and agility. Here one recognizes one of the most common themes in tales that transpose rites of initiation: *the initiated triumphs on account of what he has learned*. What he knows is worth at least as much as what he is capable of doing. If external assistance can be had, whether from men, gods, or animals, so much the better. A trustworthy dream may decide the career of a leader and the fate of a people. This helps explain why the solving of a riddle should qualify a novice to be a leader of men, and also why failure carries with it so grave a sanction as death. He who can read the thoughts of others, who can decipher the meaning of obscure words, who is able to interpret the signs that animals exchange among themselves, such a man is born to conquer. This conception appears still in the historical era—in India, for example, where one finds investiture ceremonies that are straightforward transcriptions of ancient tests of entitlement to rule.[29] It is hardly surprising that nothing similar is to be found among the Greeks, who, as I say, seem already to have lost the Indo-European word for "king" in prehistoric times. Legends alone can tell us about tests of kingship, which are distinguished from others more by their degree than by their nature.

What practical significance could the trials by which young men demonstrate their fitness for marriage or for exercising power, or both, have had? Here, once again, we are forced to rely on tales that must be interpreted with the greatest caution.

In the theft of cattle, no transposition can be detected. At the very most we can identify certain cases where, in order to avoid portraying the hero as a mere marauder, a legend tries to ennoble his deed by making it particularly difficult and, as a consequence, heroic. Iphiclus's oxen were guarded by an invincible dog; the ones that Hermes stole belonged to Apollo. The test seems to serve as a prelude to entering a higher age cohort or else to being named a leader. It hardly ever figures as a part of nuptial trials.

The footrace, by contrast, seems to have been the most common test for all those hoping to marry. Legends retained the memory of certain prospective brides of exceptional swiftness who were defeated by sufficiently agile and vigorous suitors. It is probable that there was a time when every marriage depended on the result of a race, in which not only young men but also young women had to take part. The story of Atalanta suggests this; also a curious survival, the Olympic custom described by Pausanias.[30] He says that there was a college of sixteen women who wove a robe for Hera every four years and sponsored a race for girls and young women in the great stadium at the goddess's games in Olympia. The youngest ones ran first, then the ones who were a bit older, then the oldest; they ran with their hair let down, their tunics pulled up above the knee, their right shoulder bared. The winners received laurel crowns and a share of the ox sacrificed to Hera; they were allowed to dedicate their statues. The women who supervised them were divided into two choruses, and arranged for two dances to be held, the one called Hippodamia's dance, the other Physcoa's. Here we find a trace of one of the religious colleges that were the only survival, in Greece, of female age cohorts, with their initiations and initiatrices, their ritual obligations, their tests of judgment and ability. The feats that young women were required to accomplish from time immemorial subsequently became gifts in the form of offerings to goddesses: the young *arrhephoroi* embroider for Athena, the children of Olympia for Hera.

Penelope's web is certainly another one of these works of elaborate craftsmanship on which eligibility for marriage sometimes depended. Weaving a web is the test imposed by Tarchetius on his daughter and her servant girl as the condition of their marrying—an episode left dangling, with no conclusion, in the incoherent story in which Plutarch inserted it.[31] But the Homeric legend reversed the terms of the original implication: according to the old custom, a young girl will not be able to marry until she has completed her task; according to the *Odyssey*, Penelope refuses to marry before she has completed her task. These preliminary tests must have had an intrinsically sacred character in archaic times. Penelope gives her work an extrinsic significance, however, when she describes it as a shroud for old Laertius. Everywhere there appears a concern with providing an external and specific justification for practices that archaically were thought to have immediate effect. Proper names appear in contexts where to begin with, we may be quite sure, they had no place. Here again, however, certain associations of ideas are instructive. The college at Olympia is placed under the protection of Hippodamia and Hera; it was said to have been established by Hippodamia, who wished to thank Hera for having arranged her happy marriage to Pelops. In this explanation, more clearly than the one given by the *Odyssey*, we can still discern the prenuptial character that the two tests, the footrace and the making of a masterpiece, originally possessed.[32] It crops up again in other, much less well known rites. The races run by the Dionysiades in Sparta and the Anthesteriades in Rhodes were probably organized by colleges analogous to the one in Olympia. Among the events of the Apaturia, the Athenian festival where the names of marriageable young men and women were officially recorded, there was a race at night by torchlight. The Libyan battle of the maidens, who Herodotus says were forced to fight one another on the shores of Lake Tritonis, seems to have been a prelude to collective marriages.[33]

Nevertheless we will certainly not have exhausted the religious significance of the race by describing it as a test that makes it possible to identify young men and women who are qualified for matrimony. To suppose otherwise would be to fall into the same error as did those scholars who attributed to the Spartan assembly responsibility for deciding whether or not to expose misshapen children, acting as a sort of court of appeal. The race has an intrinsic value. Here one thinks also of the rite of *circumambulation* (amphidromy), which welcomed a newborn child into the family. An officiant carried the baby in his arms while walking around the family altar, a circuit identical to the one traversed by a newlywed woman. The amphidromy of the young bride is attested by vase paintings, if not by texts.[34] At first the race must have been a means for acquiring something, the exact nature of which escapes us. Vigor? Immunization against baneful influences? Certain beneficial qualities? All these things are present in the rite of circumambulation,[35] but we must not forget that every race among athletes in Greece took place on a course or track of some sort. There are many possible explanations. None finds confirmation in the historical record, which proves that the notion of the rite's immediate efficacy was soon forgotten. Other justifications were therefore found, and it became a test. Deprived of its magical value, in other words, it could only be seen as a competition. Frazer may be cited in this connection once more, as a reminder that often the King and Queen of May were chosen following a contest of strength and agility.[36] Once the traditional structure of age cohorts had collapsed, it was no longer understood that young people took part in a kind of game, not a competition. It may be, however, that the element of rivalry was introduced in such trials earlier than we are inclined to suppose. What we may be sure of is that our legends retained a memory of the valorous youth who won the race, of the royal fiancée whom he thereby won in turn, and of the supreme alliance that their wedding represented. The pedagogic character of these accounts is evident: they were intended to inspire docility and zeal in novices, so that they would enthusiastically obey the directions given them by their initiators.

We need to examine particularly closely those tales that involve the abduction of a fiancée. They contain an element that scarcely figures elsewhere, hostility between the young woman's father and her admirers. This hostility underlies the themes of *pursuit* and the *risk of death*, both of which are found in the marriage of Hippodamia: unlucky suitors are put to death by the father, but the father must kill himself or be killed on his first failed attempt. This is the same dual risk that we found in the story of the riddle. Evenus pursues Marpessa and her abductor, and if he kills himself when he sees that she has eluded his grasp, it is no doubt because he too has made a pact with the suitors: the victor will kill the vanquished. And indeed this is the version attested by a fragment of Bacchylides and a scholium of Tzetzes.[37] A half-forgotten hostility is yet perceptible in Pausanias's account of the departure of Penelope and Odysseus for Ithaca, pursued by Icarius. Here the drama has taken on a wholly moral character: a young woman, forced to choose between her father and her husband, chooses her husband, but without doing anything that could injure her father.[38] A legendary litotes of the same kind transformed Laertes's abject condition into a voluntary retreat from the world, as we saw in Chapter 2. The sequence of events is sometimes relaxed as well: Peleus accidentally kills his father-in-law, Eurytion, after marrying Antigone; Amphitryon kills Electryon, also by accident, before marrying Alcmene. The conquest of a fiancée is everywhere bound up with the conquest of power and colored by the *affectus* of mistrust and hatred that the rite of Nemi requires. Nothing similar exists in the competitions in which several or more young men vie with one another for the hand of a young woman. We are therefore presented with two different mythic groups. They are not two stages in the development of a single theme, but two distinct themes:

1. The race for the hand of a fiancée. This contest brings together all competitors. The vanquished are not punished. There is no hostility. In *simple nuptial rites* of this kind, a healthy sense of rivalry animates the suitors.

2. The abduction of the fiancée, who is pursued by her father. This contest sets the father and future son-in-law against each other. The one who is defeated will die. Here *nuptial rites are combined with a rite for the conquest of power.*

---

It is perplexing, then, to see Atalanta, in the version preserved by Apollodorus and Hyginus, treat her suitors as Oenomaus treats his daughter's suitors. Where one expects to find only a nuptial trial, one finds instead a young woman imposing the pact of Nemi on her admirers.[39] Must we suppose that the tale of Atalanta involves a myth of conquest whose political elements have been overshadowed by sentimental ones? Hippomenes[40] was a conqueror who risked his life in adventure, like Oedipus, like Pelops, like Turandot's fiancé. It remains to be explained why Atalanta should have taken it upon herself to carry out the execution of unsuccessful suitors. The Greeks seldom attributed the behavior of a praying mantis to their young daughters. I do not think it is necessary to imagine that there may have once existed a regime of female kingship and to search in this tale for traces of an archaic gynecocracy. To account for this curious legend, I propose instead a hypothesis that others will perhaps be able to develop more fully than I am able to do here.

We may begin by asking whether Atalanta was originally one of these demoniacal creatures whose love is dangerous, like the Siren or the Sphinx, whom the poets made more and more charming without their ceasing to be maleficent. Ovid depicts her as capable of every kind of seduction, and though he excuses her from having to kill with her own hand, she nonetheless dispatches her suitors to their death no less resolutely than proud Turandot herself. The humanization of Atalanta may have begun early, and then quickly have been elaborated under the influence of a confusion that had arisen in the meantime between her and her homonym, the daughter of Iasus, huntress of Calydon.[41] The Homeric Sirens and the Sphinx of the painters of the fifth century reached the border of humanity without being able to cross it, held back by the admixture of animality in their natures that persisted in popular memory. Literature later made the Sphinx a daughter of Laius, or a pirate, or a highway robber, eradicating the monstrous traits of the incubus and leaving her only physical strength and an air of menace. Circe, once exorcised, becomes Odysseus's lover and friend. Atalanta may be related to Circe, and more closely than it would appear at first sight. For at this juncture another detail of the legend springs to mind. Both Atalanta and Hippomenes, immediately after their first and final marriage, are transformed into lions.[42] The poets justified this metamorphosis by saying that the two lovers profaned a sacred place, either a grove of the Great Goddess, Cybele, or a sanctuary of Zeus Callinicos. Subsequently they had to explain further that Hippomenes had been encouraged in this sacrilege by Aphrodite, displeased at having been forgotten in a sacrifice. All these inventions were keys, as it were, belatedly invented in order to open locks whose mechanism was no longer understood. Circe's love transformed men into animals; wolves and lions wandered around her palace.[43] The Sphinx is a woman-lion. It will be recalled, too, that Thetis, the other fiancée conquered by the winner of a wrestling competition, is a sea goddess capable of assuming many different forms, which is to say a sort of magician; also that the fortunate lover—Odysseus, Peleus, Hippomenes—prevails not by his strength or his swiftness, but by cunning and knowledge.

We need to try to explain why the character of the legend changed so rapidly. The Boeotian Atalanta soon came to be confused, as I say, with the Arcadian Atalanta, a secondary or minor deity (πάρεδρος) associated with Artemis, the goddess par excellence of initiations. In the meantime, an entire pedagogic literature had grown up around initiations. The same concern for instruction may be detected in the story of Atalanta, so long as one takes care to divide it into its three component episodes, then to isolate the second one, which over time came to obscure the two others:

1. Atalanta's challenge to the suitors.
2. Hippomenes's cunning and triumph.
3. Transformation of the two lovers into lions.

The first and third episodes are the remnants of a tale of a female magician who is more or less an incubus. The second comes from the education given by initiators, who aimed to provide novices with perfect models of accomplished young men and women. The moment an edifying theme of this kind was imported into a foreign context, it could not help but modify the coloring of the tale as a whole. Atalanta became a young woman who was no longer ferocious, merely fierce. At the same time her prowess in running was given greater emphasis, to the point that it effaced the mysterious aspect of her character: the risk that she obliges her suitors to run appears to be regulated by a spirit of fair play, and the femme fatale becomes an athlete. Perhaps there were versions, now lost, in which Hippomenes alone was transformed into a lion. When the legend acquired a sentimental cast, the poets seem to have wanted to unite the two lovers in a single destiny. Stripped of what I believe are alien elements, the second episode describes simply a race analogous to the one won by Alexidamas. The only difference is that the fiancée takes part in it herself, which is to say that the tale has its origin in a literature of instruction intended for adolescents of both sexes, whereas the others speak solely of trials undergone by young men.

---

In tales involving the abduction of a fiancée, one detail certainly has a liturgical significance, namely, *the procession in an ox-drawn cart*. It is often represented by painters and sculptors, especially those who have portrayed the legend of Pelops. It has rightly been remarked that on all such monuments Hippodamia resembles, not a young woman who is disobeying her father, but a goddess who is making herself manifest. The artists seem to have understood that they were not recreating an attempt to escape or flee in the bourgeois sense; their purpose was to recall a religious ceremony that once radiated grandeur and magnificence. As it happens, the procession in an oxcart does figure in liturgies of the historical period. But the ancient rite underlying it, as one must cannot help but suspect, had to be explained by legends invented in an era when its primitive meaning had been forgotten. An outstanding case is the Boeotian festival of reconciliation, the Daedala.

The lesser Daedala [Δαίδαλα μικρά] was celebrated exclusively by the Plataeans, at intervals whose duration remains uncertain.[44] On the appointed day, the people exposed pieces of stewed meat in an oak grove. The crowd waited until a raven swooped down to snatch a piece and took note of the tree on which it then settled to consume its feast. This tree was felled and a crude statue was carved from it and dressed as a bride; it was then wrapped up in veils and placed on an oxcart, which was led to the bank of a river and then brought back to town. The image used for this festival was conserved along with other such images from later editions until the celebration by all the people of Boeotia of the great Daedala [Δαίδαλα μεγάλα], which took place every sixty years. On that occasion all the statues were carried on wagons to the summit of Mount Cithaeron and burned in a bonfire. Our sources do not say whether the driver of the cart in each of the smaller festivals played a role alongside the statue carved from oak [ξόανον]; Nilsson, for his part, thinks there was no husband next to the bride. Nevertheless the etiological legend evidently implies the presence of a couple. Pausanias and Plutarch say that Zeus was angry with Hera and sought to play a trick on her. On the advice of the king of Plataea, Cithaeron, he dressed a wooden statue in women's clothes, wrapped it up in veils, and put it on an oxcart. Then he told Hera that he intended to marry Plataea, daughter of Asopus. The goddess in her anger tore the veils and clothes from the statue and saw at once that it was a hoax; delighted to discover that Zeus did not mean to be unfaithful to her, she roared with laughter and reconciled with Zeus. The image that this tale seeks to justify is that of a man driving a wagon alongside a tree trunk disguised as a bride. This rite, attached only later to the cycle of Zeus and Hera, is taken from one of the so-called May marriages mimicking the wedding of vegetal powers, a magical ceremony designed to produce each spring the same result that the mythical wedding itself had produced. The Plataean rite, at the time that Pausanias recorded it, was no longer perceived as a spring fertility rite, since it was no longer celebrated every year. Probably it became detached from the rhythm of the seasons precisely because, once it came to be associated with the legend of Zeus, it took its place among a set of festivals whose primitive magical character had faded from memory. The procession in an oxcart of husband and wife (or at least one of the two) plays an important role in marriages of springtime. Frazer compared Greek Daedalas with a number of liturgies of similar import, attested in other countries and spanning many centuries: the Roman festivals of Cybele, where a statue of the goddess, promenaded on an oxcart, was then bathed in the Almo; the procession of the goddess Nerthus, honored in northern Germany during Tacitus's time, whose priest was also her husband; the popular festivals of Autun, in ancient Gaul, mentioned in the sixth century by Gregory of Tours; the Swedish rites noted by Grimm, where a god of fertility is paraded in the company of a young woman who is called his wife.[45] All these ceremonies have an identical general meaning: a sacred marriage will render the land fertile. They are instances, in other words, of sympathetic magic. As late as the nineteenth century, farmers in the Campine region of Belgium, so that they might have an abundant harvest, had intercourse with their wives in the fields, as Demeter had lain with Iasion in a field that had been plowed three times.

It is very probable that Pisistratus's famous ruse is the altered memory of a sacred marriage of the same kind. It will be recalled how Herodotus related the story. Pisistratus, having been driven out of Athens, devised a plan for his return in collaboration with Megacles. They dressed up a tall and beautiful young woman named Phya, from the deme of Paeania, as Athena,[46] and drove her on a chariot into the city, preceded by heralds who announced to the crowds of onlookers at intervals along the route that the goddess wished to see Pisistratus restored to her citadel. It is stupefying to see Aristotle accept a story that Herodotus himself had already found absurd. Not only does he reproduce Herodotus's version, but mentions another one (attested, he says, by "some historians"), which differs from the first simply in the detail that the young woman is a Thracian flower-seller from the deme of Collytus.[47] Cleidemus, the first Athenian historian of Attica, recounts moreover that Pisistratus had married his younger son Hipparchus to this Phya, who was the daughter of one Socrates.[48]

Still another version occurs in the *Stratagems of War* by Polyaenus, who says that Pisistratus, returning to Attica from Euboea and finding it necessary to do battle at Pallene, killed the first adversaries he met. "But as he advanced he encountered many more. Then he ordered his men to crown themselves with olive wreathes and not to kill these latest enemies, but to say that a truce had been agreed to with the first ones. This story was believed, peace was made, and the city was handed over to Pisistratus. Pisistratus then climbed into a chariot; alongside him was a tall, beautiful woman named Phya wearing armor similar to that of Pallas Athena, thus giving the impression that Athena was bringing him back herself. Pisistratus continued on his way undisturbed and took back control of Athens."[49] Eduard Meyer feels sure that Polyaenus's source was not Aristotle, because Aristotle placed the story of Phya at the beginning of the second tyranny, whereas in the *Stratagems* it is associated with the victory at Pallene, which was supposed to mark a third and final seizure of power. Beloch suggests another candidate, Ephorus of Cyme. Neither Beloch nor Meyer notices that Polyaenus stitched together two deceptions. The first one led to the victory at Pallene itself, and since this ruse succeeded, there was no need for the second one. But the compiler was determined to leave out nothing, and with the stratagem of the *false treaty* he combined that of the *false Athena*[50]—the latter following one of the sources I just mentioned, without it being possible to decide which one, for he gives only Phya's name and the sources differ only with regard to her profession or trade. Polyaenus, like Cleidemus, says that Pisistratus rode in the chariot alongside Phya. Herodotus does not actually say this, but he implies it,[51] and it is evidently thus that Aristotle understood his account.[52]

Such are our traditions concerning a story that was, as Herodotus says, "the most ridiculous story that anyone could imagine being told of the Greeks, who were considered to be more intelligent than foreigners, less naive and freer from foolishness—and all the more ridiculous since the Athenians were said to be the cleverest of the Greeks."[53] The most curious thing is that almost all modern historians have accepted the account at face value, as Aristotle did, and repeated it with the greatest seriousness. Meyer, following Beloch, has the merit of having rejected it.[54] He sees it as the rationalization of a fable that circulated among the people during the lifetime of Pisistratus, which said that Athena herself had personally escorted her favorite to the Acropolis. This story vividly transposed an actual event: the decisive victory achieved by the tyrant near the sanctuary of Athena Pallenis, which helped to establish Attica's preeminent position among Greek states. After the fall of the tyranny, what until then had been regarded as a providential miracle came to be despised as an ignoble subterfuge. "The story of Phya," Meyer says, "is nothing other than a variation on a historical account concerning the victory at Pallene, which may have been poetical in origin, but which was presented in a mythical fashion."[55] No more than Meyer do I believe the story of the false Athena. But a fable is not invented without reason, and the Greeks were not in the habit of dressing up abstract ideas that they were fully capable of expressing without embellishment as absurd tales.

If the disguised woman had been little more than a bystander, a figure of no consequence, it is hard to understand why anyone in the next century would have still known her name. Popularly, she was known as Growth—a wholly suitable name for a queen of spring. Let us suppose that Pisistratus had surreptitiously returned to Attica when an agrarian ceremony was being held; that with the aid of Megacles he succeeded in making himself acclaimed by his partisans, first, and then by the assembled multitude, passing through the crowd on an oxcart next to a young woman who represented the new year of growth and fertility; and that his prestige in the eyes of the people subsequently grew, as a result both of the audacity of such a gesture and of the sort of consecration that the ceremony itself conferred. The woman's personal name, which would have been of no interest to anyone, would not have been remembered, only a generic name. Her association in the popular mind with vegetation was never forgotten; indeed, she was said to have been a flower-seller.[56] And because agrarian festivals are always an occasion for nuptial rites, Pisistratus was said to have married the beautiful Phya to his son Hipparchus. This detail is as preposterous as the fable of the false Athena, for Pisistratus, whose concern for advancing his own interests had never been encumbered by gratitude to anyone else, could only have acknowledged the deceitfulness of the whole business by consenting to so unequal a marriage. Perhaps some memory of a festival of fruitfulness and vegetation survived in Paeania, at Collytus, which would explain why Phya was said to have been born there. But the procession itself must have disappeared sometime between the sixth and the fifth centuries; otherwise this liturgy would not have been so easily confused with an Olympian epiphany. We should not be in the least surprised that the biography of a tyrant such as Pisistratus came to be so largely populated by legends. The biography of his contemporary Cyrus met with the same fate.[57]

Moreover, since Pisistratus and his supporters did much to promote the cult of Athena in Attica, it would hardly be surprising if the goddess were to have been substituted in popular memory for an ephemeral Queen of May. The tyrant's victory near the temple of Athena Pallenis might have had the further effect of causing the story of Phya to be incorporated in the Olympian cycle. If this is correct, however, the episode can indeed be dated to the peaceful beginning of the second tyranny, as both Herodotus and Aristotle maintain. Beloch and Meyer accept only a single exile of Pisistratus and a single return to power, the second and last reign beginning after Pallene, which Beloch dates to about 550 and Meyer to 546 or 545.[58]

———————————————

The accounts concerning marriage by abduction seem therefore to have been nourished by quite ancient beliefs and rites. Each of the sentiments that inspired these rites gives a particular coloring to the legend that results from them. Together they serve to make the young husband a *conqueror*, chosen from among many others. On closer examination of these accounts we have discovered five things:

1. The belief in the magical efficacy of the *race*, which is mysterious for us, but which nonetheless may not have been for Greeks of the archaic period.
2. The memory of trials that, at the end of adolescence, prepared young men and women for *marriage*.
3. The idea that whoever passed the most difficult tests was fit to be entrusted with *political power* as king.
4. The belief that blessings rained down upon the earth following *sacred marriages* of springtime and the procession of a sacred oxcart carrying the daemon of vegetation with his or her assisting deity, who will enact the magical wedding. The role of the king being to render the land fertile, it comes as no surprise that his marriage to a hereditary princess (the sense in which this convenient term should be understood I shall consider in a moment) should be likened to one of those fertility spells that, in the spring, must immediately exert its power over nature as a whole.
5. The special meaning of the term *circumambulation*, probably equivalent to a seizure or taking of possession.

Whereas the theft of cattle is simply the insertion into a legend of a real event borrowed from archaic life, and whereas the trial of the race is a barely altered memory of adolescent rites of passage, the theme of abduction in a chariot can be fully grasped only if it is seen to conceal a symbolism having mystical significance, thoroughly imbued with religious feeling.

It may seem puzzling not to find any place reserved here for the memory of actual marriages by abduction. But nothing similar seems to have existed in Greece.[59] And no legend bears the least trace of its most characteristic trait, namely, the resistance feigned by the young woman.

---

Earlier, in drawing up a classification of the tests for winning the hand of a princess, I postponed for separate consideration the fourth and final group, in which marriage follows combat with a monster. This theme is also encountered outside any nuptial context, but in that case it has a civic significance: *the hero delivers his country from peril* and earns the gratitude of all its people. One thinks of the labors of Heracles, which have parallels in the legends of other countries. Dumézil has studied the legends of ancient Rome, all of them colored by the memory of historical events. "Where an exploit has the greatest possible national value," he rightly remarks, "which is to say where the threefold [adversary] is less a monster than 'the traditional enemy,' there the setting becomes localized, albeit vaguely, at the border or just beyond."[60] We find this motif in the account of Oedipus's battle against the Thebans' mortal enemy, the Sphinx.

When the combat is a prelude to a marriage, the narrative schema is generally the following: the hero saves a woman who has been surrendered to a monster, and thus gains power. Tales of this type are rather complex. Possession of the crown is linked to possession of a princess, who moreover is a scapegoat (pharmakos), offered up by the community to a mysterious and frightening power that in the popular mind is imagined to be an extraordinary animal.

Andromeda and Laodamia are scapegoats who owe their salvation to the higher will of the gods. Let us use very general terms that are capable of expressing both the archaic sentiment, such as it existed when the right of expulsion first arose from it, and the feeling a Greek of the classical period must have had reading or listening to a tale that he no longer supposed to have any liturgical basis. Someone watching a play by Euripides, for example, no longer recognized in the beautiful princess rescued by Perseus a sister of those poor souls who were hunted down during the Thargelia after all the sins of the community had been laid upon their heads. He nonetheless was still aware of the miraculous character of the rescue. Now, it is impossible to read Greek legends without being struck by the number of cases in which persons who have been sacrificed are spared, in the first place, and then promoted to a higher destiny. Scholars who have studied sources that speak of the pharmakos have paid little attention to this aspect of the problem because they have approached it at the level of the cult, not of the legend. Once legends are taken as a starting point, one notices that events unfold as though the malefic elements transmitted by the community to the person selected for expulsion charge him with a neutral force that the will of the gods then polarizes. If the gods rule against the victim, his death will be frightful; but if they rule in his favor, his promotion to a higher destiny is assured. An alternative of this sort surely must have appealed to a people with a taste for risk who felt that the willingness to court danger confers an entitlement, a people whose sense of justice convinced them that gratuitous suffering of any kind deserves to be compensated. Nevertheless a conception of this sort could only have been formed rather late—if not later than the composition of the legends themselves, then, at the very least, later than the grouping together of their primary elements. Now, the kernel of such tales is just this, the election of the saved pharmakos. We are therefore led once more to insist on the ambivalence of all those elements that crystallized to form the notion of a scapegoat. Sacralization led either to utter ruin or to a stunning reversal of fortune. This ambivalence has a highly archaic character. Perhaps it is what needs to be taken into account if we are to explain a peculiar detail of the rite of Nemi, one of the strangest among them, in fact, and the only one that Frazer did not study: the *fugitive slave* who will succeed the old king if he can break off a branch of the sacred tree. The fugitive slave, like the pharmakos, is a culprit and an outlaw. He faces an alternative: either to be killed by his master, the King of the Wood, or to become himself the new King of the Wood. An alternative of the same kind forms the basis of tales concerning the saved scapegoat.

In the legends of exposed infants, the gods' instruments are animals and ordinary men and women. In the case of young women delivered up to monsters, the intervention of the gods is decisive in a hero's triumph. Moreover, it is the hero's good fortune to have the monster for a rival, for the victim, quite against her will, has been promised to whoever can slay it. The beneficent force with which she is charged, having been marked for death, first, and then saved, is transmitted to her rescuer, who becomes king. The poets gave themselves free rein and in their own various ways embellished the central theme, which could still be made out: *the taking of power is linked to marriage.*

Frazer, it will be recalled, accounts for the frequency of this theme by positing the institution of female inheritance. We have discovered nothing that disconfirms this hypothesis, but neither have we found anything that confirms it. Ultimately, it seems to me unnecessary. If the conquest of a wife and the conquest of power are almost always found together, this may be explained by at least two other reasons.

The first is the *interdependence of initiations*.[61] The same tests permitted both marriage and accession to a higher class. Traces of these practices were still perceptible in historical Greece. The youthful suitors of the *Odyssey* have all the characteristics of an age cohort: they are called κοῦροι; they compete with one another, then they sit down together to eat food that they have prepared themselves.[62] The same vocabulary is used in reference to initiations and marriage. If the Danaids became the very symbol of noninitiates, as Harrison rightly points out, this is because, in refusing to marry, they remained ἀτελεῖς γάμου [uninitiated in marriage].[63] In historical Greece, the new *couroi* and *courai* were solemnly inducted into the phratry before being allowed to marry. There can be no doubt that the phratry itself carried on a prehistoric tradition that enjoyed only a limited place in the public life of city-states. The Ionian and Dorian festivals dedicated to Apollo, the Apaturia and the Apellai, incorporated what was left of archaic initiations: a ceremony marking the admission of young men and women into the class of marriageable persons.[64] In the historical period, the selection procedure took into account only age, but more anciently it must have involved a trial in the true sense. At Rhodes, young women entitled to marry bore a special name. Entry into the class of marriageable persons was often accompanied by simultaneous marriages.[65] In Crete, all those who had been graduated from the class of children were married at the same time.[66] For an ambitious young man, marriage marked the beginning of a new phase in his career, presenting him with the opportunity to prove his talents as a commander of men. This explains the existence of legends that are at once political and sentimental.

Perhaps one day it will be possible to deepen this line of speculation. Westermarck was struck some time ago by the fact that, in certain countries, husbands and wives were styled as kings and queens. Yet he refused to see this as a survival from a time in which marriages were contracted solely by sovereigns. Those who took up the question later, noticing the aristocratic character that marriage had retained in many places (at Rome, for example), suspected that it would be necessary to reconsider the hypothesis, rejected by Westermarck, that the ritual celebration of marriage was a ceremony originally reserved for kings and queens—a magical rite, intended to stimulate the productive forces of nature—that was then gradually extended to the aristocracy and, finally, to the lower classes.[67]

The second reason why marriage and conquest are brought together in legend is the *sacred marriage of springtime*, enacted or symbolized by a royal couple. In the ancient agrarian festivals of which some record has come down to us, the amusing and picturesque aspects eventually became preponderant, with the result that the original meaning of the festivals was lost. Yet everything we know about primitive Indo-European kingship leads us to believe that the king was charged with transmitting to the earth the fecundity with which he was endowed. "Sovereignty and Fecundity," Dumézil remarks, "are interdependent powers and so amount to two aspects of Power."[68] One finds the immediate effect of a good king's action on nature still being described in barely rationalized terms by Odysseus to Penelope in the *Odyssey*,[69] where the marriage of a princess is called θαλερὸς γάμος [youthful (or joyous) marriage].[70]

Additionally, in prehistoric Greece, it is possible that political power was transmitted through women, by means of the wedding of a hereditary queen with an elective king. The strongest argument in favor of this theory seems to me not the succession of a father by his son-in-law, which I prefer to explain otherwise, but the succession of a maternal grandfather by his bastard grandson, accompanied by the hostility of the grandfather's brother toward the younger man.

---

How do the legendary elements we have just studied come together in the story of Oedipus?

Oedipus acquires power jointly with the princess and following the most difficult trial of all, the battle with a monster. This feat did not liberate Jocasta personally; it was not her, but the youth of Thebes whom the Sphinx threatened. Thus the poet decorates Oedipus with a prestige that is twofold: by prevailing at a moment of *national* crisis he is the savior of a country; at the same time he triumphs in a test that, indirectly, is a *nuptial* test.

Here the themes of the monster and of the princess, bound up with each other elsewhere, are separate. Oedipus defeats the monster without any divine assistance. The feat itself seems to consist solely in the solving of a riddle. A more schematic, more cerebral treatment of the theme—yet accompanied by the same wealth of sentimental invention and vivid detail that one finds in the legend of Perseus and Andromeda—can hardly be imagined.

Of the marriage of Oedipus and Jocasta the poets say nothing, no doubt because they wished to avoid having to deal with the subject of incest and also because the whole suspense and narrative thrust of their accounts turns on the *discovery* of the double crime Oedipus has committed. A few scattered clues nonetheless permit us to recover the religious meaning that such weddings must have had primitively—weddings between a conqueror and a queen, not between a son and his mother, for this latter aspect, which gives the Oedipus legend its particular color, was developed independently of the theme of marriage between sovereigns.

The lost epic known to us through the Pisander scholion was centered on the cult of Hera *gamoastolos* (or *gamēlia* or *teleia*), who was honored during the Daedalas. When the Boeotian cult of Hera appeared for the first time, in 480,[71] its original significance seems already to have been completely forgotten; no one any longer saw in it the memory of a sacred marriage of springtime. Nevertheless the visit of the young king and his wife, traveling in a horse-drawn chariot, to the goddess's sanctuary still carries a faint echo of tales of nuptial abduction and of vernal processions. One is put in mind once more of the Minyan version of the legend reported by Nicolaus of Damascus, which we considered in Chapter 2, without managing to give a satisfactory explanation for it: Oedipus encounters Laius, who is traveling from Thebes to Delphi in the company of Epikaste, at Orchomenos; he kills the king and his herald, but spares the king's wife. The presence of Epikaste interferes with any plausible reconstruction of subsequent events. Might this version be a survival of an archaic mythopoeia in which the procession of a king and queen in a chariot had retained something of its old ritual meaning?

Finally, a few remarks that will perhaps be useful to those who wish to compare similar tales from other lands. For it is in popular traditions and chivalric romances that traces of royal trials must be sought. One will find many curious things in Töpfer's dissertation on the king in German folktales.[72] The author scours such stories for details that either agree with or contradict the German historical past. He does a poor job isolating themes that are descended from an archaic substratum, but they do not go unnoticed in his summaries of the tales. Thus he helpfully classifies the tests by which a young prince or an adventurer proves his fitness for kingship: by picking a fruit, or by bringing back healing water, or by bringing back a golden bird, and so on. The tests generally come in threes and success is often rewarded by marriage. The adventurer marries the daughter of the king (she is sometimes locked away in a castle tower) because he has run faster than her, or solved a riddle; if he fails, he is liable to be put to death. Memories of classical legends—very distant, very much altered—play a greater role in these tales than Töpfer supposes, for he has not recognized that these Germanic princesses are spiritual daughters of Atalanta and Danaë. In a tale such as *Der turm Frönn* [The Frönn Tower],[73] whose subject is roughly the same as that of *Der treue Johannes* [Faithful John], one encounters once more the themes of the exposed infant, the battle against a dragon, and the winning of a bride, not to mention a survival of the young knight's vigil of arms—all of them contaminated at the outset by the biblical story of Joseph, sold into slavery by his brothers.[74] All these themes evidently derive from more ancient works. But there is one detail in particular whose great interest Töpfer seems not to have appreciated and that has its deepest roots in the social substratum from which primitive legends issued: the king in German tales is charged with responsibility for waging war and yet is incapable of doing so. A young adventurer triumphs in his place and will succeed him. "The German king was a military commander by birth," Töpfer notes. "But this conception is wholly foreign to the legend. The king must be passive, because in most cases the hero is someone else."[75] How can one read these lines without recalling Schurtz's distinction between the peacetime leader, who occupies a hereditary office, and a wartime leader, whose position is elective?[76] The king does not surrender his crown to the hero, for he lives on as king during the period of his eclipse. There seems to have been a time when tribes had a permanent chief who, in moments of danger, yielded his position momentarily to an adventurer whom chance had brought forth. The incapacity of the king in German folktales does not come from the classical tradition, however. Among the Greeks, the king is from the same social class as the one who triumphs over him. The conqueror, after having undergone a series of trials, is substituted for the one whom he has defeated; never has he been in the king's service, nor are the trials he has undergone ever described, as they frequently are in German tales, as services rendered to the king. Perhaps a comparativist will be able to make better use of this observation than I can myself.

# CHAPTER 6

# Incest with the Mother

ike the murder of one's own father, the theme of sexual union with one's own mother has been explained with reference to two different principles, one sociological in nature, the other psychological. Those who argue for the first type of explanation interpret incest as the memory of an ancient social order, since overturned, in which marriage was permitted between persons from the same family. For psychoanalysts, who argue for the second, a dual myth arose from the action of the libido, which encourages a son to desire his mother and to see his father as a rival. My own view is that while subconscious tendencies may have helped to establish the enduring appeal of a legendary theme of this sort, they did not create it. As for the mythopoetic role of pure memory, it seems to me to have had no effect whatever, for the memories of primitive societies did not last longer than two generations. It is true that memory may be sustained by certain states of mind that revive it, a point that I shall come back to later, in the final chapter. For the moment it will be enough to state precisely what we know about incest in reality and in legend.

The origin of the incest taboo is unknown. Freud sees it as a transposition of infantile repression, which explains nothing, for why would the child repress a desire that his mother inspires in him? Would he do this if he did not live in a world in which an incest taboo already existed and was constantly reinforced?

The further back one goes in tracing archaic societies to their primitive state, the more numerous and constraining incest taboos are found to be. One is therefore very unlikely to be right in supposing greater sexual freedom among pre-Hellenic populations, within the family, than existed during the historical period. It is very possible that these peoples tolerated sexual promiscuity prior to marriage. Nevertheless we may be certain that marriage between a father and daughter or between a mother and son was not permitted.

The incest taboo exists among all peoples, but it does not always assume the same form. Marriage between a brother and sister is sometimes allowed. It was the rule in certain royal families, even among civilized peoples well into the historical period.[1] In Athens, for example, a brother could marry his consanguine sister, though not his uterine sister. Marriage between father and daughter must have often occurred in societies where, on the one hand, paternal heredity was unknown, and, on the other hand, older men could reserve for themselves those women who pleased them most[2]—a practice of no psychological interest, since husbands and wives were equally ignorant of their own parentage. Father-daughter incest is prohibited in patrilinear systems. Mother-son incest is everywhere prohibited and nowhere attested.[3]

In legends, various types of incest appear, with very different nuances.

1. *Amorous feeling of a father for his daughter* figures in the tales of Oenomaus and Evenus. This theme, in Greek tales, seems to me to be a late addition motivated by the need to explain a father's hostility toward his future son-in-law. But it may come from older tales, now lost, of the type later popularized by Perrault's version, *Peau d'Ane* [Donkeyskin]. The father's love is always unrequited, for the daughter spurns his advances and no marriage is consummated.

2. *Adelphic polyandry*, the marriage of a woman to two or more brothers, frequently occurs and confers a privileged status on any male issue. This secondary theme has no place in Greek legends, but it plays a prominent role in medieval traditions.

3. *Mother-son incest* is exceedingly rare. Only the legend of Oedipus is well known in Greek literature. Otherwise there remain but a few brief

allusions to the tales of Menephron and Arcas. In other literatures, the only character who marries his mother is the Irish hero Lugaid. I see no conclusions to be drawn from this strange story, which seems to have been contrived simply for the purpose of cataloging all imaginable cases of incest.[4]

Comparing legends involving incest with the historical record is therefore bound to be futile. And I believe that in order to demonstrate the effectiveness of the sociological method on this point (or more likely its ineffectiveness), it would be necessary to study each particular case in minute detail. With regard to the special case of mother-son incest, things become clearer when one concentrates, not on hypothetical primitive customs, but on the entire set of Greek beliefs associated with the theme of *marriage between man and the earth*—a marriage that, in magical practices, has a sexual dimension and that, more generally, has a symbolic affinity with the theme of marriage to one's own mother. In what follows I shall cite a number of examples taken from Roman history, but the events they describe take place in lands that were so profoundly Hellenized that they may be considered to be merely an extension of Greek history.

---

At the moment when Oedipus learns of the death of Polybus, whom he has taken to be his father, and believes that he has been delivered finally from the danger of having committed patricide, but not from the oracle that threatens him with incest, Jocasta says to him:

> What is there to fear for a man who regards life as a matter of chance, knowing that nothing can be foreseen? It is best to trust to luck, as far as one may. Have no fear of marrying your mother. *Many men have slept with their mothers in dreams as well [as in oracles].* He who considers such things to be of no importance will put up with [the vagaries of] life most easily.[5]

Psychoanalysis, as everyone knows, has had a field day with these lines. "The myth of King Oedipus, who killed his father and took his mother to wife," Freud says, "reveals, with little modification, the infantile wish, which is later opposed and repudiated by the *barrier of incest.*"[6] Moreover, Jocasta's remarkable claim that many men have slept with their mothers in dreams could not help but capture the attention of a physician who sees dreams as a refuge where shameful feelings can find free expression. Echoing down the ages, the tale of a queen whose fate deeply moved Odysseus is taken to provide evidence for the doctrine of the subconscious. But the lines she is given to speak in *Oedipus the King* do not have the meaning that Freud imagines them to have; or, rather, they allude to something altogether different than the nocturnal explosion of sexual urges that are tamed finally by the light of day. The one revelatory dream of a hidden self in Greek literature is that of Io in *Prometheus Bound*:

> Visions constantly visited me at night in my maiden chamber and caressed me with comforting words: "O very blessed maiden, why do you still remain a virgin when the one who wishes to marry you is the greatest of all? Zeus has been struck by your arrow of desire and longs to share his bed with you."[7]

A psychoanalyst would say that the visions came, not from Zeus, but from Io herself, who was eager to marry while remaining determined not to lower or demean herself in any way. As for sexual union with one's own mother, it is possible that such a thing may sometimes be desired. Nevertheless, whether the desire is realized, dreamed, or simply declared, it is equivalent, I believe, to a sacred marriage that symbolizes taking possession of the earth.

In the *Oneirocritica* [Interpretation of Dreams], Artemidorus of Ephesus, who lived in the second century of our era, devotes a long chapter to the dream of intercourse with one's mother. The subject, he says, was much discussed among ancient interpreters of dreams. Where Artemidorus expresses his own view, he is careful to rely on examples that are never borrowed from literature; all of them are due to the actual experience of people who wrote down their dreams and observed their consequences.

Such dreams must be distinguished, Artemidorus says, according to the manner in which intercourse takes place. When it is performed in the normal way, and with a living mother,[8] this signifies hatred of the father and rivalry with him if he is in good health, and a wish for the father's death if he is sick.[9] A dream of sleeping with one's mother is apt to be a favorable sign, particularly for artisans, whose trade is called their "mother," as well as for public figures and all those who aspire to power, for *the mother represents one's country.* Just as a man who follows the precepts of Aphrodite will have an obedient and happy partner, so too a leader who makes love to his mother in a dream can count on being respected and loved by his subjects.[10] When a dream unites a mother and son who live apart, it promises the dreamer, the son who has gone away to a foreign land, that he will one day return home, if his mother is there; or that, if she is not, he will rejoin her wherever she lives. If he is ill, the dream means that he will get well again, for *nature is our common mother.*

The situation is different when the mother is deceased:

For a sick man to dream that he has intercourse with his dead mother is a sign of death, for *the earth is called mother.*

For a man who has brought suit over rights to land, for one who wishes to purchase land, and for one who wishes to cultivate land, it is good to dream that he is pleasurably united with his dead mother.... Such a dream means that a person living abroad will return to his native land.

But a man who has the dream in his native land will leave it, for having committed such a crime, he cannot remain near his mother's home; he will be exiled or he will go away of his own volition....

[If the union does not occur normally, the dream portends only sorrow.] If the mother lies upon the dreamer, so that he possesses her from underneath, it is a sign of death, for earth lies upon the dead [and not upon the living]....[11]

To have intercourse with a goddess or to be possessed by a god foretells death to a sick man.... But it is a good omen when a man is in good health, so long as the dream gives him pleasure....

Intercourse with Artemis, Athena, Hestia, Rhea, Hera, or Hecate means that death will soon come to the dreamer, even if the dream is agreeable, for these goddesses are august and inspire awe....[12]

A man dreamed that he was beating his mother; he was a potter, and the dream was advantageous to him, for [the earth, which a potter shapes by beating, is called "mother," and so] it alluded to his skill as an artisan.[13]

For a man who aspires to power, then, to dream of marrying one's mother is a promise either of success or death, for the maternal breast is an ambiguous symbol, which Artemidorus crudely translates by saying that the dreamer must lie on top of his mother and not beneath her.[14] Furthermore, the sacred marriage of the conqueror[15] is mentioned elsewhere than in Artemidorus's dream book. Several curious stories allude to this tradition; they differ from one another according to the degree of reality they grant to it, ranging from a simple play on words to actual incest.

Diogenes Laertius, speaking of Periander, the tyrant of Corinth, says: "Aristippus, in the first book of his work *On the Luxury of the Ancients*, accuses him of incest with his mother, Cratea. The thing was done secretly, and he took pleasure from it. When it became public knowledge, however, he was most bitterly annoyed and conducted himself in a way that gave offense to everyone."[16] It is quite pointless to wonder whether anything in this story is authentic. Was the tyrant's mother really called Authority [*Krateia*]? In no other source is her name mentioned. It is rather as though this anecdote were simply the sort of illustration one finds in the *Oneirocritica*, with the mother being given a striking name in order to emphasize the gravity of the portent. Read in the context of Artemidorus's analysis, the phrase Aristippus uses, καὶ ὃς ἤδετο [and he took pleasure from it], no longer seems a romantic embellishment in the least. For this detail constitutes the very reason for Periander's success: the satisfied lover is a master whom the nation willingly obeys. Nevertheless we do not know whether Aristippus associated sexual union with the seizure of power, since to begin with his account was no more than a romantic theme that would later be embroidered. One is tempted to suppose he did, because similar crimes were imputed to Periander by other writers. Herodotus, for example, says that he made love to the dead body of his wife Melissa.[17] Here, however, it is a mother who is enamored of her son: συνῆν αὐτῷ λάθρα [she slept with him secretly], without the knowledge of the Corinthians probably,[18] though Parthenius, in the *Erotica Pathemata* [Sorrows of Love], gives another interpretation: Periander's mother tricks him into sleeping with her, in the dark, so that he will not know the identity of his partner. Periander takes great pleasure in the encounter, but demands to know the woman's name. Finally he sees her face; the discovery infuriates him and makes him cruel. The mother kills herself.[19] In each of these accounts we have reason to suspect the coincidence of two traditions, one concerning Periander the tyrant, the other Periander the sage.[20] Neither of the narrators draws attention to the symbolic meaning of intercourse with one's mother.

Such an act, from the moment it actually takes place, is a crime whose consequences must be suffered by its perpetrators. It passes, in other words, from the realm of magic to the realm of morality, for now it is judged with reference to the norms of bourgeois life. The same transition occurs here as in the case of both Oedipus and Nero—the same forgetting of a meaning that remains perfectly clear so long as sacred marriage is enacted only in dreams.

All the themes of Artemidorus's account are found in the story Herodotus tells of the tyrant Hippias. Exiled from Athens for twenty years, Hippias brought the Persian army to Marathon in hopes of being restored to power:

> The night before arriving there, he had a dream in which it seemed to him that he slept with his mother, from which he concluded that he should return to Athens, reclaim his crown, and so die an old man in his native land. . . . But as he was giving orders he began to sneeze and cough more violently than usual; and as he was well on in years, many of his teeth were loose, and the violence of his fit caused one of them to fall out. It landed in the sand, and though he looked hard to find it, it was nowhere to be seen. "This land is not ours," he lamented to those who were with him, "we will not succeed in making it submit; all of it that will be mine, my tooth now claims as its share."[21]

Hippias's interpretation accords with the one advanced by Artemidorus. Sexual union with one's mother signifies either possession of the land or death. Hippias equably accepts the two branches of the alternative, recognizing that either outcome will be agreeable: ruling over Attica *or* dying there after a happy old age. The loss of the tooth he nonetheless must find distressing because, if the earth has received this part of his person, the oracle communicated by his dream will no longer be obliged to grant him conquest of any more land than what his tooth presently occupies. This is why he tries to recover the tooth, in order to obtain from destiny the total fulfillment of the oracle's promise—for an oracle foretells the future and in this way imposes a sort of constraint. Union with one's mother, Artemidorus says, represents either return to one's *native land* (favorable omen) or *burial* in its soil (fatal omen). In the event, however, assuming (as Artemidorus does) that Hippias died at Lemnos on his return from Marathon, neither branch of the alternative was realized. This is why Herodotus relates the story of the tooth, quite obviously an invention to justify the dream: having been borne out with regard to this fragment of Hippias's person, it is excused from any further obligation as regards the rest. A more recent tradition, recounted by Cicero and Justin, maintains that Hippias died at Marathon—in which case Artemidorus's interpretation is confirmed after all.[22]

Livy relates an analogous story about the Tarquins and their cousin Lucius Junius Brutus. The old tyrant Tarquinius, filled with foreboding by a terrible apparition, sent to Delphi two of his sons, Titus and Arruns, along with his nephew Brutus, who concealed great cunning beneath a veneer of stupidity. Brutus made an offering to Apollo of a golden staff, which he disguised by inserting it into a hollowed-out stick from a dogwood tree. Then from the depths of the cavern came a voice in response to Titus's petition: "The supreme power in Rome shall belong to that one of you young men who will be the first to give a kiss to his mother."[23] Titus and Arruns agreed between themselves to keep the matter secret so as not to alert their brother Sextus, who had remained behind in Rome. But Brutus at once fell to the ground and kissed it, knowing that the earth is the mother of all men.

Livy knew there was a limit to the liberties he could take, both with regard to the stick filled with gold and the story of the oracle: they are introduced by a cautious *dicitur* [it is said], in the one case; a circumspect *ferunt* [they say] in the other. The theme of an apparently dull and unambitious younger son who surpasses his older brothers was well known; equally so the theme of the *clever ruse*, here of an apparently ordinary offering that concealed a valuable gift to the god. As for the oracle itself, it is no more than a copy of Hippias's dream, a Greek invention (the mention of Delphi would have sufficed to indicate this) following the Athenian revolution of 514, which could then rather naturally be aligned with the Roman revolution of 509.

In a sense the Tarquins were the Italian Pisistratids, raised by a father who reigned as tyrant but destined never to reign themselves. Hippias received a dream, Titus an oracle. The *omen* was fallacious in both cases, for the Greek because he derived only the smallest possible satisfaction from it, for the Roman because a rival, profiting by his quick-wittedness, succeeded in turning the oracle's promise to his own advantage. The basic theme, of *misleading portents*, belongs to a literature that Herodotus's own inventory allows us to describe in a summary manner. It involves oracles and dreams that have to be interpreted with caution, calmly and deliberately, for their true meaning is the opposite of the one that emerges from an initial and overly confident reading. Here are the various instances, following more or less the order in which Herodotus presents them:

1. The oracles of Apollo at Delphi and of Amphiaraus at Thebes tell Croesus, king of Lydia, that if he makes war on the Persians he will destroy a great empire. The empire will turn out to be, not that of the Persians, but his own.[24]

2. Delphi warns Croesus to beware the day when a mule will be king of the Persians. He is defeated by Cyrus, son of a mere military officer and a Median princess.[25]

3. The Lacedaemonians ask the Pythian priestess whether they ought to attack the Arcadians. She discourages them in this ambition, but then says: "I will give you Tegea, to pound the earth with your dancing, and its fertile plain for you to survey and measure out with a line." The Lacedaemonians therefore marched against Tegea, leaving the rest of Arcadia in peace, but they were defeated and taken captive, and made to cultivate the land for their conquerors.[26]

4. Cambyses, having left Persia on an expedition to Egypt, dreams that his brother Smerdis now sits on the royal throne; he sends a trusted deputy to kill his brother, then learns that a Magian named Smerdis has been proclaimed king in his absence. Cambyses does not resist: the oracle has been fulfilled.[27]

5. Cambyses knows from the oracle that he will die at Ecbatanes, which he understands to be Agbatana in Media; in fact it was to be Agbatana in Syria.[28]

6. Delphi tells the Siphnians to beware a wooden host and a scarlet herald. Failing to understand the oracle, they are caught by surprise when the Samians arrive on boats painted vermillion.[29]

7. The daughter of Polycrates, tyrant of Samos, dreams that her father, raised aloft, is washed by Zeus and anointed by the sun. Polycrates is killed and his body hung on a cross.[30]

8. The Pythian priestess warns Arcesilaus, king of Cyrene, that if he finds earthen pots in the oven he should not bake them; and that if he does, he should not go to the place where the tides wash ashore. Having taken a fortress, he piles up wood around it and sets the logs on fire;

then, too late, he understands that he has done what he ought to have refrained from doing. Fleeing Cyrene, which he supposes to be the place surrounded by the sea, he takes refuge in Barce, where he is killed.[31]

9. In 514, the night before the Panathenaea, the annual festival celebrated in Athens in honor of its patron goddess, Hipparchus sees in a dream a tall, handsome man who says to him:

Τλῆθι λέων ἄτλητα παθὼν τετληότι θυμῷ·
οὐδεὶς ἀνθρώπων ἀδικῶν τίσιν οὐκ ἀποίσει

[Bear unbearable woes, O lion, bear them with a patient heart;
No man does wrong without his injustice being punished]

—an allusion to his impending downfall, which the tyrant misconstrues as urging him to act daringly. Moreover, he interprets the second line as referring to his enemies, when in fact the unjust man is none other than himself.[32]

10. The Scythians send to Darius a bird, a mouse, a frog, and five arrows. Darius interprets this as an act of surrender, whereas it is actually a harbinger of his own death.[33]

11. A solar eclipse occurs at the moment when the bridging of the Hellespont ordered by Xerxes is complete. On consulting local astrologers who assure him that the event foretells the destruction of the Greek cities, Xerxes leads his army onward to its defeat.[34]

12. In 450, the Pythian priestess gives the Athenians a fearsome oracle predicting that Athens will be destroyed in a conflagration. When they come back to her, hoping for a more favorable answer, she says that only a wooden wall will survive the fires and that "divine Salamis will cause the death of many women's children"—a sinister reply that Themistocles correctly interprets as portending the Athenians' ultimate triumph over the Persians.[35]

13. Hippias's dream,[36] which we considered earlier.

Let us now classify these stories. In every case except (12), the initial interpretation is optimistic, inspiring in the dreamer or in his consultant a false sense of confidence that leads to his downfall.[37] In two cases it is not a person, but a city, that is led into grievous error: Lacedaemonia (3) and Siph-nus (6). In all the other cases the person is a king or a tyrant: Croesus, twice fooled (1 and 2); Cambyses, twice also (4 and 5), Polycrates (7), Arcesilaus (8), Hipparchus (9), Xerxes (11), Hippias (13). Darius makes a false analogy concerning the messages of the Scythians (10).

In only one case (12) is there an initially pessimistic interpretation, subsequently contradicted by good fortune. Shortly after this episode the Athenians were to give yet another proof of their shrewdness. An oracle having advised them before the battle of Salamis to seek the assistance of their son-in-law, they understood what was meant and called upon Boreas, husband of the Athenian Orithyia.[38]

What are we justified in concluding from this analysis? The theme of the wrongly interpreted portent is frequently encountered in the folklore of all countries. Apart from the eleventh story, which may be authentic (for there was a solar eclipse in 481, and royal astrologers always interpreted shooting stars, for example, in a fashion favorable to their masters), the others might have been in circulation long before they became attached to a proper name. It seems to me certain, however, that a literature inspired by democratic ideas had gotten hold of them before Herodotus, malevolently ascribing to tyrants and kings the most disastrous errors and using them to show, first, that if oracles are wrongly interpreted, it is because those who consult them are arrogant and reckless; and, second, that the pretensions of despots are often thwarted just when they seem to be sure of triumphing. No one will fail to notice that the list I have drawn up includes, apart from four tyrants and a king punished by madness who died (Cambyses), the names of three kings who waged war against Greek states (Croesus, Darius, Xerxes). The list even provides us with a counterexample: the only story that does not tell of hopes dashed, but to the contrary of anxieties dispelled, involves the Athenians. We may therefore venture to suggest with some confidence that, between 500 and 450, it was the Athenians themselves who published a collection of misleading portents meant to illustrate the excesses of monarchs.

It is impossible to know who had the idea of adding the Tarquins to the roster of deceived—in the case of Brutus, undeceived—tyrants, nor when this was done. All that we can say is that the Tarquinian traditions were influenced by the literature that grew up around the Greek tyrants of the sixth century. Tarquinius, in order to persuade Sextus to confront the aristocracy, summoned his son's messenger and ushered him into the garden of his house, where he proceeded silently to lop off the heads of the tallest poppies with a stick; according to Herodotus, Thrasybulus acted in a similar fashion to warn Periander (according to Aristotle, Periander in order to warn Thrasybulus).[39] The details of all these stories remained unsettled so long as a suitable figure with whom they could be associated had not been found. Once that person was found, however, such tales came to be subject to several different influences.

There can be no doubt that the prophecy cunningly obtained by Brutus was derived directly from Hippias's dream. It was designed to please republican Romans, exactly as the story of the wooden wall, by analogy with Hippias's dream, must have pleased democratic Athenians: in both cases the enemy of the tyrant has the leading role. By the beginning of the first century BCE it had already have been naturalized as a Roman tale, for on two occasions Caesar turned the auspicious resonances of the Greek original to his own personal advantage.

All of this casts light on two classical Greek texts. The first is Jocasta's declaration in *Oedipus the King*: "He who considers such things to be of no importance will put up with [the vagaries of] life most easily."[40] There is a tragic irony in these words. Jocasta attaches little credit to oracles, complaining that they are always gloomy and filled with dark foreboding. Considering the one concerning Oedipus, she moves at once to dismiss the second branch of the alternative that faced Hippias, death, which she says is best not thought of if one wishes to live a happy life. But the audience already knows that it is the first branch that has been affirmed, for Oedipus has come to power—a happy outcome when intercourse with one's mother is merely a dream, but a baleful one, at least in the eyes of the Greeks of the fifth century, when it is a reality.[41]

The second passage occurs at the beginning of the ninth book of *The Republic*. There Plato expounds the psychology of suppressed desires, which in dreams break free of the shackles with which they are bound by reason. At this moment, he says, for the desiring part of the soul, "released from all sense of shame and all rational thought, there is nothing that it will shrink from doing, not even *wishing to sleep with one's mother* or with anyone else, man, god, or beast, or committing the foulest murder, or not abstaining from any kind of food."[42] These "terrible, savage, uncontrolled desires" exist in all of us, but whereas the disciplined man is able to tame and master them for the most part, the tyrant habitually surrenders himself to them and, when he is awake, acts in ways that most people only allow themselves to imagine when they are dreaming. Implicit in this brief passage is a whole doctrine of the subconscious. Plato certainly anticipated Freud in speaking of the "passionate" or "appetitive" part of our nature, which a sensible person aims neither to starve nor to overindulge.[43] Nevertheless I think that the detail of sexual union with one's mother was not suggested to Plato by any psychological observation, but by historical tradition: he has in mind Hippias's dream, Periander's incest. A very ancient association of ideas reminded him of the two constituent elements of this tradition, only now the order was reversed: whereas Artemidorus says that a man will reign if he dreams that he will marry his mother, Plato says that he will marry his mother because he is a tyrant.

The meaning of the conqueror's dream becomes wholly apparent when we consider an episode in Plutarch's life of Julius Caesar. Plutarch says that the night before Caesar crossed the Rubicon, he dreamed of having intercourse with his mother. Suetonius, reporting the same dream, places it in the year 66, when Caesar left for Spain as quaestor. The nocturnal vision disturbs Caesar, but the soothsayers he consults reassure him that one day he will reign over the entire world, for the mother he saw submitting to his will was none other, they say, than the earth, mother of all mankind. There is every reason to believe that Caesar's confusion on awakening was feigned; that, if he recounted this dream, he did so deliberately, being perfectly familiar with its classic interpretation and knowing that no one would dare to mention in his presence the second branch of the alternative, which contemplated a senile, toothless Hippias near death. Caesar also knew the oracle given to Tarquinius's sons and intended full well to be a new Brutus. It was this ancient story (later retold by Livy) that gave him the idea of leading people to believe that he had dreamed the dream of conquerors; it was this same dream that gave him the idea, again in Suetonius's account, of crying "Teneo te, Africa!" [I hold you fast, Africa!], when, on disembarking there, he stumbled and fell to the ground. Brutus had had the presence of mind to do it on purpose; Caesar, to reverse the implication of what might have seemed to be a fatal portent. If, as I believe, Caesar recounted the story to inspire confidence in his lucky star, it must be placed in 49, as Plutarch would have it, and not in 66. Suetonius trivialized the episode by putting it at the beginning of a triumphant career; also by promising the dreamer dominion over the whole world. This promised far too much: the mother, Artemidorus said, represents *the country*—Italy in this case. It was for control over Italy that Caesar set out to contend with Pompey. Indeed, in all the examples that interest us here, including that of Oedipus himself, there are only men who seek to make themselves master of their own country.[44]

Nero, like Periander, was supposed to have slept with his mother. In both Tacitus and Suetonius the story is nothing more than a romantic interlude. Tacitus says that, according to Cluvius, it was Agrippina who made advances, whereas according to Fabius Rusticus it was Nero. Elsewhere Tacitus expresses his own view, that Agrippina had arranged everything. Suetonius, for his part, agrees with Fabius Rusticus.[45] One can only marvel at the presumption of modern historians who dare to assign responsibility in a story so obscure that, had we been alive then ourselves, still we would have hesitated to declare an opinion. If Nero himself called attention to so vile a deed, it very probably was not unwittingly. He knew Greek literature. Did he wish to imitate Periander and so have in Agrippina a second Cratea? Was he resolved to assert his authority over both his mother and the country, trusting that, with Agrippina's assistance and in keeping with the principles of Artemidorus, his power in Rome would be consolidated and lastingly assured? If so, we may surmise that he had grown weary of deferring to an overbearing mother and contending with an often disobedient populace. One is led at any rate to suspect as much from the romanticized plot summarized by the two historians, and also from a curious detail noted first by Suetonius and then by the Byzantine monk John Xiphilinus, that Nero brought into his harem a woman who was the very image of Agrippina. Xiphilinus adds that Nero was deeply attached to her and that, while making love to her or showing her off to others, he used to say that he was making love to his mother.[46] The phrase used by Xiphilinus, τῇ μητρὶ ὁμιλοίη, recalls the phrase used by Plutarch in connection with Caesar's dream, τῇ μητρὶ μίγνυσθαι [to lie with his mother].[47] Would Nero have *acted out* intercourse with his mother, and so given it the symbolic meaning it has in Artemidorus's dream book? Tacitus reports, apparently following Cluvius, that Nero's mistress, Claudia Acte, turned him against Agrippina by telling him that his soldiers would refuse to serve under the command of a man guilty of sacrilege. This is probably correct, not because his soldiers had many moral scruples, but because in all countries incest inspired superstitious fears, being thought to cause droughts, ruin harvests, and bring about the death of young animals and human beings. Nero himself would not have known much about popular beliefs of this sort. Acte, a freedwoman, would have understood them far better than he.

The role of Oedipus was one of Nero's favorites in the theater, and shortly before his death he recited this verse (the only one known to us) from a lost poem, *Oedipus Banished*, in which incest is recalled by an odd locution:

Οἰκτρῶς θανεῖν μ' ἄνωγε σύγγαμος πατήρ

[My co-husband, my father, orders me to die a miserable death].[48]

Xiphilinus also relates that Nero stripped Agrippina's dead body of its clothing and said, "I didn't know that my mother was so beautiful."[49] Was this remark meant to recall Periander, who did not shrink from making love to his living mother and to his dead wife? Even if not, we cannot infer that he had never seen his mother naked before, for after having had Plautus executed he said, in much the same spirit, "I didn't know that his nose was so long.[50]

Hubaux tries to explain the accusations of incest brought against Nero by saying that the emperor played the role of Oedipus in public so well that actor and character came to be confused in the popular mind. Hubaux recalls an anecdote related by Suetonius: once, when Nero was playing the part of a furious Hercules and, as the story required, had himself bound in chains, a young soldier, believing that the emperor was in danger, rushed forward to help him.[51] But this was a spontaneous and understandable misapprehension. To make Nero a genuinely theatrical version of Oedipus, it would have been necessary to grasp the meaning of Sophocles's text. Educated members of the audience readily distinguished between the actor and the character he played, whereas ordinary people with no knowledge of Greek understood nothing at all of the words declaimed by the emperor. What is more, we know that Nero played many other tragic roles. Why should he have identified only with Oedipus?

If Nero was vilified for being his mother's lover, it was surely because he did his utmost to lend credence to this rumor. More than this it is impossible to say. Did he suppose that he was happy because he had no misgivings or moral qualms—an Oedipus who, following Jocasta's death, was content to exercise the power that she had given him? In everything that concerns Nero it is difficult to sort out what is real from what later writers have imagined. First we must try to determine whether he had really intrigued with his mother.[52] A second, still more intractable problem is to determine whether this was in satisfaction of a desire, or whether it was a magical rite, or merely a recollection of ancient tragedies.

Comparing all these stories brings out a common trait: the hero is—or wishes to be—a conqueror, but the country in which he wishes to consolidate (or reconsolidate) his authority is in every case his native land, which, for one reason or another, he was obliged to leave for a time. Oedipus himself does nothing more than claim his rightful inheritance. In trying to establish (or reestablish) their rule, all such heroes are aided—or believe they are aided—to some degree by sleeping with their mother, whether the act is contemplated, or dreamed, or performed symbolically, or actually realized. It is difficult, I think, not to recognize a connection between these two things.

Oedipus's incest therefore leads back from a clear romantic legend to the shadowy world in which myths are elaborated, the penumbra of immediately efficacious rites. The problem we face now, then, is to determine what ritual practice, what archaic rite of possession the legendary theme of the sacred marriage of the tyrant could have corresponded to.

In order to be able to give a preliminary answer to this question, we must have a more exact idea of what supplication involved. In Homer, supplication in the form of a kiss is addressed to the earth alone (τὴν γῆν κυνεῖν [to kiss the earth]), never to persons. The shipwrecked man kisses the ground when he finally comes ashore; both Odysseus and Agamemnon kiss the ground on returning to their native lands.[53] I believe that in the beginning this was not merely an expression of affection and gratitude, but also a form of sexual union—which is to say an act of possession. This union must have had the same ambiguous character that it has in the tyrant's dream. One of the two partners will dominate the other: either the hero will rule the earth or the entombing earth will lie over him forever, for in taking possession of her he gives himself up to her at the same time. This is not a simple metaphor. From various formulas employed for the purpose of execration and malediction we know that the earth was thought to be capable of rejecting one who is accursed.[54] The person on whom a curse has been placed is generally someone who is guilty of a crime; he may also be a man of reckless ambition who, believing that he has made the earth submit to his will, fails to comprehend that he runs the fatal risk instead of falling under her sway.

The nature of supplications addressed to persons is very uncertain. Only one aspect of it has been studied: the constraint under which the supplicant places the one to whom he makes appeal. To touch the knees of a person, or his chin, was supposed to be equivalent to appropriating his strength, his very vitality.[55] This constraint had to be counterbalanced, however, for a supplicant may, after all, be unworthy. Over and above the supplicant and the one whom he beseeches there must therefore exist a higher jurisdiction. Yet no literary testimony in support of this conclusion has come down to us; every supplication of which we have knowledge is free from adjudication of any kind. The posture of the supplicant is nonetheless revelatory. He is seated on an altar or else (as in Euripides) he is *prostrate on the ground.*[56] Might the mysterious power that passes judgment on the supplicant, before it became a personal god, have been the earth itself? In an article that bears rereading, page by page, Gernet draws attention to the fact that the attitude of those who have been sentenced to punishment for various crimes is the same as that of supplicants—as well as that of Theseus and Pirithous in hell.[57] He recalls that the seated position is associated with depictions of the dead, in both rites of mourning and of initiation (the latter representing a rebirth that succeeds a ritual death), and wonders whether it might not have had its origin in a funerary practice. Undoubtedly this is possible. It is also possible, as Gernet himself is inclined to suppose, that the seated position *humbles* the one who has been sentenced.

But I would say, as against this, that the seated position symbolizes his *subjection.* To whom? To the earth. The earth was thought to be capable of exacting the punishment stipulated in execrations, and perhaps in other more inscrutable forms of vengeance as well, the explicit memory of which had been lost. It does seem, however, that it is through contact of the knees and the genital organs that a man gives the earth a power over him. For the moment these remain obscure matters, as I say, which will need to be investigated with caution. Nevertheless a few scattered shafts of light may show the way forward.

A person who leaves a bodily imprint on the ground was thought to leave something of his person there as well—something that another could retrieve and make his own. "Erase all trace of where you have sat down" was therefore a counsel of prudence that, by Aristophanes's time, had become nothing more than an admonition of propriety.[58] So, too, we may presume, an indignant man hurls an object against the ground, in order to make the earth bear witness to the injustice that has been done to him.[59] Certain stones, when one sits on them, were credited with the property of restoring virility. In Arcadia, naked boys seated on stones took part in the banquets of heroes.[60] A power capable of rehabilitating is also capable of destroying, however.

If a man delivers himself to the earth through contact of the knees and genitals with it, it becomes clear why convicts and suppliants should have assumed a seated or prostrate position. The ancient penal system seldom provided for actual executions. Typically the guilty person was placed in a situation in which normally he would have been expected to die. Between him and death, in other words, the sentence left a margin of time and chance just large enough to permit divine intervention. It is in situations of this kind, dire to the point almost of hopelessness, that tragic heroes appeal to one of the elements for help.[61] Was the idea to make punishment more easily borne, in extremis, by the person convicted of a crime by putting him in a position that would allow his vital force to be communicated to the earth? In the ordeal by leaping from a precipice and also in the ordeal by immurement, the earth itself pronounced judgment. When human beings took it upon themselves to judge and to punish, by giving themselves the power to decide the fate of the convicted person, would they have looked to the earth to ratify their sentence? And would the suppliant, who comes into physical contact with the earth at vital points of his body, have had the sense that he too, by virtue of the very attitude that he is made to assume, subjects himself to the will of a mysterious and higher power—that, in imploring the earth to show him mercy, he offers himself up to a sort of divine judgment? Appeal to the elements, in the tragedies, is always colored by a desperate temerity of this kind.

We would be less uninformed with regard to these questions if the ancients (and the moderns as well) had attached to rites of possession at least some of the interest that until now has been shown almost exclusively in agrarian rites. Even in the case of these latter rites we do not know whether or not the symbolic act of taking possession was accompanied by certain gestures of sympathetic magic. Demeter lay with Iasion in a thrice-plowed field and from their union was born Plutus.[62] This is supposed to have been a transcription, as we saw in Chapter 5, of the springtime ritual in which a farmer and his wife, spending a night together on land under their cultivation, stimulated its energies. And so that this union might be fecund and, as a consequence, efficacious in the highest degree, many peoples at the end of winter observed a period of continence during which the vital forces that would be needed to act at the right moment could accumulate to the fullest extent.[63] But could it be that intercourse between man and wife was accompanied by intercourse with the earth? Frazer mentions a Prussian tradition according to which a child is born in a field at harvest time—a fiction needed to ensure the success of the following year's harvest. In the archaic conception, would he have been born of the field itself? The horse that was fathered by Poseidon is sometimes said to have had Demeter Erinyes for a mother,[64] sometimes the earth, Gaia.[65]

Here I must pause to say a few words about beings issued from the earth following its insemination by a god. Legends of this type are likely to have been numerous, but they almost all disappeared because their crudeness was thought shocking, and so they were purged of their most offensive elements. The classical version, which says that Poseidon brought forth from the earth the first horse by striking a rock with his trident, is merely an expurgation of an archaic story conserved by only two scholiasts.[66] Similarly, Erichthonius was born of the earth and Haephestus, who had failed in his attempt to make love to Athena.[67] And by Zeus, who like Poseidon had shed his semen on the ground while sleeping, was born Agdistis in Galatia.[68]

The legend of Poseidon begetting a stallion is set in Colonus. Erichthonius is said to have built the first buildings on the Acropolis in Athens. How can one not be reminded that there was a cult of Oedipus at Colonus and another on the Acropolis, the origin of which has not in either case been satisfactorily explained?

The stallion born of Poseidon and the earth acquired a political significance very early, at a time when it was unclear who was destined to preside over Attica, Athena with her olive branch or Poseidon, protector of horses. Erichthonius was the first king of Athens. Here one cannot fail to recall that the legend of Oedipus, husband of his own mother, brings together all the themes of royal entitlement in a single tale.

Does this mean that the mysterious installation of an Oedipus cult in Colonus, attested only by the *Phoenician Women*, which is to say sometime around 410, was the result of an association of like ideas around which grew up the theme of a sacred marriage with the earth? One hesitates to go quite this far. And yet association by similarity plays a role in the synthesis of legends that until now has not been examined as carefully as it deserves to be. Oedipus's biography is an outstanding example of what such associations were capable of producing in archaic Greece. Might associations of the same kind have contributed to the spread of cults as well?

To be sure, I do not mean to say that because Poseidon had fertilized the earth in Colonus there was any express intent to associate him with an Oedipus cult. But the memory of it might have been enough for Oedipus's name to be given to a local hero-shrine,[69] to some small anonymous sanctuary whose rite recalled an episode of the Theban legend. Gruppe's penetrating study of Colonus remains an inspiration for further research.[70] Taking into consideration everything that was known about Colonus and its vicinity, he was able to show that the Semen Stone (*Thorikios Petros*) and the Hollow Pear Tree were associated with spells devised for the purpose of strengthening virility. On the one hand, this stone and the pear tree, together with the Hollow Crater and the Stone Tomb, are distinctive features of the strange landscape evoked in *Oedipus at Colonus*.[71] On the other hand, the fecundity of the soil is what guarantees kingly vigor. In the current state of our knowledge we may say that both these things seem to bear the trace of ancient superstitions, but scarcely anything more.

It may be objected that the legend of Poseidon as the sire of the first horse is perhaps not very ancient; that it may come from some equine cult of the god; that the adjective θορίκιος [having to do with sperm], like the name of the deme Θορικός [Thorikos], may be pre-Hellenic and have no connection with either the verb θρᾠσκω [to leap] or with the noun θορός [sperm];[72] that the stallion's birth may have been deduced from a folk etymology of the name of the place; that the birth of Erichthonius was not known before Euripides. Possibly so. But the only things that could be recent here are proper names and the association of legendary themes with one another. Surely the origin of these ideas is ancient. The chthonian birth of the horse was not *invented* in order to explain the name "Semen Stone." We can be sure of this because the two things are never mentioned in the same breath. But under the influence of this name (whether the etymology is true or merely a popular tradition is unimportant for our purposes here), an archaic belief was *remembered*, namely, that a god may directly fertilize the earth and bring forth from it a living being.[73] Similarly, while it is certainly not Euripides who *invented* the story of Erichthonius's birth,[74] he may well have been the first to dare to treat this vulgar fable, and the old popular superstitions that are reflected in it, as a poetical subject.

---

One would like to be able to compare the legend of an incestuous Oedipus with other such fables in order to see what features they have in common. But here we are frustrated at every turn. The story of Telephus, who comes very close to having intercourse with his mother, is known to us from a play that is only partially a copy of *Oedipus the King*. The story of Menephron is known to us through two brief allusions, one by Ovid,[75]

> Dextera Cyllene est, in qua cum matre Menephron
> concubiturus erat, saevarum more ferarum
>
> [To the right is (Mount) Cyllene, where Menephron
> lay with his mother in the manner of wild beasts];

and the other by Hyginus,[76] who names among those whose union violates the laws of nature,

> Menephrus cum Cyllene filia in Arcadia et cum Pliade matre sua
>
> [Menephron, with his daughter Cyllene, in Arcadia, and with his mother Plias],

a line that Robert proposes correcting to read:

> Menephrus cum <Atlantis> filia Pliade matre sua
> [Menephron, with <Atlantis>, whose mother was Plias].

This emendation seems entirely probable since Cyllene is the eponym of Mount Cyllene, in Arcadia, birthplace also of Plias.[77]

Finally, the *Catasterismi* of Eratosthenes relates the story of Arcas, son of Callisto and Zeus. Lycaon tempts Zeus by serving up to him as a meal the entrails of Arcas. Enraged, Zeus overturns the table, hurls thunderbolts at the house, and transforms Lycaon into a wolf while bringing Arcas back to life and having him raised by a goatherd. Once grown up, Arcas comes back to Mount Lykaion and sleeps with his own mother. The Arcadians are on the verge of putting them to death for profaning Zeus's sanctuary when they are rescued by the god himself, who places them in the heavens on account of their kinship to him.[78] This fable appears to be influenced by the one about Telephus, also an Arcadian tale. It teaches us nothing. And we learn still less from the obscure story of the Rhodian sea nymph Halia, who throws herself into the sea after being raped by her sons with Poseidon.[79]

---

The conjectures I have sketched in this chapter are so tenuous that I hesitate to add one more to their number. Nevertheless it may be informative to recall in this connection that Krappe draws attention to medieval legends in which a hero is born of an incestuous union between a brother and a sister.[80] They include Roland, Cúchulainn, Siegfried, Gawain, and Pope Gregory, among others. In their election as infants one detects the trace of an ancient memory of the marriage of the *cosmocrator* (ruler of the cosmos), who, in order to beget children worthy of succeeding to his throne, can have sexual relations only with his own sister.

Naturally I do not suppose that Oedipus, who married his mother, can be compared in this respect with Siegfried, the offspring of a brother and sister. But how can we fail to be struck by the link in the two cases between incest and conquest? Note that the link is not the same in the two cases: the election of sons issued from a consanguineous union was unknown in Greece; medieval Europe probably inherited it from the East and the royal custom in some lands of marriage between a brother and sister. As for the case of Oedipus, who comes to power by marrying his mother, it is unique in Greek legend, but not in semihistorical traditions having to do with tyrants. The symbolism of these traditions, still perfectly clear at the beginning of the Christian era, rests on archaic practices whose exact nature remains hidden to us, but that we can form some idea of from rites of supplication and from fables telling of the birth of the first horse, of Agdistis, and of Erichthonius. Probably it is this symbolism that associates Oedipus as his mother's husband with Colonus as the homeland of the first horse and with Erichthonius's legacy, the Acropolis. The association seems later to have been reinforced by some historical event in the course of which Oedipus proved himself to be the protector of the Athenians against his own compatriots, thus fulfilling in advance the promise he makes to Theseus in *Oedipus at Colonus*.[81] The scholiast on Aristides who mentions the event plainly no longer knew when it occurred. Robert suggests the expedition of Sparta and its allies led by Cleomenes in 506, in which Oedipus was seen to appear to the Athenians as Echetlos was to do a few years later at Marathon.[82] This is to forget that visions come only to people who expect them. If Oedipus was seen to appear in Attica, it is because he had already been naturalized there.

---

In this connection, finally, allow me to quote a curious epigram, which must be earlier than the fourth century since it figures on two vases of this period depicting Oedipus's tomb:

νότῳ μολάχην τε καὶ ἀσφόδολον πολύριζον,[83]
κόλπῳ δ᾽ Οἰδιπόδαν Λαίο[υ] υἱὸν ἔχω.

[I carry on my back mallow and asphodel with its many roots;
I hold in my breast Oedipus son of Laius.]

On account of the forms μολάχη (in Attic Greek μαλάχη) and ἀσφόδολος (in Attic ἀσφόδελος), and also on account of the fact that these two words are encountered in a Boeotian proverb quoted by Hesiod,[84] Robert thinks that the distich is Boeotian in origin and that it reproduces an inscription engraved on the tomb of Oedipus at Eteonos. This is unlikely, for the Boeotian form causes the isopsephism[85] that obtains in the Attic form to disappear:

μαλαχη ασφοδελος = 54 + 108 = 162.
λαιου οιδιπους = 56 + 106 = 162.

And as for Oedipus's presumptive tomb, which Robert supposes to be prior to the legend, it is almost certainly, I believe, a late development. However this may be, these lines seem clearly to be an allusion to the *dream of the tyrant*, who, after possessing his mother, is possessed in his turn and now reposes in her breast.[86]

# Endings

---

I t is easy to distinguish, in the adventures of Oedipus, between that which is a romantic invention and that which has an old religious foundation. But an analogous distinction is almost impossible to make with regard to his death and that of Jocasta.

---

Jocasta hangs herself. This suicide may be an etiological legend made to explain a very widespread myth involving girls who were hung in the trees on rope swings in order to ensure a new season of abundant vegetation.[1] If so, Jocasta might primitively have been an agrarian goddess, like Helen, Ariadne, Erigone, and Charila. But then it would be necessary to demonstrate the existence of a cult that would confirm our hypothesis, for after all not all women who hang themselves are agrarian goddesses. The death of Jocasta may be a poetical invention having no religious significance.

---

Oedipus is blind, not in Homer or Hesiod, but to begin with, it would appear, in the poets of the epic cycle. And in *Oedipus the King* he is represented as blinding himself. Now, it is impossible to read this play without having the impression that the mutilation was invented by Sophocles. Coming back on stage, Oedipus cries: ἔπαισε δ᾽ αὐτόχειρ νιν οὔτις ἀλλ᾽ ἐγὼ τλάμων [The hand that struck me was none other than my own][2]—which seems plainly to signal a departure from some other version where he was blinded by another person. One then is reminded of the scholium on line 61 of *Phoenician Women*, which says that in the *Oedipus* of Euripides the "son of Polybus" was blinded by Laius's servants.[3] Here the periphrasis employed in referring to Oedipus appears to indicate that the blinding preceded the moment of recognition, rather than coming after it; if so, it points to a mythopoeia completely different from the one that has come down to us. Another scholium, on line 26 of *Phoenician Women*, reports two more versions of the blinding, each one very different again from the one in *Oedipus the King*: "Others relate that Polybus blinded him after having heard an oracle foretelling that Oedipus would kill his father. Others, that it was his mother who blinded him."[4] It is impossible to know when these more or less credible accounts were first devised. Most critics consider them to be late inventions due to mythographers and writers of adventure tales. This seems probable, though not certain. But even if here we are dealing with a literature of recent composition and inferior quality, the number of variants leads one to suppose that the theme of *voluntary self-mutilation* was not as firmly established, in the classical version of the legend, as the ones that we studied in the previous chapters.

It also needs to be kept in mind that the episode of voluntary self-mutilation, in the Oedipus legend, is absolutely unique in Greek tragedy and epic. One therefore wonders whether it would not simplify matters if mutilation were to be dissociated from blindness.

1. *Mutilation.* In Sophocles's play it is a messenger who reports that Oedipus has put out his own eyes and says why he has done so: "Tearing the gold pins from [Jocasta's] robe, he pierced his eyeballs with them, crying out . . . that [his eyes] should never more see his terrible sufferings nor his dreadful deeds, that henceforth they will see in darkness those whom they should never have seen and fail to recognize those whom he wishes no longer to know."[5] Oedipus's first wish, in other words, is never again to see his own children. A little later the chorus objects that he would be better off dead than to live as a blind man. He justifies his resolve in a memorable passage:

I do not know with what eyes I could have looked upon my father when I met him in Hades, nor upon my wretched mother, for I am guilty of crimes against them both that I could never atone for by hanging myself. And could the sight of my children have gladdened me, begotten as they were? Not with my eyes, never. The city, its walls, the statues of the gods, the temples—from all these things I cut myself off when, having reigned at Thebes in incomparable glory, I commanded all [its people] to drive out the impious one, the one whom the gods had shown to be impure and born of the race of Laius.[6]

We may be quite certain that no one had given so detailed and so explicit a justification before Sophocles. The tragic poets insisted on the outcome of events only to emphasize what they themselves had invented. I am myself inclined to suppose that the whole theme of voluntary self-mutilation is due to Sophocles. But how then are we to explain the fact that the scholiasts and Aristotle all pass over such a remarkable innovation in silence?

If the theme predates Sophocles, the poets who had treated it before him must somehow have tried to justify the hero's desperate act, either clumsily or inadequately. If not, I find it difficult to explain the lines I have just quoted, in which the reasons for living henceforth in darkness are set forth at length and with intense feeling. It would appear that the legend developed in the following manner:

1. Oedipus reigns without losing his sight (Homer, Hesiod);
2. Oedipus dies a blind man (Aeschylus);
3. Oedipus voluntarily blinds himself (Sophocles, or an immediate predecessor of whom we know nothing);
4. The idea of voluntary self-mutilation does not come to be lastingly established, with the result that in the later mythopoeia the prior state of affairs (2) reasserts itself: Oedipus is blinded by another's hand. So long as we do not know if Euripides's *Oedipus* is older or more recent than the one by Sophocles, it is impossible for us to situate it chronologically in this sequence.

2. *Blindness.* Let us suppose that the archaic legend had known, not of Oedipus blinding himself, but of a blind Oedipus. That Homer ignored the

legend proves nothing; after all, he makes Phoenix Achilles's tutor, not Chiron. But when one tries to discover why Oedipus should have been blind, no answer is to be found.

Blindness is often a punishment, Reinach says, for the violation of a taboo concerning what lawfully may be seen or looked at. I suspect that it must additionally in certain cases have had a positive value, which is to say that it signified, not a privation, but a special aptitude. Nevertheless I do not see that the stories of two legendarily famous blind men, Homer and Tiresias, have anything in common. In a few late accounts,[7] adulterers were punished by being blinded, but it may be doubted whether these tales explain the Theban legend. Could they have derived from it at some earlier date? One thinks too of Hippias, who dreamed that he had slept with his mother and died blind; but after all, the tyrant might actually have lost his sight. Perhaps comparativists will be able to propose some more satisfactory hypothesis concerning the fabulous meaning of blindness. Greek examples are few and teach us nothing.

In the particular case of Oedipus, Mr. Severyns has proposed a beguiling explanation. The theme of blindness, he suggests, entered into legend with the word πηρός [infirm], which was applied to heroes. It frequently occurs in the expression πηρὸς τὴν ὄψιν, where it has the meaning "blind" [literally, weak in respect of sight]. This requires us to accept that at some point the specific sense came to be substituted for the general sense. I must confess, however, that I find no ancient example of πηρός alone, nor of any verb derived from it, in the particular sense of "blind."

If, in an archaic form of the legend, Oedipus had been said to be πηρός, what sort of infirmity would he have suffered from? Perhaps lameness, the infirmity that made him a malefic infant, destined to be exposed—the same infirmity that is translated by the name of his grandfather, Labdacus, and whose trace was to be preserved by the story of his wounded feet.

But πηρός often meant "impotent." By sleeping with his mother, might Oedipus have incurred the punishment that Anchises dreaded after the one night he spent in the arms of Aphrodite? The analogy is tempting, and all the more as Anchises, according to some versions, was either one-eyed or blind.

We have every reason to want to pose such questions, but in the present state of our knowledge no answer to them can be given. Perhaps one day we will learn of other legends that will make it possible to resolve problems that for the moment are intractable. In the meantime we will be well advised to set aside this line of inquiry.

---

Oedipus curses his sons. We do not know why. The scholiast on line 1375 of *Oedipus at Colonus* speaks of a few verses from the *Thebaid* relating that Oedipus's sons neglected to send their father the shoulder of an animal they had sacrificed, presenting him instead with the haunch. Once the old king noticed this,[8] he threw the piece to the ground, excoriated his sons for insulting him, and implored the king of the gods, Zeus, and all the other immortals to cause his sons to die, each by the other's hand. But what intent to insult could there have been in sending their father the better piece? Aeschylus seems therefore to have followed the *Thebaid* in treating the malediction uttered by Oedipus as a fit of madness.[9]

Again according to the *Thebaid*,[10] a blind and dethroned Oedipus calls down awful curses on sons because Polyneices offered him wine in a precious cup that had belonged to Laius, set upon a golden table that had belonged to Cadmus. Why Eteocles was thought also to be deserving of punishment we do not know. Still harder to understand is what could have been thought to be offensive about this act, unless some ancient tale had spoken of "enchanted" cups that wobble when the hand holding them is unworthy, spilling the wine. Might it be that the object referred to by the *Thebaid* imposed on the dispossessed king a *test* that he would have regarded as an affront? However this may be, it is difficult to account for his anger by reference to a suddenly reawakened memory. The tragedians, owing to their habitual tendency to give legends an abstract and moral character, discarded this garbled rationale, handed down to them from epic, and replaced it with Oedipus's expulsion from the royal house.

---

The story of the enemy brothers, Polyneices and Eteocles, probably contains no archaic element. Nevertheless it is instructive in studying the proliferation of legendary themes. Here again the guiding thread is conflict between generations. Oedipus killed his father; his own sons treat him with disrespect. The Erinyes of Laius and of Jocasta hounded the patricide; Oedipus places a curse on his sons. Legends develop through the accretion of similar motifs. There is nothing at all complicated about the association of ideas that inspires them. But only a great poet can succeed in varying episodes so artfully that listeners forget that each one is merely a variant of the one preceding. The poet who was the first to cast the Oedipus legend in the form of six synonymous but thematically distinct episodes, an author possessed of an unerring instinct with regard to the rules governing fabulous sequences, composed a striking and diversified whole. At a very early time people probably were captivated by what was most novel about it, namely, the identical weight assigned to its component parts. Later the impression of variety must have become predominant, for the general and demonstrative significance of the individual episodes themselves gradually faded in people's minds as their attention came to be concentrated on Oedipus himself, whose personal character little by little emerged from the sequence of events.

By contrast with the work of the poets, there is only arbitrariness and incoherence in the strange variations with which paradoxographers disfigured the Theban legend. From this one sees wonderfully well how the poets, who invented little or nothing, went about their work. They took a well-known theme and embellished it, then relocated it. Scholiasts, on the other hand, report a great number of alternative versions.[11] To take only the case of Oedipus, in addition to the variants we considered earlier, four themes exhibit further differences of opinion:

- PATRICIDE: "Some say that Oedipus also killed his mother."
- PEDERASTY: "Some say that Laius was killed by Oedipus because they both were enamored of Chrysippus."
- EXPOSURE: "Lysimachus says that Oedipus, having learned from an oracle that his sons would kill each other, exposed Polyneices; Castor says that he exposed both of them."[12]
- INCEST: "Antigone became suspect in the eyes of Eteocles on account of her love for Polyneices. The king accused her of having slept with his brother."[13]

# Myths and Memory

ὁ μῦθος δηλοῖ ὅτι . . . [1]

I t would, of course, be foolhardy to generalize about the prehistory of myths from the study of a single myth, however meticulous it may be. And yet I do not think I am mistaken in considering the Theban legend to be a special case, on account of the number and the clarity of its elements, on account of their vast area of dispersion, and on account, finally, of the psychological strata on which they rest. In the preceding pages we have examined several dozen themes, drawn from one or two hundred legends displaying variations of such a kind that two forms seldom appear to be in any way equivalent or synonymous. A fabulous cell, which is to say a mythic theme in the sense that I gave this term in Chapter 5, by analogy with a biological cell, never develops in isolation, and it is necessary, when one wishes to interpret it, to take into consideration its narrative context, that is, the presence of neighboring cells that modify its tone and nuance.

Furthermore, these cells are themselves neither simple nor primary realities. Each of them has several origins that can be discovered on the most cursory inspection. These sources are sometimes rather different from one another, or so it would appear at first glance. The combat with a monster, for example, arose from both the oppressing nightmare (whether nocturnal or noonday) and the fear of tormented souls. If these things in combination were able to form a unique theme, it is because a third kind of superstition saw the figures that populated dreams as ghosts.[2] Sometimes the three elements are almost perfectly exactly superimposed on one another. Beneath the theme of marriage to a princess two known rites may be distinguished, nuptial trials and springtime sacred marriages; and, beneath these rites themselves, simpler beliefs in the immediate efficacy of the race and of circumambulation. But marriage has a larger and richer significance. Moreover, it seldom appears alone, nearly always being accompanied by the theme of generational conflict. The associations of ideas that fix legendary sequences in people's minds are no less revelatory than the study of themes proper.

All those who, up to the present day, have studied the genesis of mythic tales have neglected one crucial aspect, it seems to me. They consider legendary accounts to be the *transposition of a mysterious reality*—a definition that would be accepted equally by scholars who stress the primacy of ancient ritual and by those who assert the preeminence of sun myths. Both see the creation of legends as a purely disinterested activity. Ritualists characterize it as essentially backward-looking and intended to *explain* relics of life in archaic times that have become disassociated from their religious context. It may well be, of course, that some legendary themes are purely etiological, invented to account for liturgies that had fallen into decay. All the stories that come from agrarian festivals do indeed seem to have this character and, as a consequence, a purely intellectual purpose. But it may be that we have this impression simply because such stories have come down to us in mutilated form, deprived of the conclusion that formerly had made their true meaning clear. I believe that most myths, when they first became established, were meant to *persuade*, which is to say that they were forward-looking and concerned solely with the assertion of will by some part of a community, either a dominant group or an insurgent faction. If we fail to appreciate the moralizing intentions of a tale such as the one of the young pretender who vanquishes the old king, whereas we readily discern the sermonizing element in a recent tale such as that of Griselda,[3] it is simply because the social and religious context of the Griselda story is familiar to us and not the one in which succession by murder was customary. The tale of the patricide teaches a moral, namely, that the young must replace the old; but it is a moral that had already been outmoded for centuries when the episodes of the Theban legend were still widely known in Greece. It is hardly surprising, then, that the poets of the historical period should have treated it as a palimpsest and have written over it a new lesson, the only one they knew, namely, that patricide is a crime that must be atoned for. But the old lesson, entirely different, can still be deciphered beneath the erasures.

This is why all legendary themes that have their origin in rites of initiation or rites of succession by murder are *hostile to the family*. A father persecutes his daughter, exposes his grandson. A young man kills his grandfather. A god's lover is tormented by her wicked uncle. A father does battle with his son or his daughter's suitors. All this seems quite strange to us today. But beneath these recurrent themes it is still possible to make out traces of a literature that was used by the initiators of novices to demonstrate the superiority of a system based on age cohorts over one based on family units. This must have been a relatively late literature (since it supposes the existence of a family structure that threatened the traditional class structure), but still much older than that of the poets, who did their best to reconcile the old legends with the new family morality by showing fathers to be persecutors owing to the fault of an oracle and sons to be murderers through inadvertence. The primitive text and what was written over it are clearly distinguishable. Stories of children who have been butchered may betray either a bias in favor of initiations (as in the case of Pelops, who is pieced back together by the gods and grows up to be an exceptionally handsome youth) or against them (as in the case of Medea's children, murdered by their mother's hand with no compensatory benefit of divine resuscitation). Once each of these attitudes had become unintelligible, both came to be reunited in the same legend (as again in the case of Medea, who rejuvenates Aeson and kills Pelias). In legends such as these, a single magical power is at work.

Here we encounter one of the essential reasons for the transformation of myths. A myth is modified because its original motivation is no longer understood and comes to be replaced by a new one. The myth's new purpose acts in turn upon the manner of its telling and reshapes it. Thus the Theban legend, hostile to the family in its primitive form, was subsequently reworked to accommodate a familial morality. Aeschylus's Oedipus ceased to be the conqueror that he was for Homer and Hesiod and was made instead into a criminal; indeed, so acutely is Oedipus aware of his crime in Aeschylus that he punishes himself, which he could do only by stripping himself of the rewards of his conquest. This shift in ethical point of view turns the denouement inside out, so that the story concludes with an abdication—the most typical ending in all the legends of conquerors.

The pedagogic character of myths—as pronounced in the oldest ones as in the most recent ones—went unrecognized by a tradition of exegesis that connected their origins with efficient causes, as though works of the mind had no final causes. It is curious to note that popular semantics, infinitely more clear-sighted, provides us here with a hint that it would have been wise to pay greater attention to. A myth, in common parlance today, is a way of looking at the world that transcends experience (or that at least does not look to it for guidance), a rational exercise in imagination aimed at dictating a particular form of behavior and modifying the course of future events.[4] Finality—the sense of an ultimate purpose that is essential to social myths— had by no means been eliminated from religious myths among the Greeks; to the contrary, there is every reason to believe that formerly it played a far greater role in educating the young than we can imagine today.

This leads me to propose the following definition: *A religious myth is an attempt to explain a reality that is felt to be mysterious and that is often, though not always, a rite that has begun to decay. The explanation it gives has the effect of transforming an emotion that is common to all who accept the truth of the myth into a singular event, a personal experience. This experience, once it has been undergone and internalized as an example to be followed, is colored by an* affectus *from which arises a dynamism capable of acting on all the members of the group that accepts the myth.*[5]

---

It is impossible to consider the origin and the transmission of myths without posing questions concerning the persistence and the strength of memories in the societies within which these stories were first elaborated. When van Gennep says that "legends tenaciously preserve the memory of outmoded institutions,"[6] he fails to notice that he has merely stated the conclusion of a circular argument. For it must not be forgotten that he explains legends in terms of an abiding recollection of customs that are no longer observed. If a son kills his father, this is because, in the prehistory of the peoples who transmitted this tale, kinship was traced only through the maternal line and so, as a result, a boy could have grown up far from his father and not have known him. On the same ground, Frazer detects a memory of ancient uterine inheritance in the fabulous history of the kings of Rome, in which a king was succeeded by his son-in-law.[7]

Let us try to make this explanation a bit more precise. We must accept either that at a given moment, in a society that still practiced maternal descent, stories were imagined in which such descent played a role and which were preserved intact after the institution of a male regime; or that, in a society that no longer practiced maternal descent, this aspect of the past was remembered and that it was incorporated in a new account.

The first hypothesis is by no means inconceivable. But one may wonder whether it ever had any basis in historical fact. Archaic myths are brief, schematic accounts devoid of all social context. Once the framework of a legendary complex had been established, the theme of maternal descent was inevitably its most unstable element. We see this clearly in the story of the exposed infant. It derives from initiation ceremonies in which an *adolescent* subject to the rule of a *master* was *tested*. The social context having changed, and the family system having now replaced the old class system, this new framework of social relations altered in turn the framework of the myth, so that henceforth a *newborn* was subject to the rule of his *grandfather*, who *persecutes* him for reasons of bourgeois morality or else under the influence of an oracle. Oracles and reprobation of bastards were obviously late inventions foreign to the primitive nucleus, which for its part had remained intact; so obviously were they late inventions, in fact, that one is tempted to stand van Gennep's postulate on its head and say that legends, in the course of their development, far from tenaciously preserving the memory of outmoded institutions, constantly modernize themselves by reconciling in one way or another the events they relate with the state of society at the time of their latest recounting.

As for the claim that the social group within which a myth is created deliberately archaizes and composes a legendary account by reworking customs that have fallen into disuse, this conjecture is contradicted by everything we know about the shortness and the fragility of memory in primitive societies. Halbwachs has persuasively shown that individual memory, even in civilized societies, is fortified and prolonged by collective memory.[8]

Once a social framework has been shattered, memories no longer have any foundation and rapidly subside. A discontinuity in social conditions is also accompanied by a discontinuity in the memories of the group as a whole. And while customs gradually change, the past is quickly forgotten, and all the more as no one can any longer recall the course of events up to that point, much less recall the point at which they began.[9]

Is this to say that van Genneps's proposition is wholly mistaken? What I have tried to demonstrate in this book is that many customs are incorporated in legends. But what legends record is never a *memory* pure and simple; it is always a *transposition* in which the underlying ancient state of affairs is often decipherable only on a second reading.

In order to appreciate the difference between these two points of view, mine and van Gennep's, let me insist once more on the pedagogic character of every legendary creation. If, at a given moment, someone went to the trouble of drawing attention to a custom, this was in no way to register the memory of the custom before it disappeared, but to prevent it from disappearing. A myth is a story that reduces a mysterious reality, generally a rite, to a specific experience. This experience leads to either a favorable or an unfavorable conclusion. Myths—at least in their nascent state—have a certain tendency, for they were imagined solely in order to persuade someone to do something. This is readily seen in relation to myths that transcribe rites and whose earliest morals, notably in the case of the Theban legend, came to be more or less the following:

- It is prudent to expose abnormal infants; but, if they survive, they must be treated with respect, for they have been elected by the gods.
- A young chief must be able to run swiftly and be skilled in fighting in order to vanquish the old king.
- He who is learned and courageous will be able to choose the most beautiful woman as his wife and will command the obedience of all his subjects.

Even myths that transcribe beliefs were invented for the purpose of instruction. The young man who becomes king by conquering a monster will be the one who can answer its questions, which is to say one who has well remembered the teaching of his master. This episode is not gratuitous, any more than those that come from rites are.[10]

But this lively desire to persuade could only have developed in connection with customs and rites that were beginning to be disobeyed. It may even happen that a fabulous theme argues on behalf of a particular thesis but that the same theme, with a different ending, argues on behalf of the opposite thesis. The primitive story of Oedipus tells of a young hero who defeats an old king, and all the Greek variants of this tale have the same conclusion; the story of Sohrab and Rustem, by contrast, tells of an old king who kills his young rival in the end. The story of Pelops, who is slaughtered and then brought back to life, takes a favorable view of initiations, with their rites of simulated death; the story of Medea's children is hostile to them. The vehemence with which the competing claims of these tales were pressed makes it reasonable to assume that there were sharp disputes about certain liturgies, which, though they still had some supporters, now found themselves faced with more or less numerous adversaries whose arguments were found to be more or less persuasive by a majority of the community.

All of this justifies us in saying that ancient customs were indeed incorporated in myths, but in a very different sense than the one intended by van Gennep. They did not find their way into myths by chance, as though they accidentally formed a background against which the storyteller set his tale without giving any thought to it. Instead, ancient customs were defended in myths; if they had not been defended, they would have fallen into oblivion. For the original authors of myths were not writers of romances who situated an action within a certain framework, nor were they poets who gratuitously reconstructed a past that was on the verge of disappearing; they were elders and priests who had held power in a much earlier time, champions of contested traditions of which they were also the guardians—and very interested guardians at that.[11]

Considering the life of primitive societies in its broadest sense, the only things that have survived (apart from a few utensils, constructions, and drawings) are tales invented either by elders and priests anxious to preserve ancestral privileges or by their adversaries. Although people had relatively short memories, being illiterate and ignorant of any very distant past, still they remembered these tales: each generation handed them down to the next. The ritual practices whose precept needed to be inculcated and obeyed had sometimes disappeared long before; where they persisted, their meaning had changed in the interval. In either case, the fables that had been composed to defend them continued to be told and retold.

Cut off from the lesson it originally taught and having meanwhile become gratuitous, a fable of this sort was nonetheless free to embark on a new career. At its heart was a name—the name of the mythic figure who, in his earliest incarnation, had been held up as an example of what it was necessary to do or not to do. Once brought into existence, this figure was bound to require a biography ever more rich in detail and achievement. Having begun life as a deed, and then as a series of deeds, eventually he became a person, and finally a character. Primitively independent episodes were linked together with one another in accordance with rules of combination applied in ways that we do not yet fully understand. In the Theban legend, the principle that associates these episodes is synonymy, which is to say identity or equivalence of meaning and implication; probably it played no less great a role in the formation of other legendary complexes. Myths subsequently nourished the nascent art of poetry as well as the study of human psychology, then also in its infancy; at the same time they began to be criticized in the name of a morality quite different from the one they were responsible for protecting at the moment of their invention. And so it came to pass that they acquired once more an educational purpose, only now in a new context.

---

The explanation that I am proposing has until now made no room for the subconscious tendencies that psychoanalysts see as the very source of mythopoetic activity. Yet only one myth is connected by Freud with the repressed sentiments that be believes rule the human heart: the Oedipus legend. In order to accept Freud's thesis in this particular case one would have to be sure, to begin with, that young boys were as jealous of their fathers and as enamored of their mothers as he supposes. One has only to read Freud with a modicum of care to see that his generalizations rest on a very small number of observations. It is well known, for example, that in order to explain totemism he takes it for granted that the child transfers to an animal the ambivalent feeling, compounded of admiration and hatred, that his father inspired in him. Yet he defines the infantile zoophobia resulting from such a transfer on the basis of only *two* observations, neither of which he has made himself.[12] Everything he asserts with regard to Oedipus must therefore be considered with great circumspection.

Nevertheless it is certain that, if a story pleases, this is because it gives expression to some profound tendency of human psychology. Fundamental motivations of this sort surely played some role in causing myths to become established in people's minds, if not also when they were first elaborated. Here again a fuller explanation is needed.

No one would dream of denying the reality of father-son rivalry. It has its source, I believe, much more in a will to power than in sexual desire proper, what Freud calls the libido. It is this will that gives all the legends of conflict between an old king and a young pretender a distinctive mood and atmosphere, no matter how the adventure ends. The versions in which the challenger emerges triumphant would naturally have won the support of all those whose youthfulness led them to identify emotionally with the conqueror, whereas their elders would have sternly insisted on repeating the versions in which the old king prevails. This suggests the existence of a myth that was etiological to begin with, invented to justify a custom that was beginning to be an object of dispute, and that then gave rise to two tellings that differed only in respect of their endings. One was endorsed, invigorated, and propagated by the more or less acknowledged, more or less respectable sentiments of a majority of the community. The other was no less actively propagated by a minority of elders who dreaded, and not without reason, the prospect of one day being dispossessed of their heritage by a younger generation. Subconscious tendencies appear to have stimulated proselytism in each case: they began to operate, and to have lasting effect, when it became necessary to spread a myth in order to rescue the memory of a rite from oblivion; just so, it is impossible to see how they could have created the myth itself. They worked in collaboration, not with the fabulist impulse, but with memory.

# The Pisander Scholion and Related Summaries

## A. Scholia on *Phoenician Women* 1760

Pisander Scholion [Codices M A B] (lines 1–34)
Codex Monacensis gr. 560 (lines 35–40)

Ἱστορεῖ Πείσανδρος ὅτι κατὰ χόλον τῆς Ἥρας ἐπέμφθη ἡ
Σφὶγξ τοῖς Θηβαίοις ἀπὸ τῶν ἐσχάτων μερῶν τῆς Αἰθιοπίας,
ὅτι τὸν Λάϊον ἀσεβήσαντα εἰς τὸν παράνομον ἔρωτα τοῦ Χρυσίππου,
ὃν ἥρπασεν ἀπὸ τῆς Πίσης, οὐκ ἐτιμωρήσαντο.

Ἦν δὲ ἡ Σφίγξ, ὥσπερ γράφεται, τὴν οὐρὰν ἔχουσα δρακαίνης,          5
ἀναρπάζουσα δὲ μικροὺς καὶ μεγάλους κατήσθιεν, ἐν οἷς καὶ
Αἵμονα τὸν Κρέοντος παῖδα καὶ Ἵππιον τὸν Εὐρυνόμου τοῦ
τοῖς Κενταύροις μαχεσαμένου. Ἦσαν δὲ Εὐρύνομος καὶ Ἡιονεὺς
υἱοὶ Μάγνητος τοῦ Αἰολίδου καὶ Φυλοδίκης· ὁ μὲν οὖν Ἵππιος
καὶ ξένος ὢν ὑπὸ τῆς Σφιγγὸς ἀνηρέθη, ὁ δὲ Ἡιονεὺς ὑπὸ τοῦ          10
Οἰνομάου, ὃν τρόπον καὶ οἱ ἄλλοι μνηστῆρες.

Πρῶτος δὲ ὁ Λάϊος τὸν ἀθέμιτον ἔρωτα τοῦτον ἔσχεν· ὁ δὲ Χρύσιππος
ὑπὸ αἰσχύνης ἑαυτὸν διεχρήσατο τῷ ξίφει. Τότε μὲν οὖν ὁ Τειρεσίας
ὡς μάντις εἰδὼς ὅτι θεοστυγὴς ἦν ὁ Λάϊος, ἀπέτρεπεν αὐτὸν τῆς

ἐπὶ τὸν Ἀπόλλωνα ὁδοῦ, τῇ δὲ Ἥρᾳ μᾶλλον τῇ γαμοστόλῳ θεᾷ            15
θύειν ἱερά, ὃ δὲ αὐτὸν ἐξεφαύλιζεν. Ἀπελθὼν τοίνυν ἐφονεύθη ἐν
τῇ σχιστῇ ὁδῷ αὐτὸς καὶ ὁ ἡνίοχος αὐτοῦ, ἐπειδὴ ἔτυψε τῇ μάστιγι
τὸν Οἰδίποδα. Κτείνας δὲ αὐτοὺς ἔθαψε παρατίκα σὺν τοῖς ἱματίοις
ἀποσπάσας τὸν ζωστῆρα καὶ τὸ ξίφος τοῦ Λαΐου καὶ φορῶν· τὸ δὲ
ἄρμα ὑποστρέψας ἔδωκε τῷ Πολύβῳ, εἶτα ἔγημε τὴν μητέρα             20
λύσας τὸ αἴνιγμα. Μετὰ ταῦτα θυσίας τινὰς ἐπιτελέσας ἐν τῷ
Κιθαιρῶνι κατήρχετο ἔχων καὶ τὴν Ἰοκάστην ἐν τοῖς ὀχήμασι· καὶ
γινομένων αὐτῶν περὶ τὸν τόπον ἐκεῖνον τῆς σχιστῆς ὁδοῦ, ὑπο-
μνησθεὶς ἐδείκνυε τῇ Ἰοκάστῃ τὸν τόπον καὶ τὸ πρᾶγμα διηγήσατο
καὶ τὸν ζωστῆρα ἔδειξεν. Ἡ δὲ δεινῶς φέρουσα ὅμως ἐσιώπα·        25
ἠγνόει γὰρ υἱὸν ὄντα. Καὶ μετὰ ταῦτα ἦλθέ τις γέρων ἱπποβουκόλος
ἀπὸ Σικυῶνος, ὃς εἶπεν αὐτῷ τὸ πᾶν ὅπως τε αὐτὸν εὖρε καὶ
ἀνείλετο καὶ τῇ Μερόπῃ δέδωκε, καὶ ἅμα τὰ σπάργανα αὐτῷ
ἐδείκνυε καὶ τὰ κέντρα ἀπῄτει τε αὐτὸν τὰ ζωάγρια. Καὶ οὕτως
ἐγνώσθη τὸ ὅλον.                                                   30
   Φασὶ δὲ ὅτι πετὰ τὸν θάνατον τῆς Ἰοκάστης καὶ τὴν αὐτοῦ
τύφλωσιν ἔγημεν Εὐρυγάνην παρθένον, ἐξ ἧς αὐτῷ γεγόνασι
οἱ τέσσαρες παῖδες.
Ταῦτά φησι Πείσανδρος.
Οἱ τὴν Οἰδιποδίαν γράφοντες [οὐδεὶς οὕτω φησὶ περὶ τῆς          35
Σφιγγός]· Ἀλλ ἔτι κάλλιστόν τε καὶ ἱμεροέστατον ἄλλων /
παῖδα φίλον Κρείοντος ἀμύμονος Αἵμονα δῖον. Καὶ φασιν ὅτι οὐκ
ἦν θηρίον, ὡς οἱ πολλοὶ νομίζουσιν, ἀλλὰ χρησμολόγος δύσγνωστα
τοῖς Θηβαίοις λέγουσα καὶ πολλοὺς αὐτῶν ἀπώλλυεν ἐναντίως τοῖς
χρησμοῖς χρωμένους.                                               40

Pisander relates that, owing to Hera's wrath, the Sphinx was sent to the
Thebans, from the most remote regions of Ethiopia, because they had not
inflicted punishment on Laius, who had given proof of impiety by abandon-
ing himself to a criminal love of Chrysippus, whom he had carried off from
Pisa [in the western Peloponnese].

Now, by tradition, the Sphinx was a monster with the tail of a serpent who
seized and devoured young and old [alike], among them Haemon the son of
Creon and Hippius the son of that Eurynomus who had fought against the

Centaurs. Euronymus and Eionaeus were sons of Magnes, the son of Aeolus and Philodike. Hippius, who was an innkeeper, was put to death by the Sphinx, and Eionaeus by Oenomaus, in the same way as the others as well, the suitors.

It was Laius who first conceived this forbidden passion. Chrysippus, stricken with shame, killed himself with his own sword. Then Tiresias, knowing as a seer that Laius was detested by the gods, sought to turn him away from the road that led to Apollo, and urged him instead to offer a sacrifice to Hera, the goddess of marriage; but Laius would not listen to Tiresias. He therefore went on his way, and was killed on the narrow road [or: at a crossroads], together with his charioteer, after he had struck Oedipus with his whip. After having killed them, [Oedipus] buried them with their cloaks, but he took from Laius his belt[1] and his sword and put them on. He turned the chariot around and went back to give it to Polybus. Next, having solved the [Sphinx's] riddle, he married his mother. After this he made preparations to go to offer sacrifices on [Mount] Cithaeron, accompanied by Jocasta, who rode with him in his chariot: when they came to this famous place, the crossroads, he remembered it, pointed out the place to Jocasta and showed her the belt. Though greatly distressed she yet said nothing, for she did not know that he was her son. After that there came from Sicyon an old herdsman who told him the entire story, how he had discovered him and rescued him and given him to Merope, and at the same time he showed [Oedipus] his swaddling clothes and clasps, and finally laid claim to a reward for his life. It is thus that everything came to be known.

It is said that, after the death of Jocasta and after he had blinded himself, he married a young girl, Euryganea, who bore him four children.

This is what Pisander says.

According to the authors of the *Oedipodea* [no one <else> speaks thus of the Sphinx]: "But still the handsomest and the most desirable / Is the beloved son of blameless Creon, the noble Haemon." And it is said that this one was not a monster, as most people suppose, but a soothsayer who set riddles for the Thebans and put many of them to death when they misinterpreted her prophecies.

## B. Mythographic summary placed at the head
## of *Phoenician Women*

Codex Laurentianus gr. 32.33

Λάϊος ἀπὸ Θηβῶν παραγενόμενος κατὰ τὴν ὁδὸν ἐθεάσατο Χρύ-
σιππον τὸν υἱόν τοῦ Πέλοπος· τούτου ἐρασθεὶς ἠξίου αὐτὸν παρα-
γενέσθαι εἰς Θήβας σὺν αὐτῷ· τοῦ δε μὴ τοῦτο ποιῆσαι βουληθέντος
ἥρπασεν ὁ Λάϊος λάθρα τοῦ ἑαυτοῦ πατρός· ἐπὶ πολὺ δε αὐτοῦ
θρηνοῦντος διὰ τὴν τοῦ παιδὸς ἀπώλειαν ὕστερον ἔμαθε καὶ μαθὼν              5
κατηράσατο τῷ αὐτὸν ἀνελόντι μὴ παιδοποιῆσαι, εἰ δε τοῦτο γένη-
ται, ὑπὸ τοῦ τικτομένου ἀναιρεθῆναι.

Laius, coming back from Thebes, came across Chrysippus, the son of Pelops.
Filled with passion for him, [Laius] tried to persuade him to come to The-
bes with him. But as [Chrysippus] refused, Laius carried him off, without
his father's knowledge. [Pelops], having long lamented the loss of his son,
learned later what had happened and laid a curse on the abductor [or: the
murderer of his son], so that he would not have children or, in the event he
were to have any, he would be condemned to be killed by his son.

## C. Argument (or Hypothesis) of *Phoenician Women*,
## due to Aristophanes of Byzantium

Codex Vaticanus gr. 1345

Ἐπιστρατεία Πολυνείκους μετὰ τῶν Ἀργείων ἐπὶ Θήβας καὶ
ἀπώλεια τῶν ἀδελφῶν Πολυνείκους καὶ Ἐτεοκλέους καὶ θάνατος
Ἰοκάστης. Ἡ μυθοποιία κεῖται παρ' Αἰσχύλῳ ἐν Ἑπτὰ ἐπὶ Θήβας
πλὴν τῆς Ἰοκάστης. † ... ἐπὶ Ναυσιχράτους ἄρχοντος ... δεύτερος
Εὐριπίδης ... καθῆκε διδασκαλίαν περὶ τούτου· καὶ γὰρ ταῦτα ὁ              5
Οἰνόμαος καὶ Χρύσιππος καὶ ... σώζεται †. ὁ χορὸς συνέστηκεν ἐκ
Φοινισσῶν γυναικῶν· προλογίζει δε Ἰοκάστη.

Polynices's expedition with the Argives against Thebes, the loss of the two brothers Polynices and Eteocles, and the death of Jocasta. The subject of this play is found in Aeschylus in *Seven against Thebes*, with the exception of the character of Jocasta. † . . . under the archontate of Nausicrates . . . second rank: Euripides . . . composed a play on this subject. In fact, these events, Oenomaus, Chrysippus and . . . has been preserved [more probably: <these plays> have not been preserved]. † . . . The chorus is composed of women from Phoenicia [or: Phoenician women]; it is Jocasta who recites the prologue.

# Legends and Cults
# of Twin Children

A
ll Greek legends concerning divine twins share this curious characteristic: once they are grown, the children come to the aid of their mother. Antiope, Tyro, Melanippe, and Hysipyle are the outstanding examples of a woman who is rescued from danger by her sons (though Hysipyle's sons were fathered by a mere hero, Jason, not by a god). This willingness to be of assistance at a moment of urgent need is peculiar to twins; it is foreign to Perseus, Telephus, Oedipus, and other only sons. Nevertheless I believe that it must be taken into account if we are to explain the curious legend of Cleobis and Biton. No doubt it must also be studied together with pictorial and sculptural representations of two male deities ranged on either side of a female deity, a catalog of which has been drawn up by F. Chapouthier.[1] It is probable that a very ancient cult associated two horseman *daimones* with a female deity. The ritual triad survived at Samothrace, and elsewhere with the cult of the Dioscuri, Castor and Polydeuces, who rescued their sister, Helen. *Legends* of helpful twins, which appear in several tragedies of the late fifth century, and *monuments*, none of which is earlier than the third century, nonetheless form two independent bodies of evidence. For the central figure of the monuments is not a mortal woman, but an agrarian or celestial goddess, accompanied and sometimes replaced by one simple attribute, a horn of plenty, an ear of wheat,

a star or a crescent moon. In a legend such as that of Antiope or Tyro, however, we can distinguish three distinct elements: the theme of exposed infants; the theme of twins helping a woman; and, finally, superstitions relating to twins.

In almost all countries of the ancient world, twin births were considered sometimes to be beneficent, sometimes malefic. The religious *affectus* surrounding them is never negligible. This is why fundamentally identical beliefs were able to lead to quite opposite mythic outcomes, the divinization of the dioscuric pair, on the one hand, and, on the other, the expulsion of newborn twins. Chapouthier mentions the research of Rendel Harris on popular beliefs about twins,[2] but he has no interest in comparing the triadic cult with legends of divine twins who were exposed and later, as adults, save their mother. I believe, however, that the cult and the legends have a common denominator, namely, the influence of twin births on the fertility of the soil. This effect appears still more clearly in the Phocian rite reported by Pausanias, who says that men from Tithorea went to remove earth from the tomb of Amphion and Zethus at Thebes and brought it home to lay on the tomb of the twins' mother, Antiope, in order to assure themselves of a fine harvest.[3] Here we are very probably dealing with a rite that was much more archaic than the legend and that belatedly was associated with it, but superstitions concerning twin births surely helped to fix the theme in the popular mind.

Newborn twins seem also to have been the object in Greece of a cult about which, unfortunately, we are almost wholly ignorant. It is known solely through a few monuments published and commented on in 1885 by F. Marx.[4] These are terra-cotta statuettes found at Cyzicus, Thebes, and Olympia that represent two infants, naked or swaddled, bareheaded or wearing a *pilos*.[5] Pausanias came across images of this kind at Paphnus, Brasiae, Amphissa in Locris, and Amphissa in Phocis,[6] which he took to be representations of the Dioscuri and the Cabiri. There can be no doubt that the artisans who molded these figurines had the Dioscuri in mind when they chose to show the newborns wearing the *pilos*; but these enigmatic infants certainly belong to a much more ancient religious layer than the horseman gods themselves. For want of knowing any more than this, however, we are obliged to set aside various pieces of evidence that may one day, owing to the dexterity of scholars better informed than we are, be stitched together in a plausible synthesis.

# Animal Tales in Greece

---

n 1889, August Marx published a slender volume on Greek tales that tell of friendly relations between human beings and animals.[1] He grouped the tales by zoological species: dolphin, eagle, swan, lion, dog, horse, elephant, serpent. The fundamental theme of all these accounts, he maintained, is the gratitude of an animal for a kindness that it then reciprocates. This thesis is contradicted by at least half of the tales he cites, however, for in them the animal acts, not out of gratitude, but out of simple affection for a human being. Marx also neglected to take into consideration fables in which a newborn is either saved by animals or honored by them (Zeus and Plato by bees, Midas by ants, and so on),[2] probably because, in all these cases, the animal acts without any apparent reason, since no gratitude can possibly be felt toward a human infant.[3] Furthermore, and unfortunately again, Marx limits the scope of his inquiry by basing it on a preconceived idea. Rather than consider only *grateful* animals, it would have been better to examine all those tales that concern *benevolent* animals.

To see the matter clearly, it will be necessary to put to one side the majority of tales that deal with serpents. Here Marx rightly perceived that the serpent represents someone who is deceased, a mysterious ancestor who must be both feared and revered. If a serpent grants to a few privileged persons the power of understanding the language of animals and of seeing into the future, this is owing to its special acquaintance with the afterlife and its secrets. These accounts constitute a separate category that needs to be studied as a function of older conceptions concerning *souls*. Nevertheless, in certain serpent tales, one does find themes that are common to tales about other animals.

Each of these tales is colored by popular attitudes in ancient Greece toward the various species. Thus the lion was appreciated for its strength and generosity, the dog for its loyalty, the swan and the horse for their superior morality, the dolphin for its tenderness. But these animals have one trait in common, namely, the gift of *recognition*—not, strictly speaking, in the sense of gratitude, but in the sense of discernment, for it is a question, not of an animal being recognized for its own particular virtues, but of recognition by the animal, which is able to tell who is its friend, to designate that person as worthy of particular favor, and, having chosen him, to show him the kindness that is due to him—no less gratuitously, it would appear, than when it saves a newborn abandoned to his fate on a mountainside.

I believe that all such stories, of which the French folktale *Chat botté* [Puss in Boots] is a modern descendant, derive from a very old legendary stock that translates popular beliefs in a tribe's animal protector. In the French version, the cat chooses the youngest son of a miller, makes him first a fictive Marquis of Carabas and then an actual king; but the hero, having been elevated by the cat's special favor, proves to be an ingrate deserving of punishment. P. Saintyves has collected similar versions of this story, where the hero's ingratitude is atoned for by the community, which presents the benevolent animal with a funeral vault.[4] Curiously, the same theme is encountered in the pseudo-Virgilian *Culex* (where a shepherd builds a burial place for the gnat that saved his life),[5] and in the Greek story of Krisamis (where the hero kills an eel, who later, in a dream, asks him for a tomb; Krisamis forgets the eel's request and perishes miserably along with his entire race).[6] Nevertheless we do not possess, in Greek, a true folktale in the modern sense of the term—unless perhaps the *Hymn to Hermes*; all that we know of Hellenic folklore has come down to us in the form of summaries and allusions, stripped of their narrative context by compilers such as Aelian and Pliny, who selectively emphasized those elements that they considered to have a factual basis, excising the most absurd details and admitting only that which seemed to them not to offend common sense. Almost all the stories of animals that have reached us were rationalized in this fashion. In order to make them acceptable, the animal is presented as the beneficiary of an act of kindness who wishes to show its gratitude. The original theme of gratuitous recognition on the part of the animal, far from being a late motif, as Marx supposes,[7] is surely closer to an archaic stock than the wholly moral notion of repaying a benefactor that developed later as a consequence of observations of the higher animals, such as horses and dogs, which are in fact capable of remembering people who treat them well or badly.

Rationalization of another kind may be detected in tales in which a god, assuming the form of an animal, conceals his identity in order to save a mortal whom he loves.[8] Here we may readily agree with Marx that the sentimental details that enliven tales of amorous animals are of recent invention. What is archaic is the preferential designation by an animal of a human being—what might be called, so long as we do not wish to give these words too precise a meaning, *ordeal by the animal of a clan*. In saying this much I do not imagine for a moment that totemism in the strict sense is implicated, only a very ancient conception according to which a clan is led to consider itself to have been selected for protection by an animal. With regard to prehistoric Greece, at least, it is for the moment impossible to develop this line of argument more fully.[9]

The form of election I have just described is perfectly apparent in the account of the infancy of Ptolemy Soter, who, having been exposed on a shield by his father Lagus, is protected, and then nursed, by an eagle that kills quails in order to feed their blood to the newborn. Hubaux and Leroy interpret the eagle as a doublet of the phoenix.[10] This is very probably correct. The Ptolemies certainly tried to exploit the myth of the phoenix for the purpose of surrounding their newly founded dynasty with the brilliant aura of immortality radiated by the bird-king. It is also probable that Soter propagated this legend as a means of pointing out his resemblance to Achaemenes, founder of the Persian royal house, who claimed to have been nursed by an eagle; Achaemenes's infancy, in its turn, recalled that of Gilgamesh, itself related to that of Perseus. In all these stories, as well as the story of Aristomenes's escape from captivity and that of Rhodopis, the Egyptian Cinderella, the eagle appears in order to announce the higher destiny that awaits those whom it takes under its protection. The dolphin is content simply to save friendly mortals from danger. A snake watches over Erichthonius, also over Illyrius, youngest son of Cadmus. Certain birds and dogs kill barbarians while sparing Greeks; certain scorpions kill foreigners while wounding only slightly members of the native population (or vice versa).[11] It will be obvious that these traditions bear comparison with historical accounts of the Ophiogeneis in Cyprus, also of the Psylli in Libya, who seem to have practiced until quite late an ordeal of legitimacy by subjecting newborns to the bites of snakes.[12] But Marx, who discusses such traditions in passing, did not see that they hold the key to all the texts he had so patiently assembled.

Animal fables are therefore associated with a corpus of beliefs about the nature of animals. It is impossible for us to determine, on the basis of surviving fragments, how deeply and widely these beliefs were held. The only theme that can be clearly isolated in the fables themselves is that certain animals are able to recognize certain human beings and, by saving them in earliest childhood at a moment of grave peril, to single them out for a glorious career or merely a happy life. Anything more than this is conjecture.

Marx wondered to what extent the tales whose outlines we glimpse beneath the summaries left us by Aelian and Pausanias were encumbered with moral intentions by the Lessings of antiquity. The question is interesting, but poorly posed. Two phases must be distinguished in the evolution of these tales. In the form that they are known to us today they teach a lesson: the importance of kindness and its eventual reward. But beneath this edifying tendency, secular in origin, one can still make out traces of a kind of religious propaganda that must have acted much more anciently. It very much resembles the kind that is at work in European folktales such as *The Fairies* (first published by Perrault as *Les fées*), *Sleeping Beauty* (also published by Perrault, as *La Belle au bois dormant*), and *Frau Holle* (from the Grimms' *Hausmärchen*), which were devised to inculcate respect for fairies. The ancient Greek tale of Pindus, prince of Emathia, resembles the German tale and the two French tales point by point, with the added detail of Pindus's romantic conquests ("Women preferred his bed to the honor of becoming goddesses").[13] The modern tales teach the honor that is due to fairies, the Greek tale the honor that is due to animals. All of them show how abundant are the blessings showered upon those who submit to received morality, and how severe the punishments that await those who disobey it; the happy fates of the good sister who is generous to fairies and the good brother who is generous to animals stand in pointed contrast to the ultimate punishment of the wicked sister and wicked brothers.[14]

This comparison enables us to draw a conclusion. It is not at all unreasonable to suppose that animal worship was every bit as prevalent in ancient Greece as devotion to fairies was in seventeenth-century France. We know that, in certain French provinces 150 years ago, meals were still offered to fairies on the eve of a new year and to the so-called *ventrières* who were believed to protect women during childbirth.[15] These feasts, which carry an echo of the ancient Greek theme of theoxeny, show how difficult it was to eradicate old popular beliefs even after seventeen centuries of Christianity. Archaic feasts dedicated to the animal of a clan, which had fallen out of favor in the religion of classical Greece, became similarly incongruous later, and during the medieval period in Germany were transformed into *Märchen*; and since these tales were told to children, they came to be animated by a moral purpose. But the lesson itself remained in a state of perpetual evolution, whose course the fable traced in its turn. Precepts of a purely liturgical character gradually gave way to counsels of a general kind. Little by little the theme of the animal's discernment faded away, until finally it was replaced by the theme of gratitude, accompanied by a moral of a quite different character: be good to others so that you may be good to yourself. In the form that the tales are known to us today, the ritual obligations from which they sprang are wholly absent, having been supplanted by motives borrowed from the new ethic into which they were incorporated.[16]

# The Religious Significance of Spoils in the Homeric Poems

The arms of Laius play a role, as we have seen, in the epic traditions related to Oedipus.[1] Until a thorough study has been made of the religious significance of conquered arms and armor among the Greeks, however, we will have to content ourselves with the few brief notes that I bring together here.

S. Reinach, in an article on the thirty-seventh of Plutarch's *Roman Questions*,[2] examined the malefic character of spoils among the Romans and the Celts. "Why is it," Plutarch asks, "that of all the offerings made to the gods it is customary to allow only spoils of war to disintegrate with the passage of time, rather than moving them [before they fall apart] or repairing them?"[3] Spoils were taboo, Reinach replies, because in using the weapons and body armor of a vanquished adversary, it was believed, one risked being infected by misfortune. Thus spoils were destroyed or else offered to the gods; they came to be used only when utilitarian motives finally prevailed over ancient religious conceptions. Reinach did not extend to the Greeks the researches he had made about Latin and Celtic traditions. A cursory reading of Homer will nonetheless be of interest in this connection.

No prohibition attaches to spoils in Homer. Every combatant seeks to profit by plunder; indeed, he tries almost as hard to seize his enemies' armor as to kill them. Two rather different cases may be distinguished in the Homeric accounts. In the first, one seeks to possess the armor of an adversary because one wishes to make use of it oneself, this in the same utilitarian spirit that was so late to emerge in Rome. In the second case, there is no proportion between the service that spoils can render and the price that a conqueror must be prepared to pay for them; indeed, he is all the more ready to risk mortal injury in order to have them as his adversary is willing to sacrifice his life in order to keep them. But this happens only when the one who is slain is a man of outstanding valor. Here it would appear that we find the same religious belief that is attested by the Roman conception concerning the malefic character of spoils—except that Homeric heroes had, as it were, reversed its terms. Whereas the Romans thought that a defeated soldier's misfortune spread to all the objects that he used by a sort of contagion, the ancient Greeks thought that, at least in certain cases, defeat is an accident that in no way casts doubt upon the excellence of a warrior, which imparts to his armor a beneficent power that an adversary seeks to make his own by capturing it.

In the *Iliad*, three main ideas may be detected:

1. *The material value of armor.* Seizure of a slain adversary's armor is almost always considered in Homer to be something that goes without saying.[4] Nevertheless many warriors meet their deaths without any mention of spoils; stock phrases are employed instead to indicate that the wound sustained by a fallen combatant is fatal. Thus a phrase such as σκότος ὄσσε κάλυψεν [darkness enfolded his eyes] or δούπησεν δὲ πεσών, ἀράβησε δὲ τεύχε' ἐπ' αὐτῷ [he fell with a thud, and his armor came crashing down upon him][5] is more commonly met with than ἀπ' ὤμον τεύχε' ἐσύλα [he stripped the armor from their shoulders].[6]

Occasionally the reasons that account for the material value of a combatant's armor are given. Achilles takes that of Amphimachus the Carian, for example, because it is made from gold (2.872–875). Each leader keeps in his hut the weapons and armor taken from the enemy in order to be able to replenish his own supply of instruments of war in case they are shattered in battle; Ideomenus, leader of the Cretans, maintains an entire arsenal (13.260–265).

It sometimes happens that the self-interested pursuit of spoils distracts soldiers from the purpose of combat, which is carnage. Hector urges his men not to dally on the field of battle "out of a desire to bring back to the ships the greatest store possible" [ὥς κε πλεῖστα φέρων ἐπὶ νῆας ἵκηται], but instead to go on fighting (6.67–70). Sometimes a soldier places himself in danger because he pauses to strip a fallen foe of his armor. Elephenor is fatally injured while trying to remove the armor from Echepolus, slain by Antilochus (4.457–470); Ajax narrowly escapes being killed while despoiling the corpse of Amphius (6.615–626), Teucer while wrestling with the lifeless body of Imbrius, and Hector with the body of Amphimachus (13.182–194); Diomedes is wounded as he strips the corselet, shield, and helmet from Agastrophus (11.373–381).

2. *The importance of armor in knightly ethics.* At the beginning of Homer's poem, there is nothing to indicate any posthumous shame in a warrior's corpse being despoiled. Yet later Andromache recalls that Achilles, having killed her father Eëtion, had qualms about removing his armor (οὐδέ μιν ἐξενάριξ, σεβάσσατο γάρ τό γε θυμῷ [he did not despoil him, for his soul had reverence for him]), and instead burned him in his armor and buried them together (6.416–419). When Hector proposes that the Greeks designate a champion with whom he could do battle face to face, he lays down the following conditions: if the Greek prevails, he will be free to take the armor, but he must give back the body so that it may be cremated by the Trojans; if Hector prevails, he will return the body and hang the armor in the temple of Apollo at Ilion (7.77–86).[7] The offering of armor to a god is presented here as a sort of *neutralization*, less humiliating for the vanquished warrior than the use of his armor by the one who has taken his life. But primitively it may have had an altogether different meaning. Recall that when Diomedes kills Dolon, Odysseus holds aloft Dolon's cap and clothing and bow and spear and provisionally offers them to Athena, placing them on the branches of a tamarisk bush; later, on returning with Diomedes from their expedition against the Thracians, he reclaims them (10.458–529).

Beginning in the fifteenth book of the *Iliad*, the idea recurs several times that not only is a warrior who has been slain dishonored if his armor is taken from him, but also, and to a still greater degree, are his surviving companions if they do nothing to prevent the pillage. Hector calls upon the Trojans and their allies to protect the body of Caletor from the plundering Achaeans (15.422–428). The dying Sarpedon beseeches Glaucus not to let the Greeks despoil his corpse:

σοὶ γὰρ ἐγὼ καὶ ἔπειτα κατηφείη καὶ ὄνειδος
ἔσσομαι ἤματα πάντα διαμπερές, εἴ κέ μ' Ἀχαιοὶ
τεύχεα συλήσωσι νεῶν ἐν ἀγῶνι πεσόντα. (16.498–500)

[For to you in days to come I shall be an object of opprobrium and a cause
for shame, forever more, if the Achaeans strip me of my armor, now that I
have fallen near where their ships await them.]

Apollo heals Glaucus's wound so that he may fulfill this wish, but Patroclus is
resolved to humiliate Sarpedon in death; fighting rages on around the body,
which in the end is despoiled (16.553–561, 16.663–665). Glaucus, however,
insists that Sarpedon's armor must be retrieved and reproaches Hector for
having given up too easily (17.160–168). The same sentiments and the same
preoccupations are found in connection with the corpse and armor of Priam's
bastard son Cebriones (16.733–782), also of Patroclus himself (17.91–104,
17.125–139, 17.689–693, 18.82–93). The plunder of armor, a preliminary to the
foul deeds committed by the Greeks against Hector's cadaver, is presented
here as a deliberate insult to the Trojans' champion (22.367–371, 22.395–404).

In all these passages, armor has a symbolic significance that is indepen-
dent of its utility as an instrument of war or of its value as a commercial
object. Can it be purely by chance that none of these passages occurs prior
to the sixth book, and that they are particularly numerous in the sixteenth,
seventeenth, and eighteenth books?

3. *The magical value of certain pieces of armor.* A supernatural signifi-
cance is clearly indicated in the story of the *iron club* [σιδηρείη κορύνη] that
Ares gave to Areithous, who on this account was called the Club Man
[Κορυνήτης]; with it, he shattered whole battalions. Yet Lycurgus, king of
Arcadia, managed to kill Areithous "by guile, not by might"—which is to
say, before Areithous had time to reach for his club. Lycurgus despoiled him
of his armor and thereafter wore it himself in battle. As an old man he made
a gift of it to his squire Ereuthalion, who then felt emboldened to issue a chal-
lenge all the Greeks; none dared to fight him. Finally Nestor came forward
and succeeded in killing him (7.136–156).

Similarly, Achilles gives his armor to Patroclus and sends him into com-
bat: τύνη δ' ὤμοιιν μὲν ἐμὰ κλυτὰ τεύχεα δῦθι [Come, then, put my glorious
armor on your shoulders (16.64)]. Patroclus solemnly obeys, but takes two

spears only, refusing to accept the spear made of ash from the summit of Mount Pelion that Cheiron had given to Achilles's father, Peleus, and that only Achilles was capable of wielding (16.130–144). This weapon reappears in the *Little Iliad* in the hands of Neoptolemus, and again in the *Cypria*, where it wounds and then heals Telephus. In the *Iliad*, Hector announces that he will put on the armor he had stripped from Patroclus after killing him, and assures his men that victory will be theirs; but when he did this Zeus was angered, for in taking for himself what by right belonged to Achilles, Hector had gone too far. In order to hasten the Trojans' defeat, Zeus made the armor fit Hector's body, and at once he was filled with courage and his limbs with strength.[8] But as Thetis later tells Achilles, this armor will bring Hector grievous misfortune (18.130–133). As for Achilles himself, he cannot imagine availing himself of any armor other than the shield of Ajax (18.192–195)—proof that it was supposed to be impregnated with the valor of its original owner; since his wish cannot be granted, Thetis has Hephaestus forge him a new coat of armor. When she sets it down at her son's feet, his men all tremble with fear (19.12–14). All these passages recall tales in which arms have a special power of their own, independent of the skill or courage of the person who wields them.

The only passage in the *Iliad* from which it may be inferred that, in a more remote past—or a world less susceptible to utilitarian persuasion—booty was prohibited is the one where Odysseus offers Athena the armor taken from Dolon, draping them over the branches of a tamarisk bush before setting off with Diomedes. The plausibility of this inference, nearer to the Latin and Celtic conception of the religious significance of spoils, is confirmed by two passages in Euripides's *Rhesus*. In the first, Hector offers to Dolon the armor that he expects will be taken during his next campaign; Dolon refuses and implores him to hang it in the temples of the gods. In the second, Rhesus similarly proposes to make an offering to the gods of booty conquered by force of arms.[9] Plutarch, however, says that Lycurgus forbade his soldiers from despoiling the enemy's dead "lest, preoccupied by a desire for plunder, they forget to fight, but also so that they preserve both their poverty and the proper order of battle."[10] This tactical motive is probably a late addition. If Spartan soldiers refrained from despoiling the dead, it must have been due to more mysterious causes. The surviving Greek texts permit us no more than a glimpse of these causes; they do not allow us to describe them in detail with any confidence. We are led to suppose sometimes that a man's *valor* gives his armor a special sort of efficacy, and sometimes, to the contrary, that *death* and *defeat* charge it with a malefic impulse that may be exorcized by making an offering of it to the gods. It may also be necessary to take into consideration a factor to which Reinach nonetheless seems to me to attach undue importance, namely, the curse that a warrior lays upon his armor so that, should it fall into the hands of his enemies, they will take no advantage from it.

These few brief notes will not allow us to draw any conclusion so long as no careful study has been made of war trophies and the beliefs on which their cult rests, as well as the reasons for which the Latins, at the end of a campaign, hung their own armor in the temples of the gods,[11] something that almost never happened in Greece. Might this also have been in order to expel the evil influences they harbored?

# Notes

## INTRODUCTION

1. In its modern French form, *roi* (from Latin *rex*). Thus the play we know as *Oedipus the King* was called *Oidipous Tyrannos* by Sophocles, later latinized as *Oedipus Rex*. —Trans.

2. See Carl Robert, *Oidipus: Geschichte eines poetischen Stoffes im griechischen Altertum*, 2 vols. (Berlin: Weidmann, 1915). The second volume contains only notes.

3. Arist. *Po.* 1454b7.

4. Our idea of a myth will always have clearer contours than the ones suggested by the same myth at the time when it first took shape, which is to say at the time when decrepit rites were transposed into legendary narratives.

5. See the chapter on legendary synthesis in my slender volume *Légendes et cultes de héros en Grèce* (Paris: Presses Universitaires de France, 1942). [This work was reprinted by the same publisher in 1992. —Trans.]

6. A conception of magic described by Frazer in *The Golden Bough: A Study in Magic and Religion* (London: Macmillan, 1899; 2nd ed., rev. and aug., 1900) in which, owing to a principle of similarity (*similia similibus*), one thing is believed to be capable of acting on another at a distance. —Trans.

7. See Hermann Usener, *Götternamen: Versuch einer Lehre von der religiösen Begriffsbildung* (Bonn: F. Cohen, 1896). —Trans.

8. See Nilsson's book review in *Gött. gel. Anzeigen* 184 (1922): 37.

9. I find it impossible to follow Nilsson in seeing an "ethical" theme, different from any other, in the story of incest with the mother. "A people," he says, "that lives in a strictly patriarchal regime notices the offenses against morality, conscious or unconscious, that it commits. From this results a whole cycle of well-known motifs in Greek legend: marriage with one's mother or daughter, the murder of children by their father or mother, combat between father and son, fratricide, and, finally, the problem of bloody vengeance when the murderers are members of the family." Ibid., 39. For two of the themes assimilated by Nilsson I propose explanations (in Chapters 2 and 6, respectively) that are very different from the ones he gives and very different from each other. Nor do I think that any of the "familial" themes he groups together arises from a confrontation between a later social state and a foreign or archaic reality. However this may be, each one must be studied in isolation from the others. Their origins are poorly understood, and the moment when we will be in a position to generalize is yet very far off.

10. See Addendum 1 below.

11. See Edwin Sydney Hartland, *The Legend of Perseus: A Study of Tradition in Story, Custom, and Belief*, 3 vols. (London: D. Nutt, 1894–1896), and Murray Anthony Potter, *Sohrab and Rustem: The Epic Theme of a Combat between Father and Son. A Study of Its Genesis and Uses in Literature and Popular Tradition* (London: D. Nutt, 1902). —Trans.

12. L. W. Daly, in the entry on Oedipus in supplement volume 7 (1940) of August Friedrich Pauly, Georg Wissowa, Wilhelm Kroll, Kurt Witte, Karl Mittelhaus, and Konrat Ziegler, eds., *Realencyclopädie der classischen Altertumswissenschaft* [henceforth *RE*], 84 vols. (Stuttgart: J. B. Metzler, 1894–1980), groups the texts by episode. Daly's article concludes (col. 785) with a list of the various theories that have been proposed concerning the primitive nature of the figure of Oedipus. Daly joins with L. Deubner in "Oedipusprobleme," *Abh. der preuss. Ak. d. Wiss. phil. hist. Kl.*, no. 4 (1942): 39, following a line of inquiry suggested by Nilsson, in seeing Oedipus as the hero of a *Märchen*, without seeming to perceive that this is not an explanation, only the starting point for one.

13. M = Marcianus gr. 471 (eleventh century, Venice); A = Parisinus gr. 2712 (c. 1300, Paris); B = Parisinus gr. 2713 (1000–1050, Paris). For a comprehensive survey of the manuscript tradition, see the modern critical editions by Donald J. Mastronarde, *Phoenissae* (Leipzig: Teubner, 1988), xlv–xlviii, and James Diggle in *Euripidis Fabulae*, 3 vols. (Oxford: Clarendon Press, 1981–1994), 3:72–74. —Trans.

14. See Erich Bethe, *Thebanische Heldenlieder: Untersuchungen über die Epen des thebanisch-argivischen Sagenkreises* (Leipzig: S. Hirzel, 1891). —Trans.

15. See Deubner, "Oedipusprobleme," which contains an exhaustive bibliography of the question and the history of the hypotheses presented.

16. The texts of these three documents in the original Greek, with accompanying English translation (on the whole following the French version given by Wartelle), are reproduced in Appendix 1. The Pisander scholion itself has been reprinted by a number

of authors, notably Robert, *Oidipus*, 1:150–151, and Felix Jacoby, ed., *Die Fragmente der griechischen Historiker* [henceforth *FGrHist*], 17 vols. (Berlin: Weidemann, 1923–1958), 16 F10, 1:181–182. An earlier version of the short text found in Laur. gr. 32.33 occurs, with minor variation in wording, in Vat. gr. 909. (I am grateful to Professor Mastronarde for pointing out Delcourt's lapse, silently corrected here, in saying that Vat. gr. 1345 summarizes Aeschylus's *Seven against Thebes*. All three of the argumenta in question concern Euripides's *Phoenician Women*.) —Trans.

17. The summary of *The Phoenician Women* given by Aristophanes of Byzantium, in demonstrating the kinship of this play with *Seven against Thebes*, shows why it should be possible to summarize *Chrysippus*, the preamble to the former, in order to introduce the latter.

18. *Oenomaus*, *Chrysippus*, and *Phoenician Women*, along with *Alexandrus*, *Palamedes*, and *The Trojan Women* (performed in 415 BCE), must have composed Euripides's two great tryptichs—a pair of linked trilogies (in a sense very different than the one word had in Aeschylus's time) portraying different characters but dealing with events in which moral transgression and responsibility came to depend on each other in a new way.

19. The possibility that the sources of the Pisander scholion may be found in pre-Euripidean versions of Thebaid myth has been skeptically examined by Donald J. Mastronarde, ed., *Phoenissae* (Cambridge: Cambridge University Press, 1994), 31–38. For a vigorous defense of the position defended by Delcourt, taking issue with the arguments advanced by Mastronarde and others, see Hugh Lloyd-Jones, "Curses and Divine Anger in Early Greek Epic: The Pisander Scholion," *Classical Quarterly* 52, no. 1 (2002): 1–14; reprinted in *The Further Academic Papers of Sir Hugh Lloyd-Jones* (Oxford: Oxford University Press, 2005), 18–36. —Trans.

20. The reason Deubner gives is that Euripides would never have risked so bold an innovation. This is a feeble justification, since in *Phoenician Women* he lets Jocasta live, whereas the suicide of the mother/wife, hallowed since the *Odyssey*, was a far more venerable episode than the disfigurement of Oedipus, which does not seem to be earlier than the *Thebaid*.

21. See, for example, Herodotus 2.141; also the *Strategems* of Polyaenus (1.21.1), where there occurs a much more serious anacoluthon than the one Deubner points out here (see my discussion below in Chapter 5).

22. Deubner, "Oedipusprobleme," 5.

23. See Pl. *Smp.* 180a.

24. See Bethe, *Thebanische Heldenlieder*, 144ff.

25. The Pisander scholion says ἠγνόει υἱὸν ὄντα [she is unaware that it is her son] (l. 26), an obvious error in composition. The lines following indicate moreover that Jocasta, who was steeling herself to bear in silence her marriage with the murderer, kills herself on discovering the incest. Curiously, the scholiast's lapse seems to have escaped even the acerbic critical examination to which Robert subjected this text; see *Oidipus*, 161.

26. Deubner, "Oedipusprobleme," 8.

27. See Hom. *Od.* 19.218–231, 23.177–204, 24.331–344.

28. See E. *IT* 811–826, and Arist. *Po.* 1452b. Aristotle, however, makes no distinction between recognition in epic and in tragedy (1454b19–1455a21), and he says, altogether correctly, that recognition occurs in the *Odyssey* throughout [ἀναγνώρισις διόλου] (1459b13).

29. The *Nekyia* (literally, a calling up of spirits, or necromancy) is the name by which book 11 of the *Odyssey* was known in antiquity. The passage alluded to here tells of Odysseus's encounter with the shade of Oedipus's mother, Epikaste (Jocasta), a capsule summary of the legend (11.271–280). —Trans.

30. Suidas, once thought to be a scholar who lived in the second half of the tenth century CE, was long regarded as the compiler of the *Suda* [ἡ Σοῦδα], a vast Byzantine encyclopedia of the ancient Mediterranean world that seems first to have appeared in the following century. A certain Suidas is credited with authorship in a prefatory note, but the name is now attached to the work itself, not to its compiler, who is unknown. —Trans.

31. The entry for Πείσανδρος in the *Suda* reads: ἐποποιὸς καὶ αὐτὸς ἔγραψεν ἱστορίαν ποικίλην δι' ἐπῶν, ἥν ἐπιγράφει Ἡραϊκῶν Θεογαμιῶν ἐν βιβλίοις ξ' καὶ ἄλλα καταλογάδην [Himself an epic poet as well (i.e., like his father [Nestor of Laranda]), he wrote in sixty books of epic verse a miscellaneous history that begins with the wedding of Zeus and Hera, and other works in prose]. [Hence the title by which Pisander's epic is now commonly known, *Heroic Marriages of the Gods* (Ἡρωικαι Θεογαμίαι). —Trans.]

32. Almost all critics have decided the matter in favor of Suidas, concluding that it was Macrobius who was mistaken. Severyns has adduced fresh evidence in favor of the contrary hypothesis, however. [See Macr. 5.2.4–5 and Albert Severyns, *Le cycle épique dans l'école d'Aristarque* (Liège: H. Vailliant-Carmanne / Paris: É. Champion, 1928). —Trans.]

33. See Jacoby's commentary on the *Peisanderscholion* in *FGrHist*, 1:494, and Rudolf Keydell, "Peisandros," in *RE* 19.1 (1937), col. 146.

34. ἀντιποιησαμένου καὶ εὐεπείας, as John Philoponus says of Pisander in his commentary on Arist. *Anal. Post.* 77b32.

35. Wecklein thinks that we are dealing here with corrupt editions of the *Oedipodea* and the *Thebaid*; see *Die kyklische Thebais, die Oedipodee, die Oedipussage und der Oedipus des Euripides* (Munich: Sitzungsberichte der Bayerischen Akademie der Wissenschaften, 1901), 661ff.

## CHAPTER 1. EXPOSURE OF THE INFANT

1. See Marie Delcourt, *Stérilités mystérieuses et naissances maléfiques dans l'antiquité classique* (Paris: E. Droz, 1938).

2. See my earlier remarks in the Introduction.

3. See the discussion that follows in this chapter.

4. See Hermann Usener, *Die Sintfluthsagen* (Bonn: F. Cohen, 1899), 80ff.; Gustave Glotz, *L'ordalie dans la Grèce primitive: Étude de droit et de mythologie* (Paris: A. Fontemoing, 1904), *passim*; James George Frazer, "Moses in the Ark of Bulrushes," in *Folk-lore in the Old Testament: Studies in Comparative Religion, Legend, and Law*, 3 vols. (London: Macmillan, 1918), 2:43ff.

5. Prudently leaving anything that is not Greek to more competent researchers, I shall scarcely speak here of Romulus's beginnings, the subject of a complex knot of traditions that would first have to be disentangled (see n. 90 infra). As for the story of Moses, there can be no question of studying it in any detail here. But the system of references it contains is so rich that I feel I may be permitted to allude to it now and then where comparison of some aspect with Greek legends is particularly instructive.

6. See D. S. 2.4.

7. See Ael. *NA* 12.21.

8. See *Orat. Att.* 2.157 (ed. I. Bekker [Oxford, 1822; Berlin, 1823], 670).

9. See Paus. 8.47.3, 8.48.7.

10. See Glotz, *L'ordalie dans la Grèce primitive*, 79.

11. See the discussion of Telephus in Carl Robert, ed., *Die griechische Heldensage*, constituting the second volume of Ludwig Preller, *Griechische Mythologie*, 2 vols. (Berlin: Weidmann, 1920–1926), 2:1138–1160.

12. See Apollod. 2.7.4 and 3.9.1.

13. See Hyg. *Fab.* 100.

14. Among women, according to an old Greek proverb reported in certain manuscripts of Pausanias (10.19.2), only virgins can dive into the sea; see Marie Delcourt, "La pureté des éléments et l'invocation de Créuse dans 'Ion,'" *Rev. belge de phil. et d'hist.* 17, no. 1 (1938): 195–203.

15. See the texts in Robert, *Die griechische Heldensage*, 2:1145.

16. See Paus. 3.24.3.

17. See sch. *Il.* 1.38 A D.

18. See Paus. 10.14.2–4.

19. Τενεδίῳ πελέκει ἀποκόπτειν (Paus. 10.14.4). On the other hand, a Creto-Carian ax appears on the coins of the island along with a male/female janiform head. When these religious elements, having outlived a lost context, became unintelligible, they entered into narratives in which they took on the appearance of realistic and precise details.

20. Neither Paul Weizsäcker nor Karl Tümpel gave a proper analysis, any more than Usener or Glotz or Frazer did. See the entries on Deucalion by Weizsäcker, in W. H.

Roscher, ed., *Ausführliches Lexikon der griechischen und römischen Mythologie*, 6 vols. and Supplement (Leipzig: B. G. Teubner, 1884–1937), vol. 1, cols. 994–998; and by Tümpel, in August Friedrich Pauly and Georg Wissowa, eds., *Realencyclopädie der classischen Altertumswissenschaft* [*RE*], first series [A–Q] (Stuttgart: J. B. Metzler, 1894–1963), vol. 5.1, cols. 261–276.

21. Glotz, *L'ordalie dans la Grèce primitive*, 27.

22. See Delcourt, "La pureté des éléments et l'invocation de Créuse dans 'Ion.'"

23. See Ov. *Met.* 1.319.

24. Usener never translates λάρναξ by a word meaning "small boat," except at p. 38 of *Die Sintfluthsagen*, where he carelessly speaks of the *kleines Fahrzeug* that allows Deucalion and Pyrrha to arrive in safety. Elsewhere he mentions the role of the boat in divine epiphanies, which amounts to treating Deucalion's chest as a skiff or dingy, an equivalence for which there is no justification whatever.

25. See Pi. *O.* 9.43–45: Πύρρα Δευκαλίων τε Παρνασσοῦ Καταβάντε | δόμον ἔθεντο πρῶτον, ἄτεο δ' εὐνᾶς ὁμόδαμονε | κτισσάσθαν λίθινον γόνον [Pyrrha and Deucalion, having come down from Parnassus, first made their home, and, without the aid of a nuptial bed, established a lineage born of stones, a single race of people]. And yet in the same poem Pindar alludes to Protogeneia, the daughter of Deucalion and Pyrrha's nuptial bed. In late art, Deucalion and Pyrrha are depicted as throwing stones in old age: the artists felt more or less explicitly that, if the saved couple used this means to repopulate the planet, it is because they could no longer have children.

26. See Hdt. 4.154.

27. Glotz (*L'ordalie dans la Grèce primitive*, 56) is probably right to explain Minos's treatment of Scylla, who, out of love for him, had betrayed her father Nisus (see Apollod. 3.5.8) in terms of a question posed to the gods; that is, Minos plunges Scylla into the sea, with her feet tied to the stern of a ship, in order to learn whether he has to reward her love or punish her betrayal.

28. "The legend of Oedipus," Robert remarks, "is certainly older than all the oracles." Carl Robert, *Oidipus: Geschichte eines poetischen Stoffs im griechischen Altertum*, 2 vols. (Berlin: Weidmann, 1915), 1:11.

29. See Apollod. 3.9.1, 2.7.4.

30. See Alexander Haggerty Krappe, "Le mythe de la naissance de Cyrus," *Revue des études grecques* 43, nos. 200–201 (1930): 153–159.

31. A. *Th.* 748: θνᾴσκοντα γέννας ἄτερ σῴζειν πόλιν.

32. See S. *OT* 713, 1176.

33. Nic. Dam. fr. 15 [= *Historici graeci minores* (hereafter HGM), ed. L. Dindorf (Leipzig, 1870–1871), 1:19].

34. See Malalas, *Chron.* 2.59.0 [ed. L. Dindorf (Bonn, 1831), p. 50)].

35. See S. *OT* 715 (first oracle); 790 (second oracle). Ask any honest person how the oracle replied to Laius and—if he does not have the text of Sophocles's play in front of him—he will answer as Nicolaus of Damascus did, the two replies being superimposed in his memory.

36. With regard to Atalanta, see my remarks at the beginning of this chapter; with regard to Cypselus, see the discussion following.

37. See the texts in Robert, *Die griechische Heldensage*, 2:978nn3, 4.

38. See Pi. *Pae.* 8 [= ed. O. Schröder (Leipzig, 1908), 280]; also *Oxyrhynchus Papyri* [*P. Oxy.*] 5.841.

39. See Hdt. 5.92.

40. Regarding the practice of infant exposure (ἀπόθεσις) in Sparta, Athens, and Rome, see my *Stérilités mystérieuses et naissances maléfiques*, 36ff. [The term ἔκθεσις was used by Greek authors to signify the act of exposing a newborn child, whereas ἀπόθεσις adds to this the idea of abandonment. The basic meaning of the two terms, *apothesis* and *ekthesis*, is nonetheless the same.—Trans.]

41. See Nicolaus of Damascus, in Felix Jacoby, ed., *Die Fragmente der griechischen Historiker* [*FGrHist*], 17 vols. (Berlin: Weidmann, 1923–1958), 7 F58, 1:301. With regard to the theme of the voyage, see my remarks below.

42. Historical accuracy is not at issue in the case of Cypselus, about whose infancy we are wholly ignorant. His legend nevertheless exactly transcribes a practice that, in Herodotus's time, was probably no longer observed in Athens as faithfully has it had been in earlier times.

43. See Hdt. 5.92.5.

44. See Hom. *Il.* 12.117.

45. See Ov. *Met.* 12.524–526.

46. On the male and female character of the phoenix, see Jean Hubaux and Maxime Leroy, *Le mythe du phénix dans les littératures grecque et latine* (Paris: E. Droz, 1939), 3ff.; on the equation eagle = phoenix, see ibid., 129ff. Note, too, that Ion of Chios had written a play entitled Καινεὺς ἢ Φοῖνιξ [Caineus or Phoenix].

47. See Hom. *Il.* 13.136–139.

48. The original text reads: ΒΛΑΙΣΌΣ: Παραλυτικός [ . . . ] ὁ τοὺς πόδας ἐπὶ τὰ ἔξω διεστραμμένος, καὶ τῷ Λ στοιχείῳ ἐοικώς. Διὰ τοῦτο καὶ Λάμβδα ἐκαλεῖτο ἡ γυνὴ μὲν Ἠετίωνος, μήτηρ δὲ Κυψέλου τοῦ Κορίνθου τυράννου. See *Etymologicum Magnum* (ed. T. Gaisford [Oxford, 1848], p. 199, col. 573, ll. 23–27).

49. Like the slang expression for *boiteux* [lame, limping], "cinq et trois font huit" [five and three make eight], which will perhaps one day disappear from French without leaving any written trace. "Although the authenticity of the word [lambda] may be doubted," Mr. Fohalle tells me, "it must be kept in mind that the vowel *a*, relatively rare in Indo-European, occurs there notably in words having a popular character, particularly

in names of infirmities." Cf. Antoine Meillet, *Introduction à l'étude des langues indo-européennes*, 7th ed. (Paris: Hachette, 1934), 90.

50. See Robert, *Oidipus*, 1:59.

51. It is mentioned in D. Chr. *Orat.* 11.45 (ed. H. von Arnim [Berlin, 1893–1896], 1:127) and described in Paus. 5.17.5.

52. See, for example, the scholium on E. *Ph.* 26: Οἳ δὲ εἰς θάλασσαν ἐκριφῆναι [φασὶ τὸν Οἰδίποδα] βληθέντα εἰς λάρνακα καὶ προσοκείλαντα τῇ Σικυῶνι ὑπὸ Πολυβίου ἀνατραφῆναι [They threw Oedipus into the sea (it is said), after having put him in a chest; he landed at Sicyon and was raised there]; and ibid., 28: τινὲς δὲ εν λάρνακι βληθέντα καὶ εἰς θάλασσαν ριφέντα τὸν παῖδα προσπελασθῆναι τῇ Κορίνθῳ φασίν [Certain (mythographers) say that the child, put in a chest and thrown into the sea, washed up on the shore of Corinth]. Also Hyg. *Fab.* 66: Hunc [Oedipus] Periboea Polybi regis uxor cum vestem ad mare lavaret expositum sustulit Polybo sciente [Periboea, wife of King Polybus, found Oedipus, who had been exposed, as she was washing clothes at the shore and, with Polybus's consent, raised him]. See too the Homeric bowl published by Edmond Pottier in a triennial volume (1885–1888) issued in Paris by the Association pour l'encouragement des études grecques, pl. 8, p. 48; also reproduced in Carl Robert, "Homerische Becher," *Programm zum Winckelmannsfeste der Archaeologischen Gesellschaft zu Berlin*, vol. 50 (Berlin: G. Reimer, 1890), 76 c, and in Robert, *Die griechische Heldensage*, 2:885.

53. The relevant passages in each case are found in Delcourt, *Stérilités mystérieuses et naissances maléfiques*, 37–66.

54. See Nic. Dam. fr. 15.

55. Myth. Vat. Sec. *Fab.* 230.

56. Hyg. *Fab.* 67.

57. See Ferdinand Keseling, *De mythographi Vaticani secundi fontibus*, inaug. diss. (Halle, 1908), 62; and Robert, *Oidipus*, 1:77, 1:324.

58. Nicolaus Wecklein supposes, for Euripides's *Oedipus*, a mythopoeia in which the chariot taken from Laius and given to Polybus made recognition possible; see *Die kyklische Thebais, die Oedipodee, die Oedipussage und der Oedipus des Euripides* (Munich: Sitzungsberichte der Bayerischen Akademie der Wissenschaften, 1901), 671ff. [It is customary to refer to Oedipus's rescuer as a shepherd, but he is more accurately referred to as a groom or stableman, as Delcourt does here, speaking of a *palefrenier*. Elsewhere, in translating the Greek term in the Pisander scholion (ἱπποβουκόλος), he is called a *pâtre de chevaux*, a herdsman of horses. —Trans.]

59. See my discussion below in Chapter 5; also the note by Paul Kretschmer in *Glotta* 12 (1923): 59, who likewise feels that the two names are prior to the etiological legends that attempt to explain them. I will not follow Kretschmer, however, in suggesting that the two heroes were ancient serpent-gods.

60. Herbert Petersson (commenting on Martin P. Nilsson's review of Robert's *Oidipus*,

in *Gött. Gel. Anzeigen* 184 [1922]: 35) feels that the name cannot come from οἰδέω, οἰδάω [to swell, become swollen] and proposes that it be attached instead to *οδιοός (an unattested form constructed on the model of κυδρός), from the same root as the hypothetical *eitar, poison. The meaning would remain the same. Obviously it is impossible to conclude anything from guesses based on other guesses.

61. It was initially proposed, I believe, by August Friedrich Pott, "Mytho-etymologica (schlufs)," *Zeitschrift für vergleichende Sprachforschung* [*KZ* (= *Kuhns Zeitschrift*)] 7 (1858): 324. Robert attributes it to Wilamowitz, who simply adopted it—without citing Pott—in "Excurse zum Oedipus des Sophokles," *Hermes* 34 (1899): 77. "The linguist can examine the form of a word and indicate the possibilities that it suggests," Mr. Fohalle informs me in this connection, "but these possibilities are many and one of them may be overlooked, because a word of this kind is exposed to the most diverse accidents, for example to a folk etymology, precisely because the form is not supported by a stable value."

62. See Ael. *VH* 2.7.

63. See Robert, *Oidipus*, 1:72–73, and figure 22 there; cf. André de Ridder, *Catalogue des vases peints de la Bibliothèque Nationale*, 2 vols. (Paris: E. Leroux, 1901–1902), 2:272, no. 372.

64. All the testimonia together with a brief survey of modern interpretations may be found in Viktor Gebhard, *Die Pharmakoi in Ionien und die Sybakchoi in Athen* (Munich: Hueber, 1926).

65. Wilhelm Mannhardt was the first, I believe, in *Mythologische Forschungen* (Strassburg: K. J. Trübner, 1884), to hold that the agrarian rite was prior to the expiatory rite. His opinion was subsequently shared by Henri Hubert and Marcel Mauss, first in "Essai sur la nature et la fonction du sacrifice," *L'Année Sociologique* 2 (1898): 29–138 (see esp. pp. 102ff.), then in *Mélanges d'histoire des religions* (Paris: F. Alcan, 1909). Martin Nilsson, in the section on the Thargelia in his *Griechische Feste von religiöser Bedeutung mit Ausschluss der Attischen* (Leipzig: B. G. Teubner, 1906), 105–115, thinks that it was simply a matter of two equally old liturgies being merged together.

Georges Dumézil, in *Le festin d'immortalité: Étude de mythologie comparée indo-européenne* (Paris: P. Geuthner, 1924) sees the Thargelia, with its three main acts—expulsion of the pharmakos, procession of Eiresione, feast—as a festival of Ambrosia. According to Harpocration, Pharmakos stole the holy cups of Apollo and afterward was stoned by Achilles [see Istros *FGrHist* 334 F50 = Harpocration 180, 19, s.v. *pharmakós*]. Pharmakos is the demon thief who, in other mythologies, steals ambrosia from the gods, in punishment for which he is buried under rocks.

It is necessary on this view, then, to suppose that the eponymous Pharmakos of the rite (a rite that goes beyond the Thargelia) absorbed the story of the demon thief: the thief lost his primitive name; the ritual figure gained a biography; and a liturgy whose meaning is not fully understood arose from the merger of the two. It should nonetheless be noted that the superposition of an agrarian rite and an expiatory rite is rather frequent, and that it can be explained without invoking a very hypothetical festival, in this case of Ambrosia.

66. Ernst Riess, "Aberglaube," in *RE*, first series, vol. 1, col. 92. See also the article by August Bouché-Leclercq, "Devotio," in Charles Daremberg and Edmond Saglio, eds., *Dictionnaire des antiquités grecques et romaines d'après les textes et les monuments*, 10 vols. (Paris: Hachette, 1877–1919), 2:113–119.

67. See Liv. 27.37.5–6.

68. See Tz. *H.* 5.729.

69. The scholium on Ar. *Ra.* 730 reads: τοὺς φαύλους καὶ παρὰ τῆς φύσεως ἐπιβουλευομένους εἰς ἀπαλλαγὴν αὐχμοῦ ἢ … ἔθυον [Wretches and those whom nature had mistreated they sacrificed, in order to ward off drought and famine]. In suggesting this translation to me, Mr. Delatte advises that, in the Byzantine period, the image that previously had been conveyed by ἐπιβουλεύω was now completely erased. Yet the expression seems a very mannered one from the pen of a grammarian; in place of the present ἐπιβουλευομένους (which seems corrupt, but for which I have no correction to propose) one would have expected a perfect participle. Gebhard (*Die Pharmakoi*, 30) glosses this testimony—rather than translating it, though plainly he understands it as we do—thus: "Die Aristophanesscholien berichten von Leuten niederster Herkunft, Taugenichtsen, die zu gar nicht brauchbar waren, von Krüppeln denen die Natur eine böse Stiefmutter war" [The scholia on Aristophanes refer to people of the lowest origins, to bad persons, who are good for nothing, to the crippled, to whom nature was a cruel stepmother].

70. See Gebhard, *Die Pharmakoi*, 79–80. Let me note in passing that my explanation makes it possible to see something other than a mere romantic flourish in a detail provided by Athenaeus regarding Cratinus, who voluntarily gives his life during the purification of Attica by Epimenides. Cratinus is εὔμορφος: well-formed, handsome. Athenaeus (13.602c), used to seeing scapegoats whose appearance was altogether different, evidently thought it useful to point out so exceptional a detail, which Diogenes Laertius (1.10) does not mention.

71. Redheads are placed in the same category as persons suffering constitutional defects; see Eupolis, fragment 5 of *The Golden Race* in August Meineke, ed., *Fragmenta comicorum Graecorum [FCG]*, 5 vols. (Berlin: G. Reimeri, 1839–1857), 2:537. Nevertheless, a passage such as the one found on this subject in Adamantius's *Physiognomonica* shows that it is difficult to separate the physical notion of redness from the moral ideas that, for the ancients, were associated with it; see the Greek text in Richard Foerster, ed., *Scriptores physiognomonici graeci et latini*, 2 vols. (Leipzig: B. G. Teubner, 1893), 1:394 F.

72. See scholia on Ar. *Ra.* 730 (ἔθυον) and *Pl.* 454 (Θυόμενοι).

73. Tz. *H.* 5.735ff.

74. See Juliette Davreux, *La légende de la prophétesse Casandre d'après les textes et les monuments* (Paris: E. Droz, 1942), 53.

75. See my *Stérilités mystérieuses et naissances maléfiques*, 57. "In 1474," Krappe says, without giving any indication as to his source, "a cock was burned at Basel for having laid an egg." Alexander Haggerty Krappe, *La genèse des mythes* (Paris: Payot, 1938), 46.

76. See Gebhard, *Die Pharmakoi*, 109; also Nilsson, *Griechische Feste*, 113, and my further discussion in Chapter 5.

77. Str. 10.2.9.

78. See Jean Hubaux, "Le plongeon rituel et le bas-relief de Vabside de la basilique souterraine de la Porta Maggiore à Rome," *Le Musée belge* 27, no. 1 (1923): 31. Living birds, and even attached wings, would have cruelly hampered a strong swimmer otherwise capable of surviving a dangerous leap of this sort. Nilsson (*Griechische Feste*, 111) explains the presence of bird feathers by their magical value.

79. See Ar. *Ra.* 730–733 and *Eq.* 1405–1408; also Serv. *Verg. Aen.* 3.57.

80. Henri Hubert and Marcel Mauss, *Sacrifice: Its Nature and Functions*, trans. W. D. Halls (Chicago: University of Chicago Press, 1964), 60. "The infant saved from the waters and the vindicated woman," Glotz remarks, "will always bear the mark of divine consecration" (*L'ordalie dans la Grèce primitive*, 16).

81. Glotz renders the word *arca*, used by Livy in a passage (*History of Rome* 27.37.6) concerning the excommunication of a monstrous child (*vivum in arcam condidere provectumque in mare proiecerunt* [They put it alive in a chest, carried it out to sea, and threw it overboard]), by the French word *arche*—a mistranslation, since *arche*, under the influence of the description given by the author of Genesis, no longer signifies a chest, but instead a boat.

82. Glotz, *L'ordalie dans la Grèce primitive*, 22.

83. Regarding the various signs, see my *Stérilités mystérieuses et naissances maléfiques*, 54ff. See, too, Henri Gaidoz and Eugène Rolland, eds., *Mélusine: Recueil de mythologie, littérature populaire, tradition & usages,* 11 vols. (Paris: Librairie Viaut, 1878–1912), of which volumes 5–7 and 9 contain more than two dozen curious notes concerning children who were early speakers, even children who spoke before birth.

84. Only one text might be imagined to suggest as much, a note by Hesychius of Alexandria (s.v. ἐκ λάρνακος · νόθος). This does indeed seem to mean that *one who comes out from a chest* is always a bastard. But is it an expression that was current in the language? Or is it the translation of a parody of some sort, perhaps a comic passage mocking the pretensions to virtue of an Auge, or a Danaë, or a Semele? Nothing can be deduced from these three words in the absence of any context.

85. See Appendix 2, concerning legends and cults of twin children.

86. See Glotz, *L'ordalie dans la Grèce primitive*, 4, 9. Recall the proverb θεοῦ θέλοντος κἂν ἐπὶ ῥιπὸς πλέοι˘ [God willing, one could even sail on a hurdle], which Aristophanes converted into κέρδους ἕκατι κἂν ἐπὶ ῥιπὸς πλέοι [If money could be made (from it), one would even sail on a hurdle] (*Pax 699*).

87. Polydorus was belatedly given as a son to Cadmus, solely for the purpose of attaching Laius to the line of the Agenorides. Polydorus is mentioned for the first time in the catalog with which Hesiod's *Theogony* closes (line 978). Pindar knew only of Cadmus's daughters.

88. See Hom. *Od.* 12.235–259.

89. See Hyg. *Fab.* 7.

90. One might object that Romulus's childhood is a scholarly invention, and that it was in any case embellished in its different versions under the influence of Sophocles's *Tyro*. Soltau goes much further, arguing that this tragedy is the sole source of the traditions concerning the birth of the founders of Rome; see Wilhelm Soltau, "Die Entstehung der Romuluslegende," *Archiv für Religionswissenschaft* 12 (1909): 101–125. But Sophocles must have treated the sentimental version that later found its way into Apollodorus, in which the twins and their mother are persecuted by Sidero, the cruel stepmother. The antipathetic role of Amulius must come from somewhere else. For Antiope, see Robert, *Die griechische Heldensage*, 2:117n6.

91. Hubaux and Leroy (*Le mythe du phénix*, 167) give an ingenious interpretation of the episode relating Gilgamesh's rescue on the back of an eagle, which transcribes a very particular ordeal. For our purposes here, it is not necessary to distinguish this episode from the others.

92. Justin (1.4) relates that the child was suckled by a bitch, the Persian word for which is *spako*. Herodotus (1.107–122) says that he was nursed by a foster mother named *Spaka*. Here one detects here the same rationalizing impulse that transformed the she-wolf [*lupa*] that suckled the Roman twins into a peasant woman named *Lupa*.

93. See Appendix 3, concerning animal tales in Greece.

94. This is the case with Sargon, Semiramis, Cyrus, and Cypselus. The oracle says that Eëtion is scorned even though he is worthy of many honors.

95. See Ael. *NA* 1.57; Str. 13.1.14; Luc. 9.902–906.

96. See Prop. 4.10.39–41; *AP* 9.125; Jul. *Ep.*, no. 191 (ed. J. Bidez [Paris, 1924]); Claud. *in Rufin.* 2.112.

97. See Robert, *Die griechische Heldensage*, 2:1119, 1171; E. *Rh.* 926–931; Apollod. 3.15.4; [Hesiod], *Aegimius* (ed. A. Rzach [Leipzig, 1908]), fragment 185.

98. I thank J. Hubaux for drawing my attention to the role played by water in the legend of Ilia [= Rhea Silvia, daughter of Aeneas, mother of Romulus and Remus]. In Ennius, after Ilia has given birth to the twins, Amulius throws her into the Tiber, who marries her. Naevius speaks not of the Tiber, but of the Anio, whom Ovid also refers to as Ilia's husband. See the entry on Ilia by Kurt Latte in *RE*, first series, vol. 9, cols. 999–1000.

99. See n. 128 below.

100. Henri Jeanmaire, *Couroi et courètes* (Lille: Bibliothèque universitaire, 1939), 283–284.

101. See Hom. *Il.* 6.130–137.

102. It may be objected that Paris, though he had been brought up in the mountains, is a very poor hero. But one must not judge here solely on the basis of a few passages in the *Iliad*. Sophocles and Euripides both remained faithful to the archaic sentiments that imbued the theme of a rearing in the wilderness. No sooner does Paris leave his

village of herdsmen than he immediately triumphs at athletic competitions, surpassing the most brilliant achievements of his brothers. One may well wonder, independently of any terrifying oracle, whether an archaic mythopoeia did not represent him as having been reared in the mountains, like Achilles and Jason, and assured of a shining destiny. Hecuba's dream has no more chance of being ancient than the threat to Laius in the story of Oedipus. Robert has very persuasively shown (*Die griechische Heldensage*, 2:977) that primitively the bulwark of Troy was not Hector, but Paris, whose character and role were subsequently degraded for reasons that elude us. This alteration is strongly pronounced in the *Iliad*. Might the nymph Oenone, whom Hellenistic romances describe as Paris's lover, have initially been his "nurse"? The more one examines this legend, the more one is led to see traces of an initiation rite in it. The hero has two names: the herdsmen call him Paris when they discover him, and then Alexander after his rout of the cattle-thieves. Might this be a memory of the new name that novices received after having successfully endured their trials? Might the "judgment" of Paris—in which Hermes, god of initiations, brings forward the three goddesses [Hera, Athena, Aphrodite], whom archaic monuments represent simply as three young girls, without any distinguishing attributes—be a memory of the marriages that accompanied passage into the ranks of adults (see Chapter 5 of the present work)? The whole story of Paris/Alexander could profitably be reconsidered, it seems to me, from this point of view.

103. For a characteristic example of this quality of *aitia*, see n. 65 supra in connection with the story of Pharmakos.

104. See Hyg. *Fab.* 87, 252.

105. Hyginus (fable 186), following Euripides in part, relates that the twins were then falsely presented to Metapontus, king of Icaria (tentatively identified by Cuper with Italy), by his wife Theano, who was barren, as his own. Later, however, Theano has children by Metapontus and threatens the twins, either through her own sons (per Hyginus) or her brothers (per Euripides, fragment 495 in August Nauck, *Tragicorum Graecorum Fragmenta*, 2nd ed. [Leipzig: B. G. Teubner, 1889]). There are difficulties with this story. How are we to explain the presence of Melanippe and her sons in Italy? On this point see Ulrich von Wilamowitz-Moellendorff, *Herakles*, 2nd ed., 2 vols. (Berlin: Weidmann, 1895), 1:10n22, and Robert, *Oidipus* 2:171n33. Only one thing is clear, namely, that the story involves a *transplantation* (a point to which I shall return below) and *hostility toward the family*, for the twins kill their mother's father, Aeolus.

106. See n. 129 infra, a striking example from Oppian.

107. Mr. Severyns rightly reminds me of the birth of the twin sons of Boucolion, who made love to Abarbarea: ποιμαίνων δ' ἐπ' ὄεσσι μίγη φιλότητι καὶ εὐνῇ [while grazing his sheep he shared (her) favors and (her) bed] (Hom. *Il.* 6.25). But here it is a nymph we are talking about. When a mortal woman is visited by a god, either the place is not specified or, when it is, it is an upstairs room (ὑπερώιον εἰσαναβᾶσα [being led to the upper floor]).

108. See Usener, *Die Sintfluthsagen*, 100ff. One may, I think, disregard both the explanation

proposed by Erich Bethe in *Thebanische Heldenlieder: Untersuchungen über die Epen des thebanisch-argivischen Sagenkreises* (Leipzig: S. Hirzel, 1891), 73, which sees Oedipus's chest as an anticipation of the torture of parricides, who are thrown into the sea in a sack; and the one advanced by Robert (see *Oidipus*, 1:255, and *Die griechische Heldensage*, 2:885), who, relying on Aristophanes's χειμῶνος ὄντος [during the winter] (*Ra.* 190), suggests that the infant's sufferings represent the tribulations of the *Jahresgott* Oedipus—a deity of vegetation—during that season. One has only to reread the passage from *The Frogs* to see that here Aristophanes, without the warrant of any accepted tradition, is casting about for some detail that might make Oedipus seem pitiable. None of the fables we are considering here is set in a seasonal context. If one is absolutely determined to find such a context in *Oedipus the King*, recall that there Oedipus was probably born in the spring, for the two shepherds meet when the flocks are brought up into the mountains, which is to say about the middle of May.

109. The object is called κίστη [wicker basket] by Apollodorus (3.14.6.4); κιβωτός [chest] by Pausanias (1.18.2); τεῦχος [vase, urn] by Euripides (*Ion* 273).

110. See Paus. 1.27.4.

111. Jeanmaire, *Couroi et courètes*, 264. [Jeanmaire uses the French word *ciste*, which derives from Greek κίστη (see n. 109 supra) via Latin *cista* and corresponds to the English word *cist*, used here, as elsewhere, to indicate a kind of chest. —Trans.]

112. See Paus. 7.19.

113. See Georges Dumézil, *Le crime des Lemniennes: Rites et légendes du monde égéen* (Paris: P. Geuthner, 1924). Aphrodite, in order to punish the women of Lemnos for having neglected her cult, afflicts them with an evil smell; their husbands leave them and take up with Thracian concubines; in their rage the Lemnian women kill their husbands and remain alone until the arrival of the Argonauts, whom they marry. It is an etiological legend, in other words, concerning an annual festival in which men and women separate on the occasion of a retreat marking a solstice or an equinox, after which a sacred vessel departs for Delos and brings back new fire to Lemnos, signifying the rebirth of joy.

114. See V. Fl. 2.242–305.

115. See my attempt below in Chapter 5 to explain this absurd fable.

116. See Dumézil, *Le crime des Lemniennes*, 46.

117. Usener (*Die Sintfluthsagen*, 103) sees Eurypylus as god of the Wide Gate through which the dead pass but once. It is curious that he did not think to consider the etymology of Hypsipyle, nor even to compare the two names—to say nothing of the fact that another Eurypylus is a son of Telephus, who was subjected to the trial of the chest.

118. See V. Fl. 2.267.

119. See Ap. Rhod. 1.620–626, and the scholium on line 623.

120. It is certainly older than the identification asserted by Valerius Flaccus between Thoas

the Lemnian and his homonym Thoas, king of Tauris, a purely literary character. The floating chest sometimes lands at Oenoë, sometimes at Chios (ruled by Oenopion), sometimes in Crimea. It is surprising that Robert (*Die griechische Heldensage*, 2:854) should consider this last version to be the most ancient.

121. Even the historical Cypselus is brought by Eëtion to Olympia, then to Cleonae (probably the territory of Cleonae in the Argolid), before coming back to Corinth. The stay in Olympia may have been invented to explain the existence of an Olympian votive offering that was called the "Cypselus chest."

122. See Hubaux, "Le plongeon rituel," 5–81, and Jeanmaire, *Couroi et courètes*, 326ff. There one will find most of the narratives in which the theme of the "leap" occurs.

123. Perhaps a tablet bearing the old name was submerged as well. Inscriptions speak of a name that henceforth was to be hidden "in the depths of the sea." Some scholars recognize only the cleansing aspect of the ceremony; see, for example, Paul Foucart, *Recherches sur l'origine et la nature des mystères d'Eleusis* (Paris: C. Klincksieck, 1895), 29.

124. See Christian August Lobeck, *Aglaophamus; sive, De theologiae mysticae Graecorum causis libri tres*, 2 vols. (Königsberg: Borntraeger, 1829), 2:1007ff.

125. Plu. *De sera num. vind.* 23 [= 563f]; see also the excellent analysis in Hubaux, "Le plongeon rituel," 40ff.

126. See Str. 10.2.9, and my discussion earlier in this chapter.

127. These elements are clearly present in legends in which a young girl is thrown into the sea and claimed by a monster of the deep. Alcyone and Andromeda, miraculously saved scapegoats, both enter upon a new life. Others are less lucky, though Dictynna, Britomartis, Leucothea, and Enalus's anonymous lover all receive some measure of compensation after death, living among the Nereids or else being honored by sailors.

128. "The investiture of young princes comes to them from the sea," Charles Picard says in "Néréides et sirènes: Observations sur le folklore hellénistique de la mer," *Annales de l'École des hautes études de Gand* 2 (1938): 127–153. This conclusion is correct, but it results from a set of facts whose complexity Picard wholly fails to grasp. On the one hand, not all leaps are probative in the strict sense. The one made by Theseus is an ordeal of familial legitimation, in which the hero gives proof that he is descended from Poseidon, as we saw earlier. On the other hand, investiture comes to young princes from both the mountains and the sea. To say that the Nereids are *courotrophes*, nurses and tutors of a young male prince, the *couros*, is accurate only so long as the same quality is recognized in nymphs. "It was customary in the divine and heroic society of primeval Greece," Picard maintains, "that a *couros* was raised, not by his earthly mother, but beneath the sea or on the shore" (p. 133)—to which one must add: "or in the mountains." In all the legends that I analyze here, there is nothing that specifically comes under the head of a "folklore of the sea," only a very complex, very altered set of rites transposed into legends.

129. The two themes are often found together in late romances. Oppian gave an account

(*C.* 4:237–277) of the childhood of Dionysus, in which he arbitrarily lumps together any and all themes that depend on the idea of entering into a new life. The infant god is *raised in the mountains* by Ino, Agave, and Autonoë. To take him away from Hera, they put him in a *chest* around which they dance, covering up the baby's cries by the noise of drums and cymbals. Then they *leave the country* and put the sacred chest in a small boat, which is miraculously covered in garlands. The sailors are then so filled with *terror* that they try to *drown themselves*. Bacchus is then brought to Aristaeus, who rears him; indeed, the theme of rearing in the mountains figures twice in this account, referring first to infancy and early childhood, then to adolescence. It is curious to note that, beneath the accumulation of literary detail, the religious sentiment that originally colored the narrative has survived for the most part intact, simply because the poet, for want of imagination, juxtaposes details that are no more than variants of a basic theme.

130. Note that, in the Christian tradition, entry into enclosed orders sometimes involves a funerary ceremony prior to the second birth of one who is now "dead to the world." See *Cérémonial pour la profession monastique selon la règle du B.P.S. Benoît* (Tournai, 1910), 22.

131. Jeanmaire cites a fair number of examples foreign to ancient Greek civilization; see *Couroi et courètes*, 219ff. Hubaux shrewdly analyzes the rite of simulated death as a technique of initiation among the Ndembu Lunda of Congo; see "Le plongeon rituel," 46.

132. Both the cask (*píthos*) and the chest were used for interment. The Pythagoreans were buried in terracotta coffins strewn with leaves of myrtle, olive, and black poplar; see Plin. *Nat.* 35.160.

133. On the causal overdetermination of objects in myths, and their mutual interference, see Roger Caillois, *Le mythe et l'homme* (Paris: Gallimard, 1938), 32–33.

134. See Apollod. 1.8.2.1; *Epit.* 2.10, 3.10.7.

135. See Robert, *Die griechische Heldensage*, 2:1485.

136. See Ant. Lib. 33.

137. See Paus. 6.9.

138. See Theoc. 7.78–89.

139. See Jeanmaire, *Couroi et courètes*, 153.

140. See Jacob Grimm, *Deutsche Rechtsalterthümer*, 4th ed., 2 vols. (Leipzig: T. Weicher, 1899), §461, 1:634.

141. See Frazer, *Folk-lore in the Old Testament*, 1:104–361; and for a bibliography of the subject, note 1 on page 105 of the same volume. Prominent among the realists are Jacques de Morgan and Georges Contenau; see in particular Contenau, *Le Déluge babylonien* (Paris: Payot, 1941). Among the symbolists, in addition to the work of Usener, see Georg Gerland, *Der Mythus von der Sintflut* (Bonn: A. Marcus and E. Weber, 1912). The liturgical explanation is succinctly characterized in Pierre Boyancé, *Le culte des muses chez les philosophes grecs: Études d'histoire et de psychologie religieuses*

(Paris: Boccard, 1936), 71; see also the French edition of Lord Raglan's 1933 book *Jocasta's Crime*, translated as *Le tabou de l'inceste* (Paris: Payot, 1935), 160ff.

142. By contrast, as Mr. Herman Janssens informs me, the cist that contained the religious objects of the people of Israel bears another name. To this I would add that the Septuagint translates *tevah* by κιβωτός (ark) in the sixth chapter of Genesis, while rendering it as θίβη (basket) in the second chapter of Exodus; the Latin versions say *arca* and *thibis*, respectively. Flavius Josephus writes λάρναξ (box, chest).

143. Émile Mâle, *L'art religieux du XII^e siècle en France: Étude sur les origines de l'iconographie du Moyen Âge*, 2nd ed. (Paris: A. Colin, 1924), 49.

144. Contenau, *Le Déluge babylonien*, 83. The emphasis is mine.

145. Glotz is certainly right to explain the name that Lycomedes gives to Achilles's son in the same fashion. He is called Pyrrhos, according to the ancients either because of his red hair or because Achilles, disguised as a girl, came to Scyros under the name of Pyrrha. It remains, then, to explain this latter name. As for the details of red hair and rosy complexion, they come from the name and not the name from them. Tradition credits Thetis with devising two tests of differing character: in the one case she wishes to see whether her sons are immortal; in the other she wishes to confer immortality upon them. In the *Aegimius* attributed to Hesiod by Rzach (fragment 185), she puts them in a fountain filled with water to see if they are able to swim, but they fall to the bottom and die. This is a way of determining legitimacy by water, identical to the one that is applied elsewhere to the sons of rivers or of Poseidon (see my discussion earlier in the present chapter). According to another tradition, she places them over a fire to make them immortal. All the children die, as did the children of Medea, except for one: Thetis is surprised by Peleus, who manages to save the youngest, Achilles. In a variant of this version, Thetis gives birth to Achilles alone, and puts him in the fire overnight, as Demeter had done with Demophon; in the morning Peleus surprises her and interrupts the attempt at immortalization already underway. Thetis then leaves Peleus, goes back to the Nereids, and sends the baby to be raised by Chiron. Chiron gives the name "Achilles" to the infant, who until then had been called *Liguron* (Whining); but he was also called *Pyrisoos* (Saved from the Fire). The story of Thetis dipping Achilles into the waters of the Styx is a contamination, dating from the imperial period, of this version by the legend of invulnerable Ajax. (The relevant texts may all be found in Robert, *Die griechische Heldensage*, 2:65.) The background to these legends soon ceased to be understood. Just as the author of *Rhesus* says that the muse threw her son into the river Strymon in order to *hide her shame*, so the scholiast on Lycophron's *Alexandra* (l. 175) says that Thetis thrust her breasts into the fire to take her vengeance on Peleus because she had been treated in a way that was unworthy of her [ὡς πάσχουσα ἀνάξια ἑαυτῆς].

146. Weizsäcker, who wrote the article on Deucalion in the first volume of Roscher's *Ausführliches Lexikon* (1884–1890), does not even mention this episode. Tümpel, who treated the same topic in the fifth volume of *RE* (1903), refers to it without bothering to discuss it.

147. See Hubaux, "Le plongeon rituel," 27.

148. According to the *Etymologicum Magnum* (ed. T. Gaisford, p. 561, col. 1596, ll. 54–55): ΛΕΥΚΑΡΙΩΝ: καθ' ὑπέρθεσιν Δευκαλίων. καὶ Λευκάδιον, τροπῇ τοῦ Δ εἰς Ρ, Λευκάριον [Leucarion, by transposition (of letter) Deucalion. And Leucadion, by changing *d* to *r*, Leucarion]. The text is probably altered: the first word must be Λευκαδίων, for no transposition (ὑπέρθεσις) could extract *Deucalion* from *Leucarion*; see Hermann Usener, *Kleine Schriften*, 4 vols. (Leipzig: B. G. Teubner, 1912), 4:384. This passage occurs in an article that originally was published as "Zu den Sintfluthsagen," *Rheinisches Museum für Philologie* 56 (1901): 481–496.

149. Scholium on E. *Ph.* 26.

## CHAPTER 2. MURDER OF THE FATHER

1. See Murray Anthony Potter, *Sohrab and Rustem: The Epic Theme of a Combat between Father and Son; A Study of Its Genesis and Uses in Literature and Popular Tradition* (London: D. Nutt, 1902). Potter's conclusions are summarized in Arnold van Gennep, *La formation des légendes* (Paris: E. Flammarion, 1910), 235–242. van Gennep's claim that "legends tenaciously preserve the memory of outmoded institutions" needs to be qualified, as I try to show below in Chapter 8.

2. "[T]wo fundamental taboos of totemism," Freud insists, "[were created] from the *sense of guilt of the son*, and for this very reason these had to correspond with the two repressed wishes of the Oedipus complex. Whoever disobeyed became guilty of the two only crimes which troubled primitive society." Sigmund Freud, *Totem and Taboo: Resemblances between the Psychic Lives of Savages and Neurotics* [1913], trans. A. A. Brill (New York: Vintage, 1946), 185.

3. Hom *Od.* 11.271–280.

4. Ibid., 11.273–274.

5. Cf. Hom. *Il.* 5.151, *Od.* 22.264.

6. See Carl Robert, *Oidipus: Geschichte eines poetischen Stoffs im griechischen Altertum*, 2 vols. (Berlin: Weidmann, 1915), 1:95.

7. A certain number of relevant texts are collected in A.-J. Reinach, "Itanos et l'inventio scuti," *Rev. hist. des rel.* 60 (1909) and 61 (1910). Reinach's point of view toward them is altogether different from mine, however.

8. See Hyg. *Fab.* 170; Plu. *Quaest. gr.* 45; Ap. Rhod. 4:527–532; Plu. *Vit. dec. orat.* 843e, 843f, respectively.

9. See Hdt. 4.9; Plu. *Thes.* 4, 6. At Hom. *Od.* 21.114–117 one reads: εἰ δέ κεν ἐντανύσω διοϊστεύσω τε σιδήρου, / οὔ κέ μοι ἀχνυμένῳ τάδε δώματα πότνια μήτηρ / λείποι ἅμ' ἄλλῳ ἰοῦσ', ὅτ' ἐγὼ κατόπισθε λιποίμην / οἷός τ' ἤδη πατρὸς ἀέθλια κάλ' ἀνελέσθαι [If I succeed in stringing it and shooting an arrow through the iron, I will not be distressed that my venerable mother should leave this home and go off with another man, leaving

me behind, for henceforth I will be able to triumph in the noble competitions of my father].

10. See Albert Severyns, *Le cycle épique dans l'école d'Aristarque* (Liège: H. Vailliant-Carmanne / Paris: É. Champion, 1928), 342.

11. An analogous conflict is implicit in the legend of Apollo killing Eurytus for having proved himself to be the better archer; see Hom. *Od.* 8.224–228 and 21.32 with scholium.

12. On the religious value of spoils, see Appendix 4.

13. A triple junction where roads from Delphi and Daulis met a road from Thebes. —Trans.

14. See Hom. *Il.* 9.54.

15. Pi. *O.* 2.41–42.

16. See my article "Le suicide par vengeance dans la Grèce ancienne," *RHR* 119 (1939): 154–171.

17. Hom. *Od.* 11.272.

18. See book 74 of Pseudo-Callisthenes [The Greek Alexander Romance].

19. See H. Lamer's lengthy article on Laertes in August Friedrich Pauly and Georg Wissowa, eds., *Realencyclopädie der classischen Altertumswissenschaft* [*RE*], first series [A–Q] (Stuttgart: J. B. Metzler, 1894–1963), vol. 12.1, cols. 424–445. Lamer examines first the hypothesis of a primitive legend in which Laertes died before the return of Odysseus (as Hyginus suggests in fable 251, which mentions among those ones living who went among the dead, and who returned from the lower world, *Ulysses Laertae filius propter patrem*). He rejects it, however, on the ground that the entire poem would have had to be recast for Laertes to be absent from it, and concludes that the question need not concern us any more than where the nectar and ambrosia on which Calypso feeds come from or where she obtains the human foods that she offers to her visitors (col. 433), things that we do not wonder about for a moment. Inconsistencies of this kind "are blemishes that do not in any way detract from the beauty of the *Odyssey*" (col. 434). To reason in this manner is to assimilate a very curious survival to contrivances that are part and parcel of legend as a genre.

20. C. W. Westrup, "Le roi dans l'*Odyssée*," in *Mélanges Fournier* (1929), 772. [Reprinted as *Le roi de l'*Odyssée *et la peuple chez Homère* (Paris: Librairie du Receuil Sirey, 1930). —Trans.] Victor Bérard, by contrast, disposes of the problem as though it were merely a matter of psychology, with no political implication: "Anticlea died at that critical age when so many weak women take leave of their senses. . . . Three or four years later, it seems, Laertes, aged, bereft of hope, no longer had the will to go on living in this mansion where everything reminded him of his only son and the wife of his youth. . . . He withdrew to one of his country estates." Bérard, *Les navigations d'Ulysse*, 4 vols. (Paris: A. Colin, 1927–1929), 2:18. L. Bréhier, for his part, in "La royauté homérique et les origines de l'État en Grèce," *RH* 84 (January 1904): 1–32 and *RH* 85 (May

1904): 1–23, looks in the Homeric state for the germ of what later was to become the polis, not for survivals of more ancient institutions.

21. See Hom. *Od.* 16.139, 1.190, 11.194–195, and 24.226–228, respectively.

22. See Hom. *Od.* 11.119–137 and the prediction uttered there by Teresias concerning Odysseus's journey after killing the suitors. E. Meyer saw this prophecy as the primitive kernel or nucleus of the poem; see "Der Ursprung des Odysseus-mythos," *Hermes* 30 (1895): 240. It may just as well have been a linking detail, however, belatedly added in order to connect the *Telegony* [a lost epic poem of the Trojan Cycle] with the *Odyssey.* But Meyer is certainly right to recognize in the denouement of the *Telegony* an archaic theme that allies Odysseus with the Iranian Rustem, the Germanic Hildebrand—and with the Greek Laius.

23. Hom. *Od.* 11.187–196.

24. Delcourt refers here once again to the legendary character (*Rex Nemorensis*) famously described by Frazer in the first chapter of *The Golden Bough.* —Trans.

25. See E. *Andr.* 22–23.

26. See ibid., 1166 and 897, respectively.

27. See Hes. *Sc.* 10, Apollod. 2.4.6.

28. See Apollod. 3.13.1.

29. See O. Waser's article on Eurytus in *RE* 6.1 (1907), col. 1360.

30. See Timonax, *Scythica* fr. 2, and Carl Robert, ed., *Die griechische Heldensage,* constituting the second volume of Ludwig Preller, *Griechische Mythologie,* 2 vols. (Berlin: Weidmann, 1920–1926), 2:790; see also my discussion below in Chapter 5.

31. Thus Robert's opinion; see *Die griechische Heldensage,* 2:1438.

32. Three times, in fact, if one counts the *Narrationes Amatoriae* by Parthenius of Nicea (first century BCE), in which Odysseus unwittingly kills his son Euryalus, born of Euippe.

33. See Georges Dumézil, *Ouranós-Váruna: Étude de mythologie comparée indo-européenne* (Paris: Adrien-Maisonneuve, 1934).

34. See Apollod. 1.1.1.1, D.S. 3.47.

35. A neologism, signifying accounts of the origin and descent of kings.—Trans.

36. See Dumézil, *Ouranós-Váruna,* 44.

37. Ibid., 53–54.

38. See M. Pohlenz's article "Kronos" in *RE* 11.2 (1922), cols. 1982–2018.

39. Hes. *Th.* 464.

40. See Paus. 10.24.5.

41. See Hes. *Th.* 485–500.

42. The children eaten by Cronus before this last one, Zeus, were Hestia, Demeter, Hades, and Poseidon. On the apparent relation of the theme of swallowing up offspring to that of the succession to power, see Jane Ellen Harrison, *Themis: A Study of the Social Origins of Greek Religion* (Cambridge: Cambridge University Press, 1912), 248.

43. Paus. 5.7.10. The *archē* that the two rivals disputed may have been rule over Olympus (the throne of heaven) or government of the world. Which one is meant here matters little for our purposes.

44. See Lyc. *Alex.* 41 and Tz. *ad Lyc.*

45. F. M. Cornford argued that the Olympic games had their origin in a festival of the new year. He mentions Phorbas, Oenomaus, and Cronus as examples of old kings threatened by their successor. It is hard to understand why Cornford did not add Uranus and Laius to this list, and why he was not more impressed by the role played by generational conflict in almost all Greek legends. See Cornford's chapter "The Origin of the Olympic Games" in Harrison, *Themis*, 212–259.

46. See D. S. 4.73; also Paus. 5.13.2.

47. A scholium on line 1010 of *Phoenician Women* says: "The tragic poet Sosiphanes says that Menoeceus was killed by Laius." Surely it is not the son of Creon who is meant here, but the father of Jocasta. If this detail is accurate, Sosiphanes introduced in the Theban legend an element borrowed from the legend of Pelops, and conflict between generations would therefore figure in it three times.

48. See E. *Ph.* 63–68. —Trans.

49. See Paus. 8.14.10; also Pherecydes in the scholium on S. *El.* 509, as well as the scholium on E. *Or.* 981. The role of Myrtilus may be compared with an episode in the life of Siegfried, who likewise conquered on behalf of another.

50. See Hom. *Od.* 11.275–280. —Trans.

51. S. *El.* 504–515. No translation could capture the full richness of admirable verses. One meets with the same sentiment in Euripides, in Electra's monody (*Or.* 987–995).

52. See Severyns, *Le cycle épique dans l'école d'Aristarque*, 232.

53. See Apollod. 3.5.8.1 and Paus. 10.5.2, respectively.

54. Note that this detail was not incorporated in all mythographies. In the account by Nicolaus of Damascus, Oedipus kills Laius with his sword; see Felix Jacoby, ed., *Die Fragmente der griechischen Historiker* [*FGrHist*], 17 vols. (Berlin: Weidmann, 1923–1958), 90 F15, 3:340.

55. See S. *OT* 806–812.

56. Plu. *Quaest. Conv.* 5.2 (= 675c), alluding to Paus. 5.1.4. [The shrine of Olympia was located in the district of Pisa in Elis. —Trans.] I find it impossible to draw any conclusion from the Latin festival of *regifugium* [Flight of the King, held every 24

February], which Frazer interpreted as the survival of a test conferring kingship for the period of a year on the fastest runner; see James George Frazer, *The Magical Origin of Kings* (London: Macmillan, 1920), 264–269. Subsequently, in his commentary on Ovid, *Fasti* 2.685, he recognized that several explanations were possible; see James George Frazer, ed. and trans., *Ovid's* Fasti (London: W. Heinemann, 1931), 394–397. A. Rosenberg, in his article on *regifugium* in *RE*, second series (R–Z), vol. 1 (1914), cols. 469–472, very judiciously says that, in the absence of further information concerning the festival of 24 February, it would appear that the accounts given by Ovid and Plutarch are complementary.

57. See S. *OT* 803. In the scholium on E. *Ph.* 1 one reads: τὸ ἅρμα ὑποστρέψας [having sent back the chariot]; in Apollod. 3.5.7.3: ἐφ᾽ ἅρματος δὲ διὰ τῆς Φωκίος φερόμενος [Οἰδίπους] συντυγχάνει κατά τινα στενὴν ὁδὸν ἐφ᾽ ἅρματος ὀχουμένῳΛαίῳ [Oedipus, driving through Phocis in his chariot along a certain narrow road, came upon Laius, himself riding in a chariot].

58. See A. *Fr.* 173 and scholium on S. *OT* 733; also Robert, *Oidipus*, 1:80–94. Robert concludes a long discussion by saying that the Aeschylean version is likelier to be the more ancient of the two. Here as in many other places he argues on the basis of plausibility, marking the itineraries of the two travelers on a map for the sake of comparison. His conscientious research was inspired by the principle that "a legend in its nascent state needs topographical exactitude" (1:90). But is this really true? M. Nilsson, in *Gött. Gel. Anzeigen* 184 (1922): 41, argues convincingly to the contrary. With regard to the legend of Oedipus, it seems clear that what is primitive is the detail of a *narrow* (or *cleft*) *road*. Many Greek crossroads claimed to have been the site of the patricide. Pausanias (10.5.3) visited the place in Daulis called the cleft road (ἐπὶ ὁδὸν ἀφίζῃ καλουμένην σχιστήν), where the monument said to have been raised by Damasistratus to Laius and his servant—one of those mounds of uncut stones (λίθοι λογάδες σεσωρευμένοι) that travelers formed in honor of Hermes—was found. The identification of this mound with Laius's tomb must have been recent, as also the idea of associating the spring on the road from Anthedon to Thebes with Oedipus's ablutions following the murder (Paus. 9.18.6). These innovations would have been suggested by our poems or else by the detail of the cleft (or split) road, already a cliché in Pisander's summary (ἐν τῇ σχιστῇ ὁδῷ) whose surprising importance has not yet been completely explained.

59. I find it impossible to understand Louis Roussel's interpretation of the murder scene in *Oedipus the King*, in his article "Le récit du meurtre de Laïos dans *Œdipe-Roi* (798–813)," *REG* 42, no. 198 (1929): 361–372. If Oedipus encountered the chariot in front of him (ξυνηντίαζον), or if he stood aside, or if the horses trampled him, then Laius and his herald would not have been able to *violently shove* him off the road (πρὸς βίαν ἠλαυνέτην). Thus Roussel is obliged to translate: *angrily shouted at me to let them pass*. It would be better to take these words in their usual sense, however, and to interpret ξυνηντίαζον in the weaker sense that it often has of "to meet." If the travelers cross paths on a single road, the detail of the split no longer has any point, as Roussel himself recognizes (p. 365). He thinks that, if popular tradition placed the encounter near the modern village of Stavrodhromi, this is for a different reason, that it was a

"strategic place, celebrated by twenty battles" (ibid.). But plainly this cannot be right: popular tradition no longer had any idea in what part of Greece Oedipus killed Laius; it had retained only the detail of the split road. One last point. Roussel finds the πῶλοι δέ νιν χηλαῖς τένοντας ἐξεφοίνισσον ποδῶν [the horses' hooves, running over his heels, reddened them with blood] of *Ph.* 41–42 implausible. It is, of course, if one imagines horses *crushing the feet* of a man advancing toward them; but it is not implausible if one of the horses *injures the calf* of a man whom it leaves behind after having run into him. The exaggeration resides solely in the use of the plural "horses."

60. See Pherecyd. schol. E. *Ph.* 39.

61. See Paus. 10.5.7.

62. See Apollod. 3.5.7.5.

63. See S. *OT* 803.

64. See E. *Ph.* 39.

65. See, for example, Hom. *Il.* 17:608–625.—Trans.

66. As Pohlenz maintains in his article on Kronos in *RE* (see n. 38 supra).

67. See *FGrHist* 90 F15, 3:340.

68. Mythic ancestors of the Theban nobility who were said to have sprung up from the dragon's teeth sown by Cadmus—hence their name: literally, Sown Men.—Trans.

69. The relevant texts have been collected by Robert in *Die griechische Heldensage*; see Preller, *Griechische Mythologie*, 2:114nn6, 7.

70. See Ulrich von Wilamowitz-Moellendorff, "Excurse zum Oedipus des Sophokles," *Hermes* 34 (1899): 55–80, esp. 77ff.

71. Here is the genealogy:

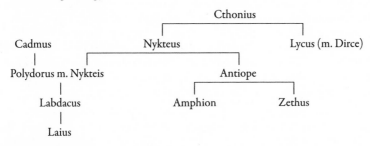

72. See Apollod. 3.5.5.

73. See Paus. 9.5.

74. See Nic. Dam. fr. 14.

75. Henri Jeanmaire, *Couroi et courètes* (Lille: Bibliothèque universitaire, 1939), 575–576; see too the discussion that follows, esp. p. 586. Taking this as a guiding thread, perhaps

one might profitably revisit the mystery of the Athenian *Lycus*, demon and local hero, whom Aristophanes mentions in passing in *The Wasps*. [Twice, at lines 389 and 819, apparently because his shrine is adjacent to the law court named after him.—Trans.]

76. The French text reads "of Theseus," evidently an inadvertent and uncorrected error.— Trans.

77. On the theme of twins who come to the aid of a woman, see Appendix 2; on the theme of the uncle who is both lover and persecutor of his niece, see my discussion above in Chapter 1 and below in Chapter 5.

78. See Hdt. 5.43: Ἐνταῦθα οἱ Ἀντιχάρης ἀνὴρ Ἐλεώνιος συνεβούλευσε ἐκ τῶν Λαΐου χρησμῶν [There (in the Peloponnese) a man from Eleon, Antichares, advised him (Dorieus) in accordance with the oracles of Laius . . . ]. Wilamowitz understands this passage as referring to oracles given to Laius, and refuses to regard Laius as a prophet or a depositary of prophecies; see Wilamowitz-Moellendorff, "Excurse zum Oedipus des Sophokles," 77–80. H. Stein, in his edition of Herodotus (Berlin, 1869), cites in support of the interpretation "oracles given *to* Laius" Hdt. 9.33, τὸ Τισαμένου μαντήιον [the oracle given to Tisamenus]; Th. 2.54, τοῦ Λακεδαιμονίων χρηστηρίου [the oracle given to the Lacedaemonians]; and S. *OT* 906, Λαΐου θέσφατα [the divine oracles given to Laius], where indeed the genitive does designate the one for whom the oracle is meant. But these examples, if one takes care to interpret them properly, prove the opposite of what Stein would have them mean. In all three cases, the provenance of the oracles is clearly indicated by the context: each time the provenance is Delphi; readers of Herodotus and Thucydides and the members of Sophocles's audience could therefore not mistake a genitive of origin for an objective genitive. Without further qualification, the phrase οἱ Λαΐου χρησμοί cannot mean anything other than *the oracles coming from Laius.*

79. See Robert, *Oidipus*, 1:10–11.

80. See Hdt. 4.149. Herodotus traces Oedipus's hereditary relation to the Aegids through the following line of descent: Polynices, Thersandrus, Tisamenus, Autesion, Theras, Oeolycus, Aegeus. Robert feels that this Cadmean lineage is a later tradition and that the Spartan Aegids claimed descent from a different Aegeus (the "Sown Man"), which is to say that in fact they came from a Theban *genos* allied to the race issuing from the dragon's teeth; see *Oidipus*, 1:565ff. Happily we do not have to take sides here in the complicated debate over the history of the Aegids.

81. See Jeanmaire, *Couroi et courètes*, 572. He regards this chapter in Herodotus as a rationalization of legends that themselves had issued from rites, and stresses the presence in the genealogy of the Aegids of an Oeolycus (Sheep-Wolf or Lone Wolf) who is father of an Aegeus, just as the Attic Aegeus has a brother named Lycus. That brings us back to the vocabulary of initiation (see my remarks of a moment ago in this connection), and it would be futile to try to uncover the historical reality hidden beneath tales associated with the first Aegids.

82. Paus. 9.5.15.

83. I find it impossible to interpret the passage in Herodotus as Robert does, placing the Furies' wrath a little after the time of the mythic Aegeus, descended from the Spartoi.

84. See Franz Studniczka, *Kyrene, eine altgriechische Göttin* (Leipzig: F. A. Brockhaus, 1890), 66; and Robert, *Oidipus*, 1:12, 1:565ff.

85. In addition to the explanation proposed by Jeanmaire, see the one found in Georges Dumézil, *Le crime des Lemniennes: Rites et légendes du monde égéen* (Paris: P. Geuthner, 1924).

86. See A. *Eu.* 904–909; also lines 785 and 815.

87. See S. *OT* 418–421. —Trans.


## CHAPTER 3. VICTORY OVER THE SPHINX

1. Henri Jeanmaire, *Couroi et courètes* (Lille: Bibliothèque universitaire, 1939), 314. In this connection see too Edwin Sydney Hartland, *The Legend of Perseus: A Study of Tradition in Story, Custom, and Belief*, 3 vols. (London: D. Nutt, 1894–1896). Hartland's astonishing erudition, while it enables him to bring together a wealth of examples, is of little help in classifying them.

2. See Hes. *Th.* 326. Speaking of Echidna, the poet says: ἣ δ᾽ ἄρα Φῖκ᾽ ὀλοὴν τέκε Καδμείοισιν ὄλεθρον [and she (Echnida) gave birth to the deadly Phix, scourge of the Cadmeans]. φῖκ᾽ schol. φίκ᾽ cod. *Rom. Casenat.* 356 σφίκ᾽ in marg. σφίγγα E φίγγ᾽ Ψ σφίγγ᾽ DF Ω c γρ. φίκα m. rec. marg. I (ed. A. Rzach [Leipzig, 1913]).

3. See Hes. *Sc.* 32–33.

4. See the entry for Βίκας in Hesychius: σφίγγας. Φῖγα· φῖκα, σφίγγα [*Sphinxes.* "Phiga": Phix, Sphinx]. See too Pl. *Cra.* 414d: Ὥσπερ καὶ τὴν Σφίγγα ἀντὶ φιγὸς σφίγγα καλοῦσιν [so in the case of the Sphinx, for example, instead of *Phix* they call it *Sphinx*]. The φιγός given by T is certainly the correct reading: its meaning is confirmed by Hesychius's note, the sole source for which moreover is the passage in Plato. B has σφιγγός, which makes no sense. Burnet is wrong to correct φιγός to read φικός in order to have the form attested by Hesiod. Fleckeisen interprets the *Pici* of Plautus (*Aul.* 701) as masculine forms of *Phix*; see *Jahr. f. Phil.* 5 (1891): 657 and cf. Ath. 5.197a. This hypothesis is all the more plausible, as we will see in what follows, because the Latins conceived of these crushing demons as male beings who tormented women, whereas the Greeks saw them as female beings who tormented men.

5. See Lasus fr. 4 [= *PLG* (ed. T. Bergk [Leipzig, 1892], 3:377]; also Apollod. 3.5.8.

6. E. *Ph.* 1019.

7. E. *Hel.* 167.

8. See Eust. 1709.39 [= ed. J. G. Stallbaum (Leipzig, 1825–1830)].

9. See Ludwig Laistner, *Das Rätsel der Sphinx: Grundzüge einer Mythengeschichte*, 2 vols. (Berlin: W. Hertz, 1889). It must not be forgotten, in judging this work, that it was

written at a time when too many scholars, satisfied with having discovered sun myths everywhere, failed to pose other questions. On p. vii of the preface to the first volume, one finds this excellent advice: "An explanation is always to be preferred that demands of the imagination of the mythic age neither a wealth [of invention], nor ways of acting, nor [other] tendencies that differ from what is characteristic of the imagination of the historical period."

10. See W. H. Roscher, *Ephialtes, eine pathologisch-mythologische Abhandlung über die Alpträume und Alpdaemonen des klassichen Altertums* (Leipzig: B. G. Teubner, 1900). Soranus of Ephesus, and after him several other ancient physicians, had long before refused to credit the existence of a crushing demon and dismissed it as the figment of a fevered imagination. Roscher took Soranus's theories as his point of departure.

11. Ilberg, in his survey *Die Sphinx in der griechischen Kunst und Sage* (Leipzig: Druck von A. Edelmann, 1896), did call attention to the *fragende Mittagsfrau* character of the Sphinx, following Laistner, but without adding any fresh insight.

12. See Georg Weicker, *Der Seelenvogel in der alten Literatur und Kunst: Ein mythologisch-archaeologische Untersuchung* (Leipzig: B. G. Teubner, 1902). Nilsson refuses to grant Sphinxes and Sirens any psychical character whatever, though without making any very persuasive argument; see his *Geschichte der griechischen Religion* (Munich: Beck, 1941), 212, and my further remarks in Addendum 2 below. [A second volume of this work appeared in 1950. —Trans.]

13. See Hom. *Od.* 12.181–201.

14. The French phrase used here, *une âme en peine*, is typically translated in later Christian contexts as "a lost soul" or "a soul in Purgatory." The notion of a permanent condition of emotional distress and mental confusion afflicting the souls of the dead nonetheless has ancient roots in Greek epic, notably Homer, where the shades are (in the words of one commentator on Hom. *Od.* 24.5–10) pathetic in their helplessness. Delcourt seems to suggest that it is the exceptionally intense inner torment of such spirits, chthonian powers of evil, that leads them to torment the living. —Trans.

15. I will recall here only two pieces of evidence: the Berlin amphora (sixth century, inv. no. 684), where a man is shown spilling his seed on a butterfly (this, says Weicker, is the oldest known Greek representation of the butterfly as a symbol of the soul), and this passage from Philostratus (*VA* 4.25) speaking of empusas, lamiae, and mormolyces: ἐρῶσι δὲ αὗται, καὶ ἀφροδισίων μέν, σαρκῶν δὲ μάλιστα ἀνθρωπείων ἐρῶσι καὶ παλεύουσι τοῖς ἀφροδισίοις, οὓς ἂν ἐθέλωσί δαίσασθαι . . . [They delight in the pleasures of Aphrodite, but still more in human flesh, and they seduce those whom they wish to devour . . . ].

16. Weicker, *Der Seelenvogel in der alten Literatur und Kunst*, 127.

17. See A. Delatte, "La musique au tombeau," *RA* 21 (1912): 318–332.

18. Epicharmus, Theopompus, and Sophron all wrote about the Sirens. One might be tempted to apply to these seductresses Ovid's lines in the *Ars Amatoria* (2:122–123): Non formosus erat, sed [erat] facundus Ulixes, et tamen aequoreas torsit amore deas

[Ulysses was not handsome, but he was a fine talker, and he made goddesses of the sea writhe with desire for him]; but these sea goddesses are only a sort of collective pronoun meant to designate Calypso, expressly named in the next sentence.

19. Herbig, in his entry for "Sphinx" [a companion essay to the one by Lesky immediately preceding] in August Friedrich Pauly and Georg Wissowa, eds., *Realencyclopädie der classischen Altertumswissenschaft* [*RE*], second series [R–Z] (Stuttgart: J. B. Metzler, 1914–1972), vol. 3.2 (1929), cols. 1726–1749, argues that the Sphinxes at Mycenae and in Crete had to have been purely ornamental. This is highly unlikely. Primitive art can scarcely be supposed to contain gratuitous motifs. These Sphinxes were probably apotropaic, like the Sirens.

20. The first element of the French word comes from the Latin *calcare* (to tread under foot, trample); the second, as in the case of the English "nightmare," from the Germanic root *mar* (demon). [In Germanic folklore, *der Alp* is a demon believed to sit on people's chests as they sleep. —Trans.]

21. Greek genealogies associate Typhon either with the Sphinx or with her mother, Echidna. [Apollodorus (3.5.8) identifies him as the father of the Sphinx. Typhon's name, the remote source of the English word "typhoon" (and more directly, with no intervening oriental influence, the French *typhon*), originally signified a violent storm. —Trans.]

22. See Laistner, *Das Rätsel der Sphinx*, 1:78–343.

23. It is true, of course, that Circe, in marrying Odysseus, regains her humanity and ceases to cast spells. The marriage of Thetis and Peleus leads to difficulties that are a result of the difference between their natures. It seems to me, too, that Atalanta may be recognized as a tamed enchantress (see my discussion in Chapter 5). But none of these stories has any psychological interest.

24. See my remark in this connection above at n. 14. —Trans.

25. The folk etymology may be found in Servius, *Verg. Aen.* 6.775: Inuus ab ineundo passim cum omnibus animalibus, unde et incubo dicitur [He is called Inuus because he has sexual intercourse indiscriminately with animals of all kinds, whence his name, from "incubus"].

26. See Saint Augustine, *De civ. Dei* 15.23: Creberrima fama est multique se expertos vel ab eis qui experti essent, de quorum fide dubitandum non esset, audisse confirmant Silvanos et Panes, quos vulgo *incubos* vocant, improbos saepe exstitisse mulieribus et earum appetisse ac peregisse concubitum [There are widespread and insistent reports, confirmed by many people, either from their own experience or from accounts of the experience of others, whose trustworthiness there is no reason to doubt, that gods of the woodland and fields who are commonly called *incubi* have often behaved improperly toward women, lusting after them and achieving intercourse with them]. John Chrysostom, by contrast, rejected the popular belief concerning incubi; the Greeks, he held, having long been instructed by philosophers to give no credit to nocturnal visions (Pl. *Cri.* 46c likens the tyranny of majority opinion to children

who conjure up goblins in their sleep), were immune to such chimera. In the end the Augustinian conception prevailed. Saint Thomas Aquinas affirmed that the demon was able to accomplish its purposes, acting sometimes as an incubus, sometimes as a succubus. See Aquinas, *Sum. theol.* 1.51, art. 6, n. 3; cf. E. Mangenot's article "Le Démon d'après les Pères," in A. Vacant, E. Mangenot, and E. Amman, eds., *Dictionnaire de théologie catholique, contenant l'exposé des doctrines de la théologie catholique, leurs preuves et leur histoire,* 15 vols. (Paris: Letouzey et Ané, 1903–1950), vol. 4, part 1, cols. 339–384, particularly col. 362.

See too the opinion expressed by F. B. H. Merkelbach, OP, in his chapter on bestiality in *Quaestiones de Castitate et Luxuria* [1926], 3rd ed. (Liège: La Pensée Catholique, 1929), 68: Ad bestialitatem reducitur concubitus cum daemone succubo vel incubo, apparente sub forma humana; quia daemon est diversae speciei cum homine. Quod peccatum addit bestialitati speciem contra religionem, scil. malitiam superstitionis; insuper aliae malitiae addi possunt secundum formam personae conjunctae, religiosae, ejusdem vel diversi sexus, sub qua daemon se ostendit. Raro daemon vere apparet; ordinario ex quadam vehementi hallucatione fit quod aliquis revera existimet se habere concubitum cum daemone [Bestiality refers to sexual union with a succubus or incubus demon, appearing in human form; because the demon is, by comparison with mankind, of a different species. This sin adds to bestiality the aspect of a crime against religion, namely, the malice of superstition; moreover, other forms of malice may be added to it, depending on what sort of person intercourse takes place with, if he or she is a monk or a nun, or if the demon assumes the form of a person of the same sex or the opposite one. The coming of the demon is quite extraordinary; usually it involves a violent hallucination in which one has the feeling of actually having sexual union with a demon].

Beliefs concerning the power of sorcerers seem to derive solely from ancient superstitions about incubi. Influenced by the Christian opposition of good to evil, however, they came to acquire a moral tone that was lacking in classical tales. In the Middle Ages the forces of evil and the forces of good were imagined to be locked in implacable and merciless combat; nothing of the sort can be found in the purely individual rivalry of Oedipus and the Sphinx, for example. But the two principles were already present in the account of Apollonius of Tyana exorcising the empusa, a text from the first century CE very strongly marked by pietism. The passage from the ancient conception to medieval superstition has not, so far as I know, been carefully studied. It may be that further research would yield interesting results. We do know at least that Bodin (*De la démonomanie des sorciers* [1580], 1.1), in order to demonstrate the existence of demons and the reality of magical powers, quoted passages in the Old and New Testaments and cited to the doctrines of the Greeks on *daimones,* in addition to Saint Augustine and the Jewish and Latin theologians. The essential traits of medieval sorcerers are the same as those of Sirens and Sphinxes: they fly, most often at night; they drink the blood of their victims; and they hunger for erotic pleasure. This is to say that their nature derives in part from the *Seelenvogel,* in part from the oppressing nightmare. I do not see that any author, not even Caillois, has noticed how illuminating it is to compare the thinking of Weicker on this point with that of Laistner and Roscher. Taken together, as I will go on to argue, they make it possible to see noonday demons—both the classical *Daemon meridianus* and the medieval *La Dame de Midi*—as tormented souls.

27. See the article by Roger Caillois, "Les Démons de midi," published in three installments in *RHR* 115 and 116 (1937). Charles Picard, in "Néréides et sirènes: Observations sur le folklore hellénistique de la mer," *Annales de l'École des hautes études de Gand* 2 (1938): 127–153, adopts the same explanation, which moreover he inspired. "The noonday demons," he says, "are the personification of the fatal disturbance associated with cases of encephalitis produced by sunstroke; this morbidity is echoed in the sometimes erotic coloring of the temptation inflicted on sailors." There can be no doubt that this is much too simple an explanation.

28. The reign of Thutmose IV is now commonly dated to the late fourteenth century, and that of Seti I to the late thirteenth century. —Trans.

29. The background to this question may be found in the entry "Sphinx (aegypt.)" by G. Roeder (1929), in W. H. Roscher, ed., *Ausführliches Lexikon der griechischen und römischen Mythologie*, 6 vols. and Supplement (Leipzig: B. G. Teubner, 1884–1937), vol. 4, cols. 1331–1332.

30. Caillois, "Les Démons de midi," *RHR* 116 (1937): 150.

31. See, for example, A. Riegler, "Romanische Namen des Alpdrucks," *Arch. f. d. Stud. d. neueren Sprachen* 167 (1935): 55–63, and the quotations he gives from Höfler's *Krankheitsnamenbuch* (1899).

32. See Laistner, *Das Rätsel der Sphinx*, 1:212. After having said that legends of female demons transcribe the nightmares of men, Laistner turns to the legends of male demons, which, he maintains, either transcribe the nightmares of women or merely reproduce those of men. He neglects a factor that I believe to be significant: the influence of medieval sorcery trials, in which the accused is almost always a woman visited by a devil. Several reasons may explain this prejudice against women. It has often been recalled that during the Middle Ages the Germans believed in the divinatory powers of women, and also that it was in Germany that the most witches were burned. I feel it is necessary to assign greater importance than is usually done to the ideas of the Latins and Saint Augustine concerning male demons that attack women, and to the influence of this doctrine on Latin scholasticism. But in European folklore the dominant image, as in ancient Greece, was of a female demon that attacks men.

33. See ibid., 1:70, 2:249. We will encounter this detail later in the tale of the Theban Sphinx.

34. Littré does not recognize the female form in French. Instead, translating from Forcellini's Latin lexicon, he gives: "*Incube, s.m.* Species of demon believed to take possession of a sleeping woman, or of a woman transported [by participation] in a witches' sabbath, for the purpose of enjoying sexual pleasure. Lat. *Incubus.*" And this: "*Succube, s.m.* Demon that, according to popular opinion, takes the form of a woman in order to have intercourse with a man."

35. The *Lore*, in the tales collected by Laistner, is at first as light as the breeze that carries

her along; then she becomes heavier and heavier, crushing whoever carries her. With the *Lai des deux amants* of Marie de France, in the twelfth century, the evolution of the myth of the Dame de Midi had come to an end, the tale having finally been transformed after two millennia into a romance.

36. O. Crusius, in "Die Epiphanie der Sirene," *Philol.* 50 (1891): 93 and plate 1 there, very rightly recognizes a σύμπλεγμα [sexual encounter (literally, entangled limbs)] between a Siren and a peasant, and not, as Michaëlis had argued in an article the year before, in *Lit. Centralblatt* (1890), between a Siren and a Satyr; see Figure 16 in the present work.

37. See fig. 8 in P. Orsi, "Nuove Antichi di Gela," *MonAL* 19 (1908): 99–102, and Orsi's comment on it there.

38. Puzzlingly, since the reproduction of this image in Figure 1 is in fact the same as the one originally published by Orsi, Delcourt describes a quite different scene in which the youth's entire body is attached to that of the Sphinx; both of his feet and legs are shown between her hindlegs, she says, his left hand is buried in her chest, and his head is turned and his gaze cast back at the face of the Sphinx. For this account I have substituted here a briefer description of the scene as it appears on the Gela vase. —Trans.

39. See Hom. *Od.* 9.415–472. —Trans.

40. Carl Robert, *Oidipus: Geschichte eines poetischen Stoffes im griechischen Altertum,* 2 vols. (Berlin: Weidmann, 1915), 2:19.

41. Delcourt translates here from Wilamowitz's review of Orsi's article, in *Lit. Zentralblatt* 60 (1909), cols. 1571–1573. —Trans.

42. L. Malten, "Das Pferd im Totenglauben," *Jahrb. d. K. d. archäol. Instit.* 29 (1914): 246n3.

43. See E. de Chanot's article in *Gaz. Arch.* 2 (1876): 77, with no precise attribution. [The reference is to a short-lived journal of the period, edited by de Witte and Lenormant, that seems to have left no trace in modern online digests. —Trans.] I do not know what became of the vase. C. H. Emilie Haspels, in *Attic Black-Figured* Lekythoi (Paris: E. de Boccard, 1936), appears to make no mention of it; see nonetheless pl. 41, fig. 4 in her book, a white lekythos with black figures held by the Louvre (CA 111, L. 28), representing a young man in the clutches of the Sphinx, between two spectators—a similar scene to the one in Figure 2 (see my further discussion below). The poor resolution of the image in *Gaz. Arch.* makes dating difficult; it is also reproduced in Henri Gaidoz and Eugène Rolland, eds., *Mélusine: Recueil de mythologie, littérature populaire, tradition & usages,* 11 vols. (Paris: Librairie Viaut, 1878–1912), 1:173.

44. See Adolf Furtwängler, *Die antiken Gemmen: Geschichte der Steinschneidekunst im classischen Altertum,* 3 vols. (Leipzig: Gesecke & Devrient, 1900), vol. 1, pl. 6, no. 32. A similar subject is represented on a chalcedony scarab in the Naue Collection at Munich, but here a griffin is shown holding down a young man beneath him (Figure 4). An exact replica of the first scarab, made from rock crystal in Crete, may be found in Furtwängler, *Die antiken Gemmen,* vol. 1, pl. 6, no. 30, and pl. 8, no. 7.

45. See Maxime Collignon and Louis Couve, *Catalogue des vases peints du Musée national d'Athènes*, 3 vols. (Paris: A. Fontemoing, 1902–1904), 1:472n1480. See also R. Weisshaeupel, *AEph* (1893), col. 15ff.; and Robert, *Oidipus*, 1:55, fig. 21, and 2:24n13.

46. See Paul Jacobsthal, *Die Melischen Reliefs* (Berlin: H. Keller), 1931, pl. 5, nos. 7 and 8; pl. 6, no. 9; also pl. 46, no. 85, and the accompanying bibliography. The first of these reliefs was considered by all its editors to come from Tenos, although the original bears on the reverse an inscription by its first owner, T. Burgon, attesting that it was discovered at Milo in 1819. Burgon took it to be a work by Hermon. All of these reliefs were produced by a local workshop that in all probability was founded around 475 BCE and remained in operation until about 440. They are evidence of a provincial but nonetheless quite charming art. Small in size (the largest of them measures 160 mm. by 197 mm. [6.24 in. by 7.68 in.]), they probably were used to decorate burial chests. The first two are now in the British Museum, the third in the Vlasto Collection in Marseille, and the last in the National Archeological Museum in Athens.

47. See Malten, "Das Pferd im Totenglauben," 245, fig. 34. A sexual encounter of the same kind seems to be depicted on the Corinthian aryballos studied by R. Hackl, "Eine neue Seelenvogeldarstellung auf korinthischen Aryballos," *Arch. f. Rel.* 12 (1909): 204–206. Here one sees a recumbent male, apparently in a swoon, turning his back on a Siren; cf. Malten, "Das Pferd im Totenglauben," 239, fig. 27. I have not been able to consult Furtwängler's article on the Sphinx of Aegina, in *Münch. Jahrb. f. bild. Kunst* 1 (1906): 4.

48. See Johannes Overbeck, *Gallerie heroischer Bildwerke der alten Kunst*, 2 vols. (Brunswick: C. A. Schwetschke, 1853–1857), vol. 2, pl. 1, fig. 8.

49. See Otto Jahn, *Archeologische Beiträge* (Berlin: G. Reimer, 1847), 112ff.

50. See ibid., pl. 1.

51. See Hetty Goldman, "Two Unpublished Oedipus Vases in the Boston Museum of Fine Arts," *AJA* 15, no. 3 (1911): 378–385, and my discussion later in this chapter.

52. Georges Nicole, *Catalogue des vases peints du Musée national d'Athènes. Supplément*, 2 vols. (Paris: H. Champion, 1911), no. 965.

53. See Haspels, *Attic Black-Figured* Lekythoi, 19.

54. Collignon and Couve, *Catalogue des vases peints du Musée national d'Athènes*, vol. 1, no. 895.

55. Concerning the four vases: (1) Louvre CA 111 (L. 28); cf. Haspels, *Attic Black-Figured* Lekythoi, pl. 41, fig. 4. The scene strongly resembles that of my Figure 2 (viz. n. 40 supra). (2) Syracuse 12085, excavated from tomb 891 at Megara Hyblaea. (3) Athens 12954 (very probably the same vase described by Nicole in his catalog as no. 965, bearing the inventory number 12965; the concordance in Nicole's edition does not include the number 12954). (4) Vienna 190.

56. See Haspels, *Attic Black-Figured* Lekythoi, 130–132, pl. 241, nos. 7–10; she dates the Haimon Painter to about 480. See also my discussion later in this chapter.

272 Notes

57. The first vase is cataloged as Mannheim 128; see H. Hoffmann, *Griechische Vasen in Mannheim* [n.p., n.d.], pl. 1, fig. 1, 4. Regarding the Princeton vase see Haspels, *Attic Black-Figured* Lekythoi, 264, pl. 33, nos. 40–41. By her reckoning, the Emporion Painter flourished around 470.

58. In all these cases an incubus dominates a prostrate youth. This may explain Circe's advice to Odysseus that he have his companions lash him to the mast by his hands and feet, in an *upright standing position*:

δησάντων σ' ἐν νηὶ θοῇ χεῖράς τε πόδας τε
ὀρθὸν ἐν ἱστοπέδῃ . . . [*Od.* 12:51–52]

[let them bind you in the swift ship hand and foot,
upright in the step of the mast . . . ]

From the moment that Odysseus is securely fastened, his position seems to have no importance among the precautions taken against the Sirens. But the poet surely thought otherwise, for the verse is repeated twice in the rest of the tale (at lines 162 and 179). In the figurative representations illustrating the Sirens episode, Odysseus is almost always naked, like the young Thebans menaced by the Sphinx; see in this connection Franz Müller, *Die antiken Odyssee-Illustrationen in ihrer kunsthistorischen Entwicklung* (Berlin: Weidmann, 1913), 31–47.

59. The entry in Suidas reads: Μεγαρικαὶ σφίγγες · αἱ πόρναι οὕτως εἴρηνται. ἴσως δὲ ἐντεῦθεν καὶ σφιγκταὶ οἱ μαλακοὶ ὠνομάσθησαν. ἢ καὶ ἀπὸ Μαίας οὕτω λεγομένης ἐν Μεγάροις · « ἀλλ' ἔστιν ἡμῖν Μεγαρική τις μηχανή » ἀντὶ τοῦ πονηρά. διεβάλλοντο γὰρ ἐπὶ πονηρίᾳ οἱ Μεγαρεῖς. [Sphinxes of Megara: This is what prostitutes are called. Whence perhaps the name "Sphinxed ones" (= debauched) given to effeminate men; this at least from what is known of Maia, so called in Megara: "but we have a kind of *Megaric* machine," which is to say *perverted* (= debauched); for she was maligned by the Megarians on account of her debauchery.] Hesychius's note, under the head Σφιγγός πράγματα παρέχων, also takes "Sphinx" to be a proper name, but here it refers to the Theban inquisitor, not the erotic demon we are interested in here. In the poem for Demetrius Poliorcetes (third century BCE) quoted by Douris of Samos and repeated in Athenaeus 6.58–63 (ed. G. Kaibel [Leipzig, 1887–1890], 2:253), nothing remains of the Sphinx's reputation as an incubus; she is solely a murderer.

60. Paus. 5.11.2.

61. See Eichler's article in *Jahresh. Österr. arch. Inst.* 30 (1937); cf. Benndorf's summary of the earliest excavations in *Anz. d. kais. Akad. in Wien, phil.-hist. Kl.* 134, nos. 5 and 6 (1897).

62. Preserved in lines 36–37 of the Pisander scholion; see Appendix 1.

63. See André de Ridder, *Catalogue des vases peints de la Bibliothèque Nationale*, 2 vols. (Paris: E. Leroux, 1901–1902), 1:186, no. 278 and fig. 29; also Scarlat Lambrino, *Corpus vasorum antiquorum*, 2 vols. (Paris: E. Champion, 1923–1928), 1:34 and pl. 46, nos. 7–9.

64. See Robert's discussion in *Oidipus*, 49; reproduction on p. 14. See too Goldman, "Two Unpublished Oedipus Vases," which dates the vase to the second quarter of the fifth century; she thinks it was very probably a children's toy illustrated with a scene from a popular nursery tale.

65. I should add that the two figures on the Boston lekythos look upon each other with what appears to be mutual fascination. One observes the same thing on the Athens lekythos, only there it is clearly the young man who is vanquished; moreover the Sphinx is larger than he is, whereas she is smaller than Oedipus on the Boston lekythos.

66. In this connection I decline to rely upon the intaglio discovered in 1915 at Thisbe in Boeotia and published by Sir Arthur Evans ten years later in "'The Ring of Nestor': A Glimpse into the Minoan After-Life and a Sepulchral Treasure of Gold Signet-Rings and Bead-Seals from Thisbe, Boeotia," *J. Hell. Stud.* 45, no. 1 (1925): 1–75; see the illustration at p. 27, fig. 31. Evans dates the scene to the fifteenth century BCE. In it one sees a young prince attacking a Sphinx. He holds a dagger in his right hand and is lunging toward her. Evans was so convinced that the hero was Oedipus and that the legend of the Swollen Foot was already extant a thousand years before Aeschylus that he expressed surprise at not detecting a limp ("[T]here is no halting in the gait of the youthful hero," he remarks). If the intaglio is authentic, it proves that there existed an archaic version in which the conqueror not only used a weapon against the Sphinx, but used a metal weapon. This theme must then have wholly vanished from the later iconography, reappearing only after the fifth century. But the authenticity of the treasure from Thisbe is so doubtful that it will be better to refrain from concluding anything from it. One may find a summary of the relevant arguments in B. S. A. Al, "De mann. et de vrouw. godheit v. d. boomcultus in d. minoïsche godsdienst," doctoral dissertation, University of Amsterdam, 1942, as well as a list of those authors who consider the Thisbe rings to be false (Coussin, Schweitzer, Nilsson, Schachermeyr) and those who hold them to be authentic (Evans, Reinach). Al himself has prudently avoided taking sides. Nilsson, for his part, considers that, of a set of pieces that is suspect in its entirety, the Oedipus intaglio is one of the most probably false ones; see his note to the text of *Geschichte der griechischen Religion*, 333.

67. See Hom. *Od.* 12.44–46. —Trans.

68. See Crusius, "Die Epiphanie der Sirene," 93.

69. See Müller, *Die antiken Odyssee-Illustrationen*, 31–47, which collects all the figurative representations of the Homeric Sirens and their suicide; for the corresponding texts, see Weicker, *Der Seelenvogel in der alten Literatur und Kunst*, 45. In the surviving literary record, mention of the Sirens' suicide does not occur before Lycophron.

70. See A. S. Murray, "A Rhyton in Form of a Sphinx," *J. Hell. Stud.* 8 (1887): 1–5 (pl. 81, p. 320); also Cecil Harcourt Smith, *Catalogue of the Greek and Etruscan Vases in the British Museum*, 4 vols. (London: British Museum, 1925), 3:344, E 696. Carl Robert has shown how far the painter was influenced by the Parthenon; his work was composed for the public of Sophocles and Euripides. See Robert, *Oidipus*, 1:50, 2:21n6.

71. See Apollod. 3.5.8.7; D. S. 4.64; scholia on E. *Ph.* 50 and 1505; a Byzantine summary of A. *Th.* [Delcourt appears to be referring here to a text now found in O. L. Smith, ed., *Scholia in Aeschylum II:2: Scholia in* Septem adversus Thebas *contiens* (Leipzig: Teubner, 1982), 3–5. —Trans.]; Hyg. *Fab.* 67.

72. See Apollod. 3.5.8.4; also Asclepiades of Tragilus, cited in the scholium on E. *Ph.* 45.

73. See Paul Hartwig, *Die griechischen Meisterschalen der Blüthezeit des strengen rothfigurigen Stiles* (Stuttgart: W. Spemann, 1893), 664, pl. 73. Hartwig attributes the work to a painter he calls the Maître à la Guirlande and whom he dates to a little after the middle of the fifth century. J. D. Beazley later attributed this work, together with the whole of this painter's production, to Douris; see Beazley, *Attische Vasenmaler des rotfigurigen Stils* (Tübingen: Mohr, 1925), 205. Beazley was seconded in this view by Hubert Philippart, who dates the work to 490–480; see Philippart, *Collections de céramique grecque en Italie,* 2 vols. (Paris: Les Belles Lettres, 1932–1933), 1:25ff.

74. See n. 58 supra.

75. See Hom. *Od.* 10:275–301. —Trans.

76. See Laistner, *Das Rätsel der Sphinx,* 1:261.

77. A queen/ogress lying in ambush near Thebes poses three questions, devours those who cannot correctly answer them, and marries the one who can. See Bernhard Schmidt, *Griechische Märchen, Sagen und Volkslieder* (Leipzig: B. G. Teubner, 1877), 143–144, 247–250.

78. Paus. 9.26.2–3.

79. Pausanias, *Guide to Greece,* trans. Peter Levi, rev. ed., 2 vols. (London: Penguin, 1979), 1:363. [Some of Levi's Greek spellings have been Latinized to match the form adopted in the present edition. —Trans.]

80. The historian Lysimachus, cited by the scholium on E. *Ph.* 26, seems to have recounted it in his *Theban Paradoxes.*

81. Robert, *Oidipus,* 1:498.

82. A. *Th.* 541: Σφίγγ' ὠμόσιτον; 777: τὰν ἁρπαξάνδραν κῆρ' ἀφελόντα χώρας. Here and below the Greek is translated by the italicized text.

83. Pi. *Fr.* 62: αἴνιγμα παρθένου ἐξ ἀγριᾶν γνάθων.

84. S. *OT* 35–36: ὅς γ' ἐξελύσας ἄστυ Καδμεῖον μολὼν / σκληρᾶς ἀοιδοῦ δασμὸν ὃν παρείχομεν.

85. S. *OT* 130: ἡ ποικίλῳδος Σφίγξ (this form of the name, I believe, occurs only here); 391: ἡ ῥαψῳδὸς κύων.

86. S. *OT* 1198–1201: Ὦ Ζεῦ, κατὰ μὲν φθίσας / τὰν γαμψώνυχα παρθένον / χρησμῳδὸν θανάτων δ' ἐμᾷ χώρᾳ πύργος ἀνέστα.

87. E. *Ph.* 48–50: ὅστις σοφῆς αἴνιγμα παρθένου μάθοι … τυγχάνει δέ πως / μούσας ἐμὸς παῖς Οιδίπους Σφιγγὸς μαθών.

88. E. *Ph.* 1505–1507: τᾱς ἀγρίας ὅτε / δυσξυνέτου ξυνετὸν μέλος ἔγνω / Σφιγγὸς ἀοιδοῦ σῶμα φονεύσας.

89. See Paus. 9.26.2, Apollod. 3.5.8.4.

90. See the scholia on E. *Ph.* 1760, ll. 35–40, in Appendix 1.

91. See the scholium on E. *Ph.* 45.

92. Robert has thoroughly cataloged the modifications to which the later poets and mythographers subjected the theme of the Sphinx, conscientiously fulfilling the promise of his book's subtitle (to provide the history of a poetic subject in Greek antiquity). For the various "romances of the Sphinx," see *Oidipus*, 1:495–503. Apart from the tale summarized by Pausanias that we examined earlier, none of them seems to contain legendary elements.

93. See Percy Gardner, "Vases Added to the Ashmolean Museum," *J. Hell. Stud.* 24 (1904): 314; also J. D. Beazley, *Corpus vasorum antiquorum. Great Britain. Oxford—Ashmolean Museum*, fasc. 1 (Oxford: Clarendon Press, 1927), 18, pl. 19, nos. 5, 8.

94. Robert cites by way of example the Sphinx of the Naxians, a column that stood next to the Temple of Apollo in Delphi, and the tomb in Lamptrai as it was reconstructed by F. Winter; see *Oidipus*, 1:52.

95. See *Oesterr. Mus. f. Kunst u. Industrie: Mon. dell'Inst.* 7, pl. 45; *Wiener Vorlegebl.* (1899), pl. 8, no. 10; Karl Masner, *Die Sammlung antiker Vasen und Terrakotten im K. K. Oesterreich Museum: Katalog und historische Einleitung* (Vienna: C. Gerold's Sohn, 1892), 336; Wilhelm Klein, *Die griechischen Vasen mit Meistersignaturen* (Vienna: C. Gerold's Sohn, 1887), 201, pl. 5; Joseph Clark Hoppin, *A Handbook of Attic Red-Figured Vases: Signed by or Attributed to the Various Masters of the Sixth and Fifth Centuries B.C.*, 2 vols. (Cambridge, Mass.: Harvard University Press, 1919), 2:28; and Beazley, *Attische Vasenmaler des rotfigurigen Stils*, 300.

96. See Robert, *Oidipus*, 1:53.

97. See Weicker, *Der Seelenvogel in der alten Literatur und Kunst*, 9; also Lesky's entry on the Sphinx in *RE*, second series, vol. 3 (1929), col. 1720.

98. See Artem. 77.14, 77.19; 78.15; 81.27; 160.14, 160.20.

99. See Erich Bethe, *Thebanische Heldenlieder: Untersuchungen über die Epen des thebanisch-argivischen Sagenkreises* (Leipzig: S. Hirzel, 1891), 17.

100. See Hes. *Th.* 298.

101. On the notion of a "threefold adversary" see Georges Dumézil, *Horace et les Curiaces* (Paris: Gallimard, 1942), 52, 88, 129–133.

102. Due to Corinna, according to the scholium on E. *Ph.* 26 (quoted in Chapter 2).

103. See E. *Ph.* 810.

104. Scholium on E. *Ph.* 1064; no source indicated.

105. Scholia on E. *Ph.* 1031 and 934; the source in both cases, if we accept Unger's correction [*Thebana Paradoxa* (Halle, 1845), 386], probably correct, is Euripides's *Antigone.*

106. See Pisander scholion, ll. 1–4 (Appendix 1); D. Chr. *Orat.* 11.8.1 (ed. H. von Arnim [Berlin, 1893–1896], 1:117); Apollod. 3.5.8.

107. Ode 13 [= fr. 36.8–9 (ed. J. M. Edmonds [London, 1922–1927], 3:163)].

108. Literally, erotic desire not in accordance with the law, which is to say an "abnormal" kind of love, apart from or outside the law.

109. I do not see even that the question has been seriously studied by scholars of mythology and folklore. One massive compendium contains only a passing mention of the tortures that served to test the physical strength and moral fiber of future leaders, this among the Indians of the Orinoco River in South America. See Gaidoz and Rolland, *Mélusine,* 4:236.

110. "Regrettably," Georges Dumézil notes, "initiations are not known to us directly through the description of rituals, nor even through myths that duplicate these rituals, but through epic accounts of this or that more or less fabulous hero in which the ancient religious material has been inserted and at the same time romanticized." Dumézil, *Horace et les Curiaces,* 30.

### CHAPTER 4. THE RIDDLE

1. See Konrad Ohlert, *Rätsel und Gesellschaftsspiele der alten Griechen* (Berlin: Mayer & Müller, 1886). Wolfgang Schultz, in *Rätsel aus dem hellenischen Kulturkreise,* 2 vols. (Leipzig: J. C. Hinrichs, 1909–1912), considers riddles to include everything that has a secondary sense or meaning: symbols, oracles, Pythagorean counsels, and so on; but he ignores all those questions, rare in Greece, that are answered by a word that must be known beforehand. Since he studies riddles in the context of an astral (and especially a lunar) mythology, he classifies them according to the natural category to which the words that solve them belong. His book, though it is not without a certain interest, adopts a perspective too different from mine to be of any great service.

2. See J. B. Friedreich, *Geschichte des Räthsels* (Dresden: Küntze, 1860); riddles that were a matter of life and death Friedreich studies separately (see note at p. 127). Curiously, the theme subsists in tales written in a light, playful style, such as Thomas Percy's ballad "King John and the Abbot of Canterbury," in which the abbot must answer three questions on pain of death: How much money is the king worth? How long does it take to go around the world? What is the king thinking?

3. See S. *Fr.* 181 and my discussion of the Sirens in Chapter 3.

4. See my discussion in Chapter 2. Schultz leaves to one side all riddles of the first type.

5. See Ludwig Laistner, *Das Rätsel der Sphinx: Grundzüge einer Mythengeschichte,*

2 vols. (Berlin: W. Hertz, 1889), 1:50, 65, 186; also *Grimms' Fairy Tales*, no. 55, "Rumpelstiltskin."

6. See Philostr. *VA* 4.25.

7. Here I take the liberty of unpacking the phrase Delcourt uses here and below, *devinettes en action*. In the narrowest sense it refers to riddles that assume the form of mysterious acts (rather than questions) needing to be interpreted, as in the tale of Turandot. —Trans.

8. For these two types of question see Laistner's chapter on *die Fragepein* in *Das Rätsel der Sphinx*, 1–78. So-called counting-out games are of the second type; an echo of them can still be heard today in the Catholic catechism (There is only one God, there are two Testaments, and so on).

9. See Chapter 3, n. 73.

10. See Hes. *Op.* 533–535:

τότε δὴ τρίποδι βροτοὶ ἴσοι,
οὔ τ᾽ ἐπὶ νῶτα ἔαγε, κάρη δ᾽ εἰς οὖδας ὁρᾶται,
τῷ ἴκελοι φοιτῶσιν, ἀλευόμενοι νίφα λευκήν.

[Then, like the Three-legged One (i.e., an old man with a staff) whose back is broken and whose head looks down upon the ground, in a like condition do they (mortals) go forth to escape the brilliant snow].

11. See Ath. 10.451–452:

εἰσὶ κασίγνηται διτταί, ὧν ἡ μία τίκτει
τὴν ἑτέραν, αὐτὴ δὲ τεκοῦσ᾽ ὑπὸ τῆσδε τεκνοῦται.

[They are two sisters, one of whom gave birth to the other, and this one, who gave birth, was born of the one she bore.]

The conundrum is explained by the fact that the names Day and Night in Greek (Hemera and Nyx) are both feminine. Schultz assumes, no doubt wrongly, that the riddle of day and night was another one of the Sphinx's riddles; see *Rätsel aus dem hellenischen Kulturkreise*, 2:67.

12. Such riddles are found in Greek folklore; see Ohlert, *Rätsel und Gesellschaftsspiele der alten Griechen*, 53ff.

13. The year of Nizāmī's death is now generally agreed to have been 1209, and his great poem *Haft paykar* (literally, seven portraits) is thought to have been composed in 1197. See the introduction to Julie Scott Meisami, ed. and trans., *The Haft Paykar: A Medieval Persian Romance* (Oxford: Oxford University Press, 1995), vii–xi, xv–xxii. —Trans.

14. Delcourt's summary of the tale differs in several important respects from Meisami's authoritative translation of the original Persian text; see ibid., 159–174. The French version on which Delcourt relies is nonetheless accurate in its essentials, or at least

sufficient for her purpose here, and I have let it stand with only a few minor changes for the sake of clarity. —Trans.

15. See Pierre Saintyves, *Les contes de Perrault et les récits parallèles: Leurs origines (coutumes primitives et liturgies populaires)* (Paris: E. Nourry, 1923).

16. I shall not attempt here to explain once more Samson's riddle in the Book of Judges (14:12–20). But it may not be beside the point to recall three things. First, the riddle involves a victory over a lion. Next, it involves a marriage. The tale even mentions the ancient practice of communal marriage: following Samson's defeat, the girl's father gives her to one of his son-in-law's friends after she had betrayed him. Finally, the thirty young men designated as Samson's companions put one in mind of age groups. At stake in this case are clothes of a particular type; Samson, having lost his wager, must obtain them by killing thirty men in Ashkelon. Now, the role played by the exchange of old clothes for new ones in the trials and ceremonies that accompany the graduation of adolescents to a higher age group is well known. All these customs—communal marriage, rites of passage, the changing of clothes through conquest—were foreign to the civilization of the Israelites. It is all the more striking to encounter them here, in connection with a riddle and as part of a larger context whose internal coherence escapes us. As for Samson's riddle itself, note that the riddles of the Old Testament are generally parables, establishing an equivalence between an image and an abstract idea; see, for example, those of Ezekiel 17 and Daniel 8, which are quite similar to dreams whose meaning needs to be worked out (Genesis 40–41). Mr. Hermann Janssens has drawn my attention to the fact that Samson's riddle may be compared to Greek conundrums insofar as the same Hebrew word may mean both "honey" and "lion."

## CHAPTER 5. MARRIAGE TO A PRINCESS

1. How many of these trials were known to the author of the *Nekyia?* Murder of the old king and winning of the queen's hand, certainly; exposure of the infant, possibly, since Oedipus did not know his parents, though his ignorance could have been contrived by other means. See Murray Anthony Potter, *Sohrab and Rustem: The Epic Theme of a Combat between Father and Son. A Study of Its Genesis and Uses in Literature and Popular Tradition* (London: D. Nutt, 1902), 83–97. We know nothing of the archaic test that would have led to conquest of the princess in this case.

2. See Carl Robert, *Oidipus: Geschichte eines poetischen Stoffes im griechischen Altertum*, 2 vols. (Berlin: Weidmann, 1915), 1:115; also Albert Severyns, *Le cycle épique dans l'école d'Aristarque* (Liège: H. Vailliant-Carmanne / Paris: É. Champion, 1928), 216.

3. See S. *OT* 577–581.

4. R. C. Jebb, one of the few critics to remark on the oddity of this "tripartite government," likens it to analogous—though historical—regimes in Argos and Troezen (Paus. 2.18.4 and 2.30.8, respectively); see the second revised edition of Jebb's translation and commentary (Cambridge: Cambridge University Press, 1897). The idea that Sophocles's "source" is to be found in polyarchies of this type seems all the

more implausible as they lack the essential characteristic of the Theban system, namely, that Oedipus alone exercises power while Creon and Jocasta alone are authorized to transmit it.

5. Delcourt says flatly that that the archaic reality was wholly unknown at the time she was writing, possibly a rhetorical overstatement in view of recent archaeological research in which she would naturally have taken a keen interest (hence my slight qualification). At all events she could not then have known of later discoveries that were to undermine the old assumptions of historical linguistics. See for example Colin Renfrew, *Archaeology and Language: The Puzzle of Indo-European Origins* (London: Jonathan Cape, 1987). —Trans.

6. James George Frazer, *The Magical Origin of Kings* (London: Macmillan, 1920), 232–233.

7. Ibid., 245, 249, 241.

8. Peleus (banished together with Telamon because they killed their half-brother Phocus) arrives in Phthia, marries Antigone, daughter of Eurytus (or Eurytion), who gives his son-in-law a third of his kingdom. Peleus then inadvertently kills his father-in-law in the Calydonian hunt. In this legend, as in so many others, one finds the theme of murder of an old king associated with that of marriage to a princess.

9. See Friedrich Pfister, *Der Reliquienkult im Altertum*, 2 vols. (Giessen: A. Töpelmann, 1909–1912). Pfister convincingly demonstrates the purely fabulous character of the genealogies of Megara, Troezen, Achaea, Thessaly, and Pylos: all proper names are either eponyms or else derive from local cults.

10. Frazer, *The Magical Origin of Kings*, 241.

11. See Hyg. *Fab.* 60, 239, 254.

12. See Carl Robert, ed., *Die griechische Heldensage*, constituting the second volume of Ludwig Preller, *Griechische Mythologie*, 2 vols. (Berlin: Weidmann, 1920–1926), 2:117n6. One might also cite in this connection the role of Amulius, who disguised himself as the god Mars in order to take advantage of his niece (Liv. 1.3.10–1.4.5; cf. Plu. *Rom.* 3), assuming that this detail does in fact come from the legend of Sisyphus and Tyro, as it may well do.

13. See Hom. *Od.* 2.122–145.

14. See ibid., 15.522, where Telemachus names Eurymachus as the most eager "to marry my mother and have the honors of Odysseus" [μητέρ' ἐμὴν γαμέειν καὶ Ὀδυσσῆος γέρας ἕξειν]. This is also the point of view of one of the suitors, who says: " . . . and his house we would have to give to his mother and to him who will marry her" [οἰκία δ' αὖτε / τούτου μητέρι δοῖμεν ἔχειν ἠδ' ὅς τις ὀπυίοι]. But in other passages Odysseus's property appears to be meant to pass to Telemachus, no matter what Penelope should decide. This is what appears to be implied by the alternative that Antinous proposes to the other suitors (16.364–392): either they kill Telemachus so that his property and treasure will go to the one among them whom Penelope chooses as a husband; or they

allow Telemachus to live, in which case he will keep all the wealth of his father [ἔχειν πατρώϊα πάντα (l. 388)], and each one of them seek in the meantime to win Penelope's hand by wooing her with gifts. Kingship in Ithaca is not at issue here, and Penelope, under this system, appears to be loved for herself.

The same conception crops up in the advice given by Odysseus to his wife on setting out for Troy (18.266–270): when their son will have become a bearded man, she should consider herself free to leave his house and to wed whomever she pleases. In this connection Penelope recalls the custom of nuptial competition (18.275–279), according to which suitors vie with one another in the form of sumptuous gifts—in contradiction of the fear expressed by Telemachus that he will have to return Penelope's dowry to his grandfather in the event that he turns out his mother. Later, in the book immediately following (19.530–534), Penelope says to Odysseus, who has come to her in disguise, that Telemachus would like to see her go so that an end may be put to the looting of his property by the suitors. Odysseus's estate passes to his son, in other words, not to his wife, the queen.

I fail to understand the reasoning of the suitor Agelaus (20.320–336). So long as there was hope that Odysseus would return to his house, Agelaus says, there was nothing wrong in stringing along the suitors; but now that it is plain he will not return, it is better that Telemachus should allow his mother to marry the one who offers the most gifts and that he should enjoy what is his by inheritance from his father. The second part is clear enough, but so long as Odysseus was still expected to come back, why go on encouraging the suitors' hopes? Or does Agelaus simply consider the feasting and carousing that doubt about Odysseus's return would have prompted to be a net gain of some sort? However this may be, it is obvious that the matrimonial regime in the *Odyssey* is a heterogeneous construction, cobbled together from pieces belonging to different periods.

15. See ibid., 1.395–398.

16. See ibid., 19.85–88.

17. Ibid., 1.386–387. Westrup rightly emphasizes that "the right of inheritance is qualified by the heir's personal aptitude for carrying out the duties of a king"; see his article "Le roi dans l'*Odyssée*," in *Mélanges Fournier* (1929): 771. But he is wrong to confuse Telemachus's incapacity with a *minority*, in the modern sense of the term. The author of the *Odyssey* contaminated the archaic system for testing a candidate's fitness for office with elements of a historically recent system of inheritance.

18. See Apollod. 3.9.2.3.

19. On the princess as reward for triumph in an athletic contest see Frazer, *The Magical Origin of Kings*, 260–263.

20. See Paus. 3.12.1–2.

21. See Pi. P. 9.117–125.

22. See Hdt. 6.126.

23. See O. Waser's entry on Eurytus in August Friedrich Pauly and Georg Wissowa,

eds., *Realencyclopädie der classischen Altertumswissenschaft* [*RE*], first series [A–Q] (Stuttgart: J. B. Metzler, 1894–1963), vol. 6.1, cols. 1359–1363.

24. See scholium on Hom. *Od.* 11.226 [= Felix Jacoby, ed., *Die Fragmente der griechischen Historiker*, 17 vols. (Berlin: Weidemann, 1923–1958), 1:76–77]. [A miscitation: Delcourt means to refer here to the scholium on Hom. *Il.* 14.323 (= 3 F13[c], 1:63–64). —Trans.] Cf. K. Wernicke's entry on Alcmene in *RE*, vol. 1, cols. 1572–1577.

25. See Hes. *Sc.* 11 and Apollod. 2.4.6.

26. See Apollod. 1.9.12, 2.2.2; and Hdt. 9.34. See too schol. Hom. *Od.* 11.290 H. Q.: ὁ γὰρ Ζεὺς εἶπε τῷ μάντει ὅτι κρατηθῆναι μέλλει ὑπὸ τοῦ Ἰφίκλου [for Zeus told the seer that he must be vanquished by Iphiclus].

27. See Frazer, *The Magical Origin of Kings*, 254–258.

28. See Heinrich Schurtz, *Altersklassen und Männerbünde: Eine Darstellung der Grundformen der Gesellschaft* (Berlin: G. Reimer, 1902), 322–328.

29. In India, Masson-Oursel observes, "Kingship appears as a wholly human institution that makes no appeal to divine right. . . . The ceremonies of the *rājasūya* require one year of preparation. The various ritual feats the sovereign must perform are to be interpreted as tests of fitness to rule: skill in drawing the bow, the symbolic raiding of at least a hundred head of cattle, the symbolic taking possession of the four cardinal directions, the execution of the Three Steps of Viṣhnu on a tiger-skin, and success in the game of dice mean either that the new prince is approved by the gods or that he possesses the qualities required of a monarch and that power is therefore rightfully his." Paul Masson-Oursel, *L'Inde antique et la civilisation indienne* (Paris: La Renaissance du livre, 1933), 105.

30. See Paus. 5.16.2–6.

31. See Plu. *Rom.* 2.35.

32. L. Weniger, in *Das Kollegium der sechzehn Frauen und der Dionysosdienst in Elis* (Weimar: Druck der Hof-Buchdruckerei, 1883), concentrated mainly on the relations between this college and the cult of Dionysus. The social importance of age cohorts in classical Greece had scarcely been recognized before the appearance of Schurtz's book two decades later (see n. 28 supra).

33. See Hdt. 4.180 as well as the entries in Hesychius for Διονυσιάδες · ἐν Σπάρτῃ αἱ ἐν τοῖς Διονυσίοις δρόμον ἀγωνιζόμεναι [Dionysiades: (Thus are called) at Sparta the young girls who compete in the race in the games held in honor of Dionysus]; for Νέαι · ἀγωνισάμεναι γυναῖκες τὸν ἱερὸν δρόμον; [The New Ones: The women who competed in the sacred race]; and for Ἀνθεστεριάδας · τάς ἐχούσας ὥραν γάμου, Ῥόδιοι [Anthesteriades: At Rhodes, girls who are of marriageable age]. See too the entry in Harpocration for Λαμπάς, and Hdt. 4.160.

34. See A. Brueckner, "Athenische Hochzeitsgeschenke," *Ath. Mitt.* 32 (1907): 81–82.

35. The meaning of this rite needs to be studied in the context of each ritual and each sequence of legendary versions to which it gives rise. This is what Delatte has done

in the case of the gathering of plants. He concludes that circumambulation, like circumscription, had first an apotropaic, then a cathartic purpose—in each case with a view to capturing a plant's characteristic properties. See Armand Delatte, *Herbarius: Recherches sur le cérémonial usité chez les anciens pour la cueillette des simples et des plantes magiques* (Paris: Les Belles Lettres, 1936; 2nd ed., Liège, 1938), 136. In most legends, appropriation—the taking possession of certain properties, qualities, or virtues—is paramount.

36. See Frazer, *The Magical Origin of Kings*, 164–165, 263–264.

37. According to B. fr. 15A (ed. J. M. Edmonds [London, 1922–1927], 3:117) [= schol. Pi. *I.* 4.92], Evenus challenged the suitors, killed them, and hung their heads on the wall of his palace or else in the temple of Apollo. According to Tz. *ad Lyc.* 161, Evenus built a temple with the heads of all those he vanquished.

38. See Paus. 3.20.11. —Trans.

39. See Apollod. 3.9.2, and Hyg. *Fab.* 185. Robert thinks that this is a late version that derives from the story of Oenomaus; see *Die griechische Heldensage*, 2:84. If this were so, the murders would be imputed to the father and not to the daughter. Robert neglects to consider a more puzzling problem, namely, how we should approach the analysis of a heterodox legend of this sort in the first place.

40. Apollodorus remarks parenthetically that the tradition according to which Hippomenes was the husband of Atalanta, rather than Melanion, is due to Euripides. —Trans.

41. Both Apollodorus (3.9.2) and Pausanias (8.35.10) confuse the two Atalantas.

42. The metamorphosis described by Ovid is also mentioned by a scholium on Theocritus 3.38a, which distinguishes the two Atalantas. See Ulrich von Wilamowitz-Moellendorff, *Hellenistische Dichtung in der Zeit des Callimachos*, 2 vols. (Berlin: Weidmann, 1924), 2:50, as well as Wilamowitz's article "Die griechische Heldensage," *Sitzungsb. d. Preuss. Ak. d. Wiss, phil.-hist. Kl.* (1925): 221.

43. See Hom. *Od.* 10.212.

44. See Paus. 9.3.3; Eus. *PE* 3.1.6, quoting Plutarch; and Martin Nilsson, *Griechische Feste von religiöser Bedeutung: Mit Ausschluss der Attischen* (Leipzig: Teubner, 1906), 50. Nilsson, in his later *Geschichte der griechischen Religion*, 2 vols. (Munich: C. H. Beck, 1941–1950), 1:404, sees the Daedala—wrongly, I believe—as an annual burnt offering without any accompanying spring wedding ritual.

45. See Frazer, *The Magical Origin of Kings*, 176–178.

46. See Hdt. 1.60. Phya is said to have been four cubits and four fingers in stature, or about 1.74 meters [= 5′8½″] tall, which is not very unusual in Europe today but which must have been in the Mediterranean world of 2,500 years ago. From the study of armor we know that human height has increased to a varying extent, depending on the country, since the end of the Middle Ages.

47. See Arist. *Ath.* 14.4.

48. See Ath. 13.609c, which quotes Cleidemus as well as Phylarcus, whose source could only have been Aristotle. From the marriage to Hipparchus, related by Cleidemus, must come the error of the scholium on Ar. *Eq.* 449, which confuses Phya with Myrrhine, daughter of Callias and wife of Hippias (see Th. 6.55). The confusion may have been favored by Myrrhine's nominal association with the plant kingdom. [Myrrhine is a variant form of the Greek word for myrtle. Phya is derived from φυή, meaning growth or stature; in the post-Homeric period the word was used of plants, in addition to people, and by the early Christian era had come to refer to a year's agricultural produce or harvest. —Trans.]

49. Polyaen. 1.21.1.

50. Another ruse, the *false wound* (a wound that Pisistratus inflicted on himself and then falsely blamed on his enemies) is mentioned in Arist. *Ath.* 14.1. Pisistratus must have been credited with quite a few tricks of this kind, which circulated anonymously.

51. The heralds "ran before them," Herodotus says. —Trans.

52. If Aristotle had understood otherwise he would have said so, since he insists on the difference between Herodotus and the other historians in the matter of the deme. Here are the texts of three accounts.

    Cleidemus: ἐξέδωκε Ἱππάρχῳ τῷ υἱεῖ τὴν παραιβατήσασαν αὐτῷ γυναῖκα Φύην, τὴν Σωκράτους θυγατέρα [Pisistratus gave in marriage to his son Hipparchus this (young woman) Phya, daughter of Socrates, who stood next to him on his chariot].

    Aristotle: γυναῖκα μεγάλην ἐξευρών . . . τὴν θεὸν ἀπομιμησάμενος τῷ κόσμῳ συνεισήγαγεν μετ' αὐτοῦ [having encountered a tall woman en route, he disguised her as the goddess (i.e., Athena) and brought her with him].

    Polyaenus: ἅρματος ἐπιβὰς παραστησάμενος γυναῖκα μεγάλην [he climbed into his chariot and placed a tall woman next to him].

53. Hdt. 1.60. [A more literal translation of the Greek would bring out Herodotus's amazement that Pisistratus and Megacles should have thought for a moment that such a scheme had any chance of fooling the Athenians. —Trans.]

54. See E. Meyer, *Forschungen zur alten Geschichte*, 2 vols. (Halle: M. Niemeyer, 1892–1899), 2:248, and K. J. Beloch, "Wann lebten Alkaeos und Sappho?," *Rhein. Mus.* 45 (1890): 470.

55. Meyer, *Forschungen zur alten Geschichte*, 2:248.

56. I hesitate here to argue on the basis of the olive wreathes that figure in Polyaenus's account, for I believe that the two stratagems he juxtaposes were primitively independent of each other.

57. See my discussion of the legends surrounding Cyrus in Chapter 1.

58. "Either we believe the story of Phya as Herodotus relates it," Beloch says, "with everything it implies and involves, or we concede that Pisistratus was sent into exile only once." I do not see that this alternative is obligatory. On the other hand, however,

I do think that it is necessary to explain the origin of fables that are not to be confused with history.

59. We must not be fooled by the formula ἐγάμουν δὲ δι' ἁρπαγῆς [They marry by abduction (i.e., by forcibly carrying off their women)] that Plutarch (*Lyc.* 15.3 = 48d) applied to the Spartans. He means simply to speak of furtive (or unacknowledged) marriages, common in all societies in which the husband continues to live, at least for a certain time, in a house shared by single men.

60. Georges Dumézil, *Horace et les Curiaces* (Paris: Gallimard, 1942), 52. Dumézil cites a number of parallels (see ibid., 129–133); many others could be found in the folklore of all countries. Dumézil sees in the combat against three monsters, or a three-headed monster, nothing more than the memory of an initiatory trial. In what follows I try to establish a much more complex origin.

61. See Jane Ellen Harrison, *Epilegomena to the Study of Greek Religion* (Cambridge: Cambridge University Press, 1921), 16–20, and the reference there to other works.

62. See Hom. *Od.* 2.96, 16.248–250, 17.174, 19.141, 22.29–30 and 121–122.

63. [Literally, not having accomplished or concluded a marriage (by analogy with the purpose of initiation ceremonies as "rites of first accomplishment," that is, of the coming to maturity). —Trans.] See the entry "Initiation (Greek)," written by J. E. Harrison, in James Hastings, ed., *Encyclopaedia of Religion and Ethics*, 13 vols. (Edinburgh: T. & T. Clark, 1908–1926), 7:322–323; also the introductory essay on Initiation by E. Goblet d'Alviella, in ibid., 7:314–319. In Suidas, under the entry for *teleia* [an epithet of gods and goddesses, meaning one who accomplishes or achieves], one reads: Ἥρα τελεία καὶ Ζεὺς τέλιος ἐπιμῶντο ἐν τοῖς γάμοις, ὡς πρυτάνεις ὄντες τῶν γάμων · τέλος δὲ ὁ γάμος [Hera *teleia* and Zeus *teleios* were honored in marriage ceremonies as the tutelary deities of marriage; and marriage is called *telos* (accomplishment)]. See too, in Julius Pollux (*Onomasticon* 3.38), the entry Ἥρα τελεία.

64. Here there is no better reference than L. Gernet, "Frairies antiques," *REG* 41 (1928): 313–359, esp. pp. 330–340.

65. *Simultaneous* marriages, in which some number of couples are married at the same time, need to be distinguished from *collective* marriages, such as the ones that are practiced in certain primitive societies, in which a preliminary ceremony serves to license quite promiscuous sexual activity (see, for example, Hdt. 4.180, which says that the Libyans living on the shores of Lake Tritonis do not cohabit, but have intercourse like animals).

66. For Rhodes, see the entry in Hesychius under Ἀνθεστηριάδας; for Crete, see Str. 10.20. Aristotle mentions the custom of scheduling simultaneous marriages in winter, but naturally he rationalizes the circumstances of its origin; see *Pol.* 1335a35.

67. See Edward Westermarck, *History of Human Marriage* [1891], 5th ed., 3 vols. (London: Macmillan, 1921), 2:261; also A. M. Hocart, *Kingship* (London: Oxford University Press, 1927), 101, and Baron Raglan, *Jocasta's Crime: An Anthropological Study* (London: Methuen, 1933), 38.

68. Georges Dumézil, *Ouranós-Váruna: Étude de mythologie comparée indo-européenne* (Paris: Adrien-Maisonneuve, 1934), 31.

69. See Hom. *Od.* 19.109–114.

70. Literally, a flowering or flourishing marriage [see Hom. *Od.* 6.66, 20.74. —Trans.]. Might it primitively have been a marriage that causes flowering, which is to say one that promotes the growth of vegetation and fruition? And might the name of the Anthesteriades in Rhodes, τὰς ἐχούσας ὥραν γάμου [girls who are of the age to marry], have had the same causal implication?

71. See Hdt. 9.51–53; also Plu. *Arist.* 11.

72. See Antonie Töpfer, *Der König im deutschen Volksmärchen*, inaug. diss. (University of Jena, 1930).

73. See Wilhelm Wisser, ed., *Plattdeutsche Volksmärchen*, 2 vols. (Jena: E. Diederichs, 1914–1927), 2:215.

74. See Genesis 37:12–36. —Trans.

75. Töpfer, *Der König im deutschen Volksmärchen*, 31–32; see also p. 64.

76. See Schurtz, *Altersklassen und Männerbünde*, 322ff.

## CHAPTER 6. INCEST WITH THE MOTHER

1. See Edward Westermarck, *History of Human Marriage* [1891], 5th ed., 3 vols. (London: Macmillan, 1921), 2:81, 88–95; and 3:184–185.

2. See Hutton Webster, *Primitive Secret Societies: A Study in Early Politics and Religion* (New York: Macmillan, 1908), 70–71.

3. What Strabo has to say in this connection about the people of Ierne (4.5.4) and the Sabaeans (16.4.25) is certainly fabulous in its origin.

4. Lugaid was the son jointly of three brothers and their sister Clothru, whom he married as an adult. From this union was born a son who succeeded his father on the throne of Ireland.

5. S. *OT* 977–983; emphasis added.

6. Sigmund Freud, *Five Lectures on Psycho-Analysis* (1910), trans. James Strachey, in James Strachey, ed., *The Standard Edition of the Psychological Works of Sigmund Freud*, 24 vols. (London: Hogarth Press, 1953–1974), 11:47.

7. A. *Pr.* 645–651. —Trans.

8. See chapter 79 of the first book of the *Oneirocritica* (ed. R. Hercher [Leipzig: B. G. Teubner, 1864], pp. 76–81), Περὶ τῆς σύγχρωτα περαινομένης καὶ ἄμα ζώσης [μητέρος] [On sexual intimacy in dreams with a still-living mother].

9. Note that Artemidorus's reasoning here is thoroughly rationalist and in no way can be construed as confirming Freudian axioms.

10. That it is the dreamer who makes love to his mother, not the same person in real life, is implicit in the Greek text: Ὥσπερ οὖν ὁ μιγνύμενος κατὰ νόμον Ἀφροδίτης παντὸς ἄρχει τοῦ σώματος τῆς συνούσης πειθομένης καὶ ἑκούσης, πάντων προστήσεται τῶν τῆς πόλεως πραγμάτων.

11. Artem. 1.79; emphasis added.

12. Ibid., 1.80.

13. Ibid., 4.2.

14. This brings us back to the problem of the incubus: in order to prevail over such a spirit, is it enough to put it back in its "natural" position, that is, by lying on top of it?

15. It would be better to speak here of the *tyrant*, in the Greek sense of the word, for we are always dealing in such cases with men who wish to rule over their own country.

16. D. L. 1.96: Ἐρασθεῖσα ἡ μήτηρ αὐτοῦ Κράτεια συνῆν αὐτῷ λάθρα · καὶ ὃς ἥδετο. Φανεροῦ δὲ γενομένου, βαρὺς πᾶσιν ἐγένετο, διὰ τὸ ἀλγεῖν ἐπὶ τῇ φωρᾷ.

17. See Hdt. 5.92.

18. If Aristippus had meant to say that Periander himself was fooled, we would expect to find here a more extended formulation; λάθρα [secretly] and φανεοῦ γενομένου [the thing having become known], without further qualification, can scarcely refer to anything other than an unnamed people—the Corinthians.

19. See Parth. 17.

20. It is thus that a thoroughly watered-down version figures in Plutarch's *Dinner of the Seven Wise Men* (2.146d): a mother falls in love with her son and kills herself—with no mention of any crime having been committed.

21. Hdt. 6.107. The manuscript reading ὁ ὀδὼν μετέχει [my tooth has as its share] is undoubtedly correct and must not be altered to read κατέχει [that contains (or retains) it].

22. See the entry Ἱππίας in Suidas; Cic. *Att.* 9.10.3; Just. 2.9.21.

23. Liv. 1.56.4–13.

24. See Hdt. 1.53.

25. See ibid., 1.55.

26. See ibid., 1.66.

27. See ibid., 3.30, 3.64.

28. See ibid., 3.64.

29. See ibid., 3.57–58.

30. See ibid., 3.124–125.

31. See ibid., 4.163–164.

32. See ibid., 5.56.

33. See ibid., 4.132.

34. See ibid., 7.37.

35. See ibid., 7.140–141.

36. See ibid., 6.107.

37. Men sometimes employ the same techniques as oracles and deceive their interlocutor by construing words in an unanticipated sense. Thus Darius kills the sons of Oeobazus, who asked that *they be left behind* (Hdt. 4.84); Athens casts into a pit, and Sparta into a well, Persian ambassadors who ask for *earth and water* (7.133).

38. See ibid., 7.189.

39. See Liv. 1.54; Hdt. 5.92; Arist. *Pol.* 1284a.

40. See n. 5 supra.

41. In the accounts of the epic poets, Oedipus remains king—a happy outcome.

42. Pl. *Rep.* 9.571b–572b; the emphasis is mine.

43. "Plato," observes Jean Paulus, "did more than anticipate [Freud], he sketched the main elements of the psychoanalytic conception (endopsychic conflict, repression, liberation of repressed tendencies)"; see *Henri de Gand: Essai sur les tendances de sa métaphysique* (Paris: J. Vrin, 1938). On the subject of Zeno's theory of dreams and the ways in which they subvert conventional morality, one would like to know more than the little that Plutarch (*De prof. in virt.* 12 [= 82f]) has to say about it.

44. See Plu. *Caes.* 32 [= 723e] and Suet. *Jul.* 7, 59; Dio Cassius (37.52) follows Suetonius.

45. See Tac. *Ann.* 14.2, 13.3; Suet. *Nero* 28.

46. See Xiph. 61.11.4.

47. It pleased Nero to substitute one lover for another. He took a concubine and a male lover, Sporus, because each one resembled his second wife, Sabina Poppaea, and he called Sporus Sabina (see D.C. 62.28.2, 63.13.1). When he played tragic roles in the theater, he wore a mask modeled on his own features while his partner wore a mask with the features of Sabina (63.9.5).

48. D.C. 63.28.5. Suetonius (*Nero* 46), no longer understanding σύγγαμος in the sense of co-husband, is led to quote a more expansive version of this line: θανεῖν μ' ἄνωγε σύγγαμος, μήτηρ, πατήρ [wife, mother, father, all order me to die].

49. Xiph. 61.14.

50. D.C. 62.14. The verb is the same in both cases, ᾔδειν.

51. See Suet. *Nero* 21.3.

52. With a view, that is, to strengthening his political authority. —Trans.

53. See Hom. *Od.* 13.354 and 4.521–522, respectively.

54. See M. Delcourt, "La pureté des éléments et l'invocation de Créuse dans 'Ion,'" *Rev. belge de phil. et d'hist.* 17, no. 1 (1938): 195–203.

55. This was still explicitly the belief of Greeks and Romans in the historical period. See the scholium on Hom. *Il.* 1.407: κεφαλῆς λαμβανόμεθα · ἐπεί ἡγεμονικόν, δεξιᾶς ἐπεί πρακτικόν · γονάτων (δι' αὐτῶν γὰρ ἐπικλᾶται τὸ σῶμα) ἐπικλᾶν σπεύδοντες τὴν ψυχὴν τοῖς λόγοις [we take the person whom we beseech by the head, because that is the part (of the body) that commands; we take it by the right hand, because that is the part that acts; we take it by the knees (for it is at the knees that the body bends) so that the soul will be moved by our words]. See too Plin. *Nat.* 11.103 [= 250]: Hominis genibus quaedam et religio inest observatione gentium. Haec supplices attingunt, ad haec manus tendunt, haec ut aras adorant, fortasse quia inest eis vitalitas. . . . Inest et aliis partibus religio, sicut in dextera; osculis aversa adpetitur, in fide porrigitur. Antiquis Graecis in supplicando mentum attingere mos erat [It has been the custom of nations to grant a sort of religious sanctity to the knees of a person. Supplicants touch them, stretch out their hands toward them, and pray to them as at altars, perhaps because some vital principle adheres in them. . . . Other parts of the body also possess a certain religious sanctity, the right hand, for instance: the back of it is kissed, or it may be extended in affirming one's faith. The ancient Greeks were accustomed to touch the chin while making entreaties]. Here and in what follows I am grateful to Mme. Demoulin-Marique, who I hope will pursue her research on this subject, still mostly unexplored.

56. See E. *IT* 973.

57. See L. Gernet, "Quelques rapports entre la pénalté et la religion dans la Grèce ancienne," *Ant. Class.* 5, no. 2 (1936): 325–339.

58. O. Weinreich, in "Ein Spurzauber," *Arch. f. Rel.* 28 (1930): 180, adds nothing to the argument made by W. Deonna in "Quelques croyances superstitieuses de la Grèce ancienne," *REG* 42, nos. 195–196 (1929): 171.

59. Achilles hurls his staff in anger to the ground (Hom. *Il.* 1.245); Dionysus's nurses, threatened by Lycurgus, throw down their wands (Hom. *Il.* 6:130–140); Demeter, caught by surprise, throws Demophon to the ground (*Homeric Hymn to Demeter* 253); Oedipus, in the Theban cycle, throws to the ground the morsel sent to him by his sons.

60. See O. Gruppe, "Die eherne Schwelle und der Thorikische Stein," *Arch. f. Rel.* 15 (1912): 359–379; also Ath. 4.149c.

61. In the ancient Greek conception, the basic elements of nature were five in number: earth, water, air, fire, and ether. —Trans.

62. See Hom. *Od.* 5.125 and Hes. *Th.* 969.

63. From the same source may come the Cypriot ceremonies in which young men imitate

the movements of women giving birth; see Martin P. Nilsson, *Griechische Feste von religiöser Bedeutung mit Ausschluss der Attischen* (Leipzig: B. G. Teubner, 1906), 369.

64. See Apollod. 3.6.8, Paus. 8.25.4–6. In this version, Demeter acquired the epithet "Erinyes" in Arcadia for her fury at having been mounted by Poseidon in the form of a stallion after she had assumed the form of a mare in order to evade him (hence the horse, Arion, to which she subsequently gave birth). —Trans.

65. This version is attributed to Antimachus by Paus. 8.25.8–10. —Trans.

66. The crude archaic version, according to a scholium on Lyc. 766, reads: ἄλλοι δέ φάσιν ὅτι καὶ περὶ τοὺς πέτρους τοῦ ἐν Ἀθήναις Κολώνου καθευδήσας ἀπεσπέρμηνε καὶ ἵππος Σκύφιος ἐξῆλθεν ὁ καὶ Σκειρωνίτης λεγόμενος [Others say that Poseidon, having fallen asleep near the rocks at Colonus outside Athens, spilled his seed (on the ground), and from this came the horse Skyphius, who is also called Skironites]. This account is repeated almost verbatim in a scholium on Pi. *P.* 55.46 (though there the horse is uniquely called Skyphius). The corresponding entry in the *Etymologicum Magnum* (ed. T. Gaisford [Oxford, 1848], p. 473, col. 1360, ll. 42–44) gives the expurgated version: ἽΠΠΟΣ ὁ ΠΟΣΕΙΔ῀ΩΝ: Ὅτι δοκεῖ πρῶτον ἵππον γεγεννηκέναι [Σκύφιον] ἐν Θεσσλίᾳ, τῇ τριαίνῃ πέτραν παίσας [Poseidon is called "Hippios" (Poseidon on horseback, or protector of horses), apparently because he brought forth the first horse, called Skyphius, by striking a rock with his trident in Thessaly]. The horse is called Arion when he is given Demeter for a mother.

67. See Apollod. 3.14.6, [Ps.-]Eratosth. *Cat.* 13, and [Ps.-]Hyg. *Astr.* 2.13, citing Euripides. Were it not for such a precise indication, in the last case, we would not hesitate to declare any such attribution to Euripides inconceivable.

68. Paus. 7.17.10. These children of the earth are, of course, monsters: Erichthonius is a snake, Agdistis is a hermaphrodite. As for the birth of Orion, who was said by Palaephatus (*Incred.* 51) to have been the son of three gods—Zeus, Poseidon, and Hermes—who shed their seed (or else urinated) on a bull's hide and caused it to be buried in the earth for ten months, the tale may well have been invented to explain Orion's name; if so, it may have been influenced, unwittingly perhaps, by the tale of the horse Arion. [The name Orion derives from the Greek *ouron*, meaning urine, whence the verb *ourein*, to urinate (also to ejaculate semen). —Trans.]

69. In the French text the Greek word ἥρῷον, which occurs, for example, at Hdt. 5.47 and Th. 2.17, is used in its romanized form, *héroon*. —Trans.

70. See Gruppe, "Die eherne Schwelle und der Thorikische Stein."

71. See S. *OC* 1595–1596.

72. Why U. von Wilamowitz should have contemptuously dismissed Gruppe's careful argument on these grounds is difficult to understand; see "Oedipus auf Kolonos" [a long essay appended to the posthumously published work by his eldest son], T. von Wilamowitz, *Die dramatische Technik des Sophokles* (Berlin: Weidmann, 1917), 325n1.

73. It may be illuminating in this connection to examine more closely the folklore of

sperm fallen to the ground, which was sometimes thought to be favorable, sometimes baleful, if we are to believe the episode of the centaur Nessus's tunic, also expurgated by Sophocles (*Tr.* 555–581). According to Apollodorus (2.7.6), Nessus advised Deianira that εἰ θέλοι φίλτρον πρὸς Ἡρακλέα ἔχειν, τόν τε γόνον, ὃν ἀφῆκε κατὰ τῆς γῆς, καὶ τὸ ῥυὲν ἐκ τοῦ τραύματος τῆς ἀκίδος αἷμα, συμμίξαι [if she wanted a love-potion to use on Heracles, she should mix the semen that he had shed on the ground with the blood that had flowed from the wound caused by the arrowhead].

74. This is what Frazer claims [or, if not Euripides himself, then another late writer] in *The Magical Origin of Kings* (London: Macmillan, 1920), 222.

75. See Ov. *Met.* 7.386–387.

76. See Hyg. *Fab.* 253.

77. Cyllene, the mountain nymph from whom Mount Cyllene takes its name, was the wife of Pelasgus, first king of Arcadia. Plias (Greek Πληιονη, also romanized as Pleias or, more straightforwardly and most commonly, Pleione), a sea nymph born on Mount Cyllene, was the wife of Atlas and bore him seven beautiful daughters, of whom Atlantis was one, immortalized in the constellation that was long supposed to take its name from her, the Pleiades (= daughters of Pleione). It is now generally believed, however, that the name of the star cluster came first and that Pleione was invented to explain it. —Trans.

78. On Arcas's childhood and the later episode with his mother, see [Ps.-]Eratosth. *Cat.* 8, 1, respectively. The *Catasterismi* (see too n. 67 supra) is now held to be due to an unknown author and wrongly attributed to Eratosthenes. —Trans.

79. See D.S. 5.55.4. —Trans.

80. See A. H. Krappe, "Ueber die Sagen von der Geschwisterehe im Mittelalter," *Arch. f. d. Stud. d. neueren Spr.* 167 (1935): 161–176.

81. See S. *OC* 616–628. —Trans.

82. According to the scholium on Aristides [ed. W. Dindorf (Leipzig, 1829), 3:560, l. 18]: ἐλθόντων ποτὲ Θηβαίων φαίνεται [Οἰδίπους] Ἀθηναίοις ἀντιπαρατάξασθαι καὶ σουβαλόντες ἐνίκησαν [when the Thebans came, it was apparent to the Athenians that Oedipus gave the order for positioning their forces: the combat was entered into and the Athenians were the victors]—a falsely specific detail that glosses a very vague allusion by Aristides to the tutelary heroes of Attica, among them ὁ ἐν Κολωνῷ κείμενος Οἰδίπους [Oedipus, he who rests at Colonus] (Ὑπὲρ τῶν τεττ., ed. Dindorf, 3:284). As for the oracle quoted by Didymus (schol. S. *OC* 57),

Βοιωτοί δ᾿ ἵπποιο ποτιστείχουσι Κολωνόν,
ἔνθα λίθος τρικάρανος ἔχει καὶ χάλκεος οὐδός

[The Boeotians advanced on Colonus, town of the horse,
where the three-headed stone and the bronze threshold enclose],

it is plainly incomplete, and, so long as we cannot judge the passage in its entirety, it would be unwise to conclude anything from it; see Carl Robert, *Oidipus: Geschichte eines poetischen Stoffes im griechischen Altertum*, 2 vols. (Berlin: Weidmann, 1915), 1:35–38.

83. Owing perhaps to a typesetter's transmission error, the first line does not scan properly as a dactylic hexameter. Delcourt herself would presumably have been aware that both of the vases she mentions have the correct spelling of the first word (νώτῳ rather than νότῳ), and that on one of them this word is followed by μὲν, fixing the defective meter. Furthermore, this is the form found in a fragment of Aristotle (no. 644 in V. Rose [Leipzig, 1886]) that includes a paraphrase by Eustathius (of Hom. *Od.* 11.538) in which the first words of the couplet are given as νώτῳ μὲν μολάχην. I am indebted to Professor Mastronarde for drawing my attention to this perplexing lapse. —Trans.

84. See Hes. *Op.* 41. [Mallow and asphodel were staples of a poor man's diet whose great value is proverbially insisted on. —Trans.]

85. A relation of equal numerical value between the letters of two words (or groups of words) in the ancient Greek notation, according to which alpha has a value of one, beta of two, gamma of three, and so on up to omega, the twenty-fourth letter of the alphabet, which has a corresponding value. —Trans.

86. κόλπῳ ἔχω [I hold in my breast] is by no means a commonplace of funerary epigrams. Moreover, the first line seems to have been composed after the second. W. Schultz was the first to draw attention to this and other isopsephisms that sharpen the point of comparisons similar to the one made here; see *Rätsel aus dem hellenischen Kulturkreise*, 3 vols. (Leipzig: J. C. Hinrichs, 1909–1912), 3:104.

### ENDINGS

1. The reference here is to the Aiora, a ceremony held on the third day of the Anthesteria, a festival of Dionysus in Attica, in honor of Erigone, who had hanged herself from grief at the death of her father, Icarius. According to Ps.-Hyg. *Astron.* 2.2, girls sitting on ropes with bars of wood attached were swung back and forth by the wind. Other accounts speak only of small female images. —Trans.

2. S. *OT* 1331.

3. "In *Oedipus*," the scholium reads, "it is Laius's servants who blind [Oedipus]: 'holding the son of Polybus to the ground, we tore out his eyes, we crushed the pupils.'" See my discussion of this point in the Introduction.

4. See the discussion in Chapter 2. —Trans.

5. S. *OT* 1268–1274.

6. Ibid., 1371–1383.

7. See for example [Ps.-]Eratosth. *Cat.* 32 and Philostr. *VA* 1.10.

8. The phrase ὡς ἐνόησε [as he understood (or was aware of) it] in no way suffices to prove that Oedipus was blind. Homer often uses this verb in the sense "to notice."

9. See A. *Th.* 967. —Trans.

10. Quoted in Ath. 11.465e–f.

11. This sentence and the one following are my own interpolation, in order to compensate for an otherwise puzzling ellipsis in the French text. —Trans.

12. This extract and the two immediately preceding are found in the scholium on *Phoenician Women* 26.

13. See scholium on Stat. *Theb.* 11.371.

## MYTHS AND MEMORY

1. "The myth shows that . . ." [or: This *fable* shows that . . . ], a formula often used by Aesop and other fabulists to introduce the moral of a story.

2. It is true that often we dream of the dead, and, when we do, these dreams are made from an older *material* that is worked on by the mood or emotion of the moment.

3. "The invention of a fierce moralist," in the words of P. Saintyves, who has brilliantly elucidated the pedagogic aspect of French folktales in *Les contes de Perrault et les récits parallèles: Leurs origines (coutumes primitives et liturgies populaires)* (Paris: E. Nourry, 1923), a work whose interest has so far not been sufficiently appreciated.

4. Thus one speaks of the "myth" of class struggle or the "myth" of a general strike. My attention was drawn to this aspect of the question by Victor Larock's remarkable essay, *La pensée mythique*, publication of which was blocked by German censorship in 1943 but which will appear at a later date. [It was in fact published by the Office de publicité in Brussels two years later. —Trans.]

5. A social myth differs from a religious myth essentially in this, that instead of explaining a given reality it seeks to create one, once again working upon the collective emotions of a group, only now in order to transform them into a form of energy, without the intercession of a legendary account.

6. Arnold van Gennep, *La formation des légendes* (Paris: E. Flammarion, 1910), 235. —Trans.

7. See James George Frazer, *The Magical Origin of Kings* (London: Macmillan, 1920), 231–235. —Trans.

8. See Maurice Halbwachs, *Les cadres sociaux de la mémoire* (Paris: F. Alcan, 1925).

9. "It suffices," Halbwachs says, "that some great event such as a war or a revolution should profoundly transform our social environment for there to remain to us, from whole periods of our past, only a very small number of memories." Ibid., 28. The same point is repeated later by way of emphasis: "The disappearance or the transformation of frameworks of memory entails the disappearance or the transformation of our memories" (p. 134); and again, more precisely: "Society deliberately consigns the ancient past to oblivion along with the entire set of values, the whole hierarchy of

persons and deeds that depended on [its memory] in order to attach themselves to the recent past, which continues up into the present" (p. 326). It may be wondered whether our own social memory is better than that of primitive societies. Tell a group of Belgians, adults or even elderly people, a story that you set in 1875 and in which you speak of the telephone, electric light, compulsory schooling, obligatory national service, and divorce. All your listeners will at once detect the anachronism in the first two cases, because they involve things that are taught in school, but less readily in the next two cases, even though compulsory schooling and national service in Belgium both date from 1911; and not at all in the last case, since no one was ever taught that divorce dates from 1886.

10. Nilsson has always considered tales to be primary, gratuitous realities on the basis of which everything else must be explained: "The legend is a free poetical work inasmuch as it was not invented for a purpose that is external to it; it tells [a story] for the pleasure of telling [it]." *Geschichte der griechischen Religion* (Munich: Beck, 1941), 17.

11. H. Webster has convincingly demonstrated that initiations, though they brutalized youths and stood in the way of progress of any kind, were perpetuated by male elders in order to maintain their authority over adolescents and to exploit women; see *Primitive Secret Societies* (New York: Macmillan, 1908), 59–66. Curiously, Webster's book complements that of Schurtz, who speaks of age cohorts and the "ethic" they embodied with a sort of nostalgic regret; see *Altersklassen und Männerbünde: Eine Darstellung der Grundformen der Gesellschaft* (Berlin: G. Reimer, 1902), 167n2.

12. See Chapter 4 ("The Infantile Recurrence of Totemism") in Sigmund Freud, *Totem and Taboo: Resemblances between the Psychic Lives of Savages and Neurotics* [1913], trans. A. A. Brill (New York: Vintage, 1946), 130–207.

## APPENDIX 1. THE PISANDER SCHOLION AND RELATED SUMMARIES

1. Technically, a baldric (French *baudrier*), a warrior's belt slung over one shoulder to hold a sword. Following standard practice in the literature I use the generic term here and in what follows. —Trans.

## APPENDIX 2. LEGENDS AND CULTS OF TWIN CHILDREN

1. See Fernand Chapouthier, *Dioscures au service d'une déesse: Étude d'une iconographie religieuse* (Paris: E. de Boccard, 1935). More than thirty years earlier, Samson Eitrem had pointed out that twins come to the rescue of a woman, either their sister or their mother; see *Die göttlichen Zwillinge bei den Griechen* (Christiania: J. Dybwab, 1902).

2. See Chapouthier, *Dioscures au service d'une déesse*, 331, and J. Rendel Harris, *The Cult of the Heavenly Twins* (Cambridge: Cambridge University Press, 1906), which contains some interesting observations. In many popular superstitions, Harris points out, only one of the twins is the son of the mother's husband; the other father is an adulterer. To my mind, however, his book makes the dioscuric tradition explain too much.

3. See Paus. 9.17.3.

4. See F. Marx, "Dioskurenartige Gottheiten," *Ath. Mitt.* 10 (1885): 81–89.

5. The *pilos*, a conical brimless hat worn by travelers, was often identified with the Dioscuri. —Trans.

6. See Paus. 3.26.3, 3.27.5; also 10.33.6, 10.38.7.

### APPENDIX 3. ANIMAL TALES IN GREECE

1. See August Marx, *Griechische Märchen von dankbaren Tieren und Verwandtes* (Stuttgart: W. Kohlhammer, 1889).

2. For Zeus, see Aes. Gibbs 509 [= Chambry 234]; for Plato, Cic. *Div.* 1.36; for Midas, Ael. *VH* 12.45, Cic. *Div.* 1.36, V. Max. 1.6.3. —Trans.

3. Stories of this type have been collected, if not studied, in E. S. McCartney, "Greek and Roman Lore of Animal-Nursed Infants," *Papers of the Michigan Academy of Science, Arts, and Letters* 4, no. 1 (1925): 15–42. Of some forty stories of "wonder children" that McCartney considers, five concern twins.

4. See Pierre Saintyves, *Les contes de Perrault et les récits parallèles: Leurs origines (coutumes primitives et liturgies populaires)* (Paris: E. Nourry, 1923), 485–490.

5. See *App. Verg.*, *Culex* 410; cf. Jean Hubaux, *Les thèmes bucoliques dans la poésie latine* (Brussels: M. Lamertin, 1930), 104–116.

6. See the entry Κρίσσαμις in Suidas and Hesychius.

7. See Marx, *Griechische Märchen*, 12–14.

8. See ibid., 19n1.

9. L. Gernet and A. Boulanger speak of the "emblematization of the clan"; see *Le génie grec dans la religion* (Paris: La Renaissance du livre, 1932), 68. P. Chantraine, studying the expression Μέροπες ἄνθρωποι [mortal men], infers from elections of this kind the existence of a prior association of human beings and deities with animals; see his contribution to *Mélanges Franz Cumont*, 2 vols. (Brussels: Secrétariat de l'Institut, 1936), 1:124. J. Bayet goes further, detecting in stories of "wonder children" the memory of a supreme power attributed to one or another animal; see his essay in ibid., 1:27. This, I believe, goes too far.

10. See Jean Hubaux and Maxime Leroy, *Le mythe du phénix dans les littératures grecque et latine* (Paris: E. Droz, 1939), 196. See also the entry Λάγος in Suidas; Ael. *NA* 12.21; Paus. 4.18.5; and Str. 17.1.33 [= 808].

11. For the contrary case see Marx, *Griechische Märchen*, 123n1.

12. See the discussion in Chapter 1. —Trans.

13. Ael. *NA* 10.48.

14. Pindus is slain in the end by his jealous brothers—a conclusion imposed by an etiological motivation foreign to the familiar animal tale: the name Pindus had to be plausibly attached to the river that ran near his tomb.

15. See the first two chapters in Saintyves, *Les contes de Perrault et les récits parallèles.*

16. Earlier, in Chapter 2, we noted the origin that Jeanmaire assigns to the wolf in fairy tales. On his view, this character may be traced back to ritual initiators wearing a wolf's mask who sought to train novices by frightening them. Only one story involving a wolf occurs in Greek tales of benevolent animals, and it takes place in a schoolroom: the young Gelon, future tyrant of Sicily, was in class when a wolf came into the room and seized his tablets; rushing off in pursuit of the robber, the roof then collapsed on his classmates. Prantl is probably right in connecting this story with German tales of the schoolmaster wolf; if so, this would tend to confirm Jeanmaire's hypothesis; see C. von Prantl, "Einige reste des thierepos bei schriftstellern des spätern altertums," *Philol.* 7 (1852): 74.

### APPENDIX 4. THE RELIGIOUS SIGNIFICANCE OF SPOILS IN THE HOMERIC POEMS

1. See my discussion in Chapter 2.

2. See the chapter "Tarpeia" in Salomon Reinach, *Cultes, Mythes, Religions* [1905–1923], 2nd ed., 3 vols. (Paris: E. Leroux, 1908–1909), 3:223–253. Reinach did not make use of a curious passage in Livy (5.30) that J. Hubaux kindly pointed out to me, in which Camillus argues against the Romans occupying Veii after having taken it, considering it *ill-fated* to inhabit a conquered territory.

3. Plu. *Quaest. rom.* 273c.

4. See Hom. *Il.* 5.25, 5.164, 5.321; 6.28; 11.100, 11.101, 11.110, 11.580; 13.579, 13.619, 13.641; 15.343; 17.60, 17.540; 21.183.

5. See, for example, ibid., 15.578 and 17.50. —Trans.

6. See, for example, ibid., 6.28. —Trans.

7. These terms are repeated to Achilles in condensed form at ibid., 22.256–259.

8. See ibid., 17.184–186, 198–212. —Trans.

9. See E. *Rh.* 179–180 and 469–470, respectively. [The play, long attributed to Euripides, is now generally thought to be spurious. —Trans.]

10. Plu. *Apoph. Lac.* 228f–229a.

11. See Ov. *Ep.* 13.50, 13.144 (in the temple dedicated to Jupiter Redux) and *Tr.* 4.8.21 (to the Lares); Prop. 4.3.71 (to the Capene gate); Hor. *Ep.* 1.1.5 (dedicated to Hercules); Luc. 1.239 (to the Penates).

# Addenda

---

1. (Intro., n. 10). This book was already in press when I became aware of [the first volume of] M. Nilsson's magisterial *Geschichte der griechischen Religion* (Munich: Beck, 1941). What he says about legends (pp. 16–23) is rather superficial, because he treats the tale as the primary datum, whose genesis has no need of being either justified or explained. On the strength of this assumption, he opposes *aitia* to tales: the *aition* seek to explain, whereas the tale, which is pure invention, seeks solely to entertain. Nilsson maintains, moreover, that "myths are partly made from the themes of tales, which have previously been humanized."

I see no reason to make a radical distinction between myths and tales. Both are made from the same themes. These themes, it seems to me, are never a result of the unconstrained play of the imagination. They always correspond to some final purpose: a *logical* purpose when the story accounts, in its own fashion, for a practice whose origin and true meaning are no longer understood; a *practical* purpose when it holds out an example to be followed or avoided. This amounts to saying that the story is always presented as a guide, either for the intellect or for personal conduct, even if the version that is known to us has been severed from its original ending. It may be told in the form of a myth, which is to say that it is treated as an explanation of actual events, or in the form of a tale, which is to say that it is treated as a poetic narrative that concludes with an immediately intelligible moral or lesson. The difference is in the handling of the constituent elements, not in the elements themselves. This is why A. H. Krappe, in asking whether the Oedipus legend is a fairy tale ("La légende d'Œdipe est-elle un conte bleu?," *Neuphilol. Mitteil.* 34 [1933]: 11), seems to me to pose a pointless question, since no matter what answer is given it will be necessary to appeal to the same arguments.

In this connection one will find it rewarding to consult what now seems to be a quite old-fashioned work, the eight-volume *Mythologische Bibliotek* (Leipzig: J. C. Hinrichs, 1907–1916), aimed at showing that all myths are meant to describe the future course of celestial bodies, particularly that of the moon. As H. Lessmann remarks in his overview of the series, "It is customary to classify sources in the following fashion: divine myths, heroic legends, tales. It would be better to adopt the following ordering: divine myths and *Märchen*, heroic legends, epics, pseudohistorical sources, local traditions to the extent that they have a mythical origin." Lessmann, *Aufgaben und Ziele der vergleichenden Mythenforschung* (1908), 25.


2. (Ch. 3, n. 12). The *psychical* character of the woman/bird has recently been cast in doubt, for reasons that do not seem to me to be sufficient, by two authors: P. Demargne, "Plaquettes votives de la Grèce archaïque," *Bull. corr. hell.* 54 (1930): 195–209, especially pp. 204ff.; and E. Kunze, "Sirenen," *Ath. Mitt.* 57 (1932): 124–141. Demargne and Kunz have indeed established that, in Minoan art, winged women are associated with the Lady of the Beasts. But it does not follow from this that other meanings must be rejected. It seems to me impossible to dismiss the many Greek texts attesting to the role of wings and flight in the beliefs of the historical period concerning frustrated souls that wander about tombs; in this connection, see particularly chapter 7 of Ernst Bickel, *Homerischer Seelenglaube: Geschichtliche Grundzüge menschlicher Seelenvorstellungen* (Berlin: Deutsche Verlagsgesellschaft für Politik und Geschichte, 1926). Kunze studied the Siren of Praisos in Crete, from the eleventh century BCE, three centuries prior to the earliest previously excavated documents; he reckons that between this first instance of a winged woman in the Mediterranean world, borrowed from the East, and later Hellenic representations, of which no example earlier than the eighth century was known to us before, there was an extended period during which the type fell into

oblivion. Does the absence of documents warrant such a sweeping assertion? Even if what Kunze claims were true, the figure of the winged woman might very well have come to be charged in the interval with new significance, nowhere apparent in Minoan religion. Since the pathbreaking researches of Zwicker and Weicker, the archaeological material has been augmented and more systematically classified, but the conclusions drawn by these two scholars owe their continuing persuasiveness to a close correspondence between texts and monuments. New discoveries can be added to earlier ones, but in no way do they contradict them.

# Index of Passages Cited

## Hesiod

## Hesychius

## Homer

# Index